THE VANISHING VISION

THE
VANISHING
VISION

The Inside Story of Public Television

JAMES DAY

UNIVERSITY OF CALIFORNIA PRESS
BERKELEY   LOS ANGELES   LONDON

University of California Press
Berkeley and Los Angeles, California

University of California Press, Ltd.
London, England

© 1995 by
James Day

Library of Congress Cataloging-in-Publication Data
Day, James, 1918–
    The vanishing vision : the inside story of public
television / James Day.
        p.   cm.
    Includes bibliographical references and index.
    ISBN 0-520-08659-7
    1. Public television—United States—History.   I. Title.
II. Title: The vanishing vision.
HE8700.79.U6D39   1995
384.55'065—dc20   94-40304
                                                                CIP

Printed in the United States of America
9 8 7 6 5 4 3 2 1

Whither is fled the visionary gleam?
Where is it now, the glory and the dream?
William Wordsworth

For Meredith, Douglas, Alan, and Ross,
who came to adulthood in the ambit of the
public medium because it was there.

CONTENTS

INTRODUCTION

It was to be a different kind of presidential election campaign. Not the 1988 Bush-Dukakis affair with its scruffy baggage of eight-second sound bites sloganizing complex issues, photo-ops conveying their own brand of distorted imagery, candidate debates that weren't debates at all, and those cleverly crafted commercials that hid far more than they revealed.

Not this time. The presidential campaign of 1992 would be different. And the difference would be PBS, public television's national programming arm. By its offer of a $5 million grant, the John and Mary Markle Foundation proposed to put PBS in a position to use the politician's most influential medium in the service of an informed electorate. The Voters' Channel—that's what Markle called their plan—included free airtime for national candidates, special shows to air voters' concerns and opinions, expert analysis and criticism to "decode" the campaign's political messages, and informative programs to look at the national problems that the candidates chose to ignore and at the probable options to solve them. Walter Cronkite, the reigning dean of news anchors, hailed The Voters' Channel as "an absolutely vital service to educate the public in the issues and personalities involved in the presidential election process."[1]

But then something happened on the way to the polls. PBS suddenly and inexplicably dropped consideration of The Voters' Channel, plumping instead for a more modest but relatively risk-free version of its own. Seeing no show of will or commitment on the part of the PBS brass, Markle withdrew its $5 million offer, PBS

1

was left to cover the election year on a severely limited scale with its own funds, and Markle's proffered $5 million, or a substantial part of it, went to the more amenable CNN to permit the commercial cable network to beef up its own planned coverage of the campaign. The voters of this country were the losers; they deserved better.

Why and how PBS turned aside The Voters' Channel and the opportunity to render a unique service—and thus to further define the singular role of public television in a confusing jumble of competing images—is the story of a medium whose place in American television broadcasting has been purposely marginalized by public policy and whose potential has been limited by its own cramped vision. For more than four decades, the public broadcasting system of this country has remained on the periphery of the playing field, its mission clouded in a vaguely defined concept of "education," its structure balkanized into more than a hundred competing fiefdoms, its financial needs grossly undermet, and its loosely joined elements neither having nor wanting strong national leadership. Unlike its counterparts in other industrial democracies, America's public system has failed in forty years to become an important part of the lives of most viewers. Its rejection of Markle's plan for The Voters' Channel underscores both the strengths and weaknesses of a system whose bright promise has thus far exceeded its less-than-bright performance.

To understand why PBS turned down The Voters' Channel, it is necessary to know that the idea for the project was born outside the blankets, so to speak—not in the precincts of the public system itself but in the offices of the Markle Foundation and its president, Lloyd D. Morrisett. The foundation's study of the 1988 presidential election had found "widespread disquiet" over the campaign. According to the study, contestants evaded issues and media handlers manipulated a compliant press, resulting in the public being "cheated." Those findings prompted Markle to work on plans to harness television's acknowledged potential for voter education for the 1992 campaign. Its logical partner was PBS. The public network had a pioneering spirit, was not bound by commercial considerations of audience size, and had the airtime to do what the others would not.

Morrisett first approached PBS in late 1989. The time was not propitious; the public network had just undergone one of its periodic reorganizations, discarding a clumsy and ineffective process of selecting programs for the national schedule by systemwide balloting. In its place, a newly installed program executive, Jennifer Lawson, was given the authority to make those selections herself. Lawson and her PBS colleagues expressed enthusiasm for the Markle proposal. With characteristic caution, however, PBS stopped short of committing itself to the project and declined to take part in funding the planning phase. Moving ahead on its own but keeping PBS fully informed, Markle put the planning phase in the hands of an independent producer, the Alvin H. Perlmutter Company. Perlmutter's thirty-year record of productions for public television has included *The Great American Dream Machine, Adam Smith's Money World,* and, with Bill Moyers, *The Public Mind* and *Joseph Campbell and the Power of Myth.*

Perlmutter completed his feasibility study in time for the annual meeting of the PBS stations in June 1990. The 132-page document was remarkable not only for the thoroughness of its research— Perlmutter had consulted more than 120 political leaders, journalists, academicians, and public broadcasters—but also for his success in harmonizing their sometimes disparate recommendations. The estimated price tag was a whopping $12 to $15 million (later pared to $12.7 million): $5 million from Markle, $3 million from PBS, and the balance to be raised from corporations and foundations. Months were wasted as PBS and its stations debated the fine points of the study. Would the offer of free airtime for national candidates put stations under pressure to extend free time to local candidates? (Most opposed the idea.) Was the Markle study really the foundation's bid to impose its will on the public network? Would Perlmutter's involvement mean the loss of editorial independence? The station concerns were summed up by the head of their lobbying group. "We're not," he said, "the kind of system where anybody can just buy their way in because they have money."[2] (He was unaware of the irony in his outburst.

Twenty-five years earlier, another "outside" group, the Children's Television Workshop, had approached a very young PBS with money and an idea called *Sesame Street.* What's more, the man who had raised the "outside" money for the children's series was the selfsame Lloyd Morrisett who was now knocking on the PBS door a second time.)

By late June of 1991, time was running out and PBS was still unwilling to make the commitment Morrisett needed before he could approach prospective donors for the additional $3 million needed to fund the project. Lawson, doubtful that the additional $3 million could be raised, proposed a scaled-down version of The Voters' Channel to fit the $8 million already in hand. But by then Morrisett's patience was exhausted; the foot-dragging, the delaying tactics, and PBS's unwillingness to commit itself to the project were too much for even his strong will. He withdrew Markle's offer of the $5 million. "It's very unclear," he noted ruefully, "how they make decisions at PBS."[3] If his frustration and anger were contained, others were less restrained. "Disgraceful," said Ward Chamberlin, president of WETA/Washington and a former vice president of PBS. "If public television doesn't do that, then what the hell good is it?"[4]

Behind the failure of PBS to accept a once-in-a-decade opportunity to define a distinct role for public television lies the tale of an institution of enormous promise mired in a self-created bureaucracy. Its human and economic resources are thinly spread over a highly fragmented system, its national leadership is divided and largely impotent, its creative energies are sapped by the inevitable competition and infighting, and its sense of purpose is clouded by parochialism and suspicion. If there is an upside to this bleak portrait, and there is, it is the marvel of those rare moments when the public system breaks free of its own bureaucracy and triumphs. We are treated in those moments to a glimpse of what it might be.

Nothing so frustrates public television's further development— not even its trumpeted paucity of funds—than its failure to formulate a clear and precise mission, a purpose that, among other things, sets it apart from the educational and cultural aims of the rising flood of "niche" cable channels. One hears an echo of this failing in Chamberlin's cry of "then what the hell good is it?" Unless it plays upon its unique strengths, public television may be compelled to relinquish its claim upon the federal treasury. The system's current practice pays tribute to the sacred concept of "localism." Each outlet fashions its mission to the needs and interests of its own community—within, of course, the broad guidelines of its FCC license. But the system does this at a cost. The concept of public-service television, and thus the justification for it, is blurred in a babel of diverse aims. Worse, when national programming, and particularly programs involving risk, must run the gauntlet of more than three hundred local outlets, each with its own self-defined purpose, only the bland will succeed. The Voters' Channel was one of the most recent victims of the system's fragmented structure.

Strong leadership can articulate a clear, precise purpose; a committee produces rhetorical mush. No better example of the former can be found than in the quality, strength, and vision of leadership given the BBC in its early days by its first director-general. An autocratic moralist with a clear notion of public broadcasting's role, Lord Reith defined a mission for that widely respected institution that remains in force more than a half-century later. The U.S. system, by contrast, has been hobbled from the outset by a federal policy, born at the dawn of radio, that entrusted the public interest to the conscience of commercial broadcasters and relegated public broadcasting to the role of a secondary and largely unessential "alternative" to the dominant medium.[5] Strong national leadership might have articulated a mission for the medium when, in 1967, it was redefined as "public" television. But Congress effectively neutered that prospect by placing "leadership" in a hydra-headed structure of competing authorities: the Corporation for Public Broadcasting to hold the money, the Public Broadcasting Service to gather and deliver the programming, and the American Public Television Stations to lobby Congress and protect the interests of the stations. If Congress reflected a benign mistrust and mild indifference toward public television by preventing the emergence of strong national leadership, it found allies among the "powerful baronies in the balkanized kingdom of 341 public broadcasting stations."[6] The system's local stations, though for different reasons, also oppose the emergence of strong national leadership. Their motives are akin to the feudal barons of earlier times who made certain that a weak and compliant king sat on the throne of England.

The seeds of the balkanized approach, sown in public television's infancy, emerged from a widespread zeal to avoid the perceived pitfalls of the three commercial networks. These monoliths were felt to be dominated by New York and Hollywood. But the noncommercial medium, like the reformed smoker turned self-righteous bore, may have moved too far in the opposite direction. To avoid a monolith, it created a bureaucratic monster—inefficient, uneconomic, and unwieldy—and pronounced it good because, above all else, it was demonstrably "democratic." But however useful democracy is for accommodating individual differences into the interests of the polity as a whole, it is decidedly inappropriate to a creative or journalistic enterprise—as any autocratic editor will be pleased to confirm. Public television's purpose is not to resolve differences but to air them, helping us to recognize, understand, and accept them. Their resolution is better left to democracy's political processes.

If public television is in crisis, and it is, the state is not an unfamiliar one. The medium has lived in crisis, uncertain of its future, ever since its awkward birth in 1952 as educational television. Then, as now, it was an aberration, an add-on to mainstream, or "real," television destined to dwell in the margins of public consciousness, and like culture generally, a matter of peripheral concern to the nation and its leaders. America's public television suffered the added handicap of arriving late on the scene and screen. In Europe and Canada, public television preceded the introduction of private commercial television, in most cases by many years, and—in what might be called the "who comes first defines the media" hypothesis—it conditioned viewer expectations by saying, in effect, "this is what television is." But in our own country, public television followed on the heels of an established system of private, profit-driven television that, for its own purposes, defined television as entertainment. Its fast-paced formats demanded less than full engagement of the viewer's mind or emotions, asking only that the eyeballs be present for the advertisers' importunities. Noncommercial educational television arrived on the scene faced not only with viewer expectations conditioned by the needs of commerce but also with an official predisposition toward a private, commercial, libertarian model of broadcasting and telecommunications that had stood for seventy years. That the public model has managed against such odds to insinuate itself into more than 40 million television homes in all fifty states, albeit irregularly, is a tribute to its perseverance if not to its quality. But as the commercial models breed and multiply, public television's efforts to serve the social and political needs of the nation are increasingly in danger of being swamped by a giant wave whose glitzy, downscale diversions are serving the needs of the advertiser first and the needs of society only incidentally if at all.

The crisis in public broadcasting is not unique to the United States, where its future has always been in doubt. The phenomenon is worldwide. A tide of laissez-faire, free-market ideology, accompanied by a fervent faith in the efficacy of the marketplace, has brought American-style private television to countries that heretofore thought broadcasting too important to be left in private hands. The seductive promise of "more channels to choose from" has governments reaching out to grasp entrepreneurial hands, not always for the stated purpose of widening viewers' choices but for the beguiling ring of money; both liberals and conservatives have touted private television as a stimulus to their countries' economies. Some countries, reluctant at first to admit private broadcasters for fear of contaminating the culture, have yielded to the inevitable as satellites overhead and out of their control have brought the unwanted images into the homes of their citizens. If private television is inevitable, they have reasoned, it is better that it be ours.

France's once-proud public system of three national networks has been undermined by the sale of the most popular of the three to private interests, leaving the remaining two in a much weaker position. And in Britain, the former Tory prime minister Margaret

Thatcher, in thrall to privatization, took aim at the BBC with a threat to open it to advertising, but managed instead to seriously wound its competitor, the country's uniquely public-service-minded system of private television. Hoping to add sterling to the national treasury, the government auctioned off the regional franchises to the highest bidder, effectively wiping out one public-service-minded broadcaster, Thames Television, and leaving most of the others so burdened with debt that their only hope of recovery lies in downscaling programming quality to boost audience size. Lost in the shuffle is any prospect that private television will be in a financial position to repeat such earlier distinguished but expensive programming triumphs as Granada TV's *Brideshead Revisited* and *Jewel in the Crown*. The BBC, meanwhile, is undergoing a radical reorganization at the hands of a new director-general who was recruited from commercial television and whose charge to make the broadcaster more businesslike has raised fears that its public-service tradition may be sacrificed to efficiency. There are perils ahead. With its Parliamentary charter up for renewal every ten years or so, one day the BBC may be hard pressed to justify continued support from a universal license fee levied upon viewers who, in increasing numbers, are switching to the private, advertiser-supported channels.

The changing situation impales the BBC and the rest of Europe's public broadcasters on the horns of a dilemma. Although some public systems are permitted limited income from advertising, all are dependent on a license fee. But as their share of audience declines, their claim to a universal license fee weakens. They know they can increase their share by copying the popular programming of their commercial competition. But they also know that it would cost them their only justification for a license fee: the uniqueness of their programming service.

In the feeding frenzy for profit that followed the breakup of national public-service monopolies and the release of channels to private entrepreneurs, the concept of public interest, once the governing ethic of broadcasting, has been largely abandoned. Particularly in countries where state-owned monopolies offered little else but a stultifying diet of good-for-you television, the breakup offers short-term benefits of broadened choice. But those of us who have who have had private, profit-driven television for a half-century know well the long-term consequences even as we try to deny them: the trivialization and commodification of life, increased incidence of violence, falling SAT scores, sensationalization of the news, and a steady erosion of political discourse.

At no time since the FCC's 1952 act setting aside television channels for "educational" use has the need been greater for a healthy and viable system of public television, a system not market driven, not drawing its sustenance from the same pockets as private television, not constrained to maximize audience size yet not satisfied to serve tiny audiences of ethnic or elitist minorities. Public television properly belongs in the media mainstream, filling a void of programming that has all but faded from the screens of the commercial medium—quality comedy, variety, light drama, even quiz shows—all without sacrifice to its established menu of "serious" investigative documentaries, innovative drama, music and dance, and shows of self-improvement. Audiences need to know that there is more to television than recycled waste and weightless trivia. They need to experience television that is no less entertaining for having substance and meaning, not just the commendable likes of *American Playhouse, Nova,* and *Great Performances,* but comedy and light entertainment of the sort that gives insight into why we behave as we do, that helps to explain the human condition. Among the industrialized democracies, ours is the only public system that is hobbled by a pinched definition of its programming role. The Reithian formula for the BBC—"inform, educate, and entertain"—calls for high-quality programming in a wide variety of forms, popular entertainment as well as the kind of high-minded fare that fills the PBS prime-time schedule. Public television should be the crucible in which American creativity is generated and nurtured, in which the full range of new and innovative forms of television is explored in relative isolation from the artistic constraints of the commercial medium. The public medium can, in the process, set higher standards for all of television to the ultimate benefit of the viewer. Substance and quality—even in popular television—offer a path to a heightened appreciation for the delights of learning and the rewards of knowing. And that, say some, is what art is all about.

Knowing, however, is not enough. The commercial media, with their cacophony of twenty-four-hour headline news, help us to know. But the flood of unassimilated and indigestible information is a prescription for thought paralysis, for confusion and indifference. What we cannot assimilate we shut out in self-protection, with consequences that could be disastrous for a self-governing society. Public television must help us to understand. It must, as E. B. White has said, "clarify the social dilemma and the political pickle"—find meaning in events of which we are aware but do not comprehend, help us toward the understanding that gives impetus and meaning to our political actions.

More than forty years ago, when television itself was still in its infancy, I undertook to bring one of the earliest educational television stations into being and onto the air. We had no model to guide us; the FCC had set aside the educational reservations the previous year, but none had yet been activated. And because Congress had made no provision for their support, we lacked money, equipment, staff, and studios. I came to the medium with no experience in television, not knowing a jump cut from a slow fade. I didn't even own a television set. But I came armed with convictions, some born of several years in public-service radio. Most, however, were a reflection of my experiences in growing up during the Great Depression.

Though I had an adolescent's natural curiosity for learning, my interest in reading was not nurtured within my own family; I have no memory of either parent's buying, borrowing, or reading a book other than the Bible. As for serious music, their interest began and ended with Jeannette McDonald and Nelson Eddy and a heavy-handed rendition of Friml's "Indian Love Call." Recalling those formative years, I am struck by the realization that the sparks igniting a love of books and music came not from my parents, caring as they were, but from elsewhere: teachers, family friends, and the local public library. But the most unusual of these influences was radio, "old-fashioned" radio. By the mid-thirties, commercial radio and the networks, not yet having abandoned the public trust for larger profits, still retained some of the feel of public-service broadcasting. (The condition would unfortunately lull Congress, the regulatory agencies, and even educators into a false belief that private broadcasters could, with minimal regulation and a sense of public trust, serve the public-interest agenda.) As an adolescent, eager to connect with a confusing and complex world, I discovered in my little bedside Philco the means of reaching beyond my limited environment. My early fondness for books was nurtured by our local NBC-owned outlet, which devoted a Sunday evening hour—during prime time, no less—to an informal book ramble with the distinguished critic of the *San Francisco Chronicle.* Joseph Henry Jackson's enthusiasms were infectious; I could hardly contain my eagerness to explore the library the following day. And so it was with music. In the days before long-playing records and CDs—a time, in fact, when radio scorned recorded music—Bach, Mozart, and Puccini came into my life through the broadcast of live concerts such as the *Bell Telephone Hour,* the *Voice of Firestone,* and the *Standard Symphony Hour.* And I haven't forgotten that America's leading commercial network once had its own symphony orchestra, one of the country's best, with the great Toscanini and regular weekly concerts. Radio, without pictures, but with words and music that stirred the imagination and respected the intellect, opened a door onto a wider and richer world for me as it must have for millions of others.

The point to be remembered is this: I did not search out these shows, radio schedule in hand, with any thought of broadening my interests or "improving" my mind. I happened upon them accidentally, the way one comes upon an exciting new book while browsing the shelves of a public library. What is most important is the fact that they were there—programs waiting to be discovered at the touch of a dial, easily available for making a difference in the lives of others as they had made in mine. Which raises the obvious question: should not public television be a presence in every home in America, universally available to serve similar ends for another generation seeking the same answers? Justification for the reserved channels should not depend solely on meeting the

needs of those whose educated tastes are unmet by other television. The public channel should simply be there, for everyone, a
presence waiting to be stumbled on by those who will one day
discover in its programs a richer world beyond the cramped walls
of their own narrow experience. The radio shows that affected my
life happened in those years when the phrase "public interest"
was more practiced than understood, years when the economic
forces of the marketplace still left breathing room for the play of
social forces. Today, the notion of the public interest has disappeared from broadcasting, driven out by the false prophets of deregulation and the competitive forces of the marketplace. We have
nothing to replace it, only a weak and inadequately supported
system of public broadcasting. It is difficult to understand how our
nation can afford to have any less concern for television's role in
the education of our young than we have for our schools and
libraries. Or why the public media, including public radio, should
be any less available to every home in America. Whoever tells our
tales, warns media scholar George Gerbner, shapes our future.[7] If
today's mythmakers and troubadours are no more than Saturday-
morning cartoons, music videos, and prime-time sitcoms, the
brightness of that future is very much at risk.

This book grows from a concern for that future. More specifically, it argues for a place in that future for a system of publicly
owned television, both effective and enlightened, whose mission
is service, not sales, and whose purpose is central, not marginal,
to the rest of the electronic medium. The argument must begin
with an effort to understand the system that now exists. The task
is not as simple as it might at first appear. I am not alone in meeting the puzzled looks of students and foreign visitors attempting
to make sense of the system's convoluted structure—*unique* is the
charitable word for it. The experience has taught me to approach
the task historically, to begin at the beginning. Only by going back
to its hobbled start at the hands of a grudging government and
by tracing the forces that have pulled and hauled at it since can
we understand what it is, why it is, and what it has the power to
become.

I have ventured to tell that story, albeit in abbreviated form, and with the omission of an important subchapter: public television's important role in supplying classrooms and organized viewing groups with programs of systematic instruction. For the purposes of my argument, it is essential to separate the mission of "instructional" television, for which effective alternatives may well be found in the newer, interactive technologies, from the broader mission of "public" television, for which no alternatives exist or are likely to emerge from an environment dominated by the pursuit of maximum profitability.

"The only good histories," Montaigne once observed, "are those written by the very men who were in command in the affairs, or who were participants in the conduct of them."[8] I was a participant in some, though not all, of the affairs described herein, but I was rarely in command of them. Those who were may feel the story might better be told by someone with less emotional investment in the outcome. Others with whom I shared this adventure may be disappointed when they search the index for their names; if their part in this history has not been properly acknowledged, it is not because their role was minor but because their part was played out beyond the sight of this particular chronicler. Montaigne's observation notwithstanding, a participant in the fighting is not likely to see the war whole, but rather only the battles waged. Moreover, a participant may not be the best judge of their import, or the most accurate and objective eye to report them. In telling the story of public television from the perspective of my own experience, I am sensitive to the biases my personal involvement brings to the account: the partiality of my own convictions, the disappointment of my own defeats, and the vision of what might have been. I urge those of my former colleagues who saw it differently, or whose contribution to the building of the medium may have been underplayed or unwittingly ignored, to add their own account to the sparse written record of this important enterprise.

In the meantime, here is mine.

A NEW MEDIUM,
AN UNCERTAIN MISSION

*Public service broadcasters must peer not to the horizon to see if the enemy
has arrived, but into their own souls.*

Willard Rowland and
Michael Tracey[1]

The years immediately following
the end of World War II were a time of renewed American confidence in the perfectibility of the human species. An enemy had
been defeated, as much by the righteousness of the cause as by
the superior industrial strength of the western democracies. On
the ruins of the war, a new world order was being erected: new
nations of Asia and Africa were being freed from the grip of empire, foundations were put in place for a European Community,
and to secure the peace, a United Nations was being created.

Anything seemed possible. America was ready to reach for the
moon. The technological and scientific advances that had
emerged from the crucible of that war, and particularly the har-
nessing of the atom, had given the nation a sense of mastery over
the world of material things, however tenuous and uncertain that
notion proved to be.

Not the least of America's postwar technological triumphs was
the emergence of television. The BBC in Britain had introduced
television much earlier, but the war had postponed its long-
promised arrival in this country. When television did finally arrive
in America, in the months following the close of the war, it spread

like a prairie fire. Sales of television sets soared as entrepreneurs, sensing a bonanza in the marketing potential of the new medium, sought available channels. First across the starting line were the three national radio networks: CBS, NBC, and ABC. Having dominated radio for decades, they were determined to secure their position in the newer and more powerful medium by grabbing the best channels in the biggest markets. They were slowed only by the FCC-imposed limit of five channels to a customer.

No one doubted or challenged the use to which television would be put. America was still in the thrall of a faith that had fashioned its policy toward radio, a faith that assumed "such considerable identity between private and public interests in broadcasting that, as in the simple models of eighteenth-century libertarianism, the best public services would emerge in a largely unfettered private enterprise." That faith had come under challenge several times before the 1950s and prior to television, most dramatically in the 1946 FCC Report (Blue Book) detailing the failure of private broadcasting to live up to its public-service obligations. After a brief but terminal increase in public-service programming, the Blue Book was largely forgotten. The nervousness it had provoked in broadcasters subsided when the Blue Book became history and not policy. What remained in the memory bank was a time much earlier when radio, with hours of unsold time to fill, had performed in accordance with the libertarian theory. Whatever the weaknesses in the theory, they could be overcome with the advent of television "through the workings of enlightened, public-spirited, private broadcasting leadership, moderate FCC oversight, and the introduction of yet another, newer technology."[2]

Confidence that enlightened private industry would serve the social needs of the nation, coupled with a not-invented-here parochialism, led the United States to reject out of hand any consideration of the form of public-service broadcasting that was commonplace in western Europe, Canada, Japan, and Australia. Public-service institutions like the BBC were widely misunderstood and generally dismissed as "state" television. Despite convincing evidence to the contrary, America moved into the age of television firm in its faith that the model developed for radio would suffice for the newer medium. It would be business as usual.

In the bonanza that followed, the FCC imposed a loosely defined and even more loosely enforced "public-interest" requirement upon those who sought entry to the new game. The rush for channels proved that the public-interest requirement was no deterrent to the entrepreneurial spirit of America's broadcasters. By 1948, only two years after the first television stations went on the air, the heavy demand for television frequencies compelled the FCC to declare a moratorium on the further issuance of licenses. The "time out" period from 1948 to 1952, commonly known as the "FCC freeze," was to be used to research a feasible way to find additional channels to meet the extraordinary demand for commercial outlets. But a group of educational activists, fearful that the powerful visual medium with its unexplored potential for teaching would be given over entirely to commerce, seized on the "freeze" to push its own agenda. The educators wanted some part of the new medium dedicated to a purpose loftier than light entertainment and more enlightening than ads for painkillers and detergent.

The precise nature of that loftier purpose was never spelled out. Television was still in its infancy, its impact unmeasured, its possibilities unknown. It seemed sufficient at the time simply to recognize the medium's potential for education and to push ahead. Curiously, there remained a residual hope that the broader public-interest needs would still be met by private television. As a consequence, there was no real sense of the need for a comprehensive national public television and radio enterprise, not even by most of those who fought to reserve the channels for education. The vision was more narrowly focused: unless some portion of the television spectrum was withheld from commercial exploitation, education might never discover the visual medium's potential for serving its special needs.

Thus the move to reserve television channels was initiated by a small handful of determined advocates, most of whom managed educational radio stations affiliated with land-grant colleges in Iowa, Wisconsin, Illinois, and other midwestern states.[3] Some years earlier, these radio stations had organized themselves into the National Association of Educational Broadcasters and under this banner had waged a successful campaign to persuade the FCC to reserve a group of FM radio frequencies for education. The fight for television reservations promised to be tougher. Far more was at stake, and powerful commercial interests wanted the valuable channels kept for their own purposes. The NAEB could not hope to counter this force without substantial help.

Help came through one of those curious coincidences of history that create unexpected alliances. At the moment when the NAEB was searching for a partner with power and deep pockets, the Ford Foundation was casting about for an appropriate cause to fulfill its philanthropic aims. Six years earlier, the Ford Foundation had been little more than a modest Detroit family foundation that served as a conduit for channeling Henry Ford's benefactions into his favorite charities. But after the death of Ford's son, Edsel, in 1943, and upon his own death four years later, the tiny organization was suddenly and dramatically transformed into the world's wealthiest foundation, with shares worth billions of dollars. Its assets exceeded the combined assets of all the country's other private foundations.

Henry Ford, who had been notoriously tightfisted, left the family very little philanthropic tradition to fall back upon. To plot a new direction, Edsel's widow, Eleanor Clay Ford, invited a small group of distinguished citizens to come up with a plan that would "put [the Foundation's] resources to work for human welfare." The group's recommendations, including one urging "cooperation with the non-commercial organizations concerned with mass communications," were quickly adopted by the trustees.[4] To carry them out, the board recruited Paul G. Hoffman and installed him as president of the newly reconstituted foundation. Hoffman had risen over the years from a Studebaker salesman to chairman of the Studebaker-Packard Corporation. In 1948, he was tapped to head the Marshall Plan for the rebuilding of a war-torn Europe, where he won a worldwide reputation for leadership.

One of Hoffman's first acts as president of the giant Ford Foundation was to subdivide it into three subsidiary funds, each with its own board and objective. One, the Fund for the Advancement of Education, was to address the "problems and opportunities in formal education from elementary grades through college level." Another, the Fund for Adult Education, was to be concerned with "that part of the educational process which begins when formal schooling is ended" or what came to be termed "liberal adult education."[5] The Fund for the Advancement of Education took several years to discover in television a potential for formal instruction. Not so with the Fund for Adult Education. It saw immediate advantage in the new medium for extended adult education. Before it could seize the advantage, however, there was the battle to secure for education some of the valuable television channels that were rapidly being claimed by commerce.

If the battle to reserve educational channels can be likened to a military engagement, its strategic planner, if not its commanding general, was C. Scott Fletcher, the man Paul Hoffman chose in 1951 to head the newly formed Fund for Adult Education. We shall have reason to meet him many times in the course of this narrative, for, as one historian has noted, "if such things could be measured, [Scotty Fletcher] has probably done more than any other person to bring public broadcasting into being and set its course."[6] Like Hoffman, with whom he was associated both at the Studebaker Corporation and in the administration of the Marshall Plan, Fletcher began his career as an automobile salesman. He left his native Australia to become Studebaker's international sales manager in the United States and then, during World War II, left the automobile business to direct the Committee for Economic Development. His appointment after the war to the presidency of Encyclopaedia Britannica Films began a lifelong interest in the media's potential for liberal adult education. A peppery, voluble man with energy to spare, Fletcher could sell ideas with the same persuasive force that he once used to sell Studebakers. His move to the Fund for Adult Education was a fitting career climax for a man descended from three generations of teachers.

Fletcher and the Ford Foundation first explored the educa-

tional potential of television shortly after Hoffman set up the
Foundation's first headquarters in his hometown of Pasadena, California, which wags were quick to dub "Itching Palms." The
Fund's first television venture was *Omnibus*, a weekly cultural magazine hosted by Alistair Cooke and produced by the Foundation's
Radio-Television Workshop. The Ford Foundation intended to
demonstrate with *Omnibus* that "high quality programming could
be made sufficiently attractive to compete for audience attention
against other commercial television programming." But even with
occasional sponsorship, the distinguished show failed to make the
Foundation's case. After gracing the network schedules for five
years, first at CBS and later at ABC, *Omnibus* was driven from the
air and into the broadcast archives by commercial competition.
Ford concluded that television's power to "contribute to the development of mature, wise and responsible citizens" was not to be
found among the commercial broadcasters.[7]

Fletcher, never an *Omnibus* booster, had long since decided that
the answer to quality programming lay not with the commercial
networks but with educational television. Even before he assumed
office, his interest had been drawn to the incipient movement by
the cadre of educational radio broadcasters organized under the
banner of the NAEB. Up to that point, this small group had led
the fight largely unaided. They had enlisted the superior strength
of the major educational organizations under a temporary Joint
Committee (later Council) on Educational Television.[8] They had
also retained Telford Taylor, former General Counsel of the FCC
and a prosecutor at the War Crimes Trial, as JCET's legal counsel.
Taylor, in the course of helping the Joint Committee on Educational Television to prepare for the FCC's channel allocation hearings, which took place in 1950–51, suggested a "monitoring
study," a record of a week's viewing of New York's seven television
channels. By showing the sheer vacuity of television's content and
its depiction of violence, the monitoring study moved the FCC to
reconsider its previous rejection of the educators' request for
channel reservations. But the JCET, challenged now to renew its
efforts to make the educators' case for channels, had, by 1951,
exhausted its funds. The NAEB turned to Fletcher for help.

Fletcher responded with a grant, the Fund's first, establishing the JCET as a permanent organization.

Even with the resources of the Fund behind it, the JCET's case might have foundered had it not been for the resolute will of a woman whose determination to see channels reserved for education earned her the honorary title "the mother protector of educational television."[9] Frieda Barkin Hennock was born in Poland and came to this country as a child. After earning a law degree from Brooklyn Law School, she became a successful criminal lawyer in New York City. When President Truman appointed her to the FCC in 1948, she became the first woman ever to serve on what was then a seven-member body. During the critical four years of the FCC "freeze" from 1948 to 1952, when educators were pounding on the FCC doors for admission to the television medium, Hennock was the only commissioner willing to lend a receptive ear to their arguments. She not only listened, she acted, ultimately arming the educators with the legal and moral platform on which to base their successful fight for the channel reservations. Friends described her as an effective champion of almost fanatical zeal, with an aggressive single-mindedness that could terrify even those whose cause she championed. I have no reason to question the description. In our only face-to-face meeting—it was 1953 and I was struggling to overcome what seemed insurmountable barriers to the activation of the channel reserved for our area—Hennock would hear nothing of discouragement. Wagging her finger in front of my nose, she virtually *ordered* me to get the station on the air. I had no immediate solutions to our problems, but I knew that it would be unthinkable to let her down.

When, in the summer of 1949, the FCC proposed a new table of channel allocations and made no provision for educational television, Hennock was the Commission's lone dissenter. Unwilling to give in to her six male colleagues, she boldly proposed that the FCC reserve no less than 25 percent of its allocations. But it would be another year before the tide would begin to turn. In March 1951, the Commission issued its *Third Notice of Proposed Rule Making*, in which there was a provision for tentatively reserving 209

channels for education, approximately 11 percent of the total allocations. Hennock had won over—or worn down—her fellow
commissioners.

The climax of the battle for educational reservations came in
April 1952. With the issuance of the FCC's *Sixth Report and Order*,[10]
the educational reservations became official, and 242 channels
were set aside for noncommercial educational use. Eighty of the
reserved channels were in the standard VHF band. The remaining
162 were in the new and largely unusable UHF band. The FCC's
historical bias toward private ownership of the airwaves was clearly
evident in the Commission's criteria for deciding which communities got educational channels. Those cities with three or more
commercial channels, which thus assured an outlet for each of the
three major networks, were allocated an additional channel for
education. But those cities with fewer than three commercial
channels received a reserved channel only if they were deemed to
be "educational centers." Worse, many of the country's major
cities, including New York, Los Angeles, Philadelphia, Washington, and Detroit, where the new medium needed a presence if it
was to send down roots and survive, were assigned the less valuable
UHF channels. The more valuable VHF channels allocated to those
cities had already been placed in the hands of private operators.
Public television was forced to enter the race with a three-legged
horse.

The inferior channel assignments were not the new medium's
only impairment. Equally handicapping was the absence of a
clearly defined mission, a particular niche into which public television could be fitted among the complex of existing privately
owned, profit-driven television stations. The *Sixth Report and Order*
gave no hint of a vision that might endow the public medium with
legitimacy and relevance. Nowhere was mention made of a national public-television system such as that which existed in every
other country with public-service broadcasting. Nor was any attempt made to fit the new medium into the broader context of
the nation's mass-communication systems. "The proposed stations," stated the order, "will be used primarily to serve the educational needs of the community; for the advancement of edu-

cational programs; and to furnish a nonprofit and noncommercial television broadcast service." The *Sixth Report and Order* might have articulated the vision of a service conceived to fill the obvious voids of the dominant market-driven media; instead it was hardly more than a grudging concession to the pressures of the educational lobby.

It does no discredit to those who fought for and won the channel reservations to note that in their view access to the new medium for "educational" purposes seemed sufficient at the time. Television was clearly an audiovisual tool, untested but with potential. At the same time, it is good to note that the educational establishment was not of one mind on the new medium, nor did it speak with one voice. Within its ranks, heated arguments were waged over the place and importance of the upstart medium in the process of teaching and learning. For every advocate of classroom television, there was an opponent. The enthusiasts, in the thrall of the new technology, envisioned an opportunity to propagate the best in teaching by using television to share the best teachers. Those opposed to television saw the tube as an unwanted intrusion into the sanctity of the classroom and a threat to cherished conventions. Moreover, they feared that teaching-by-television would lead to the need for fewer teachers. Opponents of educational television were shaken into moderating their opposition five years later, however, when the Soviets lofted a 184-pound ball named Sputnik into space. With the sudden realization that our curricula were dangerously deficient in science and math and that years would be required to train teachers, the new technology of television seemed a fortuitous blessing. The Sputnik panic spurred countless experiments in the uses of television for teaching. And yet today, after forty years of experience, the public-television fraternity remains ambivalent about the "educational" role assigned to it by the *Sixth Report.* Some of its leaders, anticipating a loss of the medium's informational and cultural role as cable increasingly moves into the territory, are lobbying for a return to public television's "educational roots."

Viewed as an act of creation, the FCC order that established a noncommercial system was lacking in any conviction that viewers needed or deserved more choice than the three dominant networks then offered. The charge gains credence from the government's failure to provide for, or even make a case for, a federal funding mechanism of the sort enjoyed by public-service broadcasting systems in every other industrial democracy. By leaving the system to fend for itself, the government first created and then abandoned what it had created; fifteen more years would pass before public television received its first dollar of support from the Congress. By limiting itself to the granting of channels for educational use, the government was spared from having to consider any proposal for the formation of a public-television system along the lines of BBC, which, of course, could challenge the dominance of privately held television.

The Commission made no effort to limit the uses of the reserved channels other than to deny them advertising revenue as a source of income—and even that was modified years later by the Reagan Administration. "The public interest," reads the *Sixth Report*, "will clearly be served if these stations are used to contribute significantly to the educational process of the nation." But then, paradoxically, it granted public broadcasters carte blanche to "transmit educational, cultural and entertainment programs," a broad, permissive, and remarkably inclusive set of rules that were not at all helpful in defining a clear and particular purpose for the public medium. The primary limitation on the channels reserved for education was the FCC's definition of those eligible to use them: "nonprofit educational organizations," some of which the report described in more specific detail.

Ironically, Commissioner Hennock, the person most responsible for translating the educators' concerns into concrete action, saw the mission of the noncommercial channels in far broader terms than they did. She understood and accepted the educators' need for access to the new medium. But she viewed the channels as more than a tool for teaching. Noncommercial television, she argued, was also a tool for improving and upgrading the quality of all television, "a beneficial complement to commercial broadcasting." With its lack of dependence on mass audiences, it could and should "provide a greater diversity in television programming." Brushing aside the arguments of those who wanted the reserved channels to be noncompetitive as well as nonprofit, she held the educational reservations to be "a means toward the goal of increasing competition and public responsibility in broadcasting." In this respect, she held views that were more advanced than those of the educators.[11]

Competition, of course, was the last thing commercial broadcasting wanted from nonprofit television. Nor did they expect to have it. Most private broadcasters opposed the educational reservations, hoping to acquire the more valuable channels for their own use. Their argument to the Commission that education would be better served if the task were left to professional broadcasters had a familiar ring. It had been used in the 1930s by private radio owners to prevent the allocation of special frequencies for education.[12] The resulting compromise had a predictable outcome: The promises made to educators were quickly forgotten just as soon as the time slots reserved for education on the privately owned radio stations became commercially desirable. Hennock's vision of a noncommercial system that would "supply a beneficial complement to commercial telecasting" had a competitive ring that the commercial broadcasters were not eager to accept. "Educational" television posed no such threat. Nor were those of us who envisioned a broader mission surprised when *Broadcasting*, the mouthpiece of private broadcasting, launched an editorial campaign against permitting the reserved channels to air "popular" shows; since educators didn't have to compete in the open market for their channels, the argument ran, they shouldn't be allowed to compete with those who did. Some commercial operators continued to hold to this view long after public broadcasting became a reality, jealously guarding their programming precincts in the hope of keeping their noncommercial cohorts confined to purely educational efforts. In Georgia, the state's association of private broadcasters filed a complaint with the FCC after the University of Georgia's public station aired *The Ox Bow Incident*. Feature films, the association argued, are not "educational"—apparently, not even when made from minor American literary classics.

Fortunately, the FCC did not agree. It was not, however, an isolated incident.

Responsibility for failing to articulate a clearer sense of mission for the new medium can easily be laid at the feet of the federal bureaucracy. Government alone has the power and the obligation to fit together the constituent pieces of the communications system, assigning to each element its proper place in an overall design that best serves the needs of the nation. Pragmatists would be quick to point out, however, that political policy is the product of compromise, an accommodation that tends to grind down the sharp edges of definition. In this case, the process produced an ambiguity that was never intended by the fervent advocates of public television.

Anne W. Branscomb, however, believes ambiguity was precisely what the government intended. In a provocative essay on public television's identity crisis, the New York attorney and communications consultant speculates that the FCC may have made a conscious effort to avoid being explicit "for fear of opening the Pandora's box of programming control."[13] Any hint of program control, she suggests, is "fraught with First Amendment connotations." Her argument points to the curiously cramped interpretation of the Constitutional guarantees of free speech that the FCC was presumably willing to accept. Unless the government had clearly intended to exercise program control by dictating what could and could not be said, the creation of one more outlet for the robust expression of ideas should have been seen as an enhancement rather than as a threat to free speech. By defining the medium's purpose and giving it a proper and useful role in the complex of existing media, the government would not have curbed its freedom to express whatever truths and heresies it might be moved to utter.

Curiously missing at the moment of public television's creation, particularly in light of the FCC's failure to provide it, is a clear and precise articulation of its aims and purposes by the system's own leadership. Nor has it come in the years since. By contrast, the first director-general of the BBC articulated the mission of Britain's public radio, and by historical extension its television, which public-service TV has honored to good effect for more than half a century.[14] The absence in this country of a similar understanding of public television's purpose offers a clue to the workings of the American system. That it grew from a radically different concept than that which produced the BBC is best illustrated, perhaps, by the absence in the American system of anything approaching the authoritarian role of the BBC's director-general.

Much of the difference between the two systems can be attributed to Scotty Fletcher's role in organizing the American system. Even before he rallied educators to storm the ramparts of the FCC and win the educational reservations, the president of the Fund for Adult Education had a vision that imprinted itself on the public system in the years following the *Sixth Report and Order*. Casting aside the kinds of centralized public systems already established throughout Western Europe, Fletcher saw "a system of independent, interrelated stations . . . [in which] each station would be locally controlled and a source of programming—both to serve the needs of each community and draw upon its resources, and to guard against the abuses and limitations of centralization."[15]

It may not be unreasonable to speculate that the new medium's fear of centralized control had its roots in the legacy of the nation's founders. When they fled the tyranny of centralized authority in seventeenth-century Europe and set up a new nation on these shores, the founders took particular care to place control of the most sensitive institutions of government—schools, police, and justice courts—in local hands. Undoubtedly, it was that legacy that led the federal government to license broadcast stations to local communities. Public television's rejection of a centralized system, on the other hand, might simply have been an acknowledgment of Congress's known opposition to a publicly subsidized national network controlled from a single base of operations. Or perhaps it was a desire on the part of its founders to avoid what they perceived as the abuses of centralized control by the three commercial networks.

How the design of a highly decentralized system of independent, autonomous stations influenced the system's search for a mission can now be clearly divined. In the absence of a centralized authority and a national spokesperson acting as the counterpart to the BBC's director-general, every local station was free to decide its own aims and purpose—within, of course, the FCC's loose framework of "educational" television. Not surprisingly, the missions of individual stations were strongly marked by such local factors as the nature and needs of the licensee institution, the primary source of the station's financial support, or, in the case of the free-standing community stations, by the need to attract viewers and viewer support.

There was an even more important corollary to the concept of a decentralized system of independent, autonomous local stations. Responsibility for activating the reservations—of converting an idea into an operating television station—was handed over lock, stock, and transmitter to the communities fortunate enough to have a reserved channel. The *Sixth Report and Order* gave no help; it reserved the channels and defined eligible licensees but provided no funds for the construction or operation of the stations. Nor were funds provided by the Congress. Whatever their resources, communities were pushed to find an institution willing to be the responsible licensee and to provide the needed dollars to construct, equip, and operate a television station. It was the democratic way: inefficient but involving, it called upon the nation's best traditions of volunteerism and community organization.

Victory was claimed in the battle for the reserved channels with the issuance of the FCC's *Sixth Report and Order* in April 1952. But the real war for educational television still lay ahead. The forces that had fought successfully for the reservations now faced the difficult task of turning an idea into reality, of converting reserved channels into operating television stations. It would take all the nursing, coaxing, and pushing that public-television advocates could bring to bear on local communities. And given the complexities of mobilizing the nation community by community, it would also take time. But time, as it turned out, was of the essence. The fight was on. Fletcher had a name for it: "the urgency-haunted struggle."[16]

2

BUILDING ON
THE BEDROCK

*These precious television assignments cannot be preserved for you
indefinitely . . . they may not even be reserved for you beyond one year
unless you can give the Commission concrete, convincing evidence of the
validity of your intent.*

Paul Walker, Chairman of the FCC[1]

For reasons that were painfully
obvious, the educators' victory in the FCC ruling of 1952 failed to
produce immediate results. Twelve months after the FCC ordered
the channels set aside for education, only one of the 242 reservations, the station in Houston, had been activated and was in
operation. Although considerable activity was stirring in a score
of communities scattered around the country, the leaders of the
movement were hard pressed to find the evidence of progress that
Chairman Walker demanded.

Fletcher, eager to commit the Fund's energies and resources to
the "urgency-haunted struggle," sought guarantees that the channel reservations would be held beyond one year, perhaps indefinitely. Without such guarantees, it was unlikely that the Ford
Foundation would grant the Fund the needed dollars. In a bold
strategic move, Fletcher, having obtained informal assurances
from the FCC that the reservations would be extended, pitched his
plan to the Foundation's board with Chairman Walker present.
He walked out of the meeting with almost $5 million to advance
the cause of educational television. His stratagem to hold the res-

ervations was capped a year later, in May 1953, with the First National Educational Television Conference. Representatives of twenty-nine communities in as many states testified to the progress they had made toward activating their reserved channels. A week later, the FCC announced its decision to hold the reservations "indefinitely." Fletcher was not one to let his Foundation role curb his natural bent for activism.

To meet his promise to Chairman Walker to "deliver" twenty to thirty new stations in the first three years, Fletcher planned action on four fronts: the Fund would continue to support the activities of the JCET, create a citizens' committee to encourage community activity, establish a national program-exchange center, and provide matching funds to help equip the first thirty stations to go on the air. The Fund's continued support of the JCET was a key element in its strategy. The Joint Committee's small staff crisscrossed the country, urging educators to take up the channel reservations, demystifying complex FCC forms for confused administrators, helping them with their arcane engineering plans, and untangling their countless legal knots.[2] By the early sixties, there was hardly an educational station on the air that did not "owe its initial progress to personal advice and help of the JCET staff during its early and critical stages."[3]

Fletcher felt that the JCET, effective though it was, was not enough. The movement needed a group of "tough, hard-hitting, really high-pressure boys"[4] to act as a sales force to promote the idea of educational television nationally. Its primary mission, however, would be the mobilization of local citizen support for the activation of the reserved channels in their communities, particularly in the larger cities. The National Citizens Committee for Educational Television was "invited into existence" in late 1952 by what one of his colleagues called Fletcher's technique of "induced initiative."[5] Marion Folsom of Eastman Kodak and Milton Eisenhower, then president of Penn State University, were recruited to co-chair the NCCET and give it high visibility. To find its executive director, Fletcher tapped into the Marshall Plan's "old boy network," choosing Robert Mullen, a vigorous and experienced public-relations man, to serve as the movement's lead salesman.

During the brief but critical two years of the NCCET's existence, Mullen hopped in and out of planes to rally interest and support for educational television in virtually every major American city. His public-relations skills, used to "mobilize public partnership," helped to create a new breed of community-sponsored public stations in the larger cities. His troops were a strike force to aid those who were struggling to mobilize their communities behind the idea of public television. If a true-believing businessman was needed to talk to skeptical local business leaders, Mullen would deliver a Leland Hazard of Pittsburgh Plate Glass or an Edward Ryerson of Inland Steel. One of his most effective strategies was the organization of an advisory committee of 106 national organizations, from the U.S. Chamber of Commerce to the NAACP, the Junior League to the AFL-CIO. Its value was proved whenever a nudge from national headquarters put a local chapter behind its community's activation efforts.

Of the almost $5 million that the Ford Foundation allocated to Fletcher for the purpose of promoting educational television, the single largest part ($3.5 million) was earmarked for grants to help equip newly activated stations. Fletcher opposed grants for equipment; the Fund's interest lay in promoting substance in programming, not in providing the tools of production. But the movement's leaders persuaded Fletcher that there would be no substance without means, including money to buy cameras, transmitters, microphones, lights, and all the complex and expensive paraphernalia that television demanded. The Fund carefully designed a matching-grant program that was deliberately "large enough to have an effect *while avoiding any tendency to retard local initiative.*"[6] To qualify, each dollar from the Fund had to be matched with two dollars raised locally—or with physical assets of an equivalent value. The maximum grant for large stations was set at $150,000, and for smaller stations at $100,000. With prudent management, the $3.5 million was to help start at least thirty new educational stations within eight years. (In fact, by 1961, when the grant money ran out, thirty-three new stations had been created.)

Fletcher framed the eligibility requirements for the Fund's capital grants with an eye to the future. Successful applicants were required to give evidence that their communities had both the means and the will to construct and operate the proposed station as well as the local resources to program it. They also had to agree to participate in a newly organized national program-exchange service and to include in their equipment purchases a kinescope recorder. This relatively crude device, used for recording television programs before the invention of videotape technology, would permit them to contribute to the proposed program exchange. The Fund's influence was felt in other ways. In choosing which applicants would receive the original equipment grants, Fletcher had a big hand in determining where new stations would be built. More important, he helped determine how they would be built. By enforcing minimal standards for equipment bought with Fund dollars, he effectively upgraded a system that was in danger of being jerrybuilt because of the pressure to stretch scarce dollars. With a hardheaded recognition of the system's fragility during those early years, the canny Fletcher saw to it that the Fund retained title to the equipment for the first eight years of a station's existence. (For some grant recipients, the eight-year term extended beyond the life of the Fund itself; in 1961 the Ford Foundation folded its Fund for Adult Education back into the parent body, ending its existence as a separate entity.)

Fletcher's deft handling of Fund resources also resulted in the creation of a new type of educational television licensee, the nonprofit community corporation. When he formed the National Citizens Committee for Educational Television and directed it to enlist the interest of community groups in the activation of their local educational channels, Fletcher virtually ensured the creation of the community stations. The community stations, notably those located in the large metropolitan centers, dominate the system today, give it much of its strength, and produce or procure most of its national programming. Fletcher's influence was also evident, though less directly, in the creation of the funding mechanism the system now relies upon for most of its support. In the mid-1950s, Fletcher funded a study of listener sponsorship, conducted by Lewis Hill, the founder and president of the Pacifica Foundation's FM station.[7] KQED/San Francisco later adopted Hill's principle of voluntary audience sponsorship and applied it to television.

Critical as the Fund's influence was on the structure of the system, its role in shaping the mission of the new medium may have left a deeper and more lasting imprint on public television's future. Among the conditions of its equipment grants to the early stations, the Fund required of its recipients that "a reasonable proportion of [its] programming should be in the area of adult education in the liberal arts and sciences."[8] By including the liberal-arts requirement in the Fund's Letter of Agreement, Fletcher may have steered the nascent system away from a much narrower focus on systematic education: slide lectures on the Age of Charlemagne, visits to the ocean habitat of the gray whale, and similar fare of the type associated with adult extension courses. The liberal arts, broadly translated, encouraged programming for adults that occasionally probed political and social issues, debated public policy, offered music and dance performance, and—when the underfunded medium could manage it—presented classical and contemporary drama. "Without the Ford Foundation's philanthropy," Jack Gould told readers of the *New York Times*, "there very probably would have been little or no noncommercial TV directed to the general audience."[9] However, the story of Ford's philanthropy might have been different had the Foundation's other subsidiary fund, and not the Fund for Adult Education, taken the lead in shaping the new medium. As it was, the Fund for Advancement of Education, whose monies were dedicated to the improvement of instruction, hesitated to leap into educational television until some time later.

By the end of 1953, the pieces of educational television's curious mosaic were in place. The Fund, under Fletcher's supervision and with the Ford Foundation's deep pockets, had established an educational medium that would evolve into a uniquely American version of public television. Months before the first station went on the air, the outlines of that design were clearly visible. At the base of the public system, its so-called "bedrock," are the inde-

pendent, autonomous stations, locally controlled, serving local
needs and local constituencies. Every other element in the system
is designed to cater to the needs of this loosely federated assembly
of independent stations—a system built from the bottom up. Europeans have difficulty understanding how our system works.
Theirs are built typically from the top down: a centralized bureaucracy, charged with creating a comprehensive program service for the nation as a whole, delivers that service through a nationwide network of transmitters that are part of the bureaucracy,
not independent of it. Even Canada, whose public system is built
in part on independent stations, organizes the stations under a
single public-service corporation. Experience on both sides of the
Atlantic has brought modest modifications to both systems in
more recent years. But in 1953, there was no question in the
minds of Fletcher and the leaders of the educational television
movement that theirs was the right plan for America.

Right or wrong, the start of America's public-television system was
faltering at best. Although all the essential elements of the plan
were in place within a year after the channels were reserved,
growth was painfully slow, even with the Fund's help. The end of
1953 saw only two stations on the air. Eight more joined the following year, and another five the year after that. Ten years would
go by before the system could boast of as many as fifty stations,
still less than one-fourth of the channels set aside for education.

The climate of the early 1950s made the new medium a tough
sell. The viewing audience was still in the thrall of conventional
television; networks were beginning to fill the screen with eye-
popping color, which offered an inducement to watch even when
the content left much to be desired. Millions of satisfied or mes-
merized viewers sat still to watch practically anything that moved
on the face of the tiny tube. If they had had cause to wish for a
more nourishing television diet, the chances are that it would not
have been for one forbiddingly labelled "educational."

The political climate was not much more welcoming to new
and untried media ventures. The country, already tied down by a
war in Korea, was being cleansed of dangerous ideas by the junior

senator from Wisconsin, Joseph McCarthy, whose illiberal storm troopers were not about to extend a welcome hand to a new medium that had "liberal adult education" as a self-described goal. The Hearst press, meanwhile, was damning the noncommercial medium as "socialism," feeding America's latent fear that educational television might become a mouthpiece for a Big Brother government. Few if any saw the new medium as a necessary corrective to the excesses of commercial media, but only because there remained in the 1950s a strongly held faith in the self-righting force of "public interest" regulation.

Those struggling worthies who sought to put down the roots of the new system faced other problems as well. Two of every three reserved channels were in the ultra high frequencies (UHF), including the key cities of New York, Philadelphia, Washington, and Los Angeles. Each of these faced the unhappy prospect of raising large sums of money to activate stations that could not be received in most homes. (Congress eased the situation somewhat with UHF several years later when it forced set manufacturers to include the higher channels on all receivers.) But even those communities that were fortunate enough to have a channel reservation in the standard VHF channels found that it was difficult at best to raise large sums of money for an untried and expensive venture. The Fund's matching-fund offer helped, but it was available only for acquiring equipment and not for meeting operational or building costs. Even to qualify for the Fund's equipment grant meant raising up to $300,000 locally among the community's committed citizens and corporations—a sizeable chunk of change in the post-war economy. The circumstances called for a remarkable feat of local ingenuity and energy. Out of it emerged today's system of public stations, some huge, boasting multimillion-dollar budgets, others barely blips on the television map. They come in all sizes and shapes. But only one can lay claim to being the first on the air.

KUHT / Houston's premiere in May 1953 as the public system's pioneer station is essentially the story of two men, both ardently entrepreneurial, unorthodox, and idiosyncratic. Dr. Walter W. Kemmerer, president of the University of Houston, KUHT's licensee institution, had the vision from which the station sprang:

he surmised that by using the educational television station for teaching, the university could save $10 million in construction costs by not building new lecture halls. Kemmerer recruited Dr. John C. Schwarzwalder from the university's radio-television department and installed him as KUHT's general manager. The vision, however, was to cost Kemmerer his presidency; a month after KUHT went on the air, he was sacked by the university trustees. Schwarzwalder survived the Kemmerer debacle and remained to shift the newly innaugurated KUHT away from its exclusive focus on instruction, while holding at bay those university forces that lusted after the television budget for what they deemed more worthy causes. Schwarzwalder, as his colleagues came to recognize, was a formidable opponent. In Houston—and later, as the first manager of the public station in Minneapolis–St. Paul—Schwarzwalder wore with self-congratulating pride his label as public television's "vice president of dissent." His targets were legion. Periodic memoranda—addressed to A Favored Few but widely disseminated—attacked virtually everyone in the system for their imagined apostasy to his rigid concept of the educational medium.[10]

Not surprisingly, the nation's first public-television station was built with the black wealth of the Lone Star State. Kemmerer created KUHT largely out of the generous philanthropies of oil millionaire Hugh Roy Cullen. Whether it was coincidence or simply the nature of philanthropy in oil-rich states, the nation's second public station was even more redolent with the smell of raw crude than was the first. Although KTHE / Los Angeles was licensed to the University of California, the station was the virtual plaything of one man, an oil millionaire. Captain Alan Hancock—the stripes were earned; he was both a master mariner and a transport pilot—was heir to a fortune extracted from oil deposits beneath Los Angeles's famed Miracle Mile. The captain was closely allied to the University of Southern California, not only as a member of its board of trustees, but through his generous benefactions, one of which was a building on the USC campus that housed the Alan Hancock Foundation.

KTHE / Los Angeles, which began operations on Channel 28 in

November 1953, was entirely underwritten with Hancock money, its studios were in the Hancock Foundation building, and its general manager was the captain's personal aide-de-camp, Dr. William Sener.[11] Not even the station's programming escaped the unmistakable mark of the captain's enterprise and versatility. KTHE aired weekly live concerts featuring the Hancock String Quartet: the captain was the cellist.

KTHE survived less than a year, doomed from the outset by its dependence for support on a single, all-too-human source. When the captain, after a tiff with the USC trustees, resigned his seat on the board and left the campus, he took with him the station's only source of funding, as well as its general manager, Bill Sener. USC was left with a television station it probably did not want and certainly could not support. After KTHE went dark in September 1954, the Los Angeles area was left without a public-television outlet for ten years—Channel 28 was not returned to the air until 1964. When it came back, however, it did so as a community station, licensed to a spirited group of Los Angeles citizens led by Dr. Lee DuBridge, president of the California Institute of Technology, supported by community-wide funding (including viewer subscriptions), and renamed KCET.

The nation's third public channel, Michigan State University's WKAR / East Lansing, was, like Los Angeles, assigned a UHF frequency, and shared with it the dilemma of putting on the air a channel that most viewers were unable to receive. In January 1954 the station began operations, but its efforts at reaching an audience on its assigned Channel 60 met with little success. A decision was made to give up the UHF channel and join forces with the operators of commercial Channel 10 in nearby Jackson, Michigan. Under their time-sharing agreement, the educators would have the daytime hours, leaving the valuable prime-time hours to the commercial operators. The arrangement soon tested the patience of both parties. After successfully negotiating the acquisition of another, lower UHF channel from a neighboring city, Michigan State withdrew from its time-sharing arrangement with the commercial station and returned to a channel of its own.

It is not by accident that the nation's first three public channels were licensed to universities. Even when, as in the case of USC, a university lacks funds to support a station's operations, it does provide an institutional structure with which to pursue the financial and legal problems of channel activation. Other applicants, hoping to get their channels up and running, were compelled to pull together a viable institutional structure before either confronting the other problems associated with the process or, in the case of state networks, negotiating at length with hard-to-convince legislators.

The first of the new breed to form its own institutional base was Pittsburgh's WQED, the nation's fourth public station. WQED was licensed to the Metropolitan Pittsburgh Educational Television, Inc., a free-standing, self-sufficient nonprofit corporation, the type of community-based group promoted by Fletcher and the National Citizens Committee for Educational Television. By choosing the community model as licensee, rather than one of the area's many educational institutions, WQED was positioned to serve equally each of the city's educational and cultural institutions. The community corporation became the organizational model for public stations in most major cities.

With its industrial money from steel, banking, and manufacturing and its strong citizen leadership, the Golden Triangle was well suited to the creation of this new breed of community-based station. Pittsburgh's mayor, David Lawrence, brought the money and leadership together under the insistent and tenacious prodding of his longtime friend, FCC commissioner Frieda Hennock. Others fell behind the mayor's leadership in a process of community organization that is uniquely American and that has over the years led to the creation of most of this country's cultural institutions. Europeans undoubtedly puzzle over the roundabout method of this process, accustomed as they are to the larger role of the state in cultural enterprises, but it has been remarkably effective in the United States given Americans' penchant for individual initiative and love of volunteerism. Typically, the process begins when a citizen with the requisite political clout and qualities of leadership becomes interested in a project to meet a particular need. He or she recruits a board of volunteers, more often than not from friends and fellow club members, which, in turn, goes to the philanthropic community for seed money. At this point, a process is under way that will, in due course, produce a new hospital, science museum, art center, orchestra, or private school. Or a public-television station.

WQED's leadership came from a crusty, civic-minded attorney, Leland Hazard, one of the city's most influential citizens, who at the time was vice president and general counsel of Pittsburgh Plate Glass. The manner in which he and his friends mobilized Pittsburgh's business and cultural leadership behind WQED served as a prototype for many of the community stations that came later. Each city had its counterpart of Leland Hazard. In Chicago it was Edward L. Ryerson, president of Inland Steel; in Boston, Ralph Lowell, a member of one of New England's most distinguished families and president of Boston Safe Deposit and Trust Company; in St. Louis, Raymond Wittcoff of the Caradine Hat Company; and in New Orleans, Darwin Fenner of the investment brokerage house that bore his name. In virtually every city where a community station exists there was at least one leading citizen willing to gamble name, reputation, and standing in the community to further what was then a largely untried and unproven new cultural institution called educational television.

WQED / Pittsburgh went on the air in April 1954. Later in the year, it was followed by new stations in Madison, Wisconsin (WHA-TV); San Francisco (KQED); Cincinnati, Ohio (WCET); St. Louis, Missouri (KETC); Lincoln, Nebraska (KUON-TV); and Seattle, Washington (KCTS-TV). At the same time, some state legislatures were beginning to see in the new medium a partial solution to the problem of spreading the state's educational resources among more of its citizens. Although Alabama was not the first to come up with the idea (an earlier plan for a New York State network died with Governor Dewey's veto), it was the first to act. The state's reserved channels, joined together under a government commission to form a statewide network, were put in the service of the state's widely scattered complex of school districts and colleges. Other states followed suit, including New Jersey, Georgia, South Dakota, Connecticut, South Carolina, and Wisconsin.

WGBH-TV began broadcasting in May 1955 as the nation's fourteenth public station. While it was not one of the earliest to go on the air, the Boston station was destined to play a special role in the public medium by becoming one of the system's brightest and most creative program producers. Much earlier, a consortium of Boston's many educational and cultural institutions had formed the WGBH Educational Foundation to serve as the licensee for a public radio station (WGBH-FM). When television came along, the Educational Foundation served as the licensee for the television station as well. WGBH-TV broadcast from makeshift facilities in a former rollerskating rink until they were destroyed by fire in 1961 and new studios were built on the edge of Harvard's playing fields. A somewhat less spectacular but nonetheless significant event occurred in the station's second year. A staff revolt, occasioned by dissatisfaction with its leadership, unseated the first general manager of WGBH, Parker Wheatly, and brought to power the young manager of its FM station, Hartford Gunn, Jr. For Gunn, it was to be the start of a distinguished career in public television, one that would have a profound influence upon the system in subsequent years. We shall have reason to return to his story later.

Boston and the other starters among the system's pioneer public stations lent the first substance to Fletcher's struggle to activate educational channels before a lack of action cost them their reserved status and caused their frequency to be reassigned to commercial use. The system was slow to start and sluggish to expand despite the Fund's aid and insistent encouragement. Station activations were fitful, haphazardly planned, and bore no correlation to the geographical distribution of the country's television homes. Viewers in some parts of the country, including New York and Los Angeles, had no access to public television's programming for a decade or more. The system's uneven, random growth resulted from the decision to leave activation of the reserved channels entirely to local initiative and local money. In each community, nothing moved until one person was fired with the zeal to organize a group to raise the needed funds. That type of leadership is not easily found. When leaders of this caliber are identified, they are often fully committed to social causes that make television seem trivial by comparison.

Faced with these and other difficulties, it may be a minor miracle that America's landscape is now dotted with more than 150 licensee institutions—community corporations, universities and colleges, public-school boards, and state networks—operating more than 350 stations, each of which is variously devoted to some form of "educational" service. Most stations are loosely federated into a national program service that they share and jointly control. But what they share is not what defines them. They are defined by their independence and autonomy, not their collectivity. This self-possessed sovereignty produces all too frequently a highly parochial approach to public television's *national* concerns, a malaise that has its roots in the system's start-up. While the fight to reserve educational frequencies drew local advocates together in a national crusade, activation of the reservations was in every case a local battle fought by local leaders to overcome purely local problems. The victors in these local wars left the field of battle flushed with the heady feeling of proprietorship; even now, they refer possessively to their station's viewers as "my audience." Medieval England's feudal lords must have felt much the same way when success in the battlefield secured their fiefdom. The danger is constantly present in public television, however, that the independent spirit born of local pride can slip easily into destructive provincialism.

Whatever their strengths and weaknesses, local stations form the heart if not the soul of the American public-television system. In both its structure and governing spirit, the whole is defined by its hundreds of diverse parts, and not by any central, cohesive core. For that reason alone, the story of each station, and the local forces that produced and shaped it, could be seen as the key to understanding the complexities of the system as a whole. To tell the story of each of the system's stations would, of course, weigh too heavily in the reader's hands and on the reader's patience.[12] I have chosen instead to tell the story of one station, knowing that it may not be typical of all, but was nevertheless among the very early stations and thus survived the problems of public television's awkward birth. More to the point, my natural desire is to tell the story I know best—the story of KQED/San Francisco. That is where public television and I first met and were to spend fifteen rewarding years together looking for answers to questions that were rarely asked.

3

QED: THE SEARCH
FOR ANSWERS

In action, KQED calls to mind the old saw about a bumblebee, which, by the laws of aerodynamics, can't fly, but, not knowing this, goes ahead and flies anyway.

George B. Leonard, Jr.[1]

In both washrooms, signs warned DON'T FLUSH DURING BROADCASTS. It was the only way we knew to keep the rumble of plumbing out of our air shows. KQED's home at the time, a ramshackle wood-and-stucco building nestled in the shabby heart of San Francisco's South-of-Market industrial district, had only two washrooms. And, unluckily for us, both opened directly onto a balcony that overlooked the production studio. The situation could be a source of embarrassment for all concerned.

For us, at least, the washroom signs were a metaphor for the improvisational, make-do state of public television in the mid-1950s. Desperately needing quarters we could afford, we found what had once been a building for a small manufacturing plant, and more recently a garage for telephone company trucks, and transformed it with our own hands into a crude but workable studio. We couldn't afford acoustic tile, so we used cast-off egg crates. Our equipment was secondhand. Our transmitter was donated by a local commercial station.[2] And our studio was wired with cable abandoned at the end of the 1964 Republican National Conven-

tion by the profligate commercial networks. Where money was
lacking, imagination and energy were substituted.

Notwithstanding its inconveniences, we were grateful finally to
have a studio we could call our own. For our first two years, we
made do with a borrowed studio of sorts, a trade-school classroom
used to train television technicians. The studio, its cameras, and
its student operators were available to us only three nights a week,
so our broadcast schedule during those years was pitifully thin—
hardly substantive enough to make a dent in the viewing habits of
our potential audience. But that didn't deter us from pitching for
money. Significantly, KQED's first live broadcast was a fund appeal,
made by me, from a makeshift studio hastily put together in the
small room that housed our transmitter. The room, in the attic of
San Francisco's Mark Hopkins Hotel, was so tiny and cramped that
the camera operator, in order to get me in the frame of the picture, had to back into and shoot from the toilet. Critics of public
television may make of this what they will.

The origins of San Francisco's public-television channel can be
traced back to the lively imagination, determination, and un-
bounded energies of one man. Unlike his counterparts in Boston,
Chicago, and Pittsburgh, Vaughn D. Seidel was not a powerful
business leader with access to the pockets of the rich. He was the
superintendent of the suburban Alameda County school district,
a true believer in audiovisual education.[3] Active in the pre-1952
movement to reserve frequencies for educational television, he
was a dedicated force in finding the means to activate Channel 9,
the valuable VHF channel reserved for the San Francisco Bay Area.
Knowing his own school district was not the best licensee to serve
the larger Bay Area, Seidel brought into being educational television's first community corporation, the Bay Area Educational
Television Association. BAETA's board, composed largely of the
heads of the Bay Area's various educational and cultural institutions, was weighty with high-mindedness but light in clout. In its
first year, it managed the purchase of a secondhand transmitter
at a fire-sale price, negotiated leases for largely unusable studio
space at the University of California and San Francisco State Col-

lege, and amassed a bank account approximating $2000 by soliciting $10 memberships from the station's projected audience.

In early 1953, however, the tide turned in BAETA's favor—two grants from local foundations gave BAETA the funds needed to hire a manager.[4] The board blithely assumed that a full-time television professional would fit all the pieces together, hire a staff, turn on the power, and light up the screens of the Bay Area with exciting, stimulating, and inexpensive fare. For better or for worse, I was the one chosen to bear this mantle of responsibility, although I was neither a television professional (my experience was in radio) nor a miracle worker. But I didn't have to be either to realize that the picture was missing some key elements.

My first priority was to find a program executive with the idealism of a reformer, the energy of a backfield runner, and the power to turn ground round into Chateaubriand. Our search began and ended with one man, Jonathan C. Rice, a former Marine combat correspondent and news photographer who, when we found him, was news chief of KTLA / Los Angeles, commercial television's most aggressive and news-oriented independent station. The hands-on television experience that he brought to our early planning, essential as it was, may have been the least of his contributions. Rice's gift for sharing his own creative spirit and nourishing it in others was the catalyst that saved us from humdrumdom. The catholicity of his interests and his amateur's love for exploring ideas, whether in music, the arts, or science, became the template for KQED's program schedule. As we sat to plot a course for the future station, neither of us knew that it was the beginning of a fifteen-year partnership that was to be firmly rooted in our shared interests and in a tacit acceptance of our respective roles: I didn't want his job; he didn't want mine.

It was clear from the outset, however, that ideas, whatever their intrinsic worth, have little value in television without the equipment to transmute them into programming. We had ideas but no equipment. Fortunately, Scott Fletcher's program of equipment grants was there to provide the leverage to loft us, and many others, onto the air. Not even that would have helped, however, without the amiable flexibility of the Fund's West Coast representative,

G. H. (Bill) Griffiths. To qualify for a grant, we knew we had to match every Fund dollar with two of our own. Griffiths, knowing that we lacked the cash, allowed us to capitalize every piece of technical equipment, functioning or not, plus "properly appraised gifts in kind" (including, incidentally, a donated piece of furniture known as a cockfight chair, which was used as set decoration). In a deal that would do credit to a tin-siding salesperson, we qualified for a desperately needed grant to acquire basic equipment.

Rice and I began work on June 1, 1953, and a year later, almost to the day, our vision became a reality. KQED was on the air, tentatively, shakily, its paid staff of eight straining to sustain a three-nights-a-week broadcast schedule. Admittedly ill prepared, we rushed into service in order to qualify for a much-needed $10,000 grant that Emerson Radio awarded to each of the first ten stations on the air. We were number six. Our name, QED—for the Latin *quod erat demonstrandum*—was suggested by my wife, Beverley, who understood those things. Its meaning—that which is to be proved—was well suited to the uncertain venture on which we were embarked.

Without a clear direction from Washington, and lacking even the precedent of an earlier station—Houston was not yet on the air when our planning began—Rice and I crafted a mission partly by instinct and partly by shared conviction. Both of us felt that the station should be a cultural institution in its own right and not simply a conveyor belt for the community's many other cultural institutions. Months before we had a studio of our own—we were still using the trade-school studio with a student television crew—Rice brazenly mounted a series of in-studio concerts with the thirty-piece Little Symphony of San Francisco. A rhapsodic critic hailed it as the "crowning glory in the short life of KQED" and "the most important local TV development of the season."[5] His words may have said more about conventional television's cultural aridity than about our concerts—in which, incidentally, even he found such "minor production flaws" as off-camera crashes and on-camera images that ranged from "crystal sharp" to "inexplicably diffused" to "frequently out-of-focus." Nothing, however, could dissuade Rice from attempting more live studio events in the years ahead—solo recitals and performances of chamber music, jazz, and dance. Each performance drew us deeper into the cultural life of the community. And that's precisely where we thought a community television station ought to be.

June 1955 was our first anniversary on the air. It was nearly our last. The board, up to its knees in debt and with prospects dim for meeting future expenses, voted to call it quits: to turn out the lights, lock the door, and wait for a more propitious time to introduce noncommercial television to the Bay Area. My "no" vote was a plea for time. Why not let the public decide? It was *their* station. Closing shop now would result not only in losing our small staff and abandoning our loyal supporters, but in the surrender of our most cost-effective fund-raising tool, the station itself. We reached a compromise: a thirty-day moratorium, during which the board would tackle the task of retiring the deficit and I, to keep us from sliding further into debt, would raise the dollars to meet six months' expenses. An additional six months of life would give us breathing room to call on a blue-ribbon citizens' committee to study our long-term economic viability and recommend remedies. If this seems an unsubtle ploy to involve community leadership in our plight, we were not the first nonprofit to use it.

With money borrowed from the parents of two of our employees, we engaged a small public-relations firm and plunged into a series of hastily planned events, all aimed at getting our hands into the community's pockets. We kicked off with an all-night telethon, its volunteer talent stretching from nuclear physicist Edward Teller to exotic dancer Tempest Storm. The telethon may have helped our image more than our bank account: after the strippers and nightclub comics, viewers could hardly think of their educational channel in the same way again. "Without realizing it," said the *San Francisco Chronicle*, "[KQED] put on the best show that has been on a San Francisco station."[6]

But the bigger show was yet to come. Our public-relations team, Curt Roberts and Len Gross, had a novel fund-raising scheme: a television auction at which donated merchandise would be displayed on camera and auctioned off to the highest bid called in by telephone. It had never been tried. With the end of the thirty-day moratorium drawing nearer, skepticism surrendered to desperation. A weary staff and corps of volunteers, having finished the telethon only three days earlier, threw themselves into a twenty-four-hour selling frenzy that ended in the predawn hours with the station closer to its goal by $6000. But something else had happened in those frenzied hours that proved more important to our future than money. We became a part of the community. Strangers called to wish us well, sent food and drink to sustain us through the tiring hours, and even showed up at the studio door to volunteer their services. The term community television suddenly had palpable meaning. That morning, as we locked the studio door and filed wearily into the foggy dawn of another day, we knew with certainty that what had begun as an act of desperation was about to become an annual KQED event, a rite of bonding with the community with tangible benefits to our bank balance.

The television auction did become an annual event, expanded from one day to ten, and did much to identify the station with the community.[7] In time, however, its charming ingenuous quality was lost in the push to squeeze more and more money out of the event. But long before that happened, and KQED Auctions became history, the highly unpredictable process produced a wealth of stories. I remember well the year (I think it was the third) that we found ourselves in possession of a pair of lavender bedsheets whose auction value had been enhanced by having been slept in by Kim Novak. The actress, then in her lavender period (her cats were even dyed lavender), had insisted that the Clift Hotel supply her with lavender sheets for an overnight stay in San Francisco. On her departure, the hotel graciously donated them, unlaundered, to the auction. The sheets were snapped up for $250 by a young man named Beale Ernst, who was then wavering between continuing his job promoting records or succumbing to his hobby of making neckties. The Kim Novak sheets tipped him to neckwear. Ernst returned the following day to give the auction dozens of neckties fashioned from the lavender sheets, all neatly labelled to remind buyers of Ms. Novak's previous presence. National publicity generated by press accounts of the episode launched Ernst on a career in fashion neckwear that eventually led him to become the nation's fourth largest supplier.

The 1955 rescue effort succeeded. But knowing that a death scene only plays once, we took seriously the recommendations of our citizens' panel and beefed up our board with business people. The position of corporate chair was turned over to a prominent civic leader and the scion of a famous San Francisco family, Mortimer Fleishhacker, Jr., and increased effort was devoted to using our airtime more effectively for fund-raising. Then as now, most of KQED's operating funds came from audience support in the form of voluntary contributions, an idea BAETA borrowed at the outset from Berkeley's KPFA radio.[8] Today, audience support is standard for most public stations. In the mid-1950s, however, most stations thought it too unreliable; only KQED dared to experiment with it. After our 1955 crisis, we sought a way to make it work more effectively and hit upon the idea of "pledging"—giving viewers a telephone number to call to declare their support of the station, with the promise of a check to follow. Pledge nights gave rise to pledge weeks when programs were interrupted with repetitious and seemingly endless pitches. Unfortunately for the hapless viewer, we discovered that income from these pitches increases in direct proportion to the time devoted to them, not to the quality of their content. In more recent years the KQED invention has become a national nuisance through semi-annual funding weeks that PBS likes to call "festivals." The necessity for them, however, remains.

Before the invention of videotape released us from the perilous high-wire act of live programming, back-to-back programming was a daily occurrence. KQED's three cameras were whipped from one part of the studio to another in the brief interval between shows (we were careful, of course, to avoid the pillar in the middle of the studio). We stretched and strained our limited resources to fill a slim weekly schedule. Because it was cheaper to produce our own simple shows than to buy programs off the shelf, our schedule was largely a pastiche of locally produced shows. Many were aimed at children, a top priority for the public medium then as now. Most were mildly instructive—storytelling, natural science, body coordination, and the like—intended, so we advertised, to make "do-ers out of viewers." This, too, was true of much of our adult programming. Television's "how to" genre offered an easily produced and popular format—needing only an expert in something, anything, who had an engaging camera presence. In the early years, the formula produced courses in a wide variety of skills: skin diving, typing, shorthand, memory training, investing, public speaking, gardening, speed reading, beginning piano, home repairs, and gift wrapping. Some were more successful than others. Rice dropped the memory-training course when the instructor forgot an appointment that he had made with us.

There was another respect in which we were strongly influenced by Pacifica radio: KPFA's practice of keeping its listeners apprised of station policy by airing a weekly report from its manager. My own effort, however, was barely begun when Rice transformed it into something else by shunting a visiting dignitary my way for an on-air interview. At the time, my report was the only live show on the schedule. The incident gave birth to a weekly half-hour interview program, ambiguously titled *Kaleidoscope*, which remained in the schedule for fifteen years. When Rice sent his secretary, Win Murphy, to be the show's producer (she later directed it as well), he inadvertently created a professional partnership that lasted longer than many marriages. We managed, over those fifteen years, to bring before our cameras a virtual *Who's Who* of leaders in the arts, entertainment, and public service, including Eleanor Roosevelt, Buster Keaton, Aldous Huxley, Bing Crosby, Norman Thomas, Robert F. Kennedy, Rube Goldberg, Alexander Kerensky, L. S. B. Leakey, Ruth St. Denis, Leo Szilard, and scores of others. In the early days, when the show was live, we never booked guests without first meeting them. We broke the rule one Labor Day in our desperation to find a subject appropriate to and available on the holiday. I had heard about a longshoreman who worked on the waterfront unloading ships by day and writing books by night. He seemed a good bet but we had no idea how to reach him. He had no telephone, so Murphy mailed a postcard inviting him sight unseen. We need not have held our collective breath. Eric Hoffer, dressed in khaki working clothes, playing his huge voice like a mighty Wurlitzer as he punctuated the air with his enormous hands, was an immediate hit and a natural performer. Murphy later turned our Labor Day triumph into a national series of twelve half-hour *Conversations with Eric Hoffer.*

On another occasion, Murphy persuaded me to interview a visiting Japanese artist. The results were disappointing; his art was esoteric and his English was beyond penetration. Murphy, however, saw in T. Mikami the makings of a successful "how to" series, instructing aspiring amateur artists in the arcane art of Japanese brush painting. At first, *Japanese Brush Painting* was a local series. Viewers were told that they would need certain tools—a brush, an ink stick, and a stone. Skeptical though he was, Rice bought out Chinatown's supply of the materials, packaged them into Japanese brush-painting kits, and offered them to our viewers at a modest price. When the show aired, we were swamped with more requests than we were able to fill. We faced a dilemma: do we disappoint the latecomers, or do we import more kits from Japan and, at the already announced price, sell them at a loss? Rice solved the problem by working the phone until he found an airline, a new one, willing to fly in more kits from Tokyo in exchange for an on-air credit to help establish its identity. Sometime later, *Japanese Brush Painting* went national, followed by a sequel, *Once upon a Japanese Time.* KQED found its way into the business of importing, packaging, and marketing brush-painting paraphernalia on a national scale.

With our interest in actively involving KQED in the political life of the community, we did not hesitate when necessary to step into the minefields of controversy, knowing that the station was at greater risk if avoiding controversy meant ducking important and significant issues. This would not have worked without the backing of a board ready to make policy but courageous enough to leave its implementation to management. Because the boundary is blurred at best, the temptation to cross it in moments of crisis is virtually irresistible. Our programming gave KQED's board ample temptation to breach the boundary, but the boundary always held. I was given, within board policy, considerable freedom to make operating decisions and even to take substantial risks, always with

the clear understanding that I bore full responsibility for the consequences. However, the viability of that relationship was, like a
marriage, put to the test in each and every crisis. The crisis in
1963 was one example.

The year was a time of particular turmoil and tension. In the
South, blacks were pressing to gain their constitutional rights; racial incidents and rallies followed one upon the other. In Dallas,
a president was felled by an assassin's bullet. The conscience of
the nation was bared like a raw nerve. In the midst of these events,
the KQED film unit produced for national release a highly provocative documentary, *Take This Hammer,* in which author James Baldwin was filmed touring the streets of San Francisco, lifting metaphorical rocks and exposing the ugly presence of racism. The
film's message was simple and direct: racism is not confined to
the Deep South, it lives everywhere, lurking even in the corners
of "America's favorite city." Advance word of the film's assault on
the city's good name sent shock waves through the ranks of the
board's civic boosters. Without examining the evidence, they an-
grily dismissed Baldwin's thesis, blaming his wrongheaded conclusions on his ignorance of the city. One board member, discreetly
couching his self-righteous cry for censorship in the rhetoric of
board policy, declared "it is not the function of KQED, in the
name of educational television, to produce inflammatory, distorted, sacrilegious, extremist programs." Another warned me of
the mayor's displeasure, apparently believing that his honor's attitude, if not a matter of policy, was at least a cause for concern.
Neither had seen the film, of course. In resolving the crisis, the
board held firm to principle, deciding that "as a practical matter
it must rely on the judgment of the staff."[9] But it wisely added
that it "may at times serve as a board of review *after* the program
has been broadcast" (emphasis added). The distinction is critical,
not only for public broadcasters but also for all not-for-profits gov-
erned by citizen-volunteer boards whose work brings them into
areas of controversy. If public broadcasters have a particular concern, it is because their decisions are on the screen, immediately
and widely visible for the world to judge.

Nothing heightens sensibilities, arouses passions, and tests the limits of board-management roles faster than the subject of sex and where to draw the lines in its treatment on "family" television. Two episodes in our experience make the point. The first was a locally produced documentary on homosexuality, *The Rejected.* If it was not the first, then it certainly was one of the earliest to treat the then taboo subject on television. Its imminent airing prompted the threatened resignation of one board member, who warned that homosexuality was a disease that could be spread by discussions about it, or worse, could be "made respectable." The board, holding to principle, left the decision to management. *The Rejected* aired both locally and nationally, the Republic held, and the skittish board member retained his seat for several more years of useful service.

The other episode involved a film series on sex education chosen by the schools to air in our television service to elementary classes. The inclusion of graphic descriptions of male and female sex characteristics and the use of terms such as "pubic hair" and "masturbation" aroused the opposition of several parental groups. One of our board members took up their cause at the next meeting, telling her colleagues that she had received "a number" of letters from "friends" protesting the series and warning that sex education was a communist plot to undermine the moral fiber of America. She did not, she added cautiously, necessarily agree with her friends. The board reacted with shocked silence, not entirely because of the allegation—that could be dismissed as cold-war hysteria—but because the member who voiced the protest brought to it the authority of celebrity. Shirley Temple Black was a living legend, and almost no one on the board had the courage to challenge her. In their hearts she was still Little Miss Marker. Struggling for an easy exit, the chair—although fully aware the series had been programmed by the schools and not by the station—proposed that the board screen the series and come to its own decision. The critical issue was whether airing it might adversely affect our public fund-raising. Fortunately, before the board was led by panic to breach the line between policy and operations, one member—a woman who, as an outstanding civic leader, was not easily awed—proposed a compromise: leave all programming decisions to management but offer the board an "informational" screening. The compromise was quickly adopted, the screening was held, but only Shirley Black attended. To her credit, and my undying gratitude, she patiently viewed the films, asked questions, and, with minor reservations, concurred in our decision to air them.

Some areas of programming, Rice and I agreed, were better left to commercial television. One was daily news. It was much too difficult and costly for us to attempt. Besides, we thought the local stations were handling it reasonably well. The situation changed suddenly and dramatically on a Friday night in 1968 when we learned that the Newspaper Guild was about to strike San Francisco's two daily newspapers. Rice and his newly hired public affairs director, former *San Francisco Chronicle* reporter Mel Wax, fearing that local television would not fill the news void, huddled over the weekend and emerged Monday morning with a plan. *Newspaper of the Air* would be a nightly news show, but an unconventional one; we couldn't afford the conventional kind. Working with what we had—reporters hired as needed off the picket lines at $100 a week, a managing editor, and a long studio table—we kicked off *Newspaper of the Air* promptly at 7:00 P.M. that first Monday evening. Bill German, the *Chronicle*'s managing editor and our managing editor as well, had assigned each reporter a story to cover. That evening, the reporters gathered around the long, rectangular table for the air show. German, seated at the head, called on each reporter in turn to tell his or her story from notes—we had no newsfilm at the time—and then subjected them to questions from him and each other. Editorial cartoonist Bob Bastian closed the night's show with a folio of witty comments on the news, drawn while the show was in progress.

In Marshall McLuhan's lexicon, *Newspaper of the Air* was "process." It was news in the act of becoming a newscast—unedited, unformed, unfinished. The show's free form was a radical departure for a medium that worships convention and avoids risk. But the audience liked it. And so, incidentally, did KGO-TV, the local ABC-owned station. Its news department copied *Newspaper*'s format—reporters talking to each other—but not its serious substance, giving birth to a commercial mutant derided as "happy talk." The distance between the genuine article and its meretricious offspring was never more sharply defined than in *Newspaper*'s coverage of the ecumenical service at Grace Cathedral following the assassination of Dr. Martin Luther King, Jr., in April 1968. German had assigned Bill Chapin to cover it. Chapin was perfectly cast as the hardbitten newsman of Hollywood cliché who's seen it all and felt nothing. But the stereotype crumbled that night. Called on to describe the scene at the service, Chapin had barely begun when he suddenly, shockingly, broke off, choked back a sob, and buried his head in his hands. It was an electrifying moment when the humanity of the storyteller was touched by the story itself and a far cry from the factitious "happy talk" that it inspired.

Newspaper of the Air died with the end of the strike nine weeks later. Efforts to revive it failed. The reporters, no longer working exclusively for us, were not about to scoop their own newspapers. Worse, our money had run out. The Ford Foundation had funded the nine-week run with a $50,000 grant, made in remarkably swift fashion by Ford's television adviser, Fred Friendly. His response to my single telephone call was vintage Friendly: no questions asked, just a demand that we do our best and "let everyone know you're doing it." Two months after *Newspaper*'s demise, Ford announced a new grant program: the Foundation was prepared to fund "innovative new series." Many suspected the tender was Friendly's veiled enticement to other public stations to follow our lead into daily news shows, and some did. But the first application into Friendly's in basket was ours. We were ready to return to the news business.

The resulting $750,000 grant allowed us to hire our own reporters and support staff, and by September of 1968 we were back on the air with a daily news show whose title, *Newsroom*, was deliberately chosen to suggest "process." The new show used more sophisticated production techniques than its hastily planned and thinly budgeted predecessor, and yet it was visibly the direct descendant of *Newspaper of the Air*. Reporters were still print-trained journalists with specific beats—city government, education, environment, and foreign affairs—and as before, they returned to the studio at airtime to sit around a table, tell their stories, and parry the questioning of their peers and of anchor Mel Wax. As the show matured, increasing use was made of news film. *Newsroom* was aggressive, interactive, and contentious journalism. Objective reporting was its aim, but not always its result: a reporter's lifted eyebrow, tone of voice, unplanned flippancy, or ad-libbed response to another's question could occasionally tilt the show in one direction or another. On the positive side, news stories were reported in depth and treated as developing strands, not as isolated, self-contained fragments of the day's events.

Predictably, *Newsroom*'s volatile format produced occasional controversy. Several days after Dr. S. I. Hayakawa took over as president of the rebellious San Francisco State College campus, he appeared on *Newsroom*. But in mid-interview, angered at the aggressive questioning, he stormed off the show with a parting imprecation to the reporters to "go to hell." The mini-drama made newspaper headlines the next day and drew a heavy volume of mail, some harshly critical of our news practices and much of it reflecting the dilemma all news shows faced in covering the student rebellions of the turbulent 1960s. Older viewers saw the riots as a metaphor for a breakdown in traditional values, a souring of parent-child relationships, for which the remedy was more discipline. The mostly younger staff of *Newsroom*, however, saw student grievances as legitimate concerns and thus found themselves swimming against the current of viewer expectations—expectations that were shaped in large measure by the images projected in more conventional news shows. Still, virtually every letter from eyewitnesses to events on the state college campus praised *Newsroom* for its "fair and accurate" coverage.

KQED paid the price for its unconventional approach to news. Corporate donors were easily put off by *Newsroom*'s aggressive style. On one occasion, the public-relations vice president of a major corporate donor, whose five-figure support check had been banked only days before, called to protest a story critical of his company aired on the previous evening's *Newsroom*. He made forcefully clear that his company did not make charitable contributions in the expectation of being booted in the corporate derriere. My reflexive response was to offer the immediate return of the check. Luckily, the offer was refused. But in a separate incident, an unwillingness to be linked with our "volatile and unpredictable" news show was the reason given by a Bay Area school district for abruptly cancelling its obligation to pay a share of our televised school service. No doubt the superintendent was beyond appreciating that volatility and unpredictability, the qualities he complained of, were the same qualities that won *Newsroom* its large and loyal following.

Scoring a beat on the conventional press, as with the bizarre story of Patty Hearst's abduction by the Simbionese Liberation Army, brought exceptional satisfaction to the show's crew. *Newsroom*'s Marilyn Baker, using contacts no one else had, managed to stay "two weeks ahead of the police in her revelations about the Hearst kidnapping case" while providing the national press and local police with "nearly every substantial clue." An envious FBI agent offered the grudging sort of praise accorded women in the business: "I wish I had that broad's connections."[10]

Newsroom's ability to be closely involved in the affairs of the community was never better served than by its part in what came to be known as the People's Park War. The dispute centered on a small patch of undeveloped property owned by the University of California and adjacent to its Berkeley campus. A group of urban poor, known as "street people," had taken over the plot and converted it into a crude park. When the University reasserted its rights by forcibly removing the park's occupants and enclosing the disputed parcel in an eight-foot steel mesh fence, a bloody melee resulted in which one person died and scores were injured. Governor Ronald Reagan sent in an armed California National Guard to restore order. *Newsroom* followed events with daily reports and film. At one critical juncture in the dispute, KQED arranged and televised a face-to-face meeting with representatives of the city, the University, and the street people. It failed. A second meeting, arranged by the University, was also aired and also failed to settle the dispute. The situation had grown steadily more ex-

plosive and was heading toward a potentially dangerous climax on
Memorial Day. On that day, a reported force of 50,000 "street
people" and their supporters planned to storm the steel mesh
fence and the National Guard troops protecting it. In a last desperate effort to avoid the feared Armageddon, Berkeley's mayor
convened an emergency session of the city council on the eve of
the planned assault and again asked *Newsroom* to cover the event.
This time he wanted the show aired statewide, not only to lower
the heat on the conflict locally, but to send a message elsewhere
to dissuade out-of-towners from trekking to Berkeley to join the
march.

That evening, an overflow crowd filled the tense council cham-
bers. Hour after hour they heard impassioned arguments on both
sides. Among the images caught by our cameras was one of a
group of teenagers, sprawled on the council room floor, looking
up in disbelief at a retired general as he warned the city council
of the imminent danger of a communist takeover by the "street
people." It was long after midnight when the meeting reached its
dramatic climax: a heart-stopping 5 to 4 vote that opened the way
for eventual settlement of the long-standing dispute. Memorial
Day's bloody conflict was averted. The next day's march was peaceful, even joyful. In a festive mood, young women who only a day
earlier were steeled to march against the loaded rifles of the National Guard laughingly stuffed flowers in the muzzles of their
rifles as the startled soldiers were pulled into the street for a spontaneous dance. *Newsroom*'s cameras brought the celebratory images to a statewide television audience. City and university officials
later cited KQED's extensive coverage of the crisis, and particularly
coverage of the crucial council meeting, as a critical factor in the
dispute's peaceful outcome.

Newsroom survived for nine years, winning Dupont-Columbia
and Peabody Awards, and giving local commercial news a run for
their audience numbers. Nicholas von Hoffman called it "report-
age of a different and higher order."[11] Three successive KQED
managements struggled to keep *Newsroom* alive, but after the Ford
grant ran out, the show's rising costs outran the station's ability

to support it without sacrificing every other local program. During the fall of 1980, over howls of protest from the audience, the show was cancelled. Several dedicated *Newsroom* fans were elected to the KQED board, pledging to reverse the decision. But it was too late. The show had spent its energy, its freshness was gone, and in some ways the show was a victim of its own success. The original ink-stained print journalists, who looked, talked, and dressed so differently from the button-neat and blow-dried reporters on the commercial channels, were a breath of fresh air in the show's early years. But not even a tough-minded team from the print press could escape the insidious power of television to reduce flesh-and-blood people to spectral personalities. In time, *Newsroom* reporters slipped inexorably into the role of self-conscious performer as their comments and responses became ever more predictable. An occasional replacement in the lineup helped. But when a bitterly fought labor dispute closed the show down for four months, its fragile internal fabric was torn. In the wake of changed relationships, both the show and its appearance took second place to its participants' overriding concern for their job security.

Newsroom was a single but significant episode in the life of one station, a tale told from a period in its history when anything and everything seemed possible, when the accretions of growth and expansion—more people, more money, more risk—had not yet clouded the vision of what public television was about. Our experience was in some respects typical of other stations and in other respects unique to a particular time and place. Each public station has its own story to tell, and each has its own face and style. The best of the stations not only reflect the character of the communities they serve, they play an integral role, shaping events as well as reporting them. At KQED, our efforts to honor that credo were played out with all the imagination and resources we could muster. But there were limits.

The most obvious was the limitation of time—not too little, but too much. The hours in our daily schedule were more than our modest staff and meager resources could possibly fill, a problem common to all broadcast stations. Commercial stations, however,

4

GO FOR BROKE

The most important dollars we spend are the gambling dollars, the dollars spent on program projects which need to be done but may not be profitable.

John F. White[1]

Network is a word that is scorned in the world of public broadcasting. It implies centralized control and lockstep programming. The very notion of networking is heresy to those who are dedicated to the proposition that public television should be decentralized, diverse, and attuned to the needs of its local audiences—in short, that it should be the antithesis of network-controlled commercial television.

Faith in the efficacy of decentralization, widely practiced in other areas of our social policy, finds expression in the noncommercial medium in the structure of PBS, the Public Broadcasting Service. The roots of a decentralized system, however, were planted years before they produced a PBS. They stretch back to educational television's early planning councils, meetings that took place before the channel reservations were a reality and long before the first educational station was on the air. The strongest voice in those planning councils—and, thus, the principal architect of the system that emerged—was the only person at the table with access to funds to make the plans a reality. As head of the Ford Foundation's Fund for Adult Education, Scott Fletcher had funded the push for channel reservations; he had provided impetus and money to stimulate the early activations; and now, while not the first to see the need, he was the first to create a national center for program exchange.

Most early planners knew that stations would be hard pressed to fill their schedules without help. As early as the summer of 1951, the NAEB produced a plan for program exchange, which it carried to the Fund the following spring and put on Fletcher's desk—only to discover that the energetic and enterprising Fletcher had already developed his own plan. Months earlier, Fletcher had been alerted to the NAEB plan and to the urgent need of "building an inventory of programs on film for use as the educational stations take the air" by his principal adviser, Robert Hudson. The same concerns were echoed several months later by a young businessman with a particular reason to be concerned. Raymond Wittcoff had volunteered to chair the effort to bring an educational station to St. Louis. Fearing that educational television in general, and his station in particular, would fail unless it could draw a significant part of its programming "from a strong and well-financed national cooperation network agency," Wittcoff proposed "a bold and forthright plan for the creation of a national educational television network."[2]

Fletcher, not one to let a good idea slip by unnoticed, acted quickly. In the summer of 1952, he invited a small group of activists to New York to discuss a plan. Characteristically, he included two new recruits to the cause, both prominent educators who until then had not been actively involved in its planning: George Stoddard, president of the University of Illinois, and Harold Lasswell, professor of law and political science at Yale. According to eyewitness reports, the discussions were "brisk and penetrating." Ideas were tossed about, argued, and refined. But through it all, Fletcher insisted on two points. First, the new organization must be autonomous (thus ruling out the NAEB's plan to put the center under its own protective wing.) The center, he said, should be a part of the mainstream of American culture, with its own board composed not of self-interested professionals but of outward-looking men and women possessing "a variety of experience, competence and command" and drawn from the broad fields of the arts, sciences, humanities, education, business, and the professions. Moreover, the members of the governing board would serve as individuals rather than as representatives of other institutions and organizations. Fletcher was equally firm on his second point: the program-exchange center would not be permitted to make its own programs or have its own production equipment. It would be expected to contract with others, primarily the local stations, for program production. Decentralizing production would accomplish two goals: ensure against the formation of a single, dominant production house and strengthen the funding of local stations by contracting with them for the production of programs.[3]

When the meeting was over, Fletcher's arguments had prevailed. They usually did. Two days later his plan was approved by the Fund board, and he immediately formed an organizing committee. True to his principles of choosing "outsiders," he named, in addition to himself, Stoddard, and Lasswell, two new recruits to the cause, Ralph Lowell of Boston and Robert Calkins of the Brookings Institute.[4] In the closing days of 1952, the five became the first board of the newly incorporated Educational Television and Radio Center—soon to be known simply as the Center. The board accepted a grant of $1.35 million for operations from the Fund for Adult Education and held its first meeting the following month to elect three more directors. To speed things along, Fletcher was named temporary president.[5]

Months earlier, Fletcher had dispatched his key consultant, Robert Hudson, off to a Cape Cod retreat to work on a plan for the proposed center. Hudson emerged a week before the Center was formed with a sixteen-page paper that laid the groundwork for the Center's programming policies: rather than a library furnishing films on demand, it would offer a regular, scheduled service of programs; and it would be "mildly directive" in choosing which programs to distribute by developing its own concept of what constituted good educational programming (instead of simply responding to what stations said they wanted).[6]

In a clear stratagem to give the Center acceptance in the academic community—and, by implication, the movement as well—the board, in the summer of 1953, chose Dr. Harry K. Newburn, president of the University of Oregon, to be its head. Fletcher's

preferred site for the Center was Chicago; it was far from the influences of New York and Hollywood and centrally located for
mailing programs to stations. Newburn, however, wishing to continue the quiet academic life he had enjoyed in Oregon, persuaded the board to locate the Center in Ann Arbor, on the campus of the University of Michigan, where it would remain for the
next five years.

Newburn could easily have been typecast as the high-school
principal that he once was: tall, graying, with squarish features, he
was sober almost to the point of dullness. Though well-regarded
as an educator, he lacked broadcasting experience. That he left
to others. When injuries sustained in an automobile accident delayed his departure by several months, Newburn dispatched his
university assistant, Lyle Nelson, to Ann Arbor to begin the process
of organizing the Center. Nelson remained with the Center for
two more years, using what one colleague called "cajolery and
good sense" to form an easy working relationship with the handful
of stations originally affiliated with the Center. In all likelihood,
Nelson's friendly humor and quick wit staved off by several years
the station revolt that ultimately erupted over Newburn's leadership.

In his determination to keep the Center staff small, Newburn
relied on temporary contract employees called "program associates," recruited from college teaching posts for a year's service as
the Center's field representatives. During their months with the
Center, they acted both as program procurers and roving ambas-
sadors, visiting the stations, seeking out and identifying possible
programs for national distribution, and arranging for their acquisition. During the five years that Newburn headed the Center, no
fewer than fifteen program associates came and went. And with
them, through the swinging doors, went whatever experience they
had accumulated in their brief time on the job. The system was
grossly inefficient.

Never in the Center's first two years did the permanent staff
number more than five. At its core was Robert Hudson, the soft-
spoken, philosophical Virginian who bore responsibility for the
Center's programming. As Fletcher's consultant, Hudson had

played a major part in the formation of the Center, contributing ideas that gave substance to Fletcher's organization plan. His experience—as a director of education for the CBS network and later as a specialist in educational radio on the faculty at the University of Illinois—brought a unique combination of expertise to Fletcher's early planning. Newburn put that experience to good use in his own organization. The Center, as Hudson saw it, was "an educational institution whose mode of expression was television."[7] Its purpose, he said, was "to inform, to educate, and to enrich the lives of viewers." Hudson's concept of education was nothing if not comprehensive. The walls of his Ann Arbor office were covered with huge sheets of butcher paper on which was meticulously diagrammed a synoptic scheme of all human knowledge. The Center's programming agenda would be built from this framework.

With the bravura of the beginner, the Center had unwisely committed itself to supplying its station affiliates with five hours of programming each week. Programming was collected from available educational film sources or from local station programs recorded off the air by the crude kinescope process that preceded videotape. Distribution consisted of making a limited number of copies of the acquired programs in the Center's Ann Arbor plant and mailing them out to the first "block" of stations for broadcast. After the first block had aired the programs, they were transshipped ("bicycled") to the next block, and so on until all the blocks had been served. Most stations had to wait weeks if not months before gaining access to a given show. The system was crude, slow, and subject to frustrating and costly errors, but in a day when distribution by leased AT&T lines would consume the entire Center budget, it was the only way to go.

The Fund's original grant of $300,000 for 150 programs—an absurd formula by anyone's standards—produced very little airable programming; the few stations then in operation were unable to meet the minimal technical requirements. Hudson turned to college production centers for much of his early programming. A handful, such as the center at the University of Michigan, had experience turning out shows for regular distribution to commercial stations. Production skills at these centers were several notches above the usual college output.

Ready or not, the Center launched the first nationwide public-television service on May 16, 1954. At the time, nationwide meant six cities—Houston, Los Angeles, Madison, East Lansing, Pittsburgh, and San Francisco. No one else had a public outlet on the air. The early shows, it is fair to say, lacked the qualities that make for riveting viewing. They included such determinedly educational fare as *Geography in Conflict, Understanding Your Child, From Haydn to Hi-Fi, Frontiers of the Sea,* and *A Prospect of Literature.*

The Center's plan to have the stations supply the bulk of the programming, unworkable in the beginning, improved as more stations joined the system. A few, mostly in the larger cities, became the Center's principal program suppliers. wQED / Pittsburgh brought the young medium the much-needed prestige of name recognition with *Heritage,* filmed visits with great artists and scientists. Its portrait of Martha Graham, *A Dancer's World,* was the first to win a national award. wTTW / Chicago contributed *Community of the Condemned,* a series on criminal justice with Cook County sheriff Joseph Lohman. Boston's wGBH, even then building a base as one of the system's future production centers, provided Boston Symphony concerts; an early how-to series, *French on TV*; a science and public-affairs series, *Of Science and Scientists*; and *Constitution and Human Rights.* And San Francisco's kQED produced several series with some of the area's eminent academics, including Mortimer Adler, Edward Teller, Glenn T. Seaborg, and S. I. Hayakawa.

The Center's two earliest "hits" (a relative term) came not from its own stations but as gifts from its putative rival, the commercial networks. In 1955, cBS-TV offered the Center a filmed interview that Edward R. Murrow had conducted with atomic physicist J. Robert Oppenheimer. cBS ran a severely cut thirty-minute version of the two-and-a-half hours and offered public television the longer version. Oppenheimer was highly controversial. A key figure in the development of America's atom bomb, he had fallen victim to the hysteria of McCarthyism and had suffered the loss of his federal security clearance, reportedly for his communist associations before the war. Predictably, public television's airing of the lengthy interview stirred expressions of both praise and outrage, awakening educational television's management to the pleasures and pains of a fully aroused audience.

Dr. Frank Baxter, the self-styled "Liberace of the Library," aroused educational television's audience in a wholly different way, drawing viewers away from *Dragnet* and *Father Knows Best* with an unlikely hook entitled *Shakespeare on TV*. The popular series, produced and aired locally by CBS's Los Angeles station, KNXT-TV, was given to the Center for its first national airing. The English professor from USC was rare, a scholar gifted with the power of popularization for whom television proved a natural milieu. His irrepressible enthusiasm for the Bard of Avon was instantly contagious and levitated him into the modest realm of educational television stardom. Baxter followed *Shakespeare on TV* with a second series, *The Written Word*, also produced and aired locally by KNXT-TV before airing nationally on educational TV.

In 1957, NBC-TV followed its competitor's lead, coming to the aid of educational television with a two-year cooperative project. For twenty-three weeks, NBC made its network lines available for a half-hour each day to deliver "live" to the Center's affiliates five educational series.[8] Three of the five series—on government, music, and mathematics—were produced and paid for by the NBC. The remaining two—on geography and on literature—were left to the Center to produce and fund. For all its good intentions, the NBC project failed to make its predicted mark on the new medium. The *New York Times* television critic found it "longer on commendable and encouraging intentions than stimulating accomplishment."[9] By the spring of the following year, the number of series had dwindled to three, and then, in the project's final fall semester, to only two. Live delivery was more of a gimmick than a necessity; none of the programs in the series contained timely or highly perishable content. Ironically, the one Center series which might have benefited from live release, *UN Review*, a summary of the week's debates in the United Nations, went out to stations by air express. None of the NBC-Center programs were seen on public television in New York City. If New Yorkers saw them at all, they saw them at odd weekend hours on NBC's own flagship station. The nation's largest city was still without a public station.

Notwithstanding the aspirations and efforts of its planners, educational television failed in its first five years to make much of an impression on America's TV viewers. The Center, the system's major source of programs, was limited not only by a meager budget, a clumsy distribution system, and a mere handful of outlets, but also by a lack of inspired leadership, an early symptom of a weakness that would plague the public medium through much of the next thirty years. Harry Newburn's interest was less in making good television programs than in making programs with "authority." The result was engagingly understated in Hudson's 1957 report to the Ford Foundation: "Criticisms that certain programs, though they may present highly qualified personnel, are somewhat dull and unimaginative have been too close to the truth."[10]

It was not that Newburn lacked opportunities for exercising leadership; they were literally thrust upon him. The Ford Foundation, seeing an opportunity to fill the movement's leadership vacuum, dumped a random assortment of projects and responsibilities onto the only national organization available to handle them. During Newburn's tenure in the presidency, the Center found itself with a Washington office, a radio arm, and duties that had little to do with programming: pushing new station activations, providing legal and technical assistance, upgrading the production skills of stations and serving as their national voice in Washington, and occasionally even acting as the system's banker by bailing out financially troubled stations. The Center had become the tentpole of the movement, a center in fact as well as name.

Harry Newburn, knowing little about television and not eager to learn, neither welcomed the Center's expanding role nor relished the leadership it thrust upon him. Oddly enough, his allies in this respect were the stations. They were, if anything, even less welcoming of the Center's expanded role, but for different reasons. While Newburn had no wish to be their leader, the stations had no wish for leadership, his or anyone else's, so long as it was outside their control. And the Center was outside their control. Fletcher had deliberately designed it that way: a free-standing, independent entity, with its own self-perpetuating board composed of prominent citizens serving as individuals rather than as representatives of any particular constituency.[11] In that respect, the Center was unique, then and now. By 1956, however, resentment over the Center's independence, coupled with what the stations perceived as Newburn's inattention to their needs—it was, more probably, his failure to understand those needs—reached a boiling point. The stations demanded and were given the opportunity to make regular representations to Newburn through a standing committee of their own chosen leaders.[12] At an early meeting with this newly elected Affiliates Committee, Newburn agreed to a three-day "retreat" where stations could air their complaints and concerns to Newburn and his staff. There was widespread feeling that Newburn's choice of Biloxi, Mississippi, as the venue was further proof of his indifference to their needs. At the time, Mississippi was a dry state.

The Biloxi meetings were stormy, matched by weather that kept the delegates and their smoldering resentments boxed up in the musty hotel. The stations' repeated refrain of "you need us more than we need you" rubbed against Newburn's usual composure like an abrasive; he was unaccustomed to having his leadership questioned. During a break on the final day, he confessed to one of the more sympathetic delegates a desire to be free of the frustrations of the infant medium and its ungrateful stations, perhaps to return to the quieter and more familiar environment of the college campus. Two months later he resigned to accept an appointment as president of Montana State College.

Newburn's departure occasioned few regrets in the public-television ranks. While most conceded that his presence had brought the upstart medium a measure of educational respectability, many felt that he had failed to marshal forces that might have brought it higher visibility and greater significance. His departure may even have been welcomed by his own board, which was now free to pursue one of its favorite goals: relocating the Center from its midwestern base in Ann Arbor to the media capital of metropolitan New York. When the board first proposed the move to New York, Newburn had sternly resisted it. Even his promise to the board to open a New York branch office went unfulfilled. Upon his departure, and without waiting to name his successor, the board went into immediate action, first dispatching a committee of three directors to consult with the station chiefs then meeting in Madison, Wisconsin. If the board expected a chorus of affirmation from the stations, they grossly misread the signals. The plan to move to Manhattan was met with angry rhetoric best characterized by the declaration of a midwestern station executive that he would never air another Center program if "his network" was taken out of America's heartland. Stunned by the vehemence of the outburst, the board committee called for a straw vote. Of the thirty stations then on the air, all but two expressed vigorous opposition to the move. The committee chair thanked the stations for their counsel. And then, exercising the very independence the stations most feared, he announced a date when the Center would move to Manhattan. The moment defined in bold relief the widening gulf between the Center and the stations it served—between an autonomous, centralized authority and an inchoate group whose goal was shared responsibility.

Whatever hope the stations may have had that Newburn's successor would temper the Center's independent role effectively ended when John F. White was named to the post. Although as general manager of Pittsburgh's WQED White came from their own ranks and had even represented the stations' interests to the Center as chair of the first Affiliates Committee, he gave a clear signal long before his appointment that he favored a strong Center, a sentiment he shared with most of the large-city station managers.

Jack White, like Harry Newburn, had migrated to television from the college campus—he had been a dean at Illinois Tech and a vice president at Case Western Reserve—but unlike the man he replaced, White came to the Center with experience in television-station management. The two men were a study in contrasts. Newburn, the older man, was pompously presidential, not fully at ease in the company of broadcasters, unable even to adapt himself to the chatty, informal mode of address typical of the television milieu. White adapted with no difficulty. His genial, hearty, outgoing personality fit the broadcaster's mold. While Newburn had sought acceptance for the new medium among his academic colleagues, White sought it among his newest peers, the broadcasting hierarchy of America's three New York–based commercial networks.

White's accession to the Center's presidency marked the close of five years of agonizingly slow growth. Seven years had gone by since the FCC had reserved 250 channels, and educational television had only thirty activated stations to show for it. Worse, the impact of the new medium was virtually impossible to measure since it was still without a presence in the key cities of New York, Washington, Los Angeles (where the ill-fated KTHE had been shuttered and not yet replaced), Detroit, and Philadelphia. By contrast, the ten-year period of White's leadership was one of dynamic growth. The number of stations grew fivefold, increasing to more than 150 by the end of decade. While the Center's role in this growth was marginal, and its president more of a coach than a quarterback, White played a critical role in the single most important addition to these numbers by bringing a public station onto the air in New York City.

The Center gave White a unique position from which to practice the art of leadership. As the occasion demanded, he could be cheerleader, nanny, or scold to the Center's affiliated stations. When a station showed signs of sinking, he kept it afloat with a loan. He mounted training programs to upgrade the stations' production skills. He chided station managers for their caution, paraphrasing a favorite Robert Frost line to remind them that the yellow line runs down the middle of the road. At the same time, he tirelessly moved his colleagues to higher levels of professional performance. Public television's historic and well-publicized paucity of funds did not deter him from pushing the entire system into the new technological age of videotape recording and color. It is worth noting that his ten-year term was one of the rare periods in public television's nearly forty-year history when it could point to undivided and undisputed leadership at the national level.

White wisely capitalized on the Center's unchallenged position at the apex of the power triangle. Under his hand what had begun as a modest mechanism for swapping programs grew into the system's principal power base, an autonomous entity filling the functional voids in a structure that had no master plan. In the absence of a plan, the stations were powerless to curb the Center's accretion of power or its tendency to declare itself the nucleus of a centralized system operating out of the Center's new Columbus Circle offices in midtown Manhattan. White's words and actions were anything but reassuring to the foes of a centralized network. Their apprehensions, first aroused by the Center's move to New York, were further fed by its decision, at White's suggestion, to add *National* to the Educational Television and Radio Center's corporate name. Even that might have seemed harmless enough had not White begun, unofficially at first, to shorten the NETRC acronym to NET, and then to add to the hubris by making casual reference to NET as "America's Fourth Network." Those for whom White's dreams of glory were a nightmare—a clear and present threat to the stations' hegemony and independence—shuddered.

White was sensitive to the stations' fears and took steps to court their confidence. During his first year in office, he fulfilled a pledge to visit every station. Later, he created a department to maintain constant contact with the stations' concerns and appointed the highly respected manager of Chicago's WTTW, Jim Robertson, to head it. One of Robertson's early tasks was to work with the Affiliates Committee to produce a new affiliation agreement that would require stations to pay for a service that had been free. The annual levy was modest, ranging from $7200 for the smallest station to $18,700 for the largest, well below the costs of a program service that was already heavily subsidized by the Center's annual operating grant from the Ford Foundation. Token though it was, the fee changed the relationship of the Center and the stations. Only the ungrateful would complain about a gift, but good business practice compels a complaint when the service fails to meet the buyer's expectations—thus for a modest outlay, a station bought the freedom to complain. Stations bought something else with their affiliation fee: exclusivity, the practice of guaranteeing one station in a multi-station market exclusive access to the

Center's programming. The practice, much honored in the world of commercial television, raised few problems in the ranks of public television while the stations were few in number. But as the system grew, and stations with overlapping signals were added in places like Seattle-Tacoma, Provo–Salt Lake City, and the metropolitan areas of New York and San Francisco, the second stations, denied Center programming, sent up howls of protest, adding a new category of enemies to those NET already had. Nevertheless, with the backing of its original affiliates, NET stuck to its guns. Although station exclusivity was abandoned in the late 1960s when PBS took over national program distribution, the issue of who gets what when has refused to die.

White's agenda, however, was topped not by the politics of power but by programming. The new administration was determined not only to raise the quality of its output, but also to widen its diversity and shake the chalkdust of the Newburn-era image from its skirts. White felt the key was in "significance." If, he told the stations, we "are to be this force in our communities and thus earn support, we must be willing to be bold and to face issues." He cautioned that "unless we provide an honest and completely free arena for debate; unless we take advantage of the peculiar freedom which is ours, we will never be this force."[13] The more timorous stations were shaken by White's call for boldness. But for others, particularly for those stations most dependent on support from their audiences, and thus in need of distinctive and exciting programming, White's challenging policy was welcome.

Bob Hudson, who had plotted the original design for the Center and shepherded it through the Newburn years as its programming chief, remained with the Center as one of three newly appointed vice presidents to translate White's credo into the promised program service.[14] With his limited resources, which included the Center's five-year $5 million Ford grant, Hudson tackled the daunting task of creating or finding quality programs. He went first to the stations. Fletcher's plan for the Center had envisioned a major production role for stations that benefited both partners: the Center would get programs, and the producing stations would earn much needed income. But it was too early in the

game; the stations were not yet ready. Stations were willing to produce programs for the Center but unwilling to accept what other
stations produced because of what they felt was its poor quality.
In an effort to improve program quality by developing the system's "production muscle," White invited a select number of stations to propose programs and promised that their production
costs would be underwritten by the Center. But of the 186 proposals submitted, only seven merited production and made it into
the Center's distribution schedule. There had to be a better way.
White had an idea.

Ford's $5 million five-year grant to the Center was "terminal";
at the end of that time the money would be gone and there would
be no more. The Foundation saw five years as time enough for the
Center to find new funders. White could imagine five years as time
enough to raise the struggling medium by its bootstraps, to make
a substantial mark on the consciousness of America's television
audience, and to attract new funders. But not with only $1 million
a year to work with. White decided on a bold and risky strategy:
go for broke. Bet the whole five-year grant on a single year—spend
now, worry later. White's wager was hedged by the hunch that
Ford's grant was terminal only because of Newburn's lackluster
performance. He persuaded himself that when the time came to
knock on Ford's door again, the Foundation would be receptive
if the Center succeeded in mounting a dazzling display of the
medium's potential. He said later that "it was the only dream you
could have."[15]

The brassy "go for broke" gamble may have saved the public
medium. From that moment on, "quality became the touchstone
of the program service."[16] Hudson restructured his staff to include
a director of programming. The rotating program associates were
dropped in favor of six permanent ones, each assigned responsibility for a particular category of programming, and each charged
with seeking out the best programming wherever it could be
found. Stations continued to be important producers, but for the
first time the Center turned outside its own constituency, and
particularly to Britain, to find "significant" programming. *An Age
of Kings*—the historical plays of Shakespeare arranged and pre-

sented in their proper chronological sequence—aired in the fall of 1961 and was the first major BBC series to hit American public television. But *An Age of Kings* had another distinction: it was the first noncommercial series to be underwritten by a corporate sponsor, the Humble Oil and Refining Company, initiating what would become public broadcasting's long-lasting symbiosis with the petroleum industry.

Viewers reveled in the consummate skill of the British cast. But the audience for the BBC series was, for the most part, an audience already disposed to educational television's demanding fare. NET needed to reach beyond the converted, to find a new audience whose appetites did not necessarily tend toward the acquired tastes of high culture. The answer was found in a Cripple Creek saloon, high in the Colorado Rockies, where a rollicking ragtime singer named Max Morath, colorfully dressed in turn-of-the-century derby and vest, pounded out rags on an upright barroom piano. KRMA / Denver turned the player and his piano into a television series. *Ragtime Era* was everything educational television was not supposed to be: upbeat, fun, and entertaining. Seated at the old-time piano, Morath played and talked, pausing between rags to share bits of historical lore. Audiences loved it. At the conclusion of the series, NET reported to its funders at the Ford Foundation that *Ragtime Era* "may ultimately be responsible for greater good to a greater number of average TV viewers than many NET programs of greater intrinsic educational significance."[17]

WGBH / Boston's *Prospects of Mankind* was more in keeping with the educational medium's image—it had significance written all over it—but the image of Eleanor Roosevelt talking with a series of world leaders brought to the public medium a measure of prestige and importance that it sorely needed. Awards also helped but had somewhat less of an effect. Two NET shows, both the work of Nathan Kroll, won awards in international competition. *Appalachian Spring* was an extension of Kroll's earlier award-winning film with Martha Graham, *A Dancer's World*. The other, *Pablo Casals Master Class*, was filmed on the Berkeley campus with the famed cello virtuoso and his students, and introduced an innovative form and technique not seen before on the television screen.

By 1962, the country was finally beginning to take notice of the upstart medium. Reliable audience studies found "regular" viewers in 10 to 25 percent of the nation's television homes.[18] These modest numbers rang no bells on the Nielsen charts, but for those engaged in the struggle to identify an audience for the public medium, it was music to eager ears. It also played well at the Foundation. Satisfied that Jack White's bold "go for broke" stroke was a success and that a decade of heavy investment in the new medium was finally paying dividends, Ford did what White hoped it would do. The Foundation gave NET a second $5.5 million grant a full two years before the original five-year grant ran out.

But success breeds it own problems, particularly when it is built out of the pockets of a single foundation. Not even the world's largest foundation—and that's what the Ford Foundation was in the 1950s—can afford to bankroll a project forever, and certainly not one in the process of rapid expansion, which was what was required as more and more local channels came on the air and demanded programming. Foundations traditionally avoid sustained support for an enterprise, preferring instead to provide "seed" money for new, often risky, projects in the expectation that once they prove themselves, long-term support will be sought elsewhere. White, knowing that NET was faced with the inevitability of a future without Ford subsidy, conceived of a plan akin to, but more audacious than, his "go for broke" gamble. Ford would be asked to make a terminal grant to NET—but *really* terminal this time—of an eye-popping half-billion dollars. That amount, wisely invested, could keep the network in business for years to come.

When White's proposal was dropped on the desk at Ford, the Foundation didn't blink. But neither did it write a check for a half-billion dollars. Instead, having asked itself some of the same questions, the Foundation proposed a radically different answer, one that was to have unexpected consequences as well as to affirm the old adage that he who pays the piper calls the tune. NET's part would soon be played in a modulated key.

5

10 COLUMBUS CIRCLE

The one heresy that public television cannot tolerate is the emergence of a strong individual or group with the resources to generate imaginative and popular programming, free of the extraordinarily dense filtering system of the sum of the stations.

Richard O. Moore[1]

Jack White's hope that his request for a half-billion dollars might get a sympathetic hearing at the Ford Foundation may have rested on a long-standing friendship with the man who was then the Foundation's president. The two men met in the late forties, when Dr. Henry T. Heald was the president of Illinois Tech and White was on his staff as a dean of students. Sometime later, Heald left Illinois Tech for the presidency of New York University, and then in 1956 he moved uptown to the Ford Foundation. When White arrived in New York City three years later, their friendship was renewed. Heald encouraged White to buy a home near his own in the exclusive suburb of Tuxedo Park, a measure of the closeness of their relationship.

Whether the Ford Foundation president actually studied his friend's half-billion-dollar proposal is moot. We do know that it was passed on to the program officer at Ford responsible for its NET grant, an irascible and blunt Midwesterner named James Armsey. Like White, Armsey had a long-standing relationship with Heald from the days when all three were together at Illinois Tech. But unlike White, Armsey had moved with Heald to New York University and then to the Foundation. In 1961, with the dissolution of the Fund for Adult Education and the departure of Scott

Fletcher, Armsey was given responsibility for the grants to public television, which at that time constituted Ford's single largest benefaction. He seemed an odd choice for the post. A man of print, both as a journalist and an avid reader, Armsey had a mild disdain for the ephemeral nature of television. But like Scott Fletcher who preceded him and Fred Friendly who followed him, Armsey used Ford's money to leverage a personal vision of the medium that would leave public television a much-changed institution.

White's dream of a half-billion-dollar golden handshake to mark the parting of the banker and its principal client was just that.[2] The Foundation had other ideas—and far, far fewer dollars in mind—when it announced that Armsey would conduct a year-long study of the future of public television to determine what role, if any, the Foundation had in that future. Over the next twelve months, the corpus of public broadcasting was poked and probed in search of answers. Foundation officers conducted lengthy interviews with the NET staff. Armsey recruited an outside expert to screen and evaluate NET's entire program output.[3] And opinions and assessments of public television's performance were solicited from a broad spectrum of prominent citizens, including Walter Lippmann and Edward R. Murrow. The investigation rubbed against sensitive nerves, particularly when the Ford study implied a subtle criticism of White and his key staff. A bad situation was made more awkward by a face-off between Armsey and White—one the investigator, the other the investigated. Each seemed to be vying for the approval of their mentor, Henry Heald. Some of us who viewed their struggle with detached amusement were led to view it as a classic case of sibling rivalry.

Tensions between Armsey and NET reached a peak during the closing days of the study. Armsey had invited the system's station managers to a three-day session and pointedly excluded NET. The announced purpose of the meeting was to probe the stations' assessment of NET's performance. Armsey prefaced the meeting with his own and the Foundation's feelings that NET should pay more attention to the quality of its productions and spend less time caring for the movement's other needs. The stations responded with predictable dissonance. Some shared Ford's feeling that NET should minimize its leadership role and strongly urged that the role be given to the NAEB, an organization over which stations had complete control. Others were unwilling even to leave NET with its programming role unless stations were given a dominant voice in program policy. But if Armsey welcomed their criticism of NET, he certainly could not have taken satisfaction from a tiny minority that seized the occasion to oppose the Ford Foundation's self-imposed role as the system's supermanager. When word of Armsey's generally hostile tone toward NET filtered back to the network's headquarters at 10 Columbus Circle, the staff felt consternation and bitterness. The prevalent feeling was one of having been betrayed by one's own sponsors.

In the summer of 1963, Armsey sent a two-page memorandum to NET entitled "Instructions for Preparation of Grant Application Letter."[4] It said, in effect, "if you want our money, here are the terms." The procedure was routine, but the terms were not. The memorandum called for NET to trim its scope radically and to focus sharply on a "clear and unequivocal commitment to the single purpose of providing a high-quality informational and cultural program service." Ford's proposed method of achieving improved program quality was artful: more money for fewer programs. NET would be limited to no more than "5 hours of new program material each week" (it had been ten), on the assumption that more money spent on fewer programs would produce higher quality. Further, "at least 50 per cent of the program service and at least 50 per cent of the program expenditures" were to be devoted to programs about public affairs and international issues. The emphasis on public affairs was a reflection of Armsey's (and, one assumes, Ford's) view of the Fourth Network as a major media outlet for airing vital issues of national and international concern.

The more-money-for-fewer-programs decree came with the corollary demand that NET relinquish its role as the movement's leadership organization—that it give up its activities in radio and instructional television and cease to represent public television's interests in Washington. The network was, in short, to dedicate itself to the "single purpose" of program production and distri-

bution. The new order forced a change in NET's relations with its
stations, including the elimination of the affiliation fee. Stations
were to receive NET's programs at no cost. Ford planned the elimination of the fee as a way of encouraging stations to form their
own organization to represent their collective interests in Washington. The memorandum's other terms were more annoying
than substantive: no more than 15 percent of the grant could be
used for administrative expense; no more than 5 percent for program promotion. Erasing all doubt about who was calling the
tune, Ford requested NET to submit "a plan and time schedule
for the reorganization of NETRC to effectuate the reorientation
and purpose and program," including a scheme of the new organizational structure, a list of job assignments, and a record of
each person's salary.[5]

White and the NET board, swallowing hard and having no other
choice, accepted Ford's stiff terms. Three weeks after Armsey's
instructional memo, a letter requesting the $6 million, jointly
signed by White and NET board chairman Dr. George Stoddard
(by now the chancellor of New York University), was sent to Heald.
Their letter promised the requisite five hours of new programs
weekly, and "with roughly fifty percent" devoted to public affairs
and "a limited amount" to be spent for publicity and promotion.
Heald's quick response was terse and to the point: "roughly" and
"a limited amount" weren't precise enough; he insisted on "no
less than" 50 percent for public affairs, and "no more than 5
percent" for promotion. Stoddard's reply thanked him for his
"helpful letter" and pledged compliance.[6]

In October 1963, the following year's grant was jointly announced by the Ford Foundation and NET. The Foundation's
press release referred to the grant and its conditions as a "major
new phase" in public broadcasting. NET, in its release, tried
bravely to put a positive spin on the new game plan by hailing the
changes as the start of "a new era." But behind the hyperbole of
the press releases was a painfully achieved result. In some quarters,
most especially at 10 Columbus Circle, it was received with mixed
emotions. On the up side was the money. There was to be more
of it, much more: NET would receive $6 million for the first year,

with successive annual reviews that held out the promise of more to come. But the grant came with spine-stiffening conditions. In addition to the limitations on its programming, NET was directed to close its Washington office and to stop all outside fund-raising except for the support of specific program projects. The Foundation clearly intended to focus the network's energies and attention on a single target: programming.

The 1964 Ford grant put public television in a whole new ball game: new rules, new players, and a realignment of the power structure. As soon as the affiliation fee was dropped, the stations lost no time in forming their own organization, ETS (Educational Television Stations), to represent their interests in Washington, originally as a division of the NAEB but later as an independent entity with its own board of elected station managers.[7] (Although it has since undergone transmutations and name changes, it continues, as APTS—the Association of America's Public Television Stations—to be the principal guardian of station interests and their Washington lobbyist.)

NET's loss of its role as the movement's undisputed leader was offset in considerable measure by the strengthening of its programming role. Not only was NET free to concentrate on programming, it was also free for the first time to enter into program production. The freedom to produce was more than a policy shift, it was a distinct departure from Ford's earlier policy as it had been formulated by Scott Fletcher. The new policy made it possible to use centralized production as the Foundation's means of upgrading program quality, and was accepted reluctantly by the stations only as a quid pro quo for gaining control of their collective destiny through ETS. The change in Ford policy was not, however, to be the final chapter in the system's historic opposition to centralized control. There were more changes yet to come.

White tackled NET's new programming challenges with renewed energy and enthusiasm, confidently promising to deliver a "strong national cultural and public affairs program service" that would be better than anything the medium had yet seen. His first step was to restructure the organization to meet the new demands. Gone was the clumsy and ineffective system of program associates;

in its place, White recruited two experienced network producers and gave them responsibility for programming—one for public affairs and one for cultural affairs. The critical public-affairs post, with its responsibility for one-half of the NET schedule, was handed to the young and energetic producer of ABC's *Howard K. Smith* news show, William Kobin. His counterpart on the cultural side was Don Kellerman. The two men, who had known each other at CBS, where Kellerman had produced *Lamp unto My Feet* and *Look Up and Live,* arrived on the job facing immediate production deadlines, and neither had much help. Kobin was limited to two producers, Paul Kaufman and Alvin Perlmutter, both of whom were on staff when he arrived and were fully occupied with their own program series. (Perlmutter's weekly *At Issue* was NET's first sustained public-affairs series.) Kellerman likewise had just two producers, Curtis Davis and Brice Howard, both program associates under the old regime. White's charge to his new program chiefs was succinct: turn the place into a real production center as quickly as you know how. On the day in December 1964 that the two men reported for work, White's goal seemed an impossible dream. But Kobin and Kellerman set to work recruiting talent and building production teams. Their success in attracting such talented professionals to public television as Jac Venza, James Karayn, David Prowitt, Jack Sameth, Jerome Toobin, and Eleanor Bunin was to have a profound influence on its future. One thing, however, remained the same: NET was still prohibited by its original charter from owning production equipment, so rather than building its own production house, the network rented studio facilities as needed, more often than not from one of its station affiliates.

Kellerman's stay with NET lasted less than a year. He resigned, reportedly after a tiff with White, and was replaced by Curtis Davis. Just prior to Kellerman's departure, Kobin was named to the new post of vice president of programming, and given overall responsibility for NET's program schedule. The public-affairs post was filled by Don Dixon, a tough-minded reporter with experience both as a foreign correspondent in Asia and a producer of network news. The three men—Kobin, Dixon, and Davis—would be responsible for public television's national programming for the remaining six years of NET's independent existence.

Change came slowly at first. New production teams were feeling their way, testing ideas, devising formats. A few series, already in NET's schedule, provided a base on which to build. One of them, *Intertel*, was a cooperative series involving public broadcasters in Britain, Canada, Australia, and the United States (for a time, NET and the Westinghouse Broadcasting Company shared the U.S. representation) to which each partner contributed one documentary each season. *International Magazine*, another import, was wholly produced by NET, demonstrating the network's enterprise as well as its limitations. Each month, an NET producer flew to London, culled from European television the stories for that month's edition, and shot the host's introductions (the show's original host, *New Statesman* editor John Freeman, was later replaced with NBC's London correspondent Robert MacNeil). The producer then flew back to the United States with the edited film under his arm and readied it for duplication, after which it was "bicycled" out to the stations. A far cry from today's instant delivery by satellite, this crude method of distribution meant that all material was dated by the time it was seen.

Of the shows already in the NET schedule, none caused more controversy, complaints, and incipient ulcers than *News in Perspective*. Its center stage was occupied, almost in the military sense, by Lester Markel, Sunday editor of the *New York Times*. Markel's despotism and curmudgeonly ways were legendary around the newspaper's editorial offices. Once each month, he hosted his editorial colleagues Max Frankel and Tom Wicker for an on-camera analysis of the month's major events. Under Markel's rules, bullying and badgering were fair game—and he did both—putting at risk everyone working on the show. On the evening the executive producer collapsed and was rushed to the hospital, it was assumed—wrongly, as it turned out—that he was the victim of the heart attack everyone thought was inevitable. Markel had that effect on those who worked with him. The producer recovered, but the show did not. Markel's combative performance drew increasingly negative comments from station programmers. When, at an annual meeting of NET's stations, a group of local managers walked in wearing large Lester Must Go! lapel badges, NET bowed to pressure and replaced Markel with the soft-spoken and courtly Clifton Daniel. But that incident did not end Markel's ties to NET. Unable to face down and fire the highly assertive Markel, White kept him on the payroll as a consultant on public-affairs programming.

Timely airing of topical shows like *News in Perspective* was impossible under NET's "bicycle" distribution system. The show took twenty-one days to make the rounds of all the stations. Later, by mailing more copies, the time was shaved to eight days. It was an expensive route to a generally unsatisfactory result. NET once made one hundred copies of a single special program memorializing the anniversary of President Kennedy's assassination in order to have it aired on every station on the anniversary date. But it still wasn't "live" television. That would require leased telephone lines (later, satellites) at a cost well beyond NET's reach. Many in the system saw no need for interconnection, and some even feared it. They remained loyal to the original concept of the Center as a "library" service in which NET supplied a broad selection of timeless programs and stations were free to select those that best suited their interests and air them whenever they wished. NET's view was quite different. It saw itself as a network, the American equivalent of the great public networks of Canada, Western Europe, and Japan, whose simultaneous release of programs stitched a nation together. In this model, interconnection was essential.

But even on a shoestring budget, NET could not afford to ignore the newer technologies that were changing the medium. In 1965, the network leased the Early Bird satellite to link classrooms in Britain and Massachusetts for a modest experiment in student exchange that was more remarkable for being done at all than for being done well. Two years later, NET joined public broadcasters in twelve countries on five continents for a more significant experiment—the first live, worldwide satellite show. *Our World* was a melange of multicultural oddities: the BBC's contribution, for example, was a filmed rehearsal session with the Beatles. The show was more notable for its technological virtuosity than for its content, notwithstanding the *Denver Post*'s judgment that the broadcast was "as distinguished an achievement as man's conquest of space."[8] President Johnson's 1967 State of the Union address provided the occasion for NET's first interconnected live broadcast. It was remembered, however, more for its format than its content. NET, introducing a new treatment of presidential address, followed Johnson's speech with two hours of comment and analysis from a panel of scholars and opinion leaders chaired by James Reston of the *New York Times*. The *National Observer* called it "a brilliant success," and the Television Academy honored it with an Emmy. But it rankled Vice President Agnew. In his 1969 Des Moines, Iowa, speech denouncing the press in general, he spoke for many politicians in excoriating the innovative format as "instant analysis."

The airing of the State of the Union address and its follow-up discussion were the work of NET's Washington news bureau. The bureau was set up after the Ford Foundation forced the closing of NET's earlier Washington office, and was put in the hands of Jim Karayn. Armed with years of news experience and a small budget, Karayn was charged with originating a regular schedule of special events from the capital. Convinced that public television needed an identifiable on-screen image of the sort the networks achieve with their news anchors (and that PBS has achieved in more recent years with Robert MacNeil and Jim Lehrer), Karayn recruited Paul Niven, an ex-CBS correspondent, to host NET's Washington-based shows. Until Niven's untimely death in a fire, his keen intelligence brought a strong presence to such NET series as *The President's Men* and *Men of the Senate*. Niven had also hosted NET's first show in color, one of the earliest extended interviews with President Nixon.

Once NET began to make its own shows, it was never far from controversy. These were the 1960s, the decade of the nation's turmoil, dissension, and disillusion, and an altogether awkward time for temporizing on the sensitive issues that engulfed the national spirit. In the South, the civil rights struggle pushed relentlessly forward: sit-ins, arrests, the March on Selma, and the murder of three civil rights workers in Mississippi. In the North, Malcolm X was felled in Harlem by an assassin's bullet. Six days of rioting in Watts left thirty-four dead and over one thousand injured. It was the decade of "the long hot summer." And if that were not enough, disillusionment over America's role in Southeast Asia was growing into despair with the mounting casualty figures.

White made no bones about NET's proposed posture in this milieu. Broadcasters, he told the affiliates, are supposed to be leaders, not followers. "It takes courage to depart from the safe and sterile, to buck strong pockets of opinion . . . if we don't have that courage, we don't belong in this business." The NET staff would be pressed to meet the challenge. On the day in November 1963 that Bill Kobin took charge of NET public affairs, events conspired to test his mettle: it was the week when a young president had been murdered in Dealy Plaza and a national mood of youthful idealism had been numbed by shock and outrage. By that time, the struggle for black equality was fixed in the national consciousness: the wave of sit-ins that began at a Woolworth's lunch counter in Greensboro, North Carolina, had fanned out through the South; James Meredith, backed by three thousand U.S. troops, had integrated "Ole Miss"; and Dr. Martin Luther King, Jr., had electrified thousands with a speech in which powerful images gave deeper meaning to the familiar words "all men are created equal." Kobin had a clear vision of the part the public-television network was to play. These events could not be ignored; they must be made comprehensible.

Not yet staffed with his own producers, Kobin relied on the stations to lay the foundations for NET's campaign of information. KQED / San Francisco's small film unit, organized and led by Dick Moore, addressed the civil rights issue with three documentaries produced in 1964 under contract to NET before the network had its own production staff: James Baldwin's controversial film tour of San Francisco, *Take This Hammer*; a film portrait of the spiritual leader of the Black Muslim movement, Elijah Muhammad, *The Messenger from Violet Drive*; and later in the year, *Louisiana Diary*, a film that documented the tortuous efforts to register black voters in that state's Iberville Parish. By 1966, NET was able to put its own production teams in the field, and its voice was beginning to be heard on the subject of civil rights. Jack Willis's *Lay My Burden*

Down looked at Alabama's rural blacks one year after the Selma-to-Montgomery march and found them no less hungry, no better educated, and no more politically powerful. Alabama's Educational Television Network declined to air the award-winning documentary, explaining that it had "insufficient educational value." Independent producer Bill Jersey's *A Time for Burning* captured the dramatic but futile efforts of a Lutheran minister in Omaha to integrate his all-white congregation with a nearby congregation of blacks in what the *New York Times* critic called "the most accomplished and sensitive hour of television this season."[9] Another KQED-produced film, *Losing Just the Same*, took a sad and searching look at the problems of an urban black family in Oakland.

The following summer, when riots erupted in Newark, killing twenty-seven people and injuring fifteen hundred, NET's cameras probed for the roots of the violence in a ninety-minute special that offered angry blacks the chance to vent their frustrations and air their grievances in a televised confrontation with the community's white leaders. The discussion was followed with an analysis by a panel of experts. A number of other specials sought to give perspective and meaning to the exploding events in the civil rights struggle: *Where Is Prejudice?*, *Who Does the Negro Think He Is?*, and a nine-part series, *History of the Negro People*, hosted by Ossie Davis. The following spring, when an assassin's bullet took the life of Dr. King, NET gathered together leaders of the black and white communities for a penetrating look in *Civil Rights: What's Next?*

In late 1967, NET introduced *Black Journal*, the first regularly scheduled black-produced series for a black audience on the American networks. The monthly show was a modest triumph for the cause of black access, yet few if any of NET's shows stirred the wrath of the affiliates with greater frequency and fervor. The protests began early, even before the show aired. Kobin looks back on the meeting where the plans were first shared with stations as one of the worst moments in his years at NET; the intensity of the stations' opposition was totally unexpected. Nor did it stop there. Predictably, perhaps inevitably, a black show for black audiences produced in the eye of a civil rights storm was bound to have moments of rage and bitterness, occasional name-calling, and fre-

quent recourse to the crude language of the street. *Black Journal*
had them all, assaulting the sensibilities of the disingenuous who
felt that "the problem" would go away if only television didn't
keep harping on it, or if the blacks would only take "a more con-
ciliatory attitude" toward whites. A small number of affiliates refused to air the show, fearing that it would contaminate their community with "a problem" it didn't have. Most did carry it, a few
fearing the reaction of a denied black audience more than the
outrage of an offended white audience. But many who did air it
pleaded with NET to "tone down the program." NET stood by its
conviction that it was a black show, produced for a predominantly
black audience, and was better judged by those for whom it was
intended. It did not go unnoticed that those who minded the gates
at the local stations were, without exception, white.

Initially, *Black Journal* was not precisely what it was advertised to
be, a black show produced entirely by blacks. Although its staff
was black, NET had assigned a highly experienced white producer,
Al Perlmutter, to oversee the show as its executive producer. The
Black Journal crew, objecting not so much to Perlmutter as to the
principle, revolted. Perlmutter dropped out and William Greaves,
an experienced black filmmaker, was brought in to replace him.
Greaves produced and hosted the series for two years. When he
left to return to independent film production, Tony Brown, a
young man from Detroit, took over as both producer and host. In
the two decades since, Brown has made the show his own (*Tony
Brown's Journal*), guided it through countless financial crises including a period of commercial-station syndication, and, with remarkable steadfastness, has kept it in front of the cameras for a
record run.

The fight for equal justice at home was matched by another
issue that challenged the courage and imagination of the public
medium. A war in the steamy klongs and forests of Vietnam was
dragging on with mounting American casualties as more and more
voices were being raised in opposition. The disaffected demanded
to be heard. In the aftermath of President Johnson's order initiating saturation bombing in Vietnam, NET offered to cover, live,
a "teach-in"—a passive form of protest customarily involving mar-

athon talk sessions with celebrity speakers—from the nation's capital. The affiliates would have none of it; even the handful of stations willing to carry the teach-in refused to give the show the prompt exposure it needed. NET settled for a documentary *about* the teach-in. The situation was symptomatic of a larger problem: in its efforts to be timely, the network often moved out ahead of its affiliates and their audiences, raising questions before anyone wanted the questions raised. NET's teach-in proposal preceded by more than a year the march on the Pentagon, the Tet offensive, and Walter Cronkite's return from Vietnam with the solemn declaration that we were losing the war. The stations, and perhaps the country, were not yet ready for the question.

Public television could hardly ignore events in Vietnam and yet, with the fighting half a world away and no program budget to bridge the distance, NET was compelled to seek other sources for its coverage. Canadian television proved to be one of the best; its correspondents, not bound by the restrictions affecting the war's participants, had free access to both sides. Offering a Canadian perspective on an American war should have been an advantage to public television's viewers, particularly when our own government was engaged in a massive cover-up of America's deepening involvement. Unfortunately, as *Mills of the Gods* demonstrated, it proved to be a problem and a provocation. The Canadian-produced documentary contained a scene in which a U.S. Air Force pilot, singing and laughing with the excited delight of a small boy with new toys, rained death and destruction on the Vietnam villages below. Affiliates and viewers, reacting with an anger that transcended simple rejection of an "outsider's" view, charged NET with airing a show that lacked "balance."

Balance became an even more heated issue with the 1968 documentary *Inside North Vietnam.* The situation began harmlessly enough. A former BBC producer, Felix Greene, had struck a deal with CBS News. In return for the first option on his film, CBS agreed to pay Greene's expenses to North Vietnam where, as a British subject, he would have access to an area closed to Americans. When he brought his completed documentary to CBS, however, the network rejected all but a few shots of captured American

pilots and released to Greene rights to the rest of the film. Greene
took his documentary to NET and screened it for Kobin and Dixon.
Neither man had any doubts about the controversy the film was
likely to arouse, particularly over the question of whether Greene
had been influenced by North Vietnamese authorities. Greene
gave NET assurances that he had been given free access to everything except military installations and that he had met with no
interference from the authorities. The film, however, was clearly
sympathetic to a people with whom we were at war, portraying
them as courageous and enterprising, bravely defending themselves against an industrial giant whose mechanized warfare was
callously indifferent to humane concerns. Greene's camera recorded images of hospitals that the North Vietnamese claimed
had been bombed by American planes, civilians torn apart by anti-
personnel bombs of a sort that our government denied using, and
bridges that were routinely bombed by day and resolutely restored
by night. Through it all, the North Vietnamese went about their
daily routines with a determination that belied the picture painted
by our government of a demoralized enemy about to surrender.

Greene pared the eighty-five-minute film to an hour, and NET
added an hour of follow-up discussion focusing on America's Vietnam policy. Political scientist Robert Scalapino supported the Administration's policy; news correspondent David Schoenbrun opposed it. By giving the show "balance," the follow-up discussion
was intended to blunt the anticipated audience reaction. But the
audience had no opportunity to react before the flak began to fly.
The loudest salvo came from the halls of Congress. Learning that
NET was planning to release *Inside North Vietnam,* thirty-three members of the House of Representatives and eleven senators shot off
a letter to NET president Jack White in which they protested in the
strongest and most uncompromising language the scheduled airing of the show.[10] None of the protesting legislators had seen the
film, nor were they aware of the planned follow-up discussion. But
that did not deter them from condemning the film as "nothing
more or less than communist propaganda." NET found itself under intense pressure; a letter from forty-four members of Congress
was not easily brushed aside, not even in the comparatively free-

wheeling days before Congress gained leverage on the public medium through federal funding. But White, in a rare assertion of public television's independence, resisted the pressures and stood his ground. Viewers, he argued, should be free to make their own judgments and not have them made for them by their surrogates in Washington. Unfortunately, viewers of 18 of NET's 133 affiliates had the option removed when the stations refused to air the show.[11]

The Greene affair had an instructive postscript. White's response to the letter from the legislators had included an offer to bring the show to Washington for a private screening for the members of Congress (not, however, before the show aired nationally). His offer was accepted, and *Inside North Vietnam* was screened in a closed session for the House Committee on Foreign Affairs. According to White, the film was applauded approvingly by the committee members.[12] The events surrounding the airing of *Inside North Vietnam* can be seen as a crucial episode in the development of public television, a moment when courageous leadership put principle above expediency. Paradoxically, Greene's documentary was neither public television's best nor most important program in that or any other year, making the protection of the principle, if more difficult, all the more essential. NET clearly believed that without the power and courage to protect its freedom, public television loses much of its meaning and most of its purpose.

Greene's documentary aired within the framework of a weekly anthology of documentaries bearing the generic title NET *Journal.* The network had its own staff of documentarians, each with a small support staff, an independent budget, and time to research and develop ideas for one or more shows a year. The staff output was augmented by documentaries from independent producers and foreign sources. NET's documentarians left few sacred cows unexamined. Jack Willis attacked the wretched conditions of poor whites (*Appalachia: Rich Land, Poor People*), the quality of New York City's parochial schools (*Every Seventh Child*), and the paradox of rising food prices and diminishing farm income (*Hard Times in the Country*). Morton Silverstein's unblinking look at the precarious situation of the poor (*The Poor Pay More* and *Justice and the Poor*) climaxed in 1972 with the explosive *Banks and the Poor*, which set off tremors in banking circles that can be felt to this day. Other filmmaker-producers, including Harry McCarthy, Bob Fresco, Arthur Ziegert, Dick McCutchen, Al Levin, and Bill Jersey, tackled the issues that shaped the decade the 1960s: drugs, the invasion of privacy, student rebellion, welfare, draft evasion, and the failures of education. A monthly consumer show, *Dollars and Sense* (later *Your Dollar's Worth*), generated its own controversy with comparative assessments of brand-name products and automobile safety standards and an occasional exposé of scams and scandals in the travel and TV repair businesses. NET built up its legal staff during this time, citing "the controversial nature of much recent programming."[13]

Given the advantages of independent funding and governance, NET didn't shrink from controversy, but neither did it deliberately court it for its own sake. Most of its public-affairs offerings were free of controversy, and many were not successful. Those that fell short of both the station's expectations and the network's own standards were aired anyway; with a budget of less than $4 million and with 260 hours annually to fill with public-affairs programming, NET had no other option. And yet, according to *Variety*, NET's public-affairs programming, including its documentaries, surpassed the combined output of the three commercial networks in quantity and, more significantly, in content.

The Ford Foundation's 1964 decree mandating that half of every programming dollar go to public affairs left the other fifty cents to cover not only the arts—music, drama, dance, and the graphic arts—but also science and children's programming, the shows most in demand by the stations. Producing more with less proved to be an art in itself, a task that first fell to Don Kellerman as director of cultural programs. In his brief time with NET, Kellerman successfully negotiated a contract with the American Federation of Television and Radio Artists that opened the way for NET to employ the union's professional acting talent. The arrangement led to the network's earliest drama production, Christopher Fry's *A Sleep of Prisoners*, followed by American Place Theater's performance of Robert Lowell's *The Old Glory: Benito Cereno* and *The*

Play of Daniel. The latter was filmed in The Cloisters, the Metropolitan Museum's medieval enclave in upper Manhattan, by another newcomer to NET, Jerome Toobin. Another medieval enclave, this time in Holland, was the setting for Kellerman's major
triumph, *Carmina Burana,* a dance special performed by the Ne-
derlands Dans Theater and produced by a newcomer to NET, Jac
Venza. The young stage designer was destined to rise to greater
heights in later years as the impresario of PBS's *Great Performances.*
Carmina Burana had another distinction: it was the first American
public-television program to be awarded the coveted Prix Italia.

NET's cultural offerings were hardly fare for the masses. Rather,
they held rigidly to NET's announced policy of helping to "culti-
vate American taste and appreciation, to examine contemporary
culture, and to give exposure to new or neglected ideas, techniques and talents."[14] The stations, however, wanted more conventional fare and challenged at every opportunity the wisdom of
NET's policy of paying more attention to culture than to audience
taste. If they hoped that Kellerman's departure would mean a
change, they misjudged his successor. Curtis Davis, who was to
remain in the cultural post for the next half-dozen years, pursued
many of the same policies and in the process put down a foundation on which public television's record of cultural achievement
was subsequently built. A soft-spoken man with a gift for talking
in complete, deliberately crafted sentences, Davis brought to his
new post a background particularly well suited to the cultural task.
He was a composer and had been a producer with Louis de Ro-
chemont Films before he joined the NET staff as one of its early
program associates.

As a seasoned veteran of NET programming, it was entirely in
character for Davis to shoot for the moon by building on Kellerman's modest beginnings. In drama, he undertook not an occasional performance but the production of a weekly series, and not
just for the season but for the whole year. NET *Playhouse* was possible to produce on a weekly basis only by juxtaposing original
productions with acquisitions and by adding a few summer repeats
for a fifty-two-week season. And even that was possible only because Davis had reached an agreement with Britain's Granada TV,

and later with the BBC, to acquire at affordable prices their high-budget dramatic productions. His triumph was applauded by most stations; a few holdouts, however, complained that "pure performance" without an academic to analyze them was a sellout to "mass entertainment."

NET *Playhouse* was launched in the 1966–67 season with Arthur Miller's adaption of Ibsen's *Enemy of the People*, followed by Tennessee Williams's *Ten Blocks on the Camino Real*, Ronald Ribman's *Fifth Horseman*, Maxwell Anderson's *Star Wagon*, the American Conservatory Theater's performance of Shaw's *Misalliance*, and four one-act plays by the La Mama Experimental Theater. Against formidable odds, Davis sustained the series for five seasons. When NET *Playhouse* died with the dissolution of the NET organization, New York's Channel 13 kept original drama alive for a brief time with *New York Playhouse*. But when *New York Playhouse* died, more than a decade would slip by before *American Playhouse* returned regular drama to the PBS schedule.

Public television's explosive growth during this period should have been a boon to NET. Instead, it was a problem. With the network's outmoded and inefficient distribution system—duplicating and mailing programs to stations—every station that was added to the system (and there were 115 by the mid-1960s) increased NET's distribution costs and reduced by a corresponding amount the dollars available for programming. With production costs rising and the Ford grant fixed at $6 million, Davis was forced to seek new and inexpensive ways of filling his allotted hours. Co-productions were a partial answer. Another alternative was to adapt simple, inexpensive formats and join them together to form a series. *The Creative Person*, a series of individual programs profiling a wide range of creative artists from Joan Baez to Nadia Boulanger, and from Antoni Gaudí to George Grosz, cost an average of $7,000 per half-hour over a forty-four-week season. The shows' budgets were ridiculously low even for those years. Slightly more ambitious and twice as long running, *Arts U.S.A.* presented "a panoramic view of U.S. cultural life in the two decades after World War II." The twice-weekly shows were sometimes didactic, always wide-ranging, highly authoritative, and mercifully inexpensive.

It was under Davis's hand that public television's durable collaboration with New York's Lincoln Center for the Performing Arts began. Much of the credit, however, must go to William Schuman, Lincoln Center's first director, whose presence on the NET board facilitated this celebrated artistic collaboration. The two institutions first joined in 1965 to present *Lincoln Center: Stage 5*, in which Anna Sokolow and Marc Bucci were challenged to choreograph a ballet and compose an opera, respectively, on the theme of a commissioned twenty-minute drama by Frank Gilroy. The high-risk gamble worked, earning *Lincoln Center: Stage 5* the 1965 Prix Italia.

Davis was not satisfied to use the medium simply to bring new audiences to existing art, important as that is. He was almost alone in believing public television had a corollary obligation to create new art, to be a patron of those who make art as well as of those who perform it. His conviction was never more convincingly demonstrated than with the NET Opera Theater project, which was bold, elitist, and uneven, but did create new art. In the late 1940s, when NBC-TV could still put the public interest ahead of profits, the network had invited the Czech-born conductor Peter Herman Adler to form the NBC Opera Company and to produce occasional operas for the small screen. Adler's approach was a modest form of chamber opera that was small and well suited to the limitations of the television screen. The NBC Opera Company survived for ten years, achieving its greatest success in 1949 with Gian Carlo Menotti's opera *Amahl and the Night Visitors*. In 1965, Curt Davis, in a modest effort to fill the void created by the disappearance of the NBC Opera Company, commissioned a production of Luigi Nono's opera, *Intolleranza*. (It may have been new art, but it went unappreciated by NET's affiliates, who were quick to make the obvious puns on Nono's name.) Davis followed his first commission a year later with the world premiere of Jack Beeson's *Lizzie Borden*, which brought director Kirk Browning, a ten-year veteran of Adler's NBC Opera Company, to the NET Opera project. Two years later, Adler himself joined, first as a consultant and later as the opera project's director.

Adler's presence helped NET forge a deal with Canada's CBC

and Britain's BBC in which each partner produced and exchanged, for a modest fee, two original operas a year, thus providing each of the public networks with a season of six original operas. NET's contributions included productions of Thomas Pasatieri's *The Trial of Mary Lincoln*, Hans Werner Henze's *Rachel La Cubana*, Leoš Janáček's *From the House of the Dead*, and Tchaikovsky's *Queen of Spades*. The Opera Project, which ended in the early 1970s with the dissolution of NET itself, might well have bowed out in a final shower of tuneful glory had NET's final commission, Duke Ellington's *Queenie Pie*, reached the air. Unfortunately, the opera, although completed just before Ellington's death, became so hopelessly entangled in his estate that it was never produced or broadcast. As a result, the Opera Project's finale was the Henze opera, which contained, confessed Davis, "not a scrap of appealing melody."[15]

Station programmers, predictably put off by Curt Davis's "advanced" tastes in music, called for more musical shows with old-fashioned, whistleable tunes. But their strongest demand was not for music but for more science programs. Science, they felt, was poorly served on the tube despite the commercial networks' popular *National Geographic* series, which later moved to PBS and became its highest-rated show. NET responded with *Spectrum*, a weekly series that NET's science editor, David Prowitt, assembled from original productions and acquisitions. *Spectrum's* efforts to blanket the broad range of the sciences were no match for the spate of science and nature programs that were to take over and dominate the PBS schedule in later years.

The latter half of the 1960s was a critical period in the development of America's public television. Under White's putative leadership and with Ford's money, the medium came alive, gained a measure of acceptance as something other than more school after school, and reached out for new audiences. Its programming frequently reached White's goal of *significance*, owing in large measure to the network's programming triumvirate of Bill Kobin, Don Dixon, and Curtis Davis. Behind the scenes, however, were NET's funders, who carefully tailored the vision of public television to fit their own goals for the medium. In laying down conditions for the 1964 grant, Jim Armsey had not only pulled the system up by its bootstraps but also reshaped its basic structure. By freeing NET to produce its own programming, he had further centralized national production, all the while reducing the stations' control over NET's programming by abolishing the affiliation fee. And yet he had pushed the stations in the direction of greater autonomy from NET's influence in matters other than programming by encouraging them to form their own national lobbying organization.

Insofar as it was Jim Armsey's own vision, it was completely in character for him to provide the coda to it. The occasion he chose was a meeting of the entire NET staff. One year had passed since the sweeping changes wrought by the 1964 grant, and Armsey wanted to explain the conditions for a second year's grant. Policy explanations, however, turned out to be only an overture to the main act. In a blistering and detailed critique of NET's programming ("a poor imitation of commercial programming" lacking in any visible overall programming philosophy), Armsey charged that NET's involvement with the international consortium that produced *Intertel* was of doubtful legality, and further, that the marketing of NET programs abroad violated a Ford policy of using its money to serve only *American* television. In a final outburst, he expressed strong opposition to the practice of corporate underwriting ("to me underwriting reads 'sponsor'; we may have to exclude it").[16] Armsey then introduced Professor Charles Siepmann, the man he had hired to screen NET's entire output for the grant year. Siepmann offered his own litany of criticism, noting that of the 195 shows he had screened, he had failed to find any "grand design" around which to build a coherent and meaningful program structure.[17]

Armsey closed the day-long session with a sweeping jeremiad on the public medium: it had no future without substantial funding; and those few stations with anything to commend them were in hopeless financial condition, while the stable ones, those with school or university ties, were operated with few exceptions by a bunch of second-raters who would like to be running commercial stations if only they had the ability. Only his parting words could lift the spirits of his stunned audience: Armsey did not expect to be handling the Foundation's public-television projects beyond the current grant.

Jack White, excluded from the meeting and angry at its outcome, shot off a sixteen-page memorandum to his chairman detailing NET's "major problems" with the Foundation, foremost of which was "Foundation interference (covert if not overt) in NET management affairs, and the negative attitude of Mr. Armsey toward [educational television] in general and NET in particular."[18] White's memo precipitated a meeting with Heald and Armsey in which White and the head of his board aired their grievances. It is unlikely that their meeting affected subsequent events; Heald had already decided to shift Armsey to full-time responsibility for the other project he was handling, the Ford Foundation's huge ($350 million) project to upgrade the quality of America's colleges and universities.

Armsey's departure occasioned few regrets at 10 Columbus Circle. His distinctive style—assertive, didactic, and blunt-spoken— ruffled feathers. And yet few would deny that he left the medium a different and palpably better institution than he found it. In addition to compelling a new and higher standard of program quality, he engineered the grant that first equipped NET and its affiliated stations with the new technology of videotape. With adequate funds to buy the professional skills needed for first-rate programming and the technical means to record consistently sharp images, public television moved into a new age of programming. More important, the changes helped to define a role for national programming in a system that was sadly uncertain of its own directions. At the same time, Armsey's policies left the system without cohesive leadership. By removing NET from a leadership role and encouraging the formation of a new station-based organization, he set the pattern that has since been followed of fragmenting public television's functions into competing entities, each with a bundle of territorial imperatives to protect and each with substantial overhead costs to be met out of already strained resources.

As it turned out, the Foundation's insistence that NET emphasize public affairs by devoting half of its program time and money to that area anticipated a shift in the Ford's own priorities. In January 1966, Henry Heald, forced to resign under pressure from the Foundation's trustees, was replaced by McGeorge Bundy, the former national-security adviser in President Johnson's White House. Bundy brought not only a well-honed intelligence, a quick wit, and a rapier-sharp tongue to the Foundation, but also a shift in emphasis from education to national affairs. But the most significant contribution of his presidency to public television was the man he chose to advise him on the Foundation's commitments to the public media. Fred W. Friendly was a neophyte in the philanthropic world, but highly experienced in the world of television, having been Edward R. Murrow's producer and partner in the CBS award-winning documentary series *See It Now*, and later the president of CBS News. His resignation from CBS News, precipitated by the network's refusal to preempt a rerun of *I Love Lucy* to carry the Senate hearings on the Vietnam War, freed Friendly to turn his awesome energies and lively imagination to the underfunded noncommercial medium. His appointment, however, sent a shudder through the system: Ford's money and Friendly's style—he was known to some at CBS as "the brilliant monster"—were an awesome, and to some a fearsome, combination.[19] One thing was certain: however he chose to play the game, public television was in for a lively time.

6

IN A FRIENDLY FASHION

Public television and radio are not just visible alternatives, they are options of sanity to the billion dollar arcade called commercial television, which makes so much money doing its worst that it cannot afford to do its best. The American public will not allow public broadcasting to perish if they know what the stakes really are.

Fred W. Friendly[1]

In the history of public television, 1967 stands out as a very special year—although it was not, as some say mistakenly, the year of public television's birth. Nevertheless, in the months of 1967 the medium was renamed and restructured, gained a new and sometimes nettlesome partner, went into long pants with its first regularly scheduled live television series, and laid the foundations for its most successful children's show.

Of the year's developments, the change in the system's name from "educational" to "public" television was certainly the most visible. It was not, however, the most significant. In the process of gaining a new name, public television had been placed "under new management." When Congress legislated the Corporation for Public Broadcasting into existence, leadership of the system shifted into its inexperienced hands. The process brought public broadcasting into a partnership with the Congress out of which would come new money, palpable political risks, and consequences the movement's founders could not have anticipated fifteen years earlier.

While politicians in Washington were tinkering with the system's structure, developments were taking place in New York that would have a profound effect on the system's programming. In one corner of Manhattan, a small cadre of highly creative people were noodling with an idea that would soon develop into public television's most popular children's television series. Their story will be told in a later chapter. Our immediate concern is with another group, the Public Broadcast Laboratory, which was working in another corner of Manhattan, creating public television's first weekly live show. PBL gave ample evidence that the Ford Foundation, little involved with 1967's other major changes, still exercised considerable influence over the medium it had virtually fathered.

PBL (the name of the show as well as the initials of the producing organization) was born of a plot hatched by Fred W. Friendly in his new role as television adviser to Ford president McGeorge Bundy. Friendly saw PBL as the answer to public broadcasting's need to grow up, to become *real* television. Shortly after joining the Foundation, Friendly visited NET's tape-duplication plant in Ann Arbor. He came away impressed with its efficiency and appalled at its necessity. Spending up to $1 million a year to make copies of programs to be mailed out to stations was, in his view, an absurdity in an age of electronic delivery. The system, he said, was riding to the moon on the pony express. The three commercial networks were covering the nation with long lines leased from AT&T and no more than a single copy of each program. And they were doing it instantaneously, not waiting until the postman trundled the tapes to more than a hundred separate stations. "A network without interconnection is not a network at all, but only a film syndicate," Friendly declared.[2]

Friendly knew that NET had little choice: the cost of leased lines would eat up its entire budget and more, leaving nothing for the programs. He recognized the dilemma, but that didn't mean he accepted it. Not surprisingly, he had an idea. Satellite technology, now an accepted part of our everyday experience, was then barely on the technical horizon, still the stuff of science fiction. (Indeed, it was the science fiction of Arthur C. Clarke that had first suggested the possibility of satellite transmission.) Friendly, a visionary then as now, foresaw in the emerging satellite technology an opportunity to bring to public television the most advanced technology and build a base of financial stability. His imagination had been stirred by something that ABC had done the previous year. The youngest of the three networks, ABC was fighting its way out

of third place in the prime-time sweepstakes and had sought FCC
approval to launch its own satellite. The new technology would
enable it to drop the use of AT&T's expensive long lines and substantially reduce its program distribution costs. To sweeten the
deal and help persuade the FCC to reverse its policy against privately operated satellites, ABC promised public television a free
ride on the "bird."

ABC's petition opened a thorny public-policy issue: should satellite technology, developed by the government with billions of
taxpayer dollars, be handed over to private interests for their own
use and exploitation? The FCC responded to ABC with a Notice of
Inquiry inviting comment from all interested parties.[3] The Ford
Foundation, first in line with comments, proposed an idea that
had sprouted in Friendly's fecund imagination: instead of allowing ABC to operate the satellite for its own benefit, why not put it
in nonprofit hands to serve not one but all three networks and
provide free interconnection service for the public system? Each
network would save a bundle on its distribution costs and since
the technology was developed at public expense it would seem
appropriate to channel those savings into public television's
strained coffers. It was a brilliant leap of imagination, a concept
worthy of one of television's most creative minds. Not only would
the satellite, operated as a public not-for-profit service, propel the
public-television system into the space age, it would also provide
the system with a steady and secure source of income—thus taking
the Foundation off the hook. What's more, it would repay in service some part of the public's multibillion-dollar investment in the
space program. Friendly even had a name for it: "The People's
Dividend."

Bundy warmed to the idea immediately and ordered a task force
from the Foundation to work day and night to draft a proposal
before the FCC's deadline. It was important, said Bundy, "lest complete control of the satellite be given away to other interested
parties without regard for noncommercial television."[4] The proposal, much of it written by Bundy himself, called for the establishment of a "Broadcaster's Non-Profit Satellite Service." In addition to providing for six commercial channels, the plan called

for five channels for noncommercial use, one for national public television and four for regional instructional services. Of course all the giant communications companies—Comsat, AT&T, Western Union, and IT&T—had good reason to make certain that the Ford satellite never lifted off the launch pad. Bundy countered with a plea for time, not only time for Ford to answer the opposition, but time for the FCC to formulate sound public policy on satellite regulation before taking precipitate action. And time is what they got—more than they needed or wanted. In a demonstration of bureaucratic torpor (induced, one suspects, by the kind of hardball common carriers sometimes play) the proposal was becalmed and ultimately forgotten, killed with kind words and bureaucratic inaction. The words of praise in the press ("a historic new watershed," "will undoubtedly stand as a historic occasion in the evolution of broadcasting")[5] framed an ironic obituary for an idea that had widened the scope of public policy and stirred hopes among public broadcasters.

The "Bundy Bird" and its aftermath were not without positive consequences, including the unusual and effective partnership forged between Bundy and Friendly, two men of widely disparate backgrounds and temperament. McGeorge Bundy, the Boston Brahmin and a descendant of the legendary Lowells, had been educated at Groton, Yale, and Harvard and had been the intimate friend and counselor of two presidents. He was a man both admired and feared for his coldly dispassionate and rational approach to matters. Fred W. Friendly, by contrast, came from the lower-middle classes of New York and Providence and graduated from Providence Business College. He had fought his way to the top of his profession, first as producer and downfield blocker for the legendary Ed Murrow (*See It Now*), then as president of CBS News. In the process, he had gained a reputation as a man of aggressive ambition whose interests of the moment were nothing less than obsessive. Few among us understood the symbiosis that drew them together, unless perhaps it fulfilled their mutual needs. Bundy drew heavily for counsel on Friendly's street smarts, not only about television but about other Ford initiatives as well, partly out of respect for Friendly's skills at selling an idea and infecting everyone within earshot with his own contagious enthusiasm. Friendly, for his part, probably found in Bundy a substitute for the departed Murrow and a link with the Establishment—someone who gave his presence respectability and status in those quarters where the self-made Friendly felt most uncomfortable.

The aftermath of the "Bundy Bird" had another payoff. In addition to capturing the attention of the nation's front pages on public television's behalf and adding fuel to the fires of concern about its economic plight, Friendly had also succeeded in making a case for the system's need for interconnection. His hope of achieving it, by pulling the public system into the realm of "real" television with a free ride on the satellite, went down with the Bundy Bird. Friendly, impetuous and impatient, was not, however, one to sit back and wait for others to shape the future—not when his restless soul hankered to do the shaping. If the satellite was not to be the answer, he had another plan.

In December 1966, the Ford Foundation announced a $10 million fund to launch "a two-year demonstration of the power of national interconnection."[6] Friendly had two objectives. One was to jettison NET's outmoded system of program distribution with a demonstration of lively and live interconnected television that would, in the modest words of its author, "mobilize the hearts and minds of the nation." The other objective was rooted in the fanciful notion that college campuses contain rich lodes of unmined television talent willing and able to parade their erudition before the cameras, a notion not shared by those of us who had worked over those tailings years before. Friendly's visits to a score of leading university campuses and meetings with their presidents produced enough commitments to form a consortium of two dozen universities. They were joined together as the Columbia University Experimental Broadcast Laboratory and headquartered on the Morningside Heights campus where Friendly, simultaneously with his Foundation responsibilities, was Edward R. Murrow Professor of Broadcast Journalism. But when Columbia's trustees realized that the university had enough problems without taking on a highly visible and experimental television program, they opted out, the consortium came unglued, and the college plan was abandoned.

Friendly, undaunted, pushed ahead with his plan "to mobilize the hearts and minds of the nation" by recasting the project as the Public Broadcast Laboratory. PBL was still to be a live, interconnected weekly television show, but without its links to college campuses. Instead, PBL was joined "administratively" to the corporate body of a stunned NET—stunned because it found that PBL was to be a "semi-autonomous" project. That seemed to mean it was to be a part of but did not belong to the network. No one, certainly not the troubled souls at NET, missed the irony of the situation: NET and PBL, both created by the Ford Foundation, and both involved in producing television programs for the same public system, had been cast as rivals, not just for broadcast time and facilities, talent, and ideas, but for Father Ford's handouts. The rivalry was ready made for breeding dissension, lowering morale, and promoting treachery. In time, it did all three.

Friendly's decision to create a new and rival production organization when the Foundation was already supporting another reveals something of the complexity, if not the perversity, of the former CBS News chief. Friendly, a former colleague of his once observed, "always came equipped with his own precipice from which to jump."[7] By creating the precipice he called PBL, Friendly clearly aimed to shake up a slumbering, self-satisfied system. His faith in NET was low because, he said, it lacked the vitality to work the miracle of reinventing public broadcasting. He aimed to do nothing less. But first he had to find the people. Public television, he complained, "has not attracted enough first-class broadcasters."[8] If PBL was to breathe life into the stodgy body of educational television, he would need men and women "with fire in their bellies." Fortunately, he knew where to find them: back at the West 57th Street headquarters of CBS News.

The first to be recruited was Avram (Av) Westin, an awardwinning producer and long-time veteran of CBS News. Westin was to be the project's executive director. He and Friendly had worked together and had, by all accounts, hit it off well. Among the others who jumped ship at CBS News to join the experimental weekly magazine show were Stuart Sucherman, Tom Kennedy, and Gerald Slater, all of whom would figure later as key players in other public-television contexts. For the rest of his team, Westin chose content specialists: for national affairs, John Wicklein, formerly a *New York Times* and ABC News reporter; for foreign affairs, Robert McCabe, and for science, Joseph Russin, both from *Newsweek*; and for the physical and natural sciences, John Osmundsen, who had been with both *Look* and *Life* magazines. Lewis Freedman, a veteran of both public and commercial television and the producer of such highly regarded shows as *Play of the Week* and CBS's innovative *Camera Three,* joined the team as cultural director. Freedman was to play an even more important role in public television's future. To supervise this high-powered team, Westin recruited Robert Hoyt from Canada, where Hoyt had been producing CBC's lively and provocative news magazine *This Hour Has Seven Days.*

One of the keys to a television magazine's success is the person who gives the show unity by tying the disparate segments together, its on-air host. PBL's host was Edward P. Morgan, an ABC anchor in the Murrow tradition, well regarded and with years of broadcasting experience, but almost all of it in radio. He was assisted, however, by two highly experienced television correspondents, Tom Pettit and Robert MacNeil, both from NBC News.

The details of how this first-class team was integrated into the PBL organizational structure might be irrelevant, of course, unless the structure affected the quality of the show. In PBL's case, it did. In attaching PBL to the NET corporate structure for administrative purposes, Friendly steadfastly refused to see PBL fully integrated with the older organization, decreeing that it was to be "a separate and distinct division" of NET. Oddly, while a committee of the NET board was given the power to appoint the PBL executive director (Westin), it was only to be *"with the advice and consent of the President of the Ford Foundation"* (emphasis added). Even more oddly, Westin was responsible to a committee of the NET board but not to the NET president, Jack White, and then only for those phases of the operation "other than content of the broadcasts."[9]

For program content, Westin reported to an Editorial Policy Board of content specialists that included both journalists and

academicians and was chaired by the dean of Columbia's Graduate School of Journalism, Edward W. Barrett.[10] Responsible to not
one but two committees—and with an actively kibitzing Ford
Foundation bankroller on the sidelines—Westin found himself
atop a hydra-headed structure that produced confusion, frustration, and anger and promoted an organizational malaise from
which PBL never fully recovered.

PBL's Editorial Policy Board proved the most debilitating. The
twelve men (there were no women) met every week while the show
was on the air to review plans with Westin and his staff, preview
segments, offer suggestions, and make policy. (The minutes of the
meetings note that Friendly was also present as a "guest.") According to its chair, the editorial board "would not attempt to
edit scripts or shows but to set broad policy . . . [to] discuss future
programming plans and review projects of [a] singularly novel or
controversial nature."[11] No matter how well constituted the editorial board, and it was one of the best, nor how well intentioned
its actions, the whole was a calamitous example of programming
by committee and proved, in the long run, to be an inevitable and
unnecessary damper on creativity.

Eleven months before the show debuted, Westin shared his concept of PBL in a memo to his staff. The show, he wrote, would
demonstrate "what responsible intellectual persons can accomplish, given free rein to their editorial and critical judgments."
As if to give meaning to its label as a laboratory, he added that
"no technique for conveying information will be overlooked and
new techniques will be developed . . . the phrase 'it can't be done
that way' will not be heard among us." The memo wound up with
the earnest proclamation: "We cannot fail because we must
not."[12] PBL would be burdened with a plethora of such heady
rhetoric.

Friendly decided to schedule the show in a Sunday evening slot
and to insist that stations carry it live. It was a deliberate effort to
lift the system by its own bootstraps. At the time, most local stations, lacking the funds to program over the weekends, did not
broadcast on Sundays. PBL's three-hour magazine would not only
fill those Sunday evening hours, but more important, by forcing

stations to light up on the weekends, it would increase public television's presence in each local community. The objective was a noble and needed prod to progress, and, for the most part, it worked. (New York's Channel 13 tried unsuccessfully to delay the show to a weekday to save Sunday transmission costs.) Unfortunately, broadcasting the program on Sunday evenings proved good for policy but disastrous for winning new audiences. The otherwise astute scheduling slotted PBL against the week's toughest commercial competition: the high-rated *Smothers Brothers Show* and Ed Sullivan's venerable variety hour *Toast of the Town*. It was a tough placement for an established show, much less a new and untried one. The prospect of airing three hours of "real" television—live, provocative, and with the promise of familiar faces and names—should have been greeted by the stations with gratitude. Instead, many were nervous and apprehensive at the thought of releasing a weekly program, sight unseen, fearing that it might contain material "unsuited" to their local audience. A few were even troubled over the show's aegis—the "liberally oriented Ford Foundation" and its resident mischief-maker Fred Friendly—and the fact that it was produced by a platoon of commercial types from the wrong side of the nonprofit fence. Station reactions ranged from a cautiously guarded wait-and-see attitude to outright skepticism.

PBL debuted on Sunday evening, November 5, 1967. Almost a month earlier, Friendly had written Westin what was "intended to be my last memorandum to you before the premiere." It wasn't the last, but it was a classic example of Friendly prose. The subject, he told Westin, was "Failure."

Don't be afraid to fail sometimes or you will fall into that ancient patter of safe ideas, the pursuit of the obvious, which leads to turgid prose and pictures for their own sake. Don't be afraid to be controversial, but don't make the mistake of believing that conflict in itself can be a base on balls to success. We expect you to be dynamic, but we also expect you to be dull, sometimes. The right to be deadly serious on certain crucial issues is part of your birthright. Remember that exposé by itself is not necessarily enlightening—street fires make an ugly glare that do not give long-term illumination. We expect you to be fair but not so balanced to every side on every subject that you become predictable. As a viewer I expect to be made to feel uncomfortable. The Ford Foundation anticipates some discomfiture, but I can assure you they can stand the heat. As a former producer, I expect to feel on numerous occasions that "I could have done it better," but I promise never to say it to you. . . . Good luck . . . you and your other associates are the ones who must put their professional reputation where our mouths are. The way for me to thank you is to leave you alone.[13]

After cautioning that "you won't be as good as your good notices say you are, and you won't be as bad as your worst critics say," Friendly warned Westin not to expect easy marks from the television press. He was prescient about that.

Tuesday morning's *New York Times* contented itself with a catalogue of critical comments from other sources, most of them negative; Friendly was quoted as saying it was a beginning but disappointing. On the other hand, Harriet Van Horne (*New York Post*) dismissed the opening effort as "bombast, pretense and warmed-over sludge."[14] If PBL's crew hoped for happier words from New York's most influential media critic, they were let down by Jack Gould's review in the Sunday *Times.* Gould wrote that PBL's premiere show failed to blaze new paths: with every advantage of money and talent, PBL "surrendered to the blight of awkward confusion and dullness." Sagging spirits at NET's headquarters were lifted by Gould's parting jab at PBL's hubris: "Supporters of public broadcasting will hope that PBL will acquire the virtue of modesty and now stop suggesting that all others in noncommercial broadcasting were sad sacks until the laboratory crashed into the breach. Without the great resources at the disposal of PBL for one evening of TV, individual stations and NET often have performed far better for a week."[15]

The reception of the premiere show was not much more welcoming among the affiliates. The show was not carried by 29 of the 119 affiliates, including the stations of the South Carolina, Alabama, and Georgia state networks. Most cited "financial reasons." But the pattern of noncarriage suggests otherwise. The premiere included a performance of Douglas Turner Ward's *Day of Absence,* the controversial off-Broadway play about people in a small Southern town who awaken one morning to find their black citizens gone and their town paralyzed. The satire, performed broadly by the Negro Ensemble Theater with the town's white citizens portrayed by black players in white face, was too much for some stations.

It was an inauspicious beginning. In a delicately phrased memo, PBL's Editorial Policy Board reacted by asserting that PBL "should be more than commercial television without restraints." Its proposed remedy was more frequent and early consultation with the Board on programming plans and a firmer Board hand in policy. "The Board feels obliged to be in on the take-offs as well as the landings (or crashes) in the case of controversial or explosive program segments . . . [and] must decline to be a buffer for that which it has not helped design."[16]

The unwieldy machinery was immediately set in motion to rescue the remainder of the season. To a degree it worked. By the time PBL capped its cameras the following spring, after grinding out twenty-six weekly Sunday-night shows, the experimental series could look back proudly on several modest successes, including a tough investigative report on the meat-packing industry, the television premiere of Pinter's *The Dwarfs,* and a remarkable film recording Dr. Martin Luther King, Jr.'s last three months of life.

Notwithstanding the occasional successes, the prevailing mood at season's end was disappointment, particularly among the members of the Editorial Policy Board. In a six-page memo to NET chairman Everett Case, they complained that PBL had not even approached its objective of being innovative and experimental. "Unhappily, our influence has been almost entirely negative . . . the staff has, in general, aimed low and has by conventional execution, often competent, shot a lot of ducks on the water." They recommended that Westin be replaced by someone "with a sounder and more sophisticated editorial judgment." Then, with a gentle swipe at the hand that fed them, the Board offered Ford a carefully worded suggestion. The term "banker," they said, "does not accurately describe the rather strong entrepreneurial hand which the Foundation exercised—and probably had to exercise—in the genesis of PBL. Looking to the future, however, we believe that a more normally remote relationship between foundation and grantee would be good for PBL—and, indeed, for the Foundation.''[17]

The seriousness, even the irreparability, of the problems between the Editorial Policy Board and the PBL staff were clearly conveyed near the close of the first season in what the Board called its basic recommendation: "Unless the present situation is soon changed, PBL's 1968–69 season should be cancelled.''[18] As summer drifted into fall, and the deadline approached for a decision, the distances between PBL, NET, and Ford were alive with flying memos as each partner staked out a position. The Editorial Policy Board wanted Westin out and even threatened to resign if he didn't go. NET wanted Westin out, too, but wanted the Editorial Policy Board removed from operations as well. Friendly, however, wanted Westin to remain, and both he and Westin wanted to be rid of the Editorial Policy Board.

In the end the "bankers" prevailed. Westin stayed and the Editorial Board resigned, replaced by a small "program advisory committee" that was to meet infrequently and deal only with policy. But there were compromises. To soften complaints against Westin's editorial judgment, Frederick M. Bohen, a former staff assistant in the Johnson White House, was made PBL's executive editor. Bohen shared Westin's authority but had specific responsibility for "program content as it affects taste, judgment and responsibility.''[19] The show itself was trimmed, cut from two hours to ninety minutes, and swapped its multi-topic magazine format for shows with a single theme. NET's position was strengthened by a change that required both Westin and Bohen to report to NET's chief executive Jack White and not directly to the NET board as Westin had done the previous year.

On the whole, PBL's second season fared better than its first. Critics had warm words for the season's opener, Arthur and Evelyn Barron's independently produced documentary *Birth and Death*. And the first of Frederick Wiseman's impressive and extensive body of cinema-verité documentaries, *Law and Order*, was praised for not portraying the Kansas City Police "as either all saints or sadists." On other Sunday nights, PBL investigated the Pentagon's decision-making process, provided television's first critical examination of the burgeoning cable industry, and probed the nature of television news. But some critics found the second season, like the first, "disappointing." Several efforts to be more experimental fell disastrously flat. A performance by Jerzy Grotowski's Polish Laboratory Theater of Wyspianski's *Akropolis*—in Polish and without subtitles—elicited load groans from the stations and a comment from the *Village Voice* that it was "grindingly tedious."[20] In another experimental approach, six independent filmmakers of disparate viewpoints made personal statements about America during the 1968 election campaign. It was summarily dismissed by one critic as a psychedelic field day with no redeeming features.[21]

By April 1969—two years and $12.5 million later—the Ford Foundation's noble if quixotic experiment came to an end. If, as some felt, PBL failed to deliver on its promise to "use television as it has never been used before," it is worth remembering that no group of television professionals could have lived up to the press puffery that preceded its launch: the show was the victim of its own hype. In one respect, PBL was nothing less than a brassy attempt to reinvent public television. Fred Friendly, impatient with what it had been, was obsessed with a vision of what it could become: a forceful, vital, and effective interconnected network, linking the nation through the shared experience of live programming. Ironically, his experiment with live programming may have had some effect in persuading Congress to provide for systemwide interconnection in its landmark 1967 Public Broadcasting Act. But if it did, the legislators acted out of a different, even contrary vision. Neither they nor the fragmented leadership of public television share Friendly's concept of networking, implying as it does the simultaneous airing of programs nationally. (Even public television's notable exception, the *MacNeil/Lehrer NewsHour*, encountered resistance from stations at the start.) Both Congress and the system itself cling to the vision of Friendly's predecessor, Scott Fletcher, who saw public television as many local outlets serviced by a national "library" from which programs best suited to individual local tastes could be "withdrawn." The interconnection, when it finally did happen, was seen primarily as the most cost-efficient means of making the library of programs available to its member stations.

The *PBL* story has a curious sidebar. In a move that is more than coincidence, both NBC and CBS mounted news magazines of their own in the fall of 1968, a year after *PBL*'s debut. NBC's *First Tuesday* was unsuccessful, disappeared, and was replaced by a series of equally unsuccessful efforts. But the CBS version, *60 Minutes*, not only survived but also rose to the top of the rating charts, and it continues to this day to serve the network and its audience. *PBL* influenced the future shape of the public system as well: stations were opened to weekend broadcasting, the way was paved for a PBS-managed network of stations, and the medium was given a much-needed infusion of talented artists and producers, most of whom would help shape the public system's future.[22]

Before that uncertain future took shape, however, the *PBL* story had one more climactic scene to play out, a tableau of intrigue and treachery brought about by the system's perverse penchant for self-dramatization. The tale began in the offices of *PBL* during the last days of its final season. As a means of memorializing Ford's two-year experiment, Fred Friendly had invited executive editor Fred Bohen and his *PBL* colleagues individually to commit to paper their thoughts on the future course of public television and the role they thought the Foundation ought to play in that future. In an atmosphere loaded with suspicion and mutual mistrust and with rumors of takeovers running rampant, Bohen's confidential memorandum, still in draft form, was stolen from his desk. It was never established by whom and for whom the memo was stolen, but whoever stole it was obviously determined to expose what they saw as the perfidy of the *PBL* upstarts by leaking the contents of the memo to *Variety*. The widely read weekly of show business snapped it up with undisguised relish and published excerpts under a front-page banner headline: "Life in Public TV Jungle."[23]

Bohen's purloined memorandum had incorporated, in addition to his own thoughts, the observations of some of his *PBL* colleagues, including Lewis Freedman's cranky complaint that "NET has the smell of stodginess and tired people, and, except for Bill

Kobin, its officers are inferior to men recruited to PBL." Stuart
Sucherman's contribution was a proposal to merge PBL into NET
"but with the establishment of top PBL personnel at the highest
administration of NET." Bohen, for his part, recommended that
Ford drop its concern for and the funding of "the vast number
of small, parochial, timid or uncompromising local ETV stations
including, perhaps, such moribund stations as Philadelphia and
Chicago."[24]

Ironically, if *Variety* had published the Bohen memo in its en-
tirety, the aftershocks would have been less intense; the full story
is usually less threatening than the headlines. Bohen, after first
noting public television's absolute lack of an organizing philosophy and after rejecting quick fixes like PBL, proposed that Ford
and the newly created Corporation for Public Broadcasting foster
a long-range solution built around two national networks, one
concerned exclusively with news and public affairs—with an emphasis upon analysis, not topicality—and the other devoted to the
arts, the humanities, and features. Both, he emphasized, would be
based in strong local stations and depend upon other local stations as "bureaus." His final recommendation was to strengthen
those key local stations that had proved themselves. Subsequent
events, notably the creation of a national public-affairs center in
Washington and the absorption of NET into the New York public
channel, both of which occurred in the months following the publication of the memo, suggested that Bohen's recommendations
received a sympathetic reading at Ford.

The melodramatic impact of the *Variety* revelations can only be
understood in the context of the times. Public broadcasting,
poised on a precipice of change, was edgy, suffering from what
the philosopher Eric Hoffer observed was the inevitable crisis of
self-esteem provoked by change. The events that began in the
critical year of 1967 came to flower in the spring of 1969. New
organizations arose and others were retired. Behind the moving
scenery, the locus of power shifted into new and untried hands.
A system that had survived on the margins of the media for fifteen
years was about to experience a rebirth, a new name, and a new
partner.

7

ONE FOR THE MONEY

Television has been fashioned into a miraculous instrument. The opportunity is at hand to turn the instrument to the best uses of American society, and to make it of new and increased service to the general public.
Carnegie Commission on
Educational Television[1]

The Public Broadcast Laboratory's two-year experiment, sponsored by Ford, was a watershed in the Foundation's relations with the public medium. Although Ford continued to pour money into public television for several more years, never again would the Foundation exercise the firm hand in the system's affairs that marked the heady days of PBL and before.

When Bundy brought Fred Friendly to the Foundation in 1966, it was rumored that his principal task was to manage Ford's fade-out from public television. If true, Friendly appears to have chosen a contrary course, adding PBL's $12 million to the annual investment of $10 million that the Foundation had already committed. Nevertheless, as early as 1963, the handwriting was on the wall, and Friendly knew it. His 1967 book referred to Ford's ten-year, $10 million annual contribution as "only a crutch" that in effect acted "to prevent educational television from finding a financially secure base of its own."[2] With the system growing, with costs rising, and with the Foundation being hit with requests for ever larger amounts, it was clear that Ford's largesse had to come to an end. The search began for alternate sources with the knowledge that it would take an uncommon amount of luck to find one whose resources could match those of the Ford Foundation.

The initiative for the new search came from an old friend of the public medium, C. Scott Fletcher. As president of the Ford Foundation's Fund for Adult Education, Fletcher had provided most of the money to get the educational channels reserved and the public television movement under way. After retiring from the Ford Foundation, he had become an executive consultant to the Educational Television Stations division of the NAEB, public broadcasting's professional association. (ETS, founded in 1964 with station funds freed by the Foundation when it forced NET to forgo its affiliation fee, wanted Fletcher to be its executive director. He was reluctant, however, to leave his retirement home in Florida.) Fletcher took up his new post fully aware that the lead item on the public-television agenda was the problem of its forward funding. He'd been around this track once before, but this time the stakes were higher; there were now more stations and programs to sustain, and their appetites had become accustomed to more expensive nourishment. Fletcher put together a plan of attack that would begin with a study of station finances and be followed by a national conference to discuss and analyze the results. The first step would clarify the extent of the problem, and the second would give it maximum visibility.[3]

The study of station finances, launched in the summer of 1964 and funded out of the U.S. Office of Education, was completed in time for a national conference at the end of the year. Most of the more than 260 persons who attended represented local stations. But in his self-described "high-handed" manner, Fletcher decreed that no station manager would be allowed to attend unless accompanied by a member of their board. Fletcher wanted a commitment from the top. He also knew the problem would need political muscle for the next step.

Deciding what the next step was going to be would be a key factor in the conference's success or failure. Most delegates favored a request to President Johnson to call a White House Conference, not only to draw national attention to the problem, but also to mobilize the force of the Oval Office behind its solution.

Ralph Lowell, patriarch of the Boston station, proposed a different approach. Reading from a prepared text—an obvious if little-used tactic to move a debate to closure—Lowell called for the creation of a small presidential commission, made up of no more than twelve distinguished citizens who would be appointed by the president. The presidential commission would study the problem, collect expert testimony, and then, not more than a year later, recommend a national policy on the future course of public television. With discussion skills honed during his years with the Fund for Adult Education, Fletcher engineered the unanimous consent of the delegates for the Lowell plan.

The delegates decided to recommend to the president the names of those who could make up the proposed commission, and to have those chosen jointly sign the letter to the president. Fletcher sent Lowell his carefully chosen list of candidates, Lowell met with them in Boston, and, in June 1965, a letter jointly drafted and signed by the members of the proposed commission was sent to the White House. But after consulting with his advisers, Johnson declined to create yet another presidential commission, feeling, perhaps, that there were already too many. Or perhaps he may have wanted to avoid creating the appearance of a conflict of interest; commercial-broadcasting properties were the source of the Johnson family fortune. The president did, however, offer to lend his support to a privately financed commission. Fletcher and Lowell turned for help to the foundations. The Carnegie Corporation, whose president, John Gardner, was a frequent adviser to Johnson and was even then under consideration for a cabinet appointment, responded with an offer of a half-million dollars to underwrite the year-long study. James R. Killian, Jr., the retiring president of the Massachusetts Institute of Technology and a former science adviser to President Eisenhower, agreed to head the study as the chair of the Carnegie Commission on Educational Television. (When Carnegie funded a second study on public television ten years later, the earlier commission was dubbed Carnegie I.) Although the president's hand was apparent in the selection of only one commissioner—the manager of Johnson's broadcast properties in Texas, J. C. Kellam—all of Killian's appointments were checked out with presidential assistant Douglass Cater to make certain they were acceptable to the White House. Sensitive to the need of courting Johnson's continued interest, Killian chose two who were close to the president: Mrs. Oveta Culp Hobby, chair of the *Houston Post* Company and a presidential adviser; and John Hayes, manager of the *Washington Post*'s television stations.[4]

The Commission and its small staff spent fourteen months visiting stations, taking testimony, conducting statistical studies, and convening conferences. In January 1967, the Commission published its findings and recommendations as a book, *Public Television: A Program for Action,* which was sold at bookstores and newsstands.[5] In addition to recommending that the system be renamed "public television," the Commission noted that it "includes all that is of human interest and importance which is not at the moment appropriate or available for support by advertising, and which is not arranged for formal instruction." In order to extend and strengthen educational television, the Commission recommended "that federal assistance be made available as a stimulus and support for local and state initiative." The Commission also proposed the creation of a second national production center and the strengthening of the first, NET—as well as support for local programming and for the production of programs by local stations for more-than-local use ("the greatest practical diversity of program production sources is essential to the health of the system"). In order to move the system toward the much-needed live interconnection of stations ("public television can never be a national enterprise until effective interconnection has been provided"), the Commission urged the Congress to permit the telephone companies to grant public television preferential rates or free access to its long lines. It also recommended that provision be made for programming research, technical research, and the recruitment and training of specialized personnel.

The most consequential of the Commission's recommendations, however, addressed the critical question of the who and how of future funding. The who part was easy; only one potential source was capable of supplying the millions that public television would need and that was the federal treasury. The how part was more difficult. Convinced that the normal budgeting and appropriations procedure of Congress was "not consonant with the degree of independence essential to Public Television," the Commission opted for a manufacturer's excise tax on television sets to generate the revenues that would go automatically into a public-television trust fund. To receive and disburse these monies, the Commission called upon Congress to create a federally chartered, nongovernmental, nonprofit corporation to be known as the Corporation for Public Television. This new organization, with a board insulated from political control, would assume the leadership position long held by NET, leading the way to "a well-financed and well-directed educational system, substantially larger and far more pervasive and effective than that which now exists."

The Commission's report was not a bestseller, nor did it provoke a much-needed national debate on communications policy. Public broadcasters, of course, welcomed it with outstretched hands, seeing in it a dim and distant vision of fiscal salvation. Only a tiny handful expressed fears that the recommended changes contained the seeds of even more serious problems ahead, among them, Joan Ganz Cooney. The creator of *Sesame Street* once told me she thought the report was a "mischievous" document. I, too, had misgivings, even beyond the worrisome political implications of funneling government money into the system. In the recommendation for multiple production centers ("more than one NET"), I saw a further diffusion of the system's resources, finances, and energies. And I feared the consequences of placing public television's leadership with a body having nothing to do with the system's only legitimate function—the making and distribution of television programs.

I was certain, given public television's well-earned reputation for endless disputation, that the Commission report would gather dust in the musty archives and never be acted upon. I was wrong. With a dispatch rarely seen on Capitol Hill, Congress incorporated most of the recommendations into a bill (the Public Broadcasting Act of 1967) that sailed through both houses virtually without opposition. The speed and success of the measure was a tribute to the lobbying skill of Douglass Cater, Johnson's legislative aide for educational matters, who shepherded the bill through both houses and into the Oval Office. President Johnson signed it into law on November 7, 1967, barely ten months after the Commission's report had been made public.

For the most part, the Commission's recommendations were embodied in the Act without substantial change.[6] What the Commission intended as the Corporation for Public Television came under heavy lobbying from the radio faction and emerged as the Corporation for Public *Broadcasting*. One of its charges remained, however, to arrange for "one or more" systems of interconnection. Congress took care to emphasize that interconnection meant "distribution" of programs, not the "lock-step" networking of commercial television. The programs distributed on the interconnection were to be aired "at times chosen by the stations." Nor was networking the only fear of the lawmakers. In their charge to the Corporation to "facilitate the full development of educational broadcasting in which programs of high quality, obtained from diverse sources, will be made available" they added the phrase *"with strict adherence to objectivity and balance in all programs or series of programs of a controversial nature"* (emphasis added).[7] It was a barbed hook, the precise meaning of which would be argued for many years to come.

Missing from the landmark legislation was the Commission's key recommendation, the provision for an excise tax to feed a trust fund "insulated" from political control. Congress did precisely what the Commission hoped it would not do; it chose to aid public broadcasting through the annual appropriations process. Despite his earlier encouragement of the Commission's work, Lyndon Johnson was unable to buy into the arguments for yet another dip into the nation's pockets—he was already bogged down with an unpopular and apparently unwinnable war in Vietnam and was publicly committed to a fiscally impossible policy of "guns and butter."[8] Nor was Congress any more disposed to accept the Commission's proposal; the lawmakers were reluctant to create yet another dedicated tax that would lie outside the control of their budgetary processes. Public broadcasters did not push the issue because they feared that it would cost them the bill and with it the Corporation for Public Broadcasting.[9] Congress, however, having chosen the appropriations route, showed an indifference to the medium's most pressing problem by authorizing a $9 million appropriation for the Corporation's first year—less than the cost of a single season of *Sesame Street*—and then did not appropriate a single dollar of it. The Corporation's initial funding was a $1 million gift from the CBS network.

Congress ignored another of the Commission's key recommendations: the composition of the Corporation's governing board. The Carnegie Commission proposed to keep it above partisan politics by proposing a board of twelve, six to be appointed by the president and those six to select six others. Congress chose instead to create a board of fifteen, all of whom were to be appointed by the president with the consent of the Senate. By specifying that no more than eight of the fifteen could belong to a single political party, Congress effectively politicized what was to have been a nonpartisan governing body, a far cry from the public-trust stewardship that the Commission had envisaged. The Commission's fears that political dabbling in public television's affairs would result were later borne out, and at no time more dramatically and destructively than during the troubled years of the Nixon Administration.

It is remarkable to note in retrospect how little public debate accompanied the adoption of legislation that so radically changed public television's relationship to government. One might expect a voice or two to warn of the dangers of putting the public system on the federal payroll or to decry the possible loss of its freedom to speak out candidly and forcefully on issues about which honest people, including politicians, honestly disagree. Instead, witness after witness appeared before the Congressional committees, eager to speak in support of the bill. Virtually no one spoke up to challenge its fundamental premise. One who did was Fred Friendly. The veteran of a time at CBS when it had the courage, the will, and the money to rock an occasional boat, Friendly brought an intimate, first-hand knowledge of the passions that are aroused when deeply held beliefs are questioned. He warned the Senate subcommittee that "we must avoid at all costs any situation in which budgets of news and public-affairs programming would be appropriated or even approved by any branch of the Federal government."[10] But his fears of government funding were not shared by others. Most were silent on the charged issue, content to take the money and run and to leave the fate of public television in the hands of legislators whose record of restraint in such matters was notoriously bad. Nor was their faith in the White House any better served. President Johnson had promised to deliver within a year of the passage of the Public Broadcasting Act of 1967 a plan for long-range, insulated funding. The promise was never kept.

In March 1969, President Johnson, fulfilling the mandate of the 1967 Act, named fifteen persons (fourteen men and one woman) to the Corporation board. Eight were Democrats, six were Republicans, and one was a declared independent. All were presumed to be, in the words of the Congressional Act, "eminent in such fields as education, cultural and civic affairs, or the arts."[11] To whatever extent any failed to meet this mandated standard, the group as a whole was nevertheless the most distinguished to fill the Corporation board seats for at least another twenty-five years. Finding someone to occupy the chair proved difficult; some thirty candidates passed it up, feeling the challenge was "not worthy of their time or effort."[12] Finally, Johnson prevailed on an old friend from his Congressional days, the former budget director, Frank Pace, Jr. A Harvard Law graduate, Pace had a long record of public service, including the post of Secretary of the Army, before leaving in the early 1950s to become chairman and CEO of General Dynamics. When the government's largest defense contractor ran into serious financial difficulties, Pace returned to public service as chairman of the International Executives Service Corps, a Peace Corps of sorts for retired executives. Knowing he would need capable hands to help with the start-up of the Corporation, Pace brought with him as his executive assistant a young lawyer who had been his associate general counsel at General Dynamics and his vice president at the IESC. Ward B. Chamberlin, Jr., proved to be what the new organization needed—a positive, self-confident, and decisive administrator, gifted with the ability to be tough when circumstances demanded and to be amiably relaxed when they did not. His personal qualities, and the circumstances of the times, positioned Chamberlin to be a major player in shaping the public-broadcasting system that emerged from the Public Broadcasting Act of 1967.

A year would pass before the board named a president to the Corporation. In the interim, Pace and Chamberlin, aided by a tiny staff, guided the inchoate Corporation through its birth pains. Little was done, however, to clarify the precise role the Corporation would assume within the growing complexity of the public medium's structure. CPB's purpose, clouded in legislative rhetoric, was to facilitate "the development of educational broadcasting." Congress directed that this goal be accomplished "in ways that will most effectively assure the maximum freedom . . . from interference with or control of the program content."[13] How these broad directives would be acted upon clearly would depend in large measure on the interpretation given them by the CPB's new chief executive.

In February 1969, a full fifteen months after the Act became law, John W. Macy, Jr., was named the Corporation's first president.[14] His selection as the chief executive officer of the nongovernmental body was a disappointment to those of us who expected someone of the stature of an Ed Murrow or Frank Stanton, an experienced television person and someone who knew and respected the medium. Macy had absolutely no experience with broadcasting; he was a bureaucrat. Except for three years as executive vice president of his alma mater, Wesleyan University, the affable, silver-haired New Englander had spent his entire adult life in government service, most recently as the chair of the U.S. Civil Service Commission, where he sought out appointees to political posts as President Johnson's "talent scout." Despite a crew-cut hairstyle that gave him the appearance of a straight-arrow military man, Macy had a warm, open, and cordial personality that might have suited the pastor of a well-to-do suburban congregation. From a family lineage that extended back to New England's early Protestant settlers he had inherited a strong work ethic and a man-

ifest sense of rectitude. If he suffered a major handicap in his new
position, it was the ominous timing of his appointment. Although
named to the post in the waning weeks of the Johnson Administration, Macy took office in the first weeks of the Nixon Administration, and would, of course, be identified with the previous
administration by the man now in the White House whose paranoia of purported "enemies" was legendary.

My own misgivings about his appointment were centered on his
lifetime of government service. Not only was there danger that he
might mistakenly view the Corporation as another agency of government, but he certainly would also look upon "public" in a
different light than I would. (Years later, Macy wrote that his long
years of government service and lack of broadcasting experience
were a "liability" that "complicated the acceptance of the corporation's leadership by the elements in the system.")[15]

All too quickly my fears were confirmed. At a meeting of the
NET stations seven months after Macy took office—and to the
amazement of those of us who thought the Corporation was supposed to stay out of programming—he handed us a list of "priority topics" for future programs. Worse, they were suspiciously
like the announced priorities of the Nixon White House. (My own
shocked reaction was to proclaim, prematurely, as it turned out,
"the death of public television as we have known it.") A short
time later, he pressed a program grant upon NET that it had not
asked for, virtually compelling public television to cover a White
House Conference on Hunger. Hunger was one of Macy's announced priorities. Another of his quasi-governmental priorities
led him to create an ill-conceived and short-lived Public Broadcasting Environment Center, whose contribution to saving the environment was the commissioning of a Louis Harris poll to un-
cover America's "most serious problem." To no one's surprise, it
turned out to be the environment.

The most visible and embarrassing episode that confirmed the
Corporation's drift into the government's embrace came in 1968
with the highly publicized Nancy Dickerson caper. It had long
since become a television tradition for the president to subject
himself to an informal roundtable conversation with the trio of

White House correspondents from the three commercial networks. This year, however, the White House insisted that the public network be admitted to the table. That much was good. But then speculation arose that Macy had allowed himself to be used by the Nixon White House by accepting what was purpotedly its choice of the news correspondent to represent public television. No one questioned Nancy Dickerson's competence as a journalist; she had been NBC's White House correspondent and had resigned the post shortly before the incident. Still, her selection rankled the other network correspondents—Howard K. Smith, Eric Sevareid, and John Chancellor—who felt that she had been too close to the presidency to be objective in her questioning. Before and during the broadcast, Dickerson remained discreetly above the fray. And although she performed her correspondent's role in a professionally competent manner, neither adding to nor diminishing the luster of public broadcasting, there were lingering concerns. Whether or not Macy had bowed to White House pressure in choosing Dickerson, it was manifestly inappropriate for the president of the Corporation to be dabbling directly in programming, especially programming that called for sensitive journalistic judgment. Few doubted the purity of his motives, but Macy was clearly out of his depth. He had simply acted as his experience had trained him to act, but unfortunately, in this particular situation, his experience was largely irrelevant. It was not a game to be played by the rules of the government bureaucrat.

Shortly after John Macy stepped into the presidency of CPB, Jack White announced his intention of resigning his post at NET. He had long felt, he said, "that any person in such a job should not hold that job for more than a decade."[16] White, however, could read the handwriting on the wall: the Ford Foundation was ending its longtime advocacy of NET as the keystone in the public television arch. The Corporation for Public Broadcasting, aspiring to the leadership role NET once had, would have no hesitation taking what it needed to achieve that end. Then, too, there were personally disquieting changes at the Ford Foundation. With the departure of his longtime friend Henry Heald, the support White had leaned on during his years at NET was gone. The Ford presidency was filled now by a man whose style and character were quite different, and who, unlike Heald, rarely dealt directly with White. McGeorge Bundy preferred to channel the Foundation's business with NET through his television expert, Fred Friendly, who, as a veteran broadcaster, had his own idea of where the public medium ought to be headed.

For a time Bundy and Friendly were supportive of White's presidency. Their support began to crumble, however, soon after Friendly created the Public Broadcast Laboratory in what White and his staff saw as a clearcut repudiation of NET's longtime leadership role in national programming. The competition between the two Ford-funded organizations cast White in a discordant role and weakened Ford's confidence in his leadership. The earlier zest in the relations between East 43rd Street and 10 Columbus Circle was gone.

White was a man well-suited to his time. The nascent educational-television movement, groping for recognition and significance, needed the kind of aggressive, confident leadership and clear sense of purpose that he was able to provide. Bob Hudson, his senior vice president and the only man to serve all three NET presidents, said of White's contribution that it was "a dynamism, a sense of motion, *a sense of mission*" (emphasis added).[17] The Ford Foundation, in much the same vein, praised White for giving the medium "a dynamic practicality and an electrifying *sense of high mission*" (emphasis added).[18] And Scott Fletcher, who had virtually invented NET, was certain that the network would not have had the support it did from the Foundation without White's leadership.[19]

During the decade of White's leadership, he had a hand in virtually every major gain the system had made—and the gains were substantial. Educational television had emerged from obscurity into a visible presence on the nation's television screens while the number of stations grew from 27 to 161. However marginal White's personal contribution may have been to the overall growth, his role was key in the single most important addition to that growth, the creation of a public station in metropolitan New

York, the nation's single largest market. And with barely enough money in the system to keep its motor running, White pushed educational television into the age of videotape and color. In programming he had promised significance, and by any measure— awards or critical and audience response—he delivered it. NET laid down a pattern for programming that even today defines public television. In the process, White, together with his principal programmers Kobin, Davis, and Dixon, set a standard of courage and independence that was rare for its time. Give me "barnburners," he urged his producers. And more often than not, they did.

White was deeply troubled by the shift in power away from NET and into the hands of an untried team with political ties to government. The shift was particularly ominous with Nixon's arrival in the White House. After less than a year in office, Nixon had made perfectly clear his lack of fondness for the media. Publicly funded television, clearly the most vulnerable area of broadcasting, was already in the White House's sights as a prime target. White shot off a warning to the affiliates at the time of his departure: "Unless a formula is found that provides insulation from political pressures . . . unless we can guarantee the independence and integrity of this powerful tool, we should forget the whole thing. . . . This country does not need a domestic USIA [the organization that operates the government's official Voice of America], and that is just what you'll have if major funding is derived from Congress solely on the basis of annual appropriation and review."[20]

One didn't need to be clairvoyant to see that the sands on which the public structure rested were shifting. Change was in the air. I was about to discover the consequences firsthand.

8

TWO FOR THE SHOW

*The present structure of public television was an accident of history and
a response to the crises of the moment, rather than part of any long-range
grand design.*

Hartford W. Gunn, Jr.[1]

The first harbinger of change
came with an invitation to breakfast from Fred Friendly. It was the
spring of 1969 and I was in New York attending the annual NET
Affiliates Meeting. There was always a portentous quality about an
invitation from Ford—partly because the majesty of its money
gave any invitation the gravity of a royal summons, and partly because, as the system's power broker, winners and losers were often
decided behind its closed doors. The ominousness of this particular invitation was underscored by the venue and the means of
getting there: I was whisked to our meeting in a sleek black Ford
Foundation limo (a Lincoln, of course) that collected me at the
Waldorf and deposited me at the Friendly residence in suburban
Riverdale. There, over scrambled eggs and toast, I learned the
purpose of the trip.

"It's time," Friendly said, "that you thought about moving up
in the world." Quickly reading between the lines, I realized that
I was being sounded out as a possible candidate for the NET presidency. But why, I wondered, was the approach being made by the
Foundation? The NET Board had a search committee to do precisely what Friendly seemed to be doing. Visibly annoyed at my
innocence of the ways of New York power politics, Friendly ex-

plained that he wanted to spare the NET board the embarrassment of a turndown should a more formal tender of the position be made.

I shared with Friendly my strong misgivings about coming to New York. It was more than a reluctance to leave my native city, difficult as that would be. I was also unwilling to exchange the management of a station for that of a network, explaining that stations, which act more or less as retailers, deal directly with the customer. Networks, on the other hand, act as wholesalers; their only path to the customer leads through the hundreds of cautious gatekeepers at the stations. The networking process, I pointed out, is more akin to politics than broadcasting. Friendly's response was a disingenuous proposal to put the local stations in New York and Washington under the NET aegis, giving the network, in effect, two stations of its own. The Foundation, of course, had no legal power to transfer the licenses. Moreover, the transfer would have been vigorously opposed, not only by the two stations affected, but also by virtually every other station in the system. They wanted NET's wings clipped, not extended.

I cannot believe my response to Friendly satisfied him, so the formal offer of the presidency, which came a week later from Norman Cousins, chair of NET's search committee, was totally unexpected. Cousins, having been told of my reservations, urged me to talk with the newly appointed president of the Corporation for Public Broadcasting before making my decision. The Corporation's addition to the public-television structure had altered the equation; the post I was considering was not the post White had vacated.

My first meeting with John Macy dispelled all doubts about taking the NET offer. I was ready to move to New York and for reasons that would have surprised Macy. Our talk revealed the readiness of the system's new leadership to yield some measure of public television's independence to the exigencies of federal funding. I found Macy's response to one of my questions particularly disquieting. After reminding him that Congress had admonished the CPB "to assure the maximum freedom" of the system "from interference with or control of program content," a caution particularly relevant to the dangers of interference by government itself, I asked if he thought that our public television should be kept as free of government interference as the BBC.[2] (This was before the BBC's freedom suffered erosion at the hands of Prime Minister Thatcher's Conservative government.) He thought a moment, said "no," then added "and I don't know why."

It was not the answer that I had hoped for from the man now responsible for defining our goals and articulating to the world what we were about. It gave me an uneasy feeling, a fear that the medium I had known for the past fifteen years was about to be smothered beneath a blanket of government bureaucracy. Without knowing it, Macy had resolved my lingering doubts. I didn't relish becoming the CPB's "right hand for programming"— Macy's description of the "new" NET presidency—for someone who felt so little need to guarantee the independence of the medium. But the NET post offered the best, if not the only, base from which to wage the battle for the freedom the public medium had enjoyed before it jumped into bed with government. It should have been clear even then that John Macy and I perceived "public" in quite different terms. Macy saw it as the "public" of public utility—accountable to government, free to act only within the rules set by federal regulation, which carried an implied message of "don't rock the boat, keep the lid on, play it cool." My perception was the "public" of the free public library, an encouragement if not a provocation to provide the broadest possible range of ideas and intellectual engagement.

New York in August can try the forbearance of the sainted, much less the tender tolerances of a reluctant immigrant from the West. Everything about my move into NET's New York headquarters in the late summer of 1969 was disorienting: Manhattan's dark, rainy afternoons; new colleagues whose cautious guardedness contrasted with the openness of my California colleagues; even the decor of my offices at 10 Columbus Circle—faux-colonial with brass pitchers and hunting prints. For a time, I felt as though I, like Alice, had fallen down a rabbit hole. I was later to discover that in one sense I had. The institutional ground on which I stood was about to give way.

Not surprisingly, my personal misgivings about the structural changes were shared by others, especially by the men and women whose creative energies produced public television's major programming. The NET staff was virtually paralyzed with a paranoia that had been ignited by the infamous purloined PBL memo suggesting that the network should be phased out. Now their fears centered on rumblings of imminent change, the most threatening of which was the rumored plan to remove program distribution from NET and to place it with a subsidiary of the Corporation's own making. Realizing that the Corporation's funding came directly from Congress, veteran producers feared that the plan would encourage the government to take a stronger hand in programming.

NET's creative staff was determined to make its voice heard through collective action. Together with the vestiges of PBL's production staff and a handful of producers from the larger stations, they formed the Association of Public Television Producers. Through their spokesperson, Alvin H. Perlmutter, the producers warned that "events of the next several months . . . may determine once and forever whether this fledgling medium goes on to become a truly 'public' network without government control or the influence of special interests, or whether . . . it degenerates into 'a domestic USIA.' "[3] Testifying before Senator Pastore's communications subcommittee, Perlmutter and fellow producer Jack Willis voiced the producers' collective concern that annual Congressional funding would result in political control of programming; that "people appointed to control public television under the Corporation for Public Broadcasting do not now fully represent the pluralistic society they are charged to serve." The producers also feared direct censorship by "the vetoes of the new panel," a reference to the yet-to-be-organized system of program distribution. Producers of public television's national programs were also concerned that the selection and distribution of their programs would fall into the hands of the same "unrepresentative" types that the president had appointed to the CPB Board, who would have the power to kill what they didn't like.[4]

The producer's fears were not unfounded. NET's fifteen-year lock on the distribution of national programming was under threat. The terms of the 1967 Act directed the CPB to "assist in the establishment and development of one or more systems of interconnection." Interconnection—linking the stations together by leased telephone company lines—was the next big step in bringing the public system into the modern world. It would replace NET's outmoded postal system with the mode of distribution used by the three commercial networks until that technology was superseded by the newer satellite technology. Pace and Chamberlin did not wait for the appointment of the Corporation's chief executive before starting work on implementing Congress's call for interconnecting the public system. Neither man, of course, had any previous experience with broadcasting. Nor did they discuss their plans with NET or seek its counsel.

The first step toward interconnection involved the Corporation in negotiations with AT&T. Congress, using its regulatory power over telephone rates, had authorized AT&T to provide public television with interconnection service at either a "free or reduced rate."[5] The giant communications monopoly rejected free access outright and balked on reduced rates. Eight months of tough negotiations produced an agreement in January 1970 for a "trial tariff" covering limited interconnection service. The arrangement—two hours a night for five nights a week—barely served public television's minimal needs. Worse, the service was second-class, including occasions when the network lines were co-opted to feed a basketball game to a sports network, leaving more than one public station high and dry without its announced network programming.

Erratic as the interconnection was, a larger issue loomed from NET's perspective: the questions of who would manage it and who would decide which programs would be fed to the stations, in what order, and at what hours. NET alone had experience with managing a network, and for a brief time the Corporation gave it the responsibility. But the new leadership was caught up in a decentralization frenzy whose aim was to give power to the local stations. That meant removing NET from its dominant role in national program production and distribution. Even in the early stages, when NET was given responsibility for managing the interconnection, Chamberlin made certain that NET did not have responsibility for deciding which programs were to be carried on the network lines. That fell to an unwieldy and temporary committee, the Interim Interconnection Management Group. Its members—representatives from NET, the Corporation, and program executives from a select group of stations—were scattered about the country. Instant decisions on schedule changes were handled by conference calls, producing an awkwardness that verged on the bureaucratically absurd, particularly when an immediate consensus was needed to preempt regular programming for an unanticipated special event and most of the committee's members could not be reached.

The importance of the IIMG's brief reign as the network's programmer lies only in what it reveals of the pattern of thinking that was dominant in the late 1960s. The system's new leadership in Washington was following what they believed was the Congressional intent of the 1967 Act, accepting as scripture the need to separate program distribution from program production. Scott Fletcher had promoted the same idea fifteen years earlier when he created the Center and barred it from producing its own programs. But when the system failed to deliver quality programming, it was scrapped and NET was permitted to both produce and distribute programs. Programming quality soared and so did tempers. Many stations resented NET's monopoly over the production and distribution system and bristled at being asked to air programs produced by NET that, in their judgment, were unsuited for their audiences, whether "left-wing documentaries," contemporary dramas on delicate themes, black-oriented programs that included street language, or whatever. Their disaffection with NET gave force to a movement for a "user-managed" network under which no single organization would have a monopoly on national program production. Decisions about which programs would be chosen for interconnection would be made democratically: the "users," not the producers, would decide. By a curious bit of reasoning, the stations defined themselves, rather than their viewers, as the "users" of the programs.

Formulation of the "user-managed" concept, however, left unresolved the question of which of the several possibilities—a station, NET, or the Corporation—would operate the leased lines on behalf of its "users." The Corporation was eliminated; by law it is prohibited from owning or operating a network or an interconnection. NET was also deemed to be out of the running; if the doctrine of separation of production and distribution was to prevail, NET's role as the major producer of national programming would presumably bar it from doing both. The only acceptable alternative appeared to be the creation of a new organization. It fell to Chamberlin, first as Pace's assistant and later as Macy's executive vice president, to coordinate the planning. The stations, still uncertain of the Corporation's intentions and fearing another centralized system like NET, were quick to let Chamberlin know that they wanted a hand in the design. He agreed to accept the counsel of a small, representative group of six station managers, three of whom were from the NET Affiliates Council, and three of whom came from the elected board of the Educational Television Stations group. (The group was quickly dubbed "the Six Pack.")[6] The group found agreement elusive; their meetings stretched over more than a year before they produced an acceptable plan for an entity to operate the public-television distribution system.

I was unaware of how far Chamberlin's planning had progressed by August of 1969, the month of my arrival in New York. I took on my new duties believing I might still make a case for NET's managing the interconnection; within the system, it was the only organization with sufficient experience, the human resources, and the administrative structure for the task. But the decision had already been made in Washington; it was not to be NET. Nevertheless, John Macy, with characteristic fairness, postponed the final decision for sixty days to allow me time to present NET's case. I was acutely aware that I was faced with the "sometimes irrational and emotional response of paranoia by the stations towards NET,"[7] but I was confident that the situation could be turned around with changes in NET's structure. My case for NET rested on two basic arguments. The first was the importance of keeping production and distribution together. To separate them would have been "to divide the indivisible and [to] inevitably limit the potential effectiveness of public television as a national instrument of communications,"[8] reducing it to television's counterpart of the United Parcel Service. The second was the danger that I saw in a reliance on a consensus of "user" stations for the selection of what went on the interconnection. "Committees don't take risks," I argued; the result would be bland programming.

My proposal was dead on arrival. The sixty-day "moratorium" on decision-making had simply been a safety valve for the pent-up frustrations at NET. Several days later, the Corporation announced that it was ready to carry out its own plan. There was no debate, no discussion. The announcement came as an unwelcome surprise to the NET board; despite its fifteen-year leadership of the movement, the board had not been consulted at any stage in the Corporation's planning. Puzzled and angry, the board's chairman, Everett Case, promptly arranged a meeting with Ford president McGeorge Bundy. Case was certain the Foundation would understand the need to keep distribution in NET's hands; they had put it there in the first place. But he found no friends at Ford. Bundy and Friendly defended the Corporation plan and even argued for the wisdom of putting production in one place and distribution in another. Friendly, showing a greater gift for rhetoric than for geography, likened it to U.S. 1, "a national electronic turnpike with inputs and outputs throughout the land."[9] Far from going "throughout the land," U.S. 1 meanders down along the Eastern seaboard in an unending clutter of fast-food franchises and service stations. At one point, Case referred to NET as a "network." Bundy reacted testily. "NET is not a network, never has been a network, and if I have anything to say about it, will never be a network." Case was visibly shaken by the outburst: had Bundy forgotten it was the Foundation itself that first suggested that NET call itself "America's Fourth Network"? Case later wrote Bundy: "I was aware, of course, of some of your reservations about NET but I was wholly unprepared to find so wide a disparity in our basic concepts of its role and function."[10]

In November 1969, the Corporation's plan went into effect: a new entity, the Public Broadcasting Service, was incorporated and given responsibility for the interconnection. The term "service" rather than "system" or "network" was chosen with deliberate care. In a memorandum to all stations, CPB explained that "network" connoted "program production activities and station time-commitments . . . [and] 'system' was deemed to encompass PTV stations and organizations beyond the realm of interconnection services." To avoid suggesting more than was intended, the neutral-sounding "service" was chosen. PBS's purpose, it explained, was "to provide the stations with high quality programming from diverse sources." PBS itself was not to be one of those diverse sources: its function was "to allocate time on the network to producing agencies and suppliers," not to produce, acquire, or commission shows. As if to underscore PBS's limited responsibilities, the plan proposed "to keep programming decisions of the new organization to a minimum." Station response was overwhelmingly positive; Chamberlin had prepared the way by circulating a memo to the stations a month earlier. One provision, however, raised the hackles of the stations. NET, because of its "present basic responsibility for five hours of programming per week and for national news and public affairs," was to be given preferential treatment for access to the interconnection. Friendly had insisted on the stipulation, either to protect the public-affairs function that NET had traditionally performed or to assuage the injured feelings of the deposed network, or both. The stations, forced to accept the despised condition, did so under protest.[11]

If a symbol was needed to mark the changed direction of the system after the 1967 Act, it could be found in the makeup of the governing board of the *Public* Broadcasting Service.[12] Only two of its nine-member board represented the public. The remaining seven were "insiders," including five elected station managers and the presidents of NET and CPB, the latter two as ex-officio members without a vote. (Later, the ex-officio members were dropped and the number of station executives was increased.) The board's composition was a clear reflection of the stations' determination to control the input by exerting control over the sources of national programming as well as by exercising their statutory power to decide which of the programs their stations would air. At least as serious, however, was the way the composition of the board reflected the public broadcasters' deep-seated distrust of public control, a distrust that was evident earlier in their attitude toward the group of distinguished citizens that composed NET's board. They were entirely public and entirely beyond the control of the stations.

Hartford N. Gunn, Jr., president and general manager of WGBH / Boston, headed a search committee of PBS board members to find an executive to head the interconnection service. Their task proved more difficult than they had anticipated, partly because the position was posted with the uninviting title of "PBS general manager." Experienced broadcasters saw little challenge and less satisfaction in a post that had no power to create, commission, or even acquire programming, only the power to schedule the delivery of programs supplied from sources over which they had no control. As the search for a manager dragged on without result, I teasingly suggested to Gunn that he draft himself for the post; no executive in the system was better qualified. He brushed aside the notion: "You and I both know that I would make more of the job than it deserves." Shortly thereafter, Gunn was named to the post not as the general manager, but with the more prestigious title of PBS president, and with a seat on the board. Those of us who knew Gunn as the man who had effectively brought Boston's public station into a position of national leadership also knew he was not one to be satisfied with simply presiding over a delivery service. If he did in fact make more of the job than the planners of PBS had in mind, the question of whether it was more than the position warranted has been effectively rendered moot by his years of leadership.

One of Gunn's first acts in the new job was his decision to locate PBS in Washington, cheek-by-jowl with the government and with the Corporation for Public Broadcasting.[13] The decision may have reflected his hope of fostering a more harmonious working relationship between the two rivals—for rivals they were destined to be. Or it may have been a gesture to ease the concern of the system's new partners in the government over the negative image of New York "liberalism" that had become attached to NET's years of dominance. Whatever its value, some of us feared that positioning the public system's sensitive programming arm so near the seat of government would create more problems than it would solve.

PBS was a masterpiece of corporate compromise, and was in effect a political solution to a programming problem. As a membership organization—every station was eligible to join—PBS accommodated the fears and aspirations of the system's many and disparate elements, empowering them to bar forever the return of centralized programming authority. To further protect against the rise of centralized authority, the members of PBS denied their own organization the power to make, buy, or contract for programming. PBS, as it was conceived in 1969, embodied the spirit of dispersed authority, its proudest boast not that it was the best but that it was the "most democratic."

The same spirit was embodied in the Corporation for Public Broadcasting; John Macy and his troops were equally passionate in their dedication to the principle of decentralized production. They found their text in the gospel according to Carnegie. The Commission had recommended "that the Corporation support at least two national production centers." If one was intended to be NET, the other, it was assumed, would be similar but located elsewhere, possibly on the West Coast to balance or offset NET's so-called Eastern bias. But Macy, with a fundamentalist's approach to the Carnegie study, read the message differently. If two production centers was a good idea, three was a better idea, and four better still. With this logic, he named the seven largest stations— New York, Boston, Washington, Pittsburgh, Chicago, Los Angeles, and San Francisco—as national production centers. Each of the seven was invited to submit proposals for programs to PBS. PBS would then decide which of the proposed programs it wanted produced for its future schedule. The list of desired programs was submitted to CPB, which would grant production funds directly to the producing stations for the designated programs. Production centers were free, of course, to circumvent the process by looking elsewhere for funding. The virtue of the process lay in CPB's peripheral role in programming: application for its program funds was decided not by a bureaucracy removed from the daily demands of broadcasting, but by PBS acting on behalf of its member stations.

The plan, however, fell apart. Macy failed to take into account the tide of egalitarianism that his own policies had let loose within the system. His announcement designating the seven largest stations as the exclusive producers of national programming was met with howls of protest from some among the two hundred or so stations excluded from the favored circle. The Corporation was charged with favoring "the fat cats" and with ignoring the everyone-is-equal ethos on which PBS was founded. Macy, true to his egalitarian principles, announced a new plan: the privilege of producing national programming was opened to every station with the will and wherewithal to supply an acceptable program or program series, whatever its size. Except for changes in the method of funding, Macy's open-door policy remains in effect today, and though national production tends still to be concentrated in the system's half-dozen largest stations, the reasons are practical and not related to policy.

Even before Macy announced his new open-door policy, he was challenged by the seven "fat cat" stations that he had named as production centers. Instead of purring with contentment, the seven, in a joint letter to the presidents of CPB and PBS, vented their anger at what they saw as the growing concentration of decision-making power in Washington.[14] Our concern (for I was one of the seven) was that the CPB, by doling out its money "piecemeal" only for programs approved "in general" beforehand, was exercising undue influence on what the production centers produced. And PBS, by asserting an illegitimate right to rule "in detail" on the content of the programs it distributed, was contributing to a trend that, if continued, would reduce the production centers to "no more than field facilities for the central office." The result would be less diversity and more uniformity, not what the Carnegie Commission had in mind. Our self-righteous outburst echoed the general malaise bred by change and by a policy of broadened participation. More players in the game meant ad-

ditional challenges to one's turf and the need to take added measures to protect it. We were a bit like the five blind men and the
elephant. Without strong central leadership to define the whole,
each of us defined the whole by the part we touched.

The Aspen Document—so-called for the place where our individual concerns became collective—set off a firestorm of reaction. Gunn rebuked us for leaking our internal squabbles to the
press, thus bringing discredit to the stations. John Macy, showing
his usual restraint, reminded us "once more that a rapidly evolving system has more than the usual number of uncertainties,
ambiguities, and imperfections."[15] Fred Friendly, however, was
considerably less restrained and branded the Aspen Document
as another example of public television's predilection for "self-
inflicted wounds." Fearing the consequences for the medium's
image in Washington, Friendly hopped a plane and met with the
chairpersons of each of our stations, warning them of the divisive
consequences of their managers' fractious behavior. But the "Aspen seven" were not alone in their fractiousness. It was pandemic
throughout the swiftly evolving system, not because it was in the
nature of public broadcasters to be difficult, but because the nature of the system made it difficult not to be. An institutional
environment in which everyone is equal is, under the best of circumstances, difficult to manage (a lesson we have long since
learned from two hundred years of democratic self-rule). The fact
that democracy has worked, although at times creakily and halt-
ingly, can be credited to strong and effective leadership: someone
in charge setting our national agenda, articulating our goals, and
bringing us together to resolve our common problems. Public
television, however, has in its determination to remain "democratic" denied itself strong leadership, favoring instead scores of
fractional "leaders," some in Washington, some scattered around
the country, each with a different agenda and a personal set of
goals. The situation was ripe for conflict and provided fertile soil
for the exercise of self interest. To no one's surprise, it also produced a bumper crop of fractious behavior.

If any among us thought that the Ford Foundation's eighteen-year
hegemony over public television ended when the two Washington-

based entities, PBS and CPB, entered the picture, we soon learned otherwise. The Foundation simply achieved its aims through more subtle methods. The shaping of PBS provides an instructive example. Conventional wisdom at the time credited its creation to the committee of station executives, the so-called Six Pack. The result was hailed as a model of democratic planning. However, in his brief history of the process, Robert Pepper concluded after examining the records of the period that "the Ford Foundation was intimately involved in creating PBS and, in fact, was with the CPB, one of PBS's two major architects."[16] He detailed the close collaboration between Chamberlin and David Davis, head of Ford's Office of Public Communications, crediting the two with being "more than any others . . . responsible for creating PBS as it finally emerged." Chamberlin, a master of corporate stratagems, knew that Ford's part in the planning of PBS, if advertised, would be the kiss of death not only among the stations whose suspicions of Ford's intentions were always verging toward paranoia, but also in the Nixon White House. With Ford's tacit agreement, its role was kept quiet. Chamberlin's success in convincing the stations that they were the authors of PBS, wrote Pepper, was a sleight of hand worthy of a master.

Such was the nature of the new order that changes in the system were generally made in the name of CPB, the seat of public broadcasting's purported leadership, whether or not the Corporation authored the idea. Macy, with little or no experience in the artful politics of public broadcasting, welcomed Friendly's counsel and drew heavily on his broadcasting experience. Whenever an idea's paternity was in doubt, fingers generally pointed to the brass-and-glass headquarters of the Ford Foundation—if not to its resident expert Fred Friendly, then to one of his colleagues in the Office of Communications, David Davis or Stuart Sucherman. The Foundation tried to play its part in key decisions with quiet discretion. Occasionally, however, decisions announced in the name of the Corporation had Ford's fingerprints all over them. Such was the case with the birth of an organization called NPACT.

During the latter half of the 1960s, the responsibility for covering national affairs out of Washington fell to NET. Over the half-dozen years, James Karayn and a small team of producers working out of NET's Washington bureau managed to build an impressive record of public-affairs programming. Acting as the public system's news presence in the nation's capital, they covered special events, arranged postmortem analysis of presidential speeches, produced occasional documentaries, and more. But in the spring of 1971 that changed, abruptly, and in a manner that told something of the Foundation's continued involvement in reshaping the structure of public television.

The first indication came with a summons to meet with John Macy, not in his office, but in the offices of the Ford Foundation, where Fred Friendly was present with his two associates, Davis and Sucherman. I had no forewarning of the meeting's purpose, but the grim looks on the faces in the room sent a clear signal that I would be leaving the meeting with less than I came with. I was not mistaken. NET's national programming functions, already trimmed by the creation of the multiple production centers, were to be trimmed still further. "It has been decided," Macy explained, with studied ambiguity as to the source of the decision, that responsibility for public-affairs programming would be better placed outside NET and its Washington bureau. The plan was to create a new Washington-based organization. The new organization would, in fact, be NET's Washington bureau, divorced from NET and independently administered. While the loss to NET of a successful programming operation was unwelcome news, I found the decision to place public television's sensitive public-affairs operations cheek-by-jowl with the sources of its government funding much more worrisome. All three commercial networks, I argued, found it prudent to headquarter their news divisions in New York and not in Washington. And without federal funding they had less to fear from the government's interfering hand than we did. Any thought that Friendly, once chief of CBS News, would be responsive to that argument vanished with his insistence the plan go forward. A week later, Macy notified me of the formation of the new organization in a letter that made clear the Foundation's complicity in the planning. The CPB's position, it said, "has the concurrence of our colleagues at the Ford Foundation."[17] Macy also made an attempt to cushion the blow to NET's badly battered self-esteem by assuring me that the change "will give you and your staff the opportunity to pursue new areas in which to exert your proven programming leadership." The flattering words did nothing to relieve my sinking feeling.

The outcome of the Ford-CPB machinations was an ill-starred and short-lived organization known familiarly as NPACT (rhymes with "impact"). Its unwieldy proper name—the National Public Affairs Center for Television—led to speculation that the acronym must have preceded the name. (Television critic Ron Powers thought that NPACT sounded like one of those global conspiracies that *The Man from U.N.C.L.E.* ferreted out and destroyed in the weekly TV series popular at the time.) To meet its need for a corporate base, NPACT was loosely attached to WETA / Washington by one of those equivocal phrases ("institutional ties") that create more problems than they solve. The two organizations shared not only production studios but a board chairman, former Time executive Sidney L. James. Because NPACT took over NET's Washington offices as well as its staff, the volatile Jim Karayn became NPACT's vice president and general manager without rising from his swivel chair.

Friendly, acutely aware of the pressing need for a strong public-television presence in the nation's capital and conscious of the fragility of WETA's public support, clearly hoped its marriage with NPACT would give the Washington station additional strength and stability. Unfortunately, good intentions and interlocking directorates did not prevent the inevitable struggle for turf. For its part, WETA had counted on the "institutional ties" with NPACT to bolster its faltering finances by bringing more national production to the station. Instead, those "institutional ties" cost WETA the only two national productions it had: *Washington Week in Review* and a weekly interview program with correspondent Elizabeth Drew, *Thirty Minutes With . . .* NPACT took over production of both.

The intentionally fuzzy ties between WETA and NPACT mirrored the vague and self-destructive relationship between *PBL* and NET two years earlier. Ironically, the seeds of both arrangements were planted in the corridors of the Ford Foundation. Fred Bohen, in his infamous purloined memo to Friendly, first proposed a Washington-based public-affairs center as a means of using the PBL experience, and perhaps even of rescuing the PBL organization. The rescue mission never materialized, but the idea remained alive, and by late 1970, both Friendly and Macy had reason to believe that the time had arrived to translate it into action. For more than a decade, NET had been the system's dominant symbol, and though it was now in decline, its alleged "Eastern liberalism" undermined public television's support from the more conservative of its patrons. Because the most obvious evidence of Eastern liberalism was presumed to be in NET's public-affairs programs, it was an easy step to conclude that, by removing responsibility for public affairs from the politically contaminated precincts of Manhattan, the system could exorcise its troublesome image. By placing this key element of its operations in Washington the system could, at the same time, strengthen its presence in the city where with congressional funding it now mattered most.

Whether 1971 was the right time, and Washington the right place, was soon open to serious question. Events were waiting to happen that would challenge the wisdom of placing NPACT in the shadow of the White House. A president who was generally hostile to the notion of a freewheeling, publicly supported television system was preparing to roll his big guns into place. And in the crosshairs of his sights would be public television's most visible and vulnerable target, NPACT.

9

THE STREET OF THE
EIGHT-FOOT CANARY

Sunny day . . .
Sweeping the clouds away,
On my way . . .
To where the air is sweet.
Can you tell me how to get . . .
How to get to Sesame Street.[1]

Neither the premiere of the Public Broadcast Laboratory nor the passage of the Public Broadcasting Act—two of the three events that marked 1967 as a very special year for the public medium—had the public impact of the third, the birth of *Sesame Street.* And while it may be fudging history slightly to pin the creation of public television's most celebrated series to our landmark year—the seeds for the series were planted in the closing months of the preceding year, and the show itself first aired in 1969, two years later—1967 was the year when the germ of an idea, unformed and untested, was developed into the reality of a people-and-puppets television show unlike anything that been seen on television.

Not surprisingly, the genesis of the show was as unusual as the show itself. Joan Ganz Cooney, a young producer of public-affairs shows for WNDT (New York's public channel was later renamed WNET), had just won her first Emmy for a documentary entitled *Poverty, Anti-Poverty and the Poor.* To celebrate her good fortune, she gathered a convivial group of friends for dinner in her Gramercy Park apartment, among them two colleagues who were destined to help lift the young producer onto the highest rungs of her profession, with honors to match. One was her boss, Lewis Freedman, programming chief at WNDT, an urbane, articulate culture maven who had grown up on Manhattan's Upper East Side in the shadow of the Museum Mile and who had been an early apprentice to the new medium of television. The other, Lloyd N. Morrisett, a lean and laconic Oklahoman with a no-nonsense manner—one writer described him as "fanatically austere"[2]—was a former psychology professor at Berkeley who had turned to philanthropy. At the time of the party, he was vice president of one of America's major philanthropic foundations, the Carnegie Corporation.

At some point in the evening, talk turned to television and to speculation about television's influence, both good and bad, on the malleable minds of the very young. Freedman, a veteran of such pioneering television triumphs as *Play of the Week* and CBS's *Camera Three*, held firm to his faith in the medium's potential. Television, he argued, was "the great educator of the future."[3] Morrisett knew very little about television, but he and the Carnegie Corporation were interested in finding and funding new approaches to early childhood education. His interest was caught by the thought that television might be useful in teaching the very young, particularly with its potential for reaching the large numbers of underprivileged children who lacked access to preschool facilities. Before the friends parted, Morrisett challenged his television friends to come up with an idea for using the medium to reach and teach the very young—the generation preparing to enter school for the first time. He set a date when the three of them could meet again, this time with some of Morrisett's Carnegie Foundation colleagues. The seed had been planted.

For fifteen years, public television had struggled to meet the demand for more and better children's programs. Local stations may have differed on the medium's mission but they agreed on one point: public television had an obligation to provide children with constructive, entertaining television fare. Commercial networks had all but abandoned the field by the mid-sixties, and the daily children's shows of an earlier era had vanished, including *Kukla, Fran and Ollie, Howdy Doody, Ding Dong School,* and *Mr. Wizard.* CBS's *Captain Kangaroo* alone remained to carry young viewers through the week toward Saturday's ghetto of animated cartoons. Children's programming had joined sports and entertainment as just another of television's profit centers.

The need, easily assessed, was tough to satisfy. Many stations produced local children's shows. Most, like KQED, managed to fill the late afternoon hours with a remarkable number of once-a-week children's shows, all live and produced on tissue-thin resources. None, however, were capable of mounting a five-day-a-week series to satisfy a young audience's television-viewing tastes. Local stations turned to NET for help but NET's hands were tied. The Ford Foundation was interested only in liberal adult education, not in children's programming. As a result, no provision was made for young audiences in any of Ford's grants to NET. The stations, in desperation, pressured NET in the early sixties to dedicate a small part of its very meager non-Ford funds toward the production of a daily children's series, *What's New*. The show was not so much a creation as a collection of disparate elements, most of them produced by local stations or acquired from foreign sources and loosely held together under its ambiguous title. The series survived until *Sesame Street* came along, but showing telltale signs of underfunding, it never caught on with its target eight- to twelve-year-old audience.

After the loss of its independent funding from affiliation fees, NET challenged the stations to reach into their own pockets to create a small discretionary fund for children's programming. The fund enabled NET to negotiate with the University of Wisconsin's WHA for the acquisition of Bob Homme's *The Friendly Giant*, an engaging series for very young viewers. But it was Pittsburgh's WQED that created the first children's show on public television to catch the fancy of children and parents alike. At a time in the mid-fifties when NET was largely dependent on local stations for its programming, WQED supplied the network with kinescopes of a locally produced series, *Children's Corner*. The show, hosted by Josie Carey, had been created and was produced by a young divinity student, Fred Rogers. Rogers also served as the voice of the puppets. In 1968, Rogers stepped from behind the scenery, doffed his jacket, donned a sweater, and, with elements from *Children's Corner*—and funding from the station's discretionary fund and the

Sears Roebuck Foundation—created *Mister Rogers' Neighborhood*.

Until 1969, NET and its affiliates struggled against formidable odds to provide more and better children's programs. Their efforts were praiseworthy, but given the pressing need and the opportunity to serve an important and largely unserved audience, it was not public television's finest hour. That honor would await the outcome of the events set in motion by the conversation at the Gramercy Park dinner party.

Freedman, Cooney, and Morrisett met several times during the spring and early summer of 1967 with Morrisett's Carnegie colleagues to toss ideas about and explore the dimensions of a vision not yet fully formed. By June, Carnegie was ready to fund a study: was it feasible to design a television series for preschoolers that could teach without sacrificing its entertainment values? New York's WNDT would be the grantee, but Morrisett wanted Cooney to conduct the study. He wrote Freedman to say that he thought she "would probably do an excellent job of carrying out the study."[4] It proved to be an understatement.

Joan Cooney, the daughter of a Jewish father and an Irish Catholic mother, was "driven by a sense of obligation from early adolescence . . . I felt I had to go off and justify my life."[5] At the age of twenty-four, with a degree in education and after a brief stint as a reporter, Cooney left her native Arizona for New York. There she worked as a publicist, first with RCA / NBC, and later with television's distinguished drama series, *The U.S. Steel Hour*. In 1962, with no production experience, she applied for and was given a position with WNDT, the newly opened public-television station in New York City. By the time she was ready to embark on the new adventure in children's programming, she had had five years' experience producing social documentaries for WNDT, some of which took her into the inner city, where she gained a heightened sensitivity to the problems of the poor, particularly the young poor. She was familiar with the problem; she set off to find some answers.

Making her way across the United States and Canada, Cooney met with psychologists, educators, pediatricians, children's-television specialists, and anyone who could provide ideas, evidence, and arguments. By October, the results were organized into a fifty-two-page report, "The Potential Uses of Television," that recommended testing and evaluating "television's potential for fostering the intellectual and cultural development of young children." The report provided the foundation on which the series was built. The recommendations contemplated an hour-long magazine show, broadcast twice (morning and afternoon) every weekday, and employing a variety of techniques including puppets, animation, music, stories, and child-involving activities. The content of the show was to be strongly cognitive in design, overtly instructional in nature, and rapid and repetitious in method. The experts with whom Cooney talked strongly recommended that the show for children be accompanied by a weekly show for the parents of the preschoolers. The idea was later dropped as unfeasible.

Cooney was influenced in her judgments on content by the experts with whom she talked, but her own instincts as a television producer spoke loudly and clearly about method. She wisely incorporated three interrelated objectives in her recommendations: first, to use television's most advanced production techniques; second, to produce the series through a national rather than a local entity; and third, to not undertake the series until it had sufficient funding to do the job properly. "If we are going to attract children to quality children's programming," she wrote, "they must have many of the production values [meaning pace, humor, professional performing talent, film inserts, animation, and so forth] to which today's young children have become accustomed." Nor did she ignore the potential of the commercial as a teaching form, disdained as they were by educators. "If we accept the premise that commercials are effective teachers, it is important to be aware of their characteristics, the most obvious being frequent repetition, clever visual presentation, brevity and clarity."[6] *Sesame Street*'s "commercials" for numbers and letters would become one of its most effective and distinguishing elements.

Although Morrisett and Cooney thought that the desired quality could only be achieved by forming their own production company, Cooney, who was still nominally a WNDT employee, felt obligated to discuss production with the station first. (The Carnegie Commission study, under way at this time, was about to recommend the decentralization of national program production.) The discussions, however, never became serious; the president of WNDT, a former vice president of CBS, failed to see the program's potential. There was another, related factor. If the proposed series was to stand up to the commercial competition, it would need an adequate production budget, not the anemic production budgets of public television's other series. Awesome as it seemed in the context of public television's lean budgets, her original estimate of $2 million had to be doubled, then tripled, and ultimately quadrupled by successive cost analyses. The final cost of $8 million for the first year's experiment, an amount only dreamed of by most public-television producers, was compared in Cooney's report to the estimated sum of $2.75 billion it would cost to send every four- and five-year-old to school at public expense.[7] It was not necessary to pretend that a season of *Sesame Street* was the equivalent of two years of formal schooling—it obviously was not—in order to make the case for an $8 million daily television show that would touch the lives of millions of children that age.

Even before Cooney's feasibility study was fashioned into a formal proposal, Morrisett began the search for the needed funds. The next eighteen months provide a cautionary tale for those who would undertake to fund an expensive production for the public medium, even one with the potential benefits of *Sesame Street.* Morrisett's persevering efforts to find partners, anyone willing to share the heavy funding burden—other foundations, the big three networks, or production companies—reaped heaps of praise and encouragement and some tentative expressions of interest, but little else. And then in the summer of 1967 the tide began to turn. The man largely responsible for the change was Harold ("Doc") Howe, the U.S. Commissioner of Education and one of Morrisett's longtime friends. The department, better known for bureaucratic torpor than bold leadership, was an improbable force for turning tides and affecting the course of events. But then "Doc" Howe was an improbable person to be occupying its highest office. At the conclusion of a meeting at which Morrisett and Cooney briefed his staff on the project, Howe's enthusiastic response was "Let's do it." He instructed his staff to explore any available means of mobilizing the government's educational resources behind the project.

In a fortunate choice, Howe put his assistant, Louis Hausman, in charge of the project. Hausman, a veteran of the commercial networks, understood the special demands of the medium, and though he was unconvinced that an educational television show, however skillfully done, could compete successfully with commercial entertainment, he thought that the idea deserved a test. (But true to the totemic traditions of the commercial medium from which he came, Hausman wanted the test put into the hands of "professionals," by which he meant the Hollywood production studios.) His television experience also brought a note of reality to the budget; he was the first to warn of the inadequacy of the original $2 million estimate, and he convinced Howe that the government's share had to be larger, large enough to give the project a fair shot at reaching its higher goal.

When 1967 drew to a close with no firm commitments on funding—Doc Howe's plan to pull together a pool of grants from several government agencies, including his own, was working, but still far from realization—Morrisett knew that only resolute action could move the project off dead center. He turned to his own foundation, persuading the Carnegie president, Alan Pifer, to make the first move. The plot was simple: If we at Carnegie show our good faith in the project by the rustle of our money, perhaps others will follow. It was risky, but it worked. In January 1968, the Carnegie board voted the first $1 million, followed three weeks later by a Ford grant of $250,000, with Ford's promise of more to follow if the project got off the ground. The final $1 million came from the Corporation for Public Broadcasting in what was one of its earliest major grants. By March of 1968, Carnegie and its new partners were ready to go public with their plans.

In the elegant environment of a Waldorf Astoria ballroom, worlds away from the underprivileged audience the series hoped to reach, Alan Pifer of Carnegie, McGeorge Bundy of Ford, and Doc Howe of the U.S. Office of Education (USOE) announced the formation of the Children's Television Workshop, together with its plan to produce a twenty-six-week television series that would take preschool youngsters on "the educational journey so vital to their lives and the well-being of the nation."[8] To no one's surprise, Joan Ganz Cooney, who had departed WNDT a year earlier to devote herself full-time to the study, was named the project's executive director. (Jack Gould of the *New York Times* was moved to comment prophetically that Cooney's appointment "automatically thrusts her into the forefront of women executives in broadcasting.")[9] The need for a corporate base for the new organization was satisfied by "affiliating" it with NET for its first year. Morrisett and Cooney, both wary of tying the Workshop too closely to what they saw as the highly bureaucratic public-television structure, signed an agreement with NET's Jack White that provided for needed administrative and legal services but assured total autonomy where it counted: in programming, personnel, and finance. Even those ties were severed at the end of *Sesame Street*'s first season, when CTW became its own corporate entity.[10] The wisdom of the move became more evident in later years when CTW's freedom to chart its own course, to move in or out of the nonprofit world, and to develop and market the products of its creative genius provided an economic base that allowed it to become a largely self-supporting institution.

Joan Cooney likes to say luck played an important part in the Workshop's ultimate success. But luck was a marginal factor in her choice of David D. Connell for the critical role of the project's executive producer. Earlier, Cooney received an offer of help from Michael Dann, at the time the programming chief of CBS-TV. "You'll need an executive producer," he told her. "Let me help you find one." Dann recommended Connell, the former executive producer of CBS-TV's children's series *Captain Kangaroo*, a highly imaginative producer and, most important, one who had mastered the special skills of producing a daily show. Cooney was to discover to her dismay that Connell had left *Captain Kangaroo* a year earlier with no thought of returning to children's programming, and certainly not to a series hobbled with an advisory board of educators. They talked not once but four times. Connell liked Cooney's openness, her thoughtfulness, and her intelligence. But he had strong reservations about her plans for a children's television series. With its platoon of educational advisers, the show was bound to be "academicked to death." She assured him that she would not allow the entertainment values to be sacrificed. "If we err, we will err on the side of entertainment."[11] This statement proved to be the turning point in their protracted negotiations.

Connell agreed to put aside the challenge of his own business to take on the much larger challenge of producing yet another program for children. This, however, was to be a program with a difference, not wholly entertainment or education, but a skillful blending of both—light enough to win young hearts away from seductive cartoons, yet freighted with enough educational content to satisfy the aspirations of its planners. It would be the toughest challenge of his professional career, and one that would need the help of the best production talent he could find. Not surprisingly, he turned first to the ranks of his former colleagues at *Captain Kangaroo.* Two, Sam Gibbon and Jon Stone, already in conversation with Joan Cooney, were quickly signed on as producers. Together with Connell, they formed the nucleus of what was to become one of the most imaginative and remarkable production teams in children's television.

Even before they were on the payroll, the three were tossed into a dizzying round of summer seminars with panels of educational advisers. For three case-hardened television producers, armed with a producer's traditional faith in their innate ability to sense what would work and what wouldn't work on the tube, meeting with "advisers" was tantamount to consorting with the enemy. But they were wrong and they were the first to admit it; the seminars proved to be one of those elements that, as everyone later agreed, "made" the television series. It was tough going at first. But as soon as each side learned to breach the barriers of the other's arcane lingo, they found that they could talk. And talk they did, hammering out a set of specific curriculum goals on which the producers' creative skills would be tested. No little part of the seminars' success was due to the organizing skills of an able young professor from Harvard, Gerald S. Lesser, who joined the Work-shop in its early stages as a consultant in developmental psychology. When Morrisett and Cooney decided to organize a Board of Advisers—the content specialists chosen to keep the television producers on track—the sandy-haired ex–New Yorker was their first choice to head it. His meticulous behind-the-scenes planning, together with his jargon-free speech, shirt-sleeves informality, and self-mocking humor, helped to minimize the predictable academic grandstanding—Lesser called it "Talmudic haggling"—expected of a group well practiced in one-upmanship. He created an unthreatening environment that not only permitted the interchange of ideas but actually encouraged it.

Out of the summer meetings came the seminal work on which the shows were built, a heavy volume detailing a wide variety of educational goals, some cognitive (teaching the child to recognize and manipulate numbers, letters and geometric shapes, and so forth) and some affective (serving the child's emotional needs by helping the child to adjust to his or her environment through teaching such values as cooperation). Setting specific educational goals gave a distinctive character and unique educational value to what could have been just another highly engaging, entertaining children's show. The goals, necessarily stated in broad strokes, gave a clear sense of overall direction but offered little help to producers attempting to focus a piece of animation or the lyrics of a song on a very specific lesson. Honing the broad goals to manageable size was left to a small corps of bright young researchers; they told the producers what to shoot for then let them know whether their pieces hit or missed the mark.

Unconventional as it was to television, the importance of research to the CTW design was never questioned, least of all by Morrisett, whose social-science background convinced him that it was integral to the production process from beginning to end. "Formative" research tested the product as it was being made, providing a means of quality control that allowed for mid-course corrections, and these corrections were followed by another test to see if the material and method successfully held the attention of the target audience. Finally, when the shows were aired, "summative" research measured whether they had, in fact, achieved what they were supposed to achieve. In addition to the tests, the Workshop's research director, Dr. Edward L. Palmer, used a fiendish device called a "distractor" to measure attention levels. Palmer had invented the distractor while studying television's effects on young children for the Oregon State System of Higher Education. The "distractor" was a portable movie screen, set at an angle off to the side of the television receiver, which showed a series of slides with random images appealing to children. Using this device, Palmer could determine from moment to moment the young viewers' attention to the program on the tube. By changing the slide every seven and one-half seconds and observing whether the eye movements of the youngsters were on the screen or the tube, Palmer developed an attention profile of each episode that resembled nothing so much as the chart of stock-market prices in a highly unstable economy—instant evidence of what held the children's attention and what didn't. Attention levels, important as they were, were combined with other modes of testing to determine levels of comprehension of the educational message.

The program's producers, at first predictably skeptical of Palmer's results, were won over when he cannily demonstrated his device, not with their own untried *Sesame Street* material, but with established children's shows that they knew and, in the case of *Captain Kangaroo*, had themselves produced. The results were shattering. What every producer knows in his heart—that kids will respond positively to being addressed directly by the show's star— was solidly debunked by tests on *Captain Kangaroo*. The distractor showed that whenever the Captain addressed his young audience directly, their collective gaze, attention, and interest shifted to the distractor slides. Even though Palmer had shrewdly chosen an episode in which Captain Kangaroo attempted the almost impossible task of holding his young viewers' attention while explaining how government works, the exercise taught some needed lessons. Even before turning out their first foot of film for *Sesame Street*, the producers were privy to invaluable insights into their prospective audience and its television behavioral patterns. Insights, however, were not always an ironclad guarantee against misjudgments—as

nell chose a young singer from the Mitch Miller show, Bob Mc-Grath, who had achieved a measure of stardom among Tokyo's teenagers while on tour in Japan. Of the four principal cast members, only the role of Mr. Hooper would be filled by a professional actor. Until his death in 1982, Will Lee, a veteran of forty years on the stage, played the role of the kindhearted candy-store proprietor.

Sesame Street's quartet of flesh-and-blood residents were soon upstaged by a motley cast of nonhumans—odd creatures artfully stitched from pieces of felt, manipulated by a company of deft hands, and bearing the implausible names of Kermit the Frog, Cookie Monster, Bert and Ernie, and Oscar the Grouch. Although puppets had been part of Joan Cooney's original plan for the show—she had suggested among other possibilities Burr Tillstrom and his Kuklapolitans—her producers saw the inanimate creatures as a limiting factor. Writing for characters with already established personalities is rough when you're trying to tackle a wide range of teaching situations. Luckily, good fortune intervened. One of the producers—which one is in friendly dispute—suggested Jim Henson and his Muppets. All of the producers knew and admired his work, even though Henson's fame was still very limited. Word was beginning to spread, however, after his several appearances on the *Ed Sullivan Show* and his participation in product commercials. Jon Stone, who worked with Henson on the ABC special *Hey, Cinderella,* had a high regard for the spade-bearded puppeteer's genius—especially his knack for creating custom-made personalities to fit the most bizarre requirements—and like his colleagues thought Henson was the only puppeteer for the project. Persuaded to place his wild-ranging imagination in the service of early childhood education, Henson joined *Sesame Street* with a bundle of ideas and a single hand puppet, Kermit the Frog. The Street's other familiar puppets-in-residence were created to meet the specific needs of the Workshop.

The Muppets gave *Sesame Street* an identity as winning as it was singular, although its singularity may have been muted somewhat after Henson introduced his own highly successful series, *The Muppet Show,* on commercial television. But only Kermit the Frog, of all the *Sesame Street* Muppets, turned up on the screen in both series. (Henson shared rights to his *Sesame Street* creations with the Children's Television Workshop. But because Kermit was created before Henson joined *Sesame Street*, he owned the frog outright.) The Muppets, of course, were a huge hit with children as well as their parents. In the process of becoming an inseparable element in the success of the series, they helped to turn Henson's career and company into a highly bankable asset. His sudden death in 1990 of what could have been an easily treatable illness shocked and saddened the millions of Muppet fans whose lives had been brightened by his wit and creativity.

Earlier, *Sesame Street* lost another of its creative stars with the untimely death of Joe Raposo, the composer of much of the show's engaging and instructive music. Raposo combined a classic composer's credentials—he had studied with Walter Piston at Harvard and the great Nadia Boulanger in Paris—with the accomplished piano fingers of a Broadway tunesmith. He turned out tunes for *Sesame Street* for five seasons, resigned for a time, then returned in 1983. But even in his absence the show was marked with his musical brand. His output was prodigious, eight pounds of music a week by his own estimate, and incredibly wide-ranging—danger music, mischief music, reverie music, slithering snake music. His youthful audience, however, identified him with his singable songs—several of which hit the popularity charts, climbed to the top, and remained there for an impressively long run. "Sing," one of his biggest hits, was recorded by a varied list of artists, including Barbra Streisand, the Carpenters, Peter Nero, and the Boston Pops. And "Being Green," Kermit's appeal for an understanding and appreciation of skin-color differences, was lofted into the ranks of the big hits with a Sinatra recording.

Eighteen months of painstaking preparation set the stage for the highly satisfying climax on the morning of November 10, 1969, when the world got its first glimpse of the eagerly awaited show. The young viewers showed wide-eyed fascination with the show's fast-paced sequences. Critical acceptance was also enthusiastic but more restrained. The *Village Voice* found reviewing the show "about as easy as reviewing the Second Coming,"[14] while the

New York Times, also despairing of the task, wrote, "It is with a feeling of helplessness that an adult tries to assess the potential impact of the Children's Television Workshop."[15] Both overcame their feelings of helplessness to endorse warmly the promising newcomer to the otherwise bleak wasteland of children's daytime television. Some critics were astute enough to recognize that *Sesame Street* was more than a breakthrough in children's television— it signaled the early rumblings of a revolution that would force a change in the way primary schools approached the education of children entering school for the first time.

The *Sesame Street* show that the children of America saw that November morning was much better than the five pilot programs that had been tested during the preceding summer on the inner-city children of Philadelphia. Research made the difference. Palmer's distractor revealed deep valleys of inattention in the pilot shows. The problem was not in the animation, film, or Muppet sequences, but in the street scenes with the four live actors. The producers recommended enlivening the street scenes by introducing Muppets. But the educational advisers were opposed; they felt that intermixing people and puppets—fantasy with reality— would risk confusing the two in the child's mind. Connell thought the risk was worth taking. "Explain to me," he asked of anyone willing to listen, "what reality means to a four-year-old in front of a television set."[16]

The producers prevailed. Henson, challenged to create several of his inimitable furry creatures to interact with the street's human population, came up with two of *Sesame Street*'s most popular and enduring characters. Oscar the Grouch, sole tenant of the street's trash can, would help the child to understand that it was perfectly all right on occasion to feel grouchy and out-of-sorts, to feel "different." And Big Bird, the lovable eight-foot canary, clumsily inept but determinedly optimistic in the face of disappointment, would reassure the child about their inability to do everything right the first time. It's "the only adult-sized object in the world," one reviewer pointed out, "that kids can feel superior to."[17] Both Oscar and Big Bird, given life with the voice and hands of Carroll Spinney, showed that educational goals need not be sacrificed for the sake of gaining the child's attention when both can be achieved in one master stroke.

Cooney felt the ideal hour for airing *Sesame Street* would be 9 A.M., the prime time for reaching preschoolers in their homes. The older children, who usually control the set, were off at school, the adult early morning lineup of shows was over, and *Sesame Street* wouldn't be in the awkward position of competing with commercial television's only program for preschoolers, *Captain Kangaroo*, which came on at 8 A.M. Some stations, however, were contractually committed to provide local school districts with an instructional television service at that hour and were reluctant to yield their time. (It did not help that nursery schools were outside the jurisdiction of the contracting school district.) With her customary resolve, Cooney and her assistant, Robert Davidson, hit the road, visited twenty-five key cities, met with station executives, and most important, talked to local school superintendents. With one significant exception they achieved the desired results: only Cooney's former colleagues at WNDT resisted the appeal. Although the station agreed to run the show twice a day, it would not or could not yield the nine o'clock hour. New York, with the country's highest concentration of day-care centers, was critical to the success of the experiment. Determined to have her 9 A.M. slot, Cooney struck a deal with a local commercial channel (WPIX) for the hour she wanted. For its first season, *Sesame Street* aired on both New York channels; by the time the second season rolled around, WNDT had come to terms with its school service and aired the series in the morning time slot.

Despite the large number of UHF stations in their lineup of 170 NET affiliates, *Sesame Street* attracted in its first week a formidable audience of 1.46 million television homes, a number destined to grow many times over in succeeding months. The result was no happy accident. Morrisett and Cooney, alert to the necessity of recruiting an audience, earmarked a sizeable 10 percent of the $8 million grant for promotion and utilization activities. Part went to a public-relations professional, Robert Hatch, then a vice president with Carl Byoir. (Hatch later became a Workshop vice president.) Hatch orchestrated a national promotional effort that culminated in a Xerox-sponsored salute to the show on NBC-TV two nights before its premiere on public television. Many who caught the NBC special tuned to their local public channel the following week for the first time.

Hatch's audience-delivering efforts exceeded expectations. But his use of conventional media meant that he was not reaching the underclass—*Sesame Street*'s target audience—which rarely depends on conventional media for its information. Working with local public stations, Hatch organized an inner-city effort in twenty selected cities. New York, however, with the nation's largest population of low-income families, demanded a special campaign. The task was given to Evelyn Davis, a quietly effective African American with more than fifteen years of experience working with New York's low-income people. Although television receivers were almost universal in poor homes by this time, most of their occupants were unaware of the educational channel. For those who had no access to a television set, Davis organized a treasure hunt for used receivers. Some of these receivers were designated for schools, some for day-care centers, and, where small viewing groups could gather in homes around the single set, day-care providers were supplied with materials and trained in the use of the programs. Davis was determined to destroy the cultural myth among low-income families that parents of poor families, poorly educated themselves, are ill-equipped to teach their own kids. "I told them: 'You are your child's first teacher . . . we're going to offer you a more organized way of doing it.' "[18] Her work paid dividends. In 1970, an independent survey of Bedford-Stuyvesant, the city's largest concentration of poor blacks, revealed that among children two to five years old, 90 percent were regular *Sesame Street* viewers. This result was replicated in other inner-city areas around the country.

Davis's early inner-city efforts in New York grew into a much larger effort, national in scope, that moved well beyond the original task of reaching new audiences for the Workshop's several series for children. Under Davis's leadership as corporate vice president for the Workshop's Community Educational Services, they developed a bold and innovative outreach program without parallel in broadcasting, helping the children of migrant farm workers and prison inmates, training low-income adults and adolescents to become child-care providers, organizing science clubs amidst the desolation of the South Bronx, forming community clubs ("Power Stations") to motivate underachievers to learn basic language arts among the rural poor in the Mississippi Delta, and more.

From the beginning the Workshop had two goals for *Sesame Street*: to teach basic facts and skills to preschoolers, and, at the same time, to attract a large and devoted audience. The latter was achieved and sustained for more than a quarter of a century, during which the series attracted the largest and most diverse audience of any PBS daily series. More critical, however, is the question of whether its educational goals were realized. That answer came from an independent research firm, the Educational Testing Service, in a four-hundred-page volume of test results and analysis at the close of the first season.[19] The ETS report validated the original hypothesis of the project: *Sesame Street* could teach—and did. The children who gained the most were those who viewed the most. And what they learned best were those skills given the most time and attention on the shows. Moreover, the presence of an adult with the child proved significant: the greatest gains were made by children who watched at home in the company of a mother or another interested and caring adult with whom to talk over the show. Race, sex, and socioeconomic status made no difference in the gains made by the children—all did equally well. Frequent viewers, often children from disadvantaged homes, surpassed the gains of children who watched only infrequently. It would have been gratifying had *Sesame Street* succeeded in narrowing the gap separating disadvantaged from advantaged children entering school for the first time. Unfortunately, using a nationally televised series to narrow the gap would require the advantaged to forgo the televised series until the disadvantaged caught up, an obvious impossibility. On the other hand, there was concern that *Sesame Street* not inadvertently widen the gap. ETS assured them it did not. Both groups made significant gains, and though the gap remained, it was a gap between two groups of which both had benefited from exposure to the show.

The first season's test results were corroborated at the end of the second season.[20] Still, critics of the series found plenty to carp at, particularly among the community of social scientists—predictably, perhaps, since nothing can tame an academic who has caught the scent of an esteemed colleague's "flawed" study.[21] Some critics called for "better" goals and then cited mutually exclusive ideas for improving them—one even suggested that *Sesame Street* teach "wisdom"—while others charged CTW with hubris for having goals at all; who were they to decide what a child should be taught? Overlooked was the obvious: a single television series, however well done, is not the sum of a child's early education. For the show's producers, confident that America's public television had finally produced a show worthy of the BBC, the bitterest pill was the BBC's refusal to air the series in Britain. Rather than praising the series, Monica Sims, BBC's director of children's programs, condemned it for dictating to children what they should learn and for placing too much emphasis on "right answers." *Sesame Street,* she declared, is "indoctrination."[22] British children were not denied the series, however. After limited exposure on the independent channels, the series began daily airings in 1986 on Britain's Channel 4.

Over the years, *Sesame Street* has worn out or won over most of its critics, most of whom, it is fair to say, are over the age of six and whose judgments, therefore, must be weighed accordingly. One reason for the show's continued popularity and its durability has been Cooney's insistence on keeping *Sesame Street* fresh by minimizing repeats and producing new material. Over a third of each season's content has never before been seen. And unlike those children's shows whose viewers outgrow the show and move on, *Sesame Street*'s viewers start younger and stay later, reason enough to keep the show fresh. But there is an even more compelling reason. *Sesame Street* was born as an experiment, and the Workshop is determined to keep it that way by continuing to try new methods, new materials, and new goals. Some changes, more cosmetic than substantive, included replacements in the cast. Yet when Will

Lee (Mr. Hooper) died in 1982, he was not replaced nor was his absence explained to the young viewers by any one of the many obvious dodges. Instead, his death became the subject of a special show, aired on Thanksgiving Day when many parents would be watching with their children, that treated the sensitive subject honestly but also gently affirmed the continuity of life by linking Mr. Hooper's death with the birth of a new baby.

The substantive changes have been less apparent but are much closer to the show's purpose, affecting what and how it teaches. Curriculum goals have been continually expanded, and more emphasis has been placed on the child's behavioral development—social attitudes, self-esteem, and coping with fear and failure—but without sacrificing basic cognitive skills. *Sesame Street* still means preparation for reading, math, and science, all of which, along with the show's recent attention to ecology and the status of women, reflect some of the current concerns of America's adult population. Similarly, the "discovery" of the large and growing Hispanic population in the United States not only introduced a shift to bilingualism but also brought two new neighbors to the street, Maria and Luis, as positive role models for Latino children.

Two years after the debut of *Sesame Street*, the Workshop launched a second series, *The Electric Company*, using fast-paced entertainment and big-name stars to motivate second- and third-graders to read. *The Electric Company* became the most widely used television program in U.S. classrooms and, though production of the series ended with its sixth season, the series continued in reruns on public television and in school classrooms for another eight years. *The Electric Company* was followed in 1980 by *3-2-1 Contact*, which sought in its twelve years to demystify science for the eight- to ten-year-old and to encourage more young people to consider science as a future career. In a somewhat similar vein, *Square One TV*, launched in 1988 and continued for five seasons, managed to make the abstractions of mathematics the subject of a highly entertaining series aimed at dispelling classic fears of the subject. The Workshop turned to the dramatic form with *Ghostwriter*, its most recent effort to motivate the eight- to ten-year-old to take an interest in reading.

CTW's two sorties into adult programming have been somewhat less triumphant. A 1974 series, *Feeling Good*, imbedded health information for young adults in an entertainment format but foundered on its own premise: viewers looking for entertainment looked elsewhere while those looking for health information found the entertainment intrusive. Though enjoying mild success in several limited areas—anti-smoking, for instance—the series achieved greater effect in a spinoff called *Latin American Health Minutes*, which capsulized preventive health-care information into one-minute messages for use on television throughout Spanish- and Portuguese-speaking Latin America. Three years later, the bicentennial of the United States was celebrated, albeit belatedly, with a nine-hour miniseries, *Best of Families*, a fictional account of two New York families at the turn of the century who were separated by class but joined by the romance of the two principals. Critics gave it good marks, but the shows failed to generate the kind of popular enthusiasm the Workshop had stirred up with its children's shows.

For the more than two decades since it began experimenting with the uses of entertainment for learning, the Workshop's production record has been remarkably high—more hits than misses—and has included series and specials produced for the commercial networks and cable. The Workshop's success has brought countless honors to Joan Ganz Cooney, its president for most of those years. Cooney is now semi-retired, having been succeeded by her former executive vice president, David Britt, but she continues to participate actively in the Workshop's affairs as the chair of CTW's executive committee. Less well known publicly has been Lloyd Morrisett's role as the Workshop's chairman since its founding. Not only was he responsible for finding the start-up money, he has continued his efforts to keep the nonprofit agency in a sound financial condition. From the beginning, he urged the staff to greater efforts at self-support, freeing the enterprise from dependence on the vagaries of federal subsidy. Federal dollars have been used primarily for the start-up of new Workshop projects.

The first step toward self-sufficiency was modest: a products di-

vision licensing the CTW name and identity to a handful of educational toys. The toys, the books, and the contracts grew until the
modest marketing had ballooned into a multimillion-dollar business. To the toys and books were added games, soft goods, and all
manner of merchandise with an appeal to children. In addition,
while the product-licensing business was growing, so were the
Workshop's magazine-publishing ventures. Monthly publications,
each tied to a Workshop series, enter two million homes as an
adjunct to the television series. One of CTW's most successful ventures has been the marketing of its several series in foreign countries. An international division placed *Sesame Street* on the television systems of nearly sixty countries on six continents. The show's
culture-free creatures are as familiar to young viewers in Brunei
as they are in Brooklyn. In more than half the countries where
the show is seen, *Sesame Street* has been adapted to fit the cultural
context of the country. The culture-free animation and Muppetry
of the original are used, but the New York street scene is replaced
with settings appropriate to the country; indigenous people and
street creatures of the country's choice make up the cast; and
curricular goals are set by local educators. France, for example,
coproduced a *Rue Sesame*, Germany a *Sesamstrasse*, Latin America
a *Plaza Sesamo*, and in the Middle East, a Hebrew version, *Rechov
Sumsum*, was coproduced in Israel and an Arabic version, *Ifta Ya
Simsim*, was coproduced in Kuwait.

Because it is determinedly nonprofit, CTW's revenues from
product licensing and foreign coproductions are reinvested in its
own programming. Some of the money goes to meet part of the
production costs of *Sesame Street*, discounting by as much as three-
quarters the cost of the series to the public stations, and some is
invested in new ventures. In this respect the Children's Television
Workshop is unique among public broadcasters: by using its own
income to discount the costs of its shows to the system, it has
become one of public television's principal program underwriters.

Success has a million mothers. CTW's success has been variously
credited to wise planning, fortuitous circumstances, and just plain
luck. Certainly time and money were a factor: CTW had both. Until
Sesame Street came along, no public-television series had ever en-

joyed the luxury of eighteen months of preparation and money in the bank to go first cabin. The hardheaded realism of the planners at the Carnegie Corporation had taken pains to see that it had both. The Workshop likes to credit its programming success to what it calls "the CTW Model," the melding of the "art" of television with the "science" of program research. In this model, producers work in close harness with researchers, a relationship whose uniqueness derives from the common knowledge that producers and researchers speak a different language—and rarely to each other. David Connell, *Sesame Street*'s original executive producer, was among the skeptics; years of experience with children's programming led him to fear that the intervention of researchers would intellectualize the material to death. To his and everyone's surprise, the model worked. Connell was the first to admit it, citing the notion of broadcaster-researcher cooperation as "the most bold experiment" in the experimental series.[23] Within the organization, the CTW model is accorded a reverence reserved for Holy Writ and finds application in all the Workshop's program efforts.

Herman Land, commissioned to do a study on the Workshop during its early years, credited the Workshop's remarkable success to its organization, through which runs "a thread of sanity." Very early in its history, the Workshop attracted a group of uncommonly talented and highly motivated people—a pioneer of the Workshop described them as "lightning in a bottle"[24]—but the critical ingredient was creative leadership. Land called it "objective management . . . management dedicated to the achievement of a social goal through rational ends."[25] CTW's leadership came primarily from two people, founding chairman Lloyd Morrisett and founding president Joan Cooney. Morrisett, a visionary with a practical streak, has a gambler's impulse to place his bets—but not until the odds have been carefully weighed. Joan Cooney's seemingly unerring sense of what works and what doesn't, and her unusual sensitivity to talent and how to recognize it, have been strengths in a business in which instinct and luck are required ingredients.

Both have wisely insisted on the Workshop's autonomy. Self-sufficient, independent of the system, and unburdened by its endemic politics, with no permanent commitment to serve the public system exclusively—although PBS has been its principal partner—and with a governing board neither politically appointed nor station-elected, the Workshop has been free to serve the single constituency it is committed to serve: its young viewers.

Unlike most children's television, the Workshop has clearly defined its goals and limited the scope of what it hopes to achieve to readily measurable objectives. Did the young viewer learn the letters of the alphabet? No need for seat-of-the-pants guesswork or recourse to oracular divination. Nor have the Nielsen numbers been the final arbiter; ratings only told how many were touched by the success or failure of the teaching. Few television programs have understood their purpose so surely, and fewer still have known with such certainty whether they have succeeded in achieving it.

Finally, the factor of timing must be taken into account. The Children's Television Workshop, with its aim to serve the educational needs of the disadvantaged, was born at a moment in the nation's life when our collective conscience was darkened with the injustice of inequality. Racial riots in Newark and Detroit months earlier were still fresh in our collective memory, and greater blows were yet to come. On March 31, 1968, President Johnson, weary of a war in Vietnam that had siphoned off resources needed for his war on poverty at home, announced his intention not to run again. The curtain on the Great Society was coming down (not, however, before it had lent its impetus and some of its funds to the creation of the Workshop). Less than a week later, the country was numbed by the assassination of Martin Luther King, Jr., on a motel-room balcony in Memphis, followed eight weeks later by the gunning down of Robert Kennedy in Los Angeles. A stunned nation was ready for palliative measures. The Workshop offered one such measure, small for a large ailment, but with the virtue of speed. By 1967, television had become pervasive, a fixture in low-income homes as well as the homes of the more affluent. Skeptical educators, fearful of the intrusive tube, were beginning to give it grudging acceptance as a potentially effective teaching tool. The tool was there, waiting to be used.

When *Sesame Street* first took to the air in 1969, *Variety* commented that "the only thing wrong with *Sesame Street* is the fact it took twenty years to get here."[26] Now that it has been around for more than a quarter of a century, affecting the lives of two generations of children, questions are being asked about its staying power—whether it can continue to maintain its freshness and originality as tastes and times change. The show's popularity on public television is already being challenged by another preschool series featuring a tubby "dinosaur" named Barney, whose simple, low-key approach is in sharp contrast to *Sesame Street*'s fast-paced, more complex production values. On the positive side is the push that the success of *Sesame Street* has given to public television to fulfill its commitment to serve young audiences. As a result, PBS has increased the number and variety of its children's programs. On the negative side is the failure of *Sesame Street* to affect the quality of children's shows on the commercial networks. Having successfully proved that children's fare could be constructive and, at the same time, meet the commercial networks' standard for popular entertainment, expectations were high that *Sesame Street* would open the door to a new approach by the networks. But ready as they are to clone a competitor's winning format, commercial television rejected the prompt and continued to address young audiences primarily as potential consumers for products of dubious social value. We stand alone among the nations of the industrialized world in treating young viewers with such casual disdain. Our indifference is compounded by an apparent reluctance to create a publicly funded system capable of balancing the questionable commercial values projected by the nation's dominant broadcasters.

10

DREAMS FROM
A MACHINE

Public Television . . . will seek vitality in well-established forms and in
modern experiment. Its attitude will be neither fearful nor vulgar. It will
be, in short, a civilized voice in a civilized community.

Carnegie Commission on
Educational Television[1]

Steeped in the self-pride of find-
ing myself president of National Educational Television, the third
to hold that post in fifteen years (or the fourth if you count the
interim presidency of Scott Fletcher), I dismissed the possibility
that I might very well be the last. NET had been the tentpole of
the public system since its creation. I was blithely unaware that
NET was being used as a bargaining chip in political games being
played out in Washington. Years later it would be revealed
(through files released by the Freedom of Information Act) that
at the time I was preparing to take office, the Corporation for
Public Broadcasting was preparing to jettison NET to win points
with the Nixon White House. The system's new leadership had
concluded that with public television, now dependent on government subsidy, its interests on Capitol Hill would be best served by
purging itself of what Congress and the stations had come to view
as a "rogue" outfit—rogue because it was independent and thus
outside the control of the stations, and because its programs were
perceived by some as "dangerously liberal." That NET was based
in New York seemed to confirm that judgment. The consensus of

negatives was supported by the fears of those stations who felt that NET's programming put their respective subsidies from state legislatures at risk. And so NET was marked for dissolution. For years it had served not only as a program producer and distributor, but as the system's principal (and virtually only) national organization, articulating public television's mission, lobbying its cause, and setting its trends. By the time of my arrival, however, the leadership role had shifted to the Corporation for Public Broadcasting and its presidentially appointed board of directors. Shortly, NET's program distribution function would be placed with another newly created agency in Washington, the Public Broadcasting Service. NET's once exclusive role as the producer of national programming had, of course, already been parceled out to the stations by the decision of the Corporation's president. What was happening to the once dominant NET organization was not so much a wipeout as a frame-by-frame fadeout.

These changes, however, did not take place at once. In the fall of 1969, NET was still the sole supplier of national programming, responsible for providing stations with five hours each week. The 1970–71 season was the first for which I bore any responsibility, and I was determined to make it an outstanding one. Fortunately, I had been given three advantages: Ford's support grant had been boosted from $6 million to $9 million, an affirmation of Friendly's confidence in NET's new leadership; we had gained several highly talented producers from the dissolution of PBL; and we had acquired our biggest audience-building series to date with the twenty-six episodes of the BBC's very popular *The Forsyte Saga.*[2]

Using a dynamic that had served us well at KQED, I convened an informal two-day rap session with the eighty or so talented members of NET's production staff. I had no agenda. My purpose was not directive but exploratory: I was curious to see how those who shaped public television's national programming interpreted its mission. What I learned was both revealing and disturbing. Most of the producers made an arbitrary distinction between the programs public television *ought* to be doing and the programs they watched and enjoyed during their off-duty hours. Clearly, they were not programming for themselves but for a public-

television audience that existed only in their imaginations. I was
reminded of an informal meeting with David Attenborough during the time he was programming chief of the BBC. After a quick
after-hours gin-and-tonic, Attenborough excused himself, explaining that he had to get home so as not to miss that evening's shows
on the BBC. I expressed surprise, noting that rarely have I known
American television executives to spend evenings at home watching the tube; programs are for "them," the great undifferentiated
mass with whom they generally do not identify. For the BBC, Attenborough responded, Them is Us and whatever was on the BBC
that night was probably the most interesting thing happening in
London. I urged my NET colleagues to emulate the BBC in this
respect, not to heed the fictional voice of "ought," but to listen
to their own voices and to create the kinds of programs they, as
viewers, would be eager to watch at home.

After an intense year of planning, marked by a burst of creative
energy, the staff produced a 1970–71 program schedule that reflected a clear and definite rethinking of our mission. The 1970–
71 programs were first shown to the station executives at their
annual spring meeting in New York and received an unprecedented standing ovation. The brightest slot in the schedule was
filled with an innovative and high-risk venture called *The Great
American Dream Machine*. The producers had planned it originally
as an entire evening devoted to a single program, appropriately
entitled *Wednesday Evening*. Budgeting realities converted the concept to a ninety-minute weekly magazine. Al Perlmutter and Jack
Willis were named co-executive producers; the partnership was a
virtual guarantee that *The Great American Dream Machine* would not
be a conventional show. Early in the planning stages, Jack Willis
suffered a serious injury in a surfing accident that left him paralyzed from the neck down and with the almost certain prospect
that he would never be able to walk again. Planning sessions were
convened around his hospital bed during the summer months and
were continued through the period of his long, slow recovery as
a dramatic sidebar to the show itself.[3] (Willis and his wife Mary
have told the story of his successful fight to walk again in both a
book and a made-for-TV movie.)

The original plan called for a rotating weekly host, which would provide an opportunity to test new talent for the star-starved public medium without signing the also-rans to long runs. But producer Sheila Nevins had a better idea: do without a live host and weave the various segments of the magazine together with graphics—pictures, drawings, and animation. It was unconventional, but it proved to be one of the elements that made *The Great American Dream Machine* a television original. Once production of the series began, Perlmutter and Willis put together a first-rate team of experienced professionals—some from NET's production staff, some specially recruited to fit the peculiar requirements of the show—and installed them in unconventional quarters in the ballroom of New York's Empire Hotel.

In the early version of the series, each show opened with a brief comedic bit of mime: two stark white faces, much like the classic masks of Comedy and Tragedy, mouthed the sounds of a full symphony orchestra. Behind the chalk-white faces were two comedians, Ken Shapiro and a little-known actor named Chevy Chase. Following their mime, Eleanor Bunin's distinctive animated graphics introduced the show's title with a nondescript machine, topped by the head of an American eagle, which huffed and puffed and turned the wondrous national dreams of everlasting peace, equality, and affluence into reality. The show itself was best described by one enthusiastic critic as "a whacky, wishful, wonderful, wise conglomeration of extravagant creations that brings dazzling mental stimulation to the screen."[4] Its eclectic contents ran the gamut from the satirically ludicrous to the culturally sublime: stripper Blaze Starr staging a charity benefit; the television premiere of Leonard Bernstein's *Mass*; a portrait of Jane Fonda produced entirely by women; comedian David Steinberg's sardonic look at California's car culture from the front seat of his convertible at a drive-in church service; and a salute to Pablo Casals on his ninety-fifth birthday. Some shows were built around a single theme: the black experience, home, love games, and death.

Some of the major talents in the humor business produced *Dream Machine*'s trenchant satire. When CBS refused to run Andy Rooney's "Essay on War," Perlmutter snapped it up, aired it, and offered Rooney a regular on-camera spot. His "Opinion" pieces brought to the show a sharp eye and a sharper tongue, as Rooney took on the Vietnam War, America's volunteer army (more non-coms than privates), gasoline prices, and sex. He found himself in good company: Alan Arkin, Linda Lavin, Stan Freberg, Jack Gilford, Richard Castellano, and the team of Joseph Bologna and Renee Taylor. One weekly segment featured Studs Terkel, live from Chicago's Tap Room, discussing life's verities over a stein of beer with a widely disparate group of "friends." With its range of talent, *The Great American Dream Machine* did not need a single star who stood above the rest. But the one performer most often identified with the series was a "lovable endomorph" named Marshal Efron. The self-styled "idiot savant," a thirty-three-year-old actor from the satirical review *The Premise,* unraveled in his "abrasive and smartest kid in the class manner"[5] the mysteries of making a lemon cream pie without lemon or cream ("exactly as Morton's makes theirs!"), the arcane scale for grading olives ("the smallest size is called 'giant' "), or the wonders of the Maytag Trashmaster ("turns twenty pounds of trash into twenty pounds of trash!").

The press greeted the January 1971 debut of *The Great American Dream Machine* with generous praise: "comes close to being what television is all about" (*Washington Post*)[6] and "almost too good to be true and too true to be bad" (*San Francisco Chronicle*).[7] The cheering was not unanimous—one critic found the show "precociously amateur and light years away from professional realization"[8]—but the naysayers were greatly outnumbered by those who found *The Great American Dream Machine* a fresh (some even thought too fresh!) image on the bland landscape of American television. NET's stations, for the most part, welcomed the show, embracing its novelty even as they shuddered at its brashness. They were particularly grateful for the fact that it brought new and younger viewers to the tube. In the land of localism, however, there are always exceptions. KTCA/St. Paul's viewers were denied access to the show because, said its manager, its airing would interfere with local programming. And while WTTW/Chicago's manager aired the show, he took pains to expurgate those parts that could offend his audience's sensitivities. Chicago's four television critics were particularly outraged over his removal of a satirical skit about an unmarried couple in bed discussing their fading affair. To mute the criticism, the manager agreed to air the piece and put its suitability to a vote of his viewers. Some 2,700 Chicago area viewers responded, voting 4–1 to support the station's decision.[9] Critic Ron Powers, however, called it a "sad mandate . . . a blow to intelligence."[10]

Popular and distinguished as it was, *The Great American Dream Machine* nevertheless created a financial dilemma. Its $100,000-an-hour budget, very high by the day's standards, consumed so much of NET's Ford grant that little was left for other programming. The clamor to meet those program responsibilities made it more and more difficult to justify NET's large investment in the one show. Efforts were made to stretch scarce dollars by cutting the second season's show to an hour and using more repeat material. But by the end of the second season, cutbacks in public television's federal funding made another season for the program little more than a wistful hope. With the last show of the 1971–72 season, *The Great American Dream Machine* slipped into the public-television archives, its demise met with the generous praise and piety customarily reserved for the recently departed.

Leo Seligsohn of *Newsday* found irony in "the untimely dismantling of 'Dream Machine.' " Its very quality—"irreverent, funny, provocative, controversial"—was cited as the unspoken cause of its demise ("With a record like that it obviously was only a matter of time before it would be cancelled").[11] The usual conspiracy theorists echoed Seligsohn's cynicism by refusing to believe that *Dream Machine* had succumbed to the natural causes of financial anemia, preferring to think that it had fallen victim to political foul play, with the trail of suspicion leading, needless to say, to the door of the Oval Office. Almost any suspicion was credible, of course, in the larcenous days of White House break-ins and wire-taps, but no evidence exists to suggest that the White House had any more contempt for *The Great American Dream Machine* than it did for NET's other programs, and there is certainly no evidence that the Administration made any effort to kill the show. The Administration's contempt was for public television itself.

The Great American Dream Machine, following in the wake of bloody riots, assassinations, and an unpopular war abroad, re-flected a moment in history when the American Dream seemed to be a tarnished ideal. This accounts in part for the way that the show was received. NET's other public-affairs offerings fared less well. Affiliates and some critics challenged the right of NET's social and political documentaries to express a point of view. Some were quick to cast NET into the role of "anti-establishment." It could be argued, however, that its weekly documentaries, especially when they veered from the well-rutted road of broad consensus, contributed to the marketplace of ideas and thus to democracy itself.

A sampling of NET's schedule for 1970, the last year of its in-dependent existence and the final period of relative calm before the Nixon Administration laid the axe to public television's public-affairs programs, offers evidence of the range and robustness of its documentary output.[12] Frederick Wiseman's *Hospital* was an un-blinking portrait of an East Harlem hospital emergency room on a busy Saturday night; it raised dustdevils of controversy and pro-duced the year's silliest negotiation: how many cries of "oh shit" by the despairing victim of a drug overdose would be permitted to remain in the final version of the film. Bob Fresco's *Trial: The City and the County of Denver vs. Lauren R. Watson* provided national television with its first actual courtroom trial. Jack Willis's *Hard Times in the Country* examined the question of why consumers were paying more for farm products while farmers were earning less. Dick McCutchen's *The Three R's . . . and Sex Education* stepped care-fully around the minefield of sex education in our public schools. *The Long Walk* gave the Navajo nation a chance to speak out can-didly about the effects of government policy on the Native Amer-ican. And a jailhouse interview with Black Panther leader Bobby Seale raised questions many wish had never been asked.

Every fourth week NET *Journal* became *Black Journal,* and on those nights one could almost hear the collective sucking in of breath along the network as the more timorous among the affili-ates waited to see what provocations the show's black producers would thrust upon the stations' predominantly white audiences.

The affiliates' sensitivity to audience reaction was such that this first national show for a black minority would have sent apprehensive shudders through the system had it done nothing more than recite the alphabet. It did more, of course, exploring issues rarely aired on national television and giving a voice to black concerns, occasionally touching raw nerves with predictable consequences. "Justice?" in which black spokespersons, including the controversial Angela Davis, charged the criminal justice system with being weighted in favor of whites, reaped a bountiful harvest of protest letters from white viewers. So, too, did a special two-part panel called "A Black Paper on White Racism."

When affiliates felt displeasure with the more provocative of its programs, they complained directly to NET, even though many felt that the network was less than responsive to their complaints. The situation changed dramatically after 1970 with PBS's appearance on the scene. Stations now had their own organization, one over which they had complete control, to intervene on their behalf with the producers of the programs they disliked. But the stations' desire to use PBS as a shield against what they called "problem programs" had limits. The stations were unwilling to go so far as to cede to PBS any real editorial power, for fear of turning the "distribution system" into a "network." No one wanted that. For a time, the stations fought to gain their own editorial control over PBS programming by demanding the right to delete at will those portions of the programs they found unacceptable.[13] It was a right that PBS did not have the power to give; program producers were bound by contracts with the artists guaranteeing that shows would be aired without alteration. Reluctant to give increased power to PBS and having failed to gain it themselves, the stations accepted a compromise agreement. For one moment, they were content to cast PBS in the role of a toothless tiger. PBS, mediating between conflicting forces, would coordinate them rather than command them. The matter was barely resolved before it was overrun by an event—not surprisingly, a NET documentary—that brought stations to the realization that the tiger might need teeth.

In October 1970, PBS had just started its first full season at the helm of the quasi-network when it found itself holding a live grenade in the form of an hour-long documentary produced by Morton Silverstein, one of NET's most experienced documentarians. With stylistic production techniques that heightened the drama but offended PBS, *Banks and the Poor* challenged the advertised claim of New York's largest banks that they "paid special attention to the needs of the disadvantaged." Both banks and savings and loan associations were charged with perpetuating slum conditions by bankrolling "slumlords," practicing discriminatory loan policies against the poor, and otherwise conducting business in ways that denied either banks or thrifts the right to call themselves friends of the poor. The real bombshell came in the documentary's closing minutes. Having been told by the head of the New York State Bar that Congress had done little to correct the bankers' discriminatory practices because so many members of both houses had bank connections, Silverstein did the unforgivable. With the "Battle Hymn of the Republic" booming in the background, he scrolled down the screen—over an image of the nation's august Capitol building—the names of almost one hundred Senators and members of the House with "bank connections." The irony was intentional.

PBS previewed the show and knew instantly that it had a "problem program" on it hands. It was provocation enough that most member stations had bankers on their boards. But the situation was made more complex by the fact that *Life*, already on the newsstands, contained a favorable review of the show. (Mort Silverstein's "considerable achievement," wrote John Leonard, "is to have brilliantly dramatized the invisible.")[14] Stations now faced the choice of explaining to local bankers why they had aired the show or to local audiences why they hadn't. PBS president Hartford Gunn handed the problem to his newly elected board, only two members of which—Gunn and myself—had actually seen the show. Nevertheless, the entire board, over my single objection, voted to reject it as "journalistically unsound."

However, in rejecting *Banks and the Poor*, the board had overlooked a rule that the stations themselves had instituted. Fearing the force of a NET-like centralized authority, they had deliberately limited PBS's editorial control. In short, PBS lacked authority to reject programs. I persuaded a reluctant board that it had no choice but to accept the program for distribution. *Banks and the Poor* was delivered to PBS stations on November 9, 1970, accompanied by a PBS disclaimer: "If any station receives inquiries regarding the content . . . or requests for an opportunity to respond," they should be sent directly to the producer and not to PBS.[15] The *New York Times* commented that "public broadcasting should stop having the jitters. . . . *Banks and the Poor* was a job well worth the doing. . . . For the layman the program was a fine and laudable example of pinpointing crucial economic practices that require wide discussion."[16] Jitters were not calmed in Texas, however, where several stations, fearing the reaction of the financial community, previewed the program for the state's banker's association—then discreetly "postponed" airing it.

Persuading PBS to distribute *Banks and the Poor* was a Pyrrhic victory; pressures were building for changes in the rules. On the one hand, Gunn was not satisfied with a passive role for PBS. On the other, stations wanted protection from having to publicly justify decisions not to air programs that stirred controversy. The solution was obvious and inevitable: invest PBS with the gatekeeper's power to keep "problem programs" out of the distribution pipeline. Gunn, in calling for steps "to assure PTV the highest quality of journalism and professionalism," was clearly determined to codify standards of journalistic practice for public television. And *Banks and the Poor* was to be his weapon. The call for standards acquired an air of urgency after Congress called CBS president Frank Stanton to Washington to account for his network's 1971 documentary *The Selling of the Pentagon.* Urged on by the defense establishment, a committee of the House grilled Stanton on the network's standards of broadcast journalism and very nearly slapped a contempt citation on him when he refused to supply the committee with outtakes from the show. The warning signs were all too evident.

The signals were not lost on Gunn. "We cannot afford to be irresponsible," he told his board. He not only called for uniform standards for all producers, but also wanted them in writing so that he would have a document to wave in front of a Congressional

committee should he be called to account for the programs that
PBS distributed. The first tentative stab at producing standards
proved to be a fiasco. The paper, rewritten by the PBS staff from
a draft by the board's most politically conservative member, demanded nothing less than absolute accuracy. Producers were required to warrant that all "facts are correct, up-to-date, and substantial ... [and that] secondary sources have not been relied
upon."[17] The demand for absolute accuracy was buttressed with a
quote from Walter Lippmann—whose name, unfortunately, was
misspelled (perhaps as a consequence of relying on secondary
sources). The draft was tabled. Gunn turned next to a panel of
professional journalists led by Elie Abel, then dean of Columbia's
Graduate School of Journalism. Instead of commandments to be
rigidly observed, the panel produced a statement of journalistic
guidelines. PBS adopted them without dissent in the spring of
1971.[18]

The new standards were barely in the books when another crisis
erupted, once more involving NET and again calling into question
acceptable standards of journalistic practice. The eye of the storm
was a twelve-minute segment of *The Great American Dream Machine*
produced by Paul Jacobs, an investigative journalist with a long
record of leftist attacks on establishment institutions. Jacobs had
videotaped interviews with three former college students, each of
whom claimed that he had been encouraged, and even aided, by
FBI agents and local police to commit illegal acts on college campuses in order to justify a crackdown on campus radicals. Four
days before the show was to air, Gunn and PBS general manager
Gerald Slater flew to New York to ask NET to voluntarily withdraw
the segment from the show. Their assertion that Jacobs's charges
"lacked documentation" was not entirely off the mark since the
FBI, by refusing to appear on the show, had left us with no "documentation" except the statements of the three self-confessed
undercover agents. Satisfied that NET's legal department had
checked on the validity of the charges, I turned down the PBS
request to withdraw the piece. I did, however, ask our producers
to incorporate into the piece portions of a late-arriving letter from
J. Edgar Hoover in which the FBI chief declared that "on the basis

of information available to this Bureau, each of the charges is totally and absolutely false in each and every particular." His denial was not surprising; the oddly qualifying phrase "on the basis of information available" was. Hoover's letter ended with an ominous threat: "We have referred this matter to the Department of Justice."[19]

We assumed that the revised version, rushed to PBS on the day before the show's scheduled airing, met most if not all of their objections. We were wrong. Hours before it was to air, PBS pulled the segment from the show, explaining that they had no time to "check out" the revised version. The hole in the *Dream Machine* was plugged with filler. The press had a field day. "Once again," cried the (Philadelphia) *Evening Bulletin*, "censorship on public TV brings into focus the disturbing aspect of its financial support by the federal government."[20] The *Memphis Press-Scimitar* saw it as a lesson "in how public TV has lost its courage since National Educational Television lost its power."[21] Though a few thought that PBS knuckled under to FBI pressure, no evidence was ever produced to prove that pressure had been applied.

What the press saw as censorship the PBS stations saw as an exercise of prudent editorial judgment. From the stations' perspective, Gunn had acted wisely and well, sparing them and the system the obvious embarrassment of having to defend an indefensible piece of muckraking journalism. The battle over the FBI segment miraculously dissolved stations' earlier reluctance to arm PBS with the power to make editorial judgments. Less than a week after the incident, the PBS board resolved that in the future final authority to make "go, no go" decisions would reside with the PBS staff when the effort to achieve consensus with the producing stations is not successful. The board action thus permanently altered the manner in which PBS discharges its program-distribution responsibilities.

Written rules, however skillfully crafted, do not change personal sensibilities. Differences over the standards most appropriate to the public medium continued long after the rules were written and are still being argued today. But in the early 1970s, standards of taste had not yet been affected (some would say liberated) by the permissiveness of today's movies, television, and cable. And so a program like the television adaptation of Ronald Ribman's *Ceremony of Innocence*, which was highly praised by critics, could draw fire from the stations for its earthy language. Or a brief moment of semi-nudity in Craig Gilbert's powerful documentary portrait of Irish author-painter Christy Brown could provoke heated protests from stations and outright rejection by the Louisville station. Timorous station executives sometimes had the sanction of local government. A Tennessee board of education, labelling NET's shows "highly inflammatory and of questionable educational value,"[22] ordered its stations to censor them more strictly. In 1970, irate citizens leveled charges of racism against the Alabama state network for refusing to carry *Black Journal* and other series aimed at black audiences. The FCC, however, ruled that the state was free to drop the black shows as "a matter of taste and judgment." (Four years later the FCC reversed itself; its threat to remove the state's licenses for discriminating against blacks brought about the needed reform.)[23]

By the close of 1971, provocative programming was dying, knocked out of the box by a White House that was bent on removing the government-funded medium from the production of public-affairs programs. Increased control over national programming by the more cautious local stations also contributed unintentionally to the smothering of controversy. By that time, NET had been stripped of its documentary unit and was no longer an independent production house but an integral part of the New York public station. Nevertheless, it attempted to keep robust journalism alive with a show called *This Week*. The show's failure to light up the night sky was not the fault of the host, a young newspaper publisher named Bill Moyers, but of the conventional anchor-man-behind-the-desk format and of the producers for not recognizing or making the best use of his unique talents. It was Moyers' first regular series for television, and he was not at all comfortable with the medium. "I am just not cut out to be a television performer," he said to me at the end of the first season, in what must have been the grossest misjudgment of his career. He was persuaded to return the following year in a new and more suitable format, *Bill Moyers' Journal,* which soon gave the lie to his modest disclaimer and set him on the path to becoming one of television's brightest and most effective performers.

With 1972's decline in bold-spirited shows, *VD Blues* qualified as the aberration of the year. From its opening moments—a funky rock band strolling the Sausalito waterfront while belting out the lyrics to "Don't Give a Dose to the One You Love Most"—Don Fouser's candid and forthright look at venereal disease turned the conventions of television upside down. He planned to target teen-agers, who formed the center of a resurgent epidemic of venereal disease, and yet resisted the blandishments of public TV. Fouser's strategy was to bring outrageous humor and irreverence to the discussion of a topic normally treated only in hushed tones. Its message was simple and direct: VD is detectable and curable. NET liked the idea and format and agreed to let Fouser produce it. More surprisingly, the 3M Corporation courageously agreed to underwrite the show's production costs. But that was before they saw the script. (How they saw the script remains a mystery; cor-porate underwriters are ostensibly barred from becoming involved in program content.) While reading the script, the eyes of the 3M executives fell on a mildly funny sketch by Jules Feiffer in which a woman patient, infected by VD and forced by her doctor to reveal her sexual liaisons, names the doctor as her sole contact. A call came immediately from 3M's offices in St. Paul to tell me that the sketch had to be deleted. The PR people were apparently con-cerned lest 3M's name be associated with a program that implied that doctors committed indiscretions with their patients. (And doctors, I later learned, are big 3M customers.) Reluctant to allow an underwriter to have a voice in the producer's plans, I politely declined. They just as politely declined to have 3M's name on the show.

Once the show was completed, *VD Blues* was previewed for sta-tion programmers on a closed-circuit system a week prior to its scheduled airing. We were surprised to learn that 3M executives, accompanied by several doctors and a public-health official, were present for the preview in the St. Paul station. We were even more surprised when they called me to ask if the 3M name could be restored to the show. It could. Fearful, however, that "a great many reasonable viewers would feel that this program openly condones promiscuity," 3M requested that the show open and close with an announcement that NET was "solely responsible for the content and method of presentation."[24]

VD *Blues* aired on October 9, 1972. Only two stations refused it: one in Jackson, Mississippi, and one in Little Rock, Arkansas. Most not only ran it but mounted local follow-up shows with experts responding to viewers' inquiries. The New York station's follow-up show, hosted by Geraldo Rivera, had to be extended from one to three-and-a-half hours to accommodate more than 15,000 telephone calls. Other cities experienced similar results. The VD *Blues* story had an O. Henry-style finish: 3M was presented later in the year with the American Medical Association's 1972 Journalism Award for its courage in underwriting such a high-risk show. The story of the award, wrote *Variety*'s Bill Greeley, was "one of those marvelous ironies which only a gimp of a medium [like] public television could supply."[25]

By the time VD *Blues* aired, public television was well along the road to what PBS president Hartford Gunn called a cohesive but decentralized system. The national schedule was no longer the sole province of NET; important programs were beginning to come from other sources, mostly the big-city stations. WGBH / Boston supplied the hugely popular *French Chef, Evening at Pops*, and the durable *Masterpiece Theater*.[26] KCET / Los Angeles, having brought Lewis Freedman, PBL's cultural chief, to the West Coast to produce *Hollywood Television Theater*, supplied a series of distinguished American-produced dramas, one of which ("Andersonville Trials") was honored with the public medium's first Emmy. In the early burst of decentralized national production, series for national distribution also came from WTTW / Chicago (Bob Cromie's *Book Beat*), KQED / San Francisco (*World Press*) and South Carolina ETV (William Buckley's *Firing Line*).

While the decentralization of national production opened avenues of opportunity for producers outside New York and resulted in a more diversified national schedule, it did not cause New York to be replaced as the principal source of national programming.

In the early months of 1971, an idea for a television series was germinated in the New York offices of NET that would result two years later in the most discussed, argued over, and written about series public television had yet produced. Nor has the argument over the series entirely subsided; *An American Family* can still provoke discussion twenty years later. The show grew out of an earlier desire by the staff to develop a series dealing with the radically changed attitudes of the young toward marriage, religion, sex, and drugs. Our first thought was a series of conventional documentaries, each treating one of the topics. But one of our producers, Craig Gilbert, thought he had a better idea. His boss, Curt Davis, brought him to my office to argue passionately for what they both believed was a superior way to deal with the cultural shift.

Gilbert, a huge bear of a man, hulking, rumpled, and with a generous growth of beard, had won an Emmy a year earlier for his documentary *The Triumph of Christy Brown*. He had started nothing substantive since. A broken marriage and the trauma of divorce had left him with self-doubts and a long list of unanswered questions about life in general and about relationships between men and women in particular. He was on the verge of quitting NET when Davis, unwilling to lose one of his best producers, handed him a challenge he couldn't refuse: give me a plan for a show you always wanted to do but for whatever reason couldn't. Gilbert thought about it during a weekend in which he "drank a lot and wallowed in self pity" over his failed marriage. Somewhere, buried in the troubling question of why men and women have such a tough time maintaining relationships, was the germ of an idea for a show. He grabbed a pencil and began making notes. The result was the outline for *An American Family*.[27]

Gilbert had a nervous habit of lighting a cigarette, taking a few puffs, stubbing it out, and lighting another. He stubbed his way through the better part of a pack while describing his "better idea": eight one-hour shows—they later turned out to be twelve—culled from intensive and intimate film coverage of a single family over the space of a year. Not necessarily a typical family, but a family whose experiences would reflect the changes that the times were wreaking on all of us. Perhaps, he reasoned, the answers he sought in his own life might be found in the lives of others. The risk was high. But the notion of treating the issue of changing values in a more dramatic, less didactic, less ordinary context than the conventional documentary form was more than tempting, it was irresistible. We decided to move ahead. The funds originally scheduled for documentaries were switched to the new project over the aggrieved cries of the documentary unit. A search was begun to find a family willing to share its life with a film crew— and several million strangers.

For two months Gilbert moved from coast to coast in a fruitless search for the right family. He started by talking with family therapists, believing that a family already in therapy might better be able to withstand the consequences of protracted television exposure. He varied his approaches, but none produced a family willing to be the subject. Despairing, he went on a blind date with a Santa Barbara newspaper reporter, shared his problem over drinks, and was led by her to the William C. Loud family of that California city: Pat and Bill and their five children, Lance, Kevin, Grant, Delilah, and Michele. Pat and Bill Loud were doubtful and hesitant at first, but during several all-night talk sessions Gilbert was able to dispel, or at least to minimize, their reservations. Filming began several nights later, on June 1, 1972. The opening sequence, a party in the Loud home to celebrate Grant's election to the student-body presidency of his high school, turned into a consolation party. Grant was defeated. And so our drama began.

Ten days later, Gilbert wrote to tell me of his satisfaction with the family:

As for the series, I am excited about its possibilities beyond any other project I have ever been involved with. At the same time, I must admit that it has triggered a series of anxieties that I guess I'll just have to live with for the next year. Before we started, I realized that the choice of the family was crucial and that all dreams or nightmares would flow from that choice. So far, we have been incredibly lucky. The family appears to be giving us precisely what we want.[28]

If Gilbert thought that he had found in the Louds of Santa Barbara a stable, down-home American family—"normal" in the positive sense of that term—he learned in short order that the Louds refused to fit the mold. Upper middle class, living close to the core of the American Dream, with a ranch-style house, swimming pool, two cars, and many of the other amenities of the Southern California "good life," the Louds were not quite the contented, integrated family unit that Gilbert had seen on his first visit. By early summer, several weeks into the shooting, hairline fissures began to appear in the marriage. And by the time the final sequence was filmed seven months later, the picture of happy domesticity had fallen into disarray. The Loud's separation and divorce did, of course, add an unexpected element of drama— particularly the scene in which Pat confronted Bill with news of her decision to divorce him—but it resulted in a grossly unbalanced series budget. Where one film crew had been budgeted for, two were now needed to follow Pat and Bill as they went their separate ways.

The principal filmmakers were the man-and-wife team of Alan and Susan Raymond. Independent filmmakers in their own right (*The Police Tapes, Bad Boys*), the Raymonds had also worked with Gilbert on his award-winning documentary *The Triumph of Christy Brown*. During the time *An American Family* was in production, they, together with Gilbert's assistant, Susan Lester, were with the Louds during most of the family's waking hours, sometimes filming, sometimes simply waiting for "things to happen." Gilbert, feeling that his additional presence would lessen the "reality" of the situation, stayed away from the house during much of the actual shooting, keeping in touch with his team by telephone and occasionally meeting with the Raymonds and the family, but leaving the Raymonds to decide what and when to film. (As a consequence, Gilbert and the Raymonds have feuded for years over the "authorship" of *An American Family*.) Over their seven months with the Louds, the Raymonds and Susan Lester developed an easy working relationship with the family, a formidable achievement in itself, living as they were in each other's pockets for most of that time. None of the crew actually lived in the Loud home, but they came and left each day, frequently after long hours together.

Three months into the filming, Pat Loud wrote a note to those involved in the production. "You have eminently justified the faith my family tacitly put in you. . . . Believe me, if anyone ever wants to muck around in my life again, it has got to be you."[29] But the family's mood had turned darker by the time the shooting ended and the finished shows were aired. More than three hundred hours of film had been shot over the seven months, and this film would be edited over the next eighteen months into twelve hour-long episodes. (Gilbert had wanted additional episodes, but his new bosses—NET had by then been absorbed into Channel 13— took account of a budget that had soared from its original $600,000 to $1.6 million and drew the line at twelve.) In late December 1972, after completion of the first two episodes, I flew to Los Angeles and joined the Loud family—Pat, her mother, and four of the children—for the press preview. Although the family had seen some of the rushes as they were being shot, this was the first time the Louds saw a completed episode. The family's reaction was generally positive. Pat thought the two episodes were true to the facts of their life, although she did have a reservation about the opening titles. *An American Family* was spelled out in great blocks of granite that slowly developed hairline cracks and crumbled. "That fries me," Pat Loud told Gilbert. "It should be taken out." It wasn't. Gilbert was solidly wed to the visual metaphor for the fragility of the American family.

The first episode of *An American Family* aired nationally on January 11, 1973, to a highly favorable critical reception: "a remarkable document" (*Newsweek*);[30] "extraordinarily interesting to watch" (*Time*);[31] "what may be the most extraordinary series ever made for the medium (*Washington Evening Star and Daily News*);[32] "unquestionably the most ambitious [project] ever attempted by public television, it may well be the most significant" (*Los Angeles Times*).[33] On the whole, the show fared far better than its subjects did. Critics tore into the family. Jim Caines (*Village Voice*) wrote that "the Louds have neither wit nor warmth . . . they are zombified."[34] Stephanie Harrington (*New York Times*) felt that it was the Loud's "crucial failures to reach out to each other across empty spaces that make this affluent middle-class family such a fragile composition of fragments."[35]

The Louds reacted with shock and anger. With their self-image under savage attack, the Louds struck back. The counterattack was directed not at the critics and their unkind words but at the producers and their unkept promises. "We weren't deceived, but we were misled," Bill Loud told a reporter. "If they had five happy shots and five sad or tragic or bizarre shots, they picked four negative shots for every one of the other." The producers, he charged, "had a preconceived, liberal, leftist view that the American way of life is wrong, that family life is wrong, that our values are wrong."[36] Pat Loud went on television to tell her side of the story. In a confrontation with a nervous, chain-smoking Craig Gilbert on Dick Cavett's late night ABC show on the evening of February 20, 1973, she accused the producer of deliberate distortion to make his point. Her most virulent anger, however, was directed at WNET and the publicity and advertising campaign that was used to introduce the series when it first aired. Particularly galling was an article by writer Fredelle Maynard, which appeared in Channel 13's own monthly magazine.

Flying, partying, quarrelling, just talking, the Louds reveal a peculiarly American faith in simple solutions, instant cure. Unhappy? Take a trip. Lonely? Give a party, set your hair. Pat's instinct in a crisis is to reach for a drink.[37]

Maynard's article would have hurt had it appeared anywhere. But showing up as it did in the producing station's own publication was too much. Pat Loud was truly "fried." And unforgiving.

In the aftermath of the series, Pat wrote a book, Bill remarried, and the children pursued their own careers. Their lives were changed forever; a whole chunk of their existence had been thrust beneath the microscope and dissected, their common experience mediated by the unblinking eye of the camera, their privacy made public property. Few families could withstand the pressures of public exhibition and hope to emerge unscathed. The Louds were not, as some critics would have it, an aberration, a clutch of California flakes worshipping at the altar of consumerism and frantically pursuing The Good Life as practiced by the self-absorbed sun worshippers of the Pacific slopes. While not *the* American family, the Louds of Santa Barbara were certainly *an* American family, and not much different from hundreds of thousands of upwardly mobile suburban strivers like themselves. "With innumerable variations," wrote John O'Connor, "the Louds are all around us."[38]

In some measure, *An American Family* mirrored the society of its time, or more accurately, that part of society whose established values had eroded under the assault of materialistic goals—the part for whom the pursuit of a "high standard of living" was and is the essence of the American Dream. Margaret Mead offhandedly burdened the series with far too much cultural weight by saying that the series was "as important for our time as were the invention of drama and the novel for earlier generations."[39] Nevertheless, *An American Family* was an undeniably dramatic and novel experiment, wholly in keeping with public television's mandate to break the mold of conventional television and search out exciting new forms. In the twenty years since its first release, the series continues to have a half-life. Alan and Susan Raymond produced a tenth-anniversary show for cable, updating the lives of the Louds, and in 1988 New York's Museum of Broadcasting held a retrospective seminar with Craig Gilbert, the Raymonds, and the two youngest Loud children. But the afterlife that was most hoped for by serious scholars has disappeared. The almost three hundred hours of film that did not find their way into the final version had been squirrelled away at WNET as a resource for future anthropologists, a trove of family lore for those who might wish to study the society of the seventies. With television's characteristic disdain for preserving its past, the administration at WNET happened upon the trove and had it destroyed.

So much for cultural history.

TWO INTO ONE
EQUALS THIRTEEN

If newness be its vice, then boldness be its virtue.

Edward R. Murrow[1]

The 1970 merger of NET and New York's WNDT / 13 was a marriage of convenience. Neither partner desired it, but neither had a choice in the matter. Both institutions were financial wards of the Ford Foundation, and the Foundation, for its own reasons, wanted them made one.

NET was a result of the Foundation's benign intervention in public television's birth and early development; Ford's Fund for Adult Education created it and Ford money sustained it through all of its twenty years. Despite its autonomy in the public system, NET necessarily danced to Ford's tune. Channel 13, ten years younger than NET, was equally vulnerable to Ford's master planning. By the late 1960s, the station's efforts to gain visibility in a market dominated by six other well-established VHF channels had exhausted its resources, leaving it a wan and undernourished institution. Ironically, each of the two institutions, situated cheek-by-jowl on New York's Columbus Circle, had what the other needed: NET had programming money and no studios; WNDT had studios and too little programming money. The station's financial burdens might have been eased had NET been willing to lease WNDT's studios for its major productions. But NET's producers, reluctant to entrust their productions to WNDT's "incompetent" studio crews, took them out of town.[2]

Fierce rivalry for the attention of the fickle New York press, the largesse of the Ford Foundation, and the loyalty of New York's viewers shaped the attitudes of their respective staffs. For ten years they glared at each across West 58th Street, the narrow canyon that separated them. Meanwhile, the Foundation, banker to both institutions, had little patience with their "competitive and sometimes combative" relationship, especially since Ford dollars fueled it. Bundy and Friendly saw in a merger of the rivals the means of wiping out wasteful competition—and something more. Both men were embarrassed by Channel 13's performance. Measured by any standard, WNDT "has remained among the weakest and most ineffective of the public broadcasting stations in the major cities."[3] Friendly felt that his efforts to wheedle millions for the public medium from the Ford board were undermined by Channel 13's lackluster performance. For most Ford trustees, the New York channel provided their only first-hand knowledge of public television. Friendly believed that a marriage of NET's production skills with Channel 13's audience reach could make the flagship station the showpiece of the public medium.

John Macy and the Corporation for Public Broadcasting had even stronger reasons for pushing the merger. The Corporation's plan for restructuring the system made no provision for a free-standing production house; instead responsibility for national program production was assigned to the PBS member stations. Folding NET into a station removed an anomaly, a production center without a station base. The move not only neatened the system's organizational chart but also helped to solve CPB's identity crisis. Before CPB and PBS came on the scene, the public-television system was generally referred to as "NET," much as it is referred to today as "PBS." (Interestingly, both terms refer to only one element in the system, not the system itself.) To establish the identity of the new entities. CPB needed to bury the long-established NET image. Merger with a local station was the answer. (The purpose in changing the station's name from WNDT to WNET after the merger was to retain the market value of NET's established reputation abroad. It did nothing to blunt the Corporation's design; a whole generation has grown up not knowing that NET once stood for more than a shortened version of the station's name.)

Years of feuding between Channel 13 and its network neighbor tended to obscure the fact that WNDT's very existence was due in large part to NET's need to have its programs seen in the New York area. In 1959, when NET moved its base from Ann Arbor to Manhattan, New York City was one of the few population centers (and the largest) in the nation without a public-television station. Establishing a national presence is virtually impossible without visibility in the nation's media center—home of the nation's leading daily newspaper, its major commercial networks, and most of its periodicals. If public television was to be more than a provincial phenomenon, it had to be seen in New York. NET's interest in establishing an outlet for its programs in New York, obsessive as it was, brooked no compromise with its goal of seeking on outlet that would be on a parity with other New York stations. Acquiring a VHF channel was an essential part of this plan. Unfortunately, none were available. All seven of New York's VHF channels, the maximum number that technical considerations will allow, were already in private hands by 1948 when the FCC put a "freeze" on the issuance of new licenses. Later, in 1952, when the FCC issued its list of reserved channels, the nation's largest city was compelled to take what was left, a largely unreceivable and therefore unusable UHF channel. For a time in the mid-fifties, a group calling itself META—the Metropolitan Educational Television Association—tried to rally support to activate the UHF channel. But the prospects for its success in competition against seven established commercial channels were not promising. META soon dropped its activation plans and turned to producing occasional programs for NET.

And then, in 1961, the break came, suddenly and unexpectedly. One of the area's seven VHF channels—licensed to WNTA / Channel 13 Newark, New Jersey—was quietly put on the market by its owners, National Telefilm Associates. The station was losing money. White, alerted to WNTA's availability by a professional station broker hired for just that purpose, hastily pulled together a

steering committee of prominent New Yorkers, taking care to include a handful of corporate heavyweights: New York Life's retired
chairman Devereux Josephs; National City Bank's retired chairman Howard Sheperd; John D. Rockefeller 3d, philanthropist and
chairman of Lincoln Center for the Performing Arts; and Arthur
A. Houghton, Jr., president of Steuben Glass. Educators were represented by the chancellor of New York University, George D.
Stoddard, and by White himself. The group incorporated itself as
ETMA, Educational Television for the Metropolitan Area, and
elected Sheperd as their chair.

ETMA had clout but lacked cash. With no more money in hand
than a $2 million pledge from the Ford Foundation, the group
bid $4 million for the New Jersey channel. Their bid was rejected.
The seller had a better offer, a bid of $8 million from a buyer who
proposed to keep the channel in commercial hands. At that level
ETMA stood little chance of staying in the bidding game. It was a
dark moment for public television. Then, with the campy theatrics
of a cavalry rescue, a young Chicago attorney named Newton Minow entered the scene to save the day. Minow, recently appointed
by President Kennedy to head the FCC, wanted desperately to see
a public channel in New York but knew that the Commission had
no choice but to grant the channel to the highest bidder. The
opportunity for an educational channel in New York would be lost.
But Minow also knew that the winning bidder, unwilling to see
money tied up indefinitely, needed speedy FCC approval. Cagily,
Minow persuaded his FCC colleagues to announce the Commission's intent to hold hearings on the desirability of securing noncommercial outlets in New York and Los Angeles, thereby post-
poning action on the winning bid until the hearings were
completed. The process could take a year or more. The high bidder read the message and withdrew, and the way was cleared for
the sale of the channel to the public group.[4]

One problem remained, however, and it was a big one. Channel
13 was New Jersey's only VHF channel. Governor Robert Meyner
was not about to let a band of marauding New Yorkers, however
high-minded, steal it away and carry it across the Hudson. Like
the state's other elected officials, he had personal reasons for

keeping a VHF channel in the state. Without it, New Jersey politicians would be forced to campaign on the VHF stations in neighboring New York state and Pennsylvania and pay a premium price for reaching, in addition to their electorate, audiences in those states. Months of legal maneuvering finally produced an accord in which Meyner dropped opposition to the transfer in return for the station's pledge to devote a portion of its scheduled programming specifically to the New Jersey audience. Legend has it that Norman Cousins's friendly games of tennis with Governor Meyner played an important part in the successful negotiations.[5]

On December 22, 1961, the deed was done. ETMA paid the channel's former owners $6.45 million, of which the largest single portion ($3.825 million) came from Ford. Seven smaller foundations gave an additional $1.375 million. The balance of $1.25 million came in contributions from New York's commercial television channels, all hoping to boost their profits by removing the New Jersey channel from commercial competition. In effect, the public was forced to buy back "the public's airwaves" in order to return them to public ownership. The situation, without precedent, gives persuasive evidence of the lopsidedness of the nation's communications policies, placing as it does private interests above the public interest.

Nine months after the transfer, on September 16, 1962, the station returned to the air as WNDT (New Dimensions in Television), this time as a public outlet with a public board, and with a new corporate name, the Educational Broadcasting Corporation.[6] WNDT's first president, Dr. Samuel B. Gould, was the former president of the University of California's Santa Barbara campus. WNDT's vice president and general manager was Richard Heffner, whom White had brought from CBS to help with the details of the transfer. White, having played a key role in both the transfer of the channel and the organization of a local public corporation to operate it, assumed WNDT would become a subsidiary of NET. The Ford Foundation, however, thought otherwise. Having given its full support to NET's efforts to win the channel and having put up a substantial part of the purchase price, the Foundation promptly

vetoed plans to merge the channel with NET. Instead, it insisted
that NET step aside and that White resign from the station board.

Two years later, events intervened to bring an end to their separation, at least for a time. Both Gould and Heffner had left the
station, and their posts, combined into the single post of president
and general manager, had been filled with a young CBS vice president, John W. Kiermaier. The station, however, was teetering on
the edge of bankruptcy, the victim of its own inability to raise
enough money to balance the books. Fearing the fallout of a failed
station in New York, NET's other affiliates urged White to organize
a rescue effort. WNDT's board welcomed the help and invited four
NET directors, including White, to return to the Channel 13
board. The station's management was placed in the hands of a joint
NET-WNDT board committee. Although WNDT's financial crisis
prompted renewed talk of a merger, Ford again vetoed the proposal. The Foundation felt the station's board could end the financial crisis by devoting more effort to fund-raising. If after a
year the board had still failed, the merger would be reconsidered.

The board succeeded, and the station was returned to a sound
financial footing. Talk of merger was temporarily muted, but NET's
lust for a linkage with the station would not die. Two years after
the rescue effort, NET proposed a modified plan for a merger,
including interlocking boards, consolidation of several overlapping departments, and cancellation of the $1.8 million the station
still owed NET for its rescue effort. But not even the network's offer
of a dowry, $1 million a year for five years for programming and
operations, could persuade Channel 13 to surrender its independence.

White's vision of a "a strong and vital flagship station" in the
New York metropolitan area haunted him throughout his tenure
at NET. As late as 1968, only weeks away from resigning the presidency, White complained that WNDT, "as presently constituted,"
was "ineffective," its programming "staid, even dull," its fund-
raising efforts "inadequate," and its service to the New York community "far below what it should be." His solution, to make the
channel a subsidiary of NET, was the only way WNDT "could be-

come more exciting, vigorous and relevant to its own community."[7]

By 1969, however, new players had come into the game, the rules had been rewritten, and talk of a merger bore a whole new meaning. The Corporation for Public Broadcasting, barely out of the chrysalis, also had merger on its mind, but its design for merger, far from embodying White's vision of a flagship station for the network, would end forever NET's hopes of hegemony over the New York scene.

The process that ultimately joined the two essentially rival organizations played out as an absurdist drama of political intrigue. The details are less important than what they represent: the public medium's readiness to sacrifice programming strength for parochial political advantage.

Merger talks between NET and WNDT were begun with their respective chairmen, Norman Cousins of NET and Ethan Allen Hitchcock of Channel 13. The two negotiators could hardly have been more mismatched. Norman Cousins was the idealistic editor, a dealer in cosmic concepts, a seeker after humanitarian solutions to global problems. Ethan Allen Hitchcock was the pragmatic corporate lawyer—uncompromising, a tiger on tiny details, and with a lawyerly skill at carving out a line of argument and defending it against the most formidable assaults of logic and reason. The two men talked past each other. Both boards, sensing an impasse, did what boards usually do to resolve unresolvable problems: they formed a committee and commissioned a study. Former Cornell president James Perkins, drafted to undertake the study, returned with a three-page memorandum whose essence was a recommendation that national program production be assigned to "at least four powerful, well-financed leadership stations."[8] One of the four, to be called PB-NY, would be a merged NET / WNDT. Everett Case, NET's former chairman and a member of the study committee, reacted with a wittily scathing memo likening the Perkins proposal to an "Oz-like fantasy" in which PB-NY was to be the voice of the Munchkins, PB-S (south) the voice of the Quadlings, PB-W (west) the voice of the Winkies, and PB-MW (midwest) the voice of the Gillikins.[9] The Perkins proposal was tabled.

Desperate to move the merger process forward, the NET board turned to Peter G. Peterson, one of its members and its most experienced power broker, and asked him to try to work out a solution with Hitchcock. The strategy paid off. Peterson (at the time chairman of Bell & Howell and later Nixon's Secretary of Commerce) and Hitchcock met, argued, exchanged countless drafts of tentative agreements, and, in a struggle of Herculean proportions, hammered out an agreement. Peterson said later that the agreement resulted from "some of the toughest negotiations I've ever experienced."[10]

The composition of the merged boards proved to be the sticking point. NET favored combining the two boards. Hitchcock was opposed, not only because the combined board would be unwieldy, but also because he saw no need to include those NET directors from outside the New York area. The WNDT chairman clearly held the trump card; as the licensee of the television channel, the station had the more irreplaceable asset. Hitchcock's arbitrariness, however, in deciding single-handedly who was to stay and who was to leave, angered members of the NET board. In a last-ditch effort to preserve its self-esteem Peterson proposed a compromise. All eighteen members of the NET board would be invited to serve, but he, Peterson, would guarantee that the requisite number of invitees would "gracefully decline the generous offer."[11] Hitchcock turned it down. The haggling over the board composition continued almost to the day the merger was publicly announced in August 1970. With patience growing thin and time running out, Hitchcock agreed to accept ten of NET's eighteen board members. Seven were deemed acceptable because they were New Yorkers (despite the fact that one, Burke Marshall, was from Yale). Another, William Schuman, declined to serve because his wife, Frances, was already on the Channel 13 board. The three out-of-towners acceptable to Hitchcock were Nobel Laureate Glenn T. Seaborg of Berkeley, University of Chicago historian John Hope Franklin, and Roger Revelle, director of Harvard University's Population Research Center. The compromise did not sit well with those dropped from consideration, especially the only two women on the NET board. Carolyn Charles, a San Francisco civic leader and trustee of Stanford University, and Patricia Roberts Harris, dean of the Howard Law School, suspected that they were rejected for reasons other than Hitchcock's explanation—that both women also sat on the boards of their respective local public stations—particularly since both had offered to resign from those boards.

Of the NET directors who survived the merged, Norman Cousins presented a special case. Although he was a ten-year veteran of the NET board and had just become chairman when the merger discussions began, he was passed over for chair of the merged corporation. Instead, in the behind-the-scenes planning at the Ford Foundation the decision was taken to balance the scales between the rival organizations by giving the chair position to WNDT and the presidency to NET. Although Cousins was invited to serve on the Channel 13 board, his leadership position was lost almost before he had the opportunity to exercise it. Bundy and Friendly, sensitive to the awkwardness of Cousins's position and perhaps feeling some responsibility for having put him into it, were eager to cushion the blow to his pride and at the same time make productive use of his energy and dedication to the public medium. Their solution did honor to public television's favorite means of solving its problems: create another organization.

In the course of the merger negotiations, the Foundation had written to Peterson promising "to recommend [to the Foundation trustees] favorable action" on a proposal to create a new body to advise on national programming. With no hint of artifice, the letter stated that Ford was "particularly pleased that Mr. Hitchcock has not only expressed enthusiasm for the concept of such a group, but has also suggested that Norman Cousins be appointed its first chairman."[12] In fact, Hitchcock had given his consent grudgingly. This became all too apparent when he and Cousins sat down to discuss specifics. Cousins envisioned a "board" of "creative and disciplined minds" focused "exclusively and intensively" on national programming—in effect, an heir to the functions of the dismissed NET board. Hitchcock, on the other hand, saw an advisory "council" with a much more limited function that would act as an adjunct to his own local station board. A flurry of testy "if-you-agree-with-this-sign-below" letters flew between their offices before the differences were ironed out and the National Programming Council was born.[13]

Cousins immediately opened an office near the United Nations on Manhattan's East Side, hired an executive secretary, and dipped into his bulging Rolodex for the names of the "creative and disciplined minds" to serve the Council. His selection was as eclectic as it was distinguished, including among others the head of a major advertising agency, a prominent industrialist, a college president, and the youthful leader of an environmental movement.[14] Unfortunately, the Council's collective expertise was wasted. Hitchcock, having grudgingly agreed to its formation to please Ford, virtually ignored its existence. He was convinced his own Channel 13 board could provide whatever counsel on national programming was needed. And so, at the end of the two-year Ford grant, the National Programming Council quietly disappeared. It had served its primary function of cushioning Cousins's ego during the transition. Its dissolution, however, cast aside a group of potential and powerful allies as though dedicated friends in high places were superfluous to the cause of public television.

As the "surviving president" of the combined corporations, I had ample cause to welcome the outcome of the NET-WNDT merger, yet my feelings were mixed. The months of negotiation had left a bitter aftertaste, particularly because of the way human resources had been scuttled to achieve a result. And while the pairing of a chairman from one organization and a president from the other had a desirable symmetry, I was fully aware that the symmetry bore the seeds of future discontents. However, with the merger behind us, there was little time for dwelling on the past and its regrets. New challenges lay ahead that had to be met, not the least of which was the task of mobilizing the resources of the combined organizations to put the New York station in the vanguard of the public system, and at the same time to make it count among its constituents in the New York metropolitan area.

Channel 13's local programming, once a matter of pride to the station's staff, had changed after the 1964 brush with bankruptcy. To rescue the station from the financial brink, WNDT president Jack Kiermaier had been forced to use draconian measures. Locally produced programming had virtually vanished from the schedule. By 1970, only two regular local shows remained, Mitchell Krause's nightly *Newsfront* and *New Jersey Speaks*, a pallid response to the requirement that Channel 13 serve the state to which it is licensed. No regular programs were specifically targeted for the 8 million people of the metropolitan area. (Ellis Haizlip's *Soul*, a variety hour featuring popular black entertainers, had by this time moved from the local to the national schedule of PBS.) The station had paid a price for its lack of local programming. While audiences for most local stations were growing, Channel 13's was not. "When Hitchcock talks about WNDT's growing audience," quipped *Variety*'s Bill Greeley, "he means they're growing older."[15] He called the station's local programming "listless," adding that its "poverty of programming and production ingenuity is an eyesore on the VHF band."[16] The *New York Times*'s Jack Gould was no kinder. Channel 13, he observed, "does not appear to have had a new idea of its own in years."[17]

Our eagerness to see Channel 13 brought to life again was exceeded only by Fred Friendly's impatience to see the result. He and the Foundation had banked, literally and figuratively, on the outcome; as part of the merger agreement, the Foundation had granted $2 million specifically for WNET's local programming. Friendly saw no reason why changes could not be made instantly— as they were at CBS. He exploded when I told him the results might not be apparent on the screen for at least a year: "We can't wait a year!" (But he did, and, with characteristic generosity, said later that the wait had been worth it.) I proceeded by my own method, the only one I knew. I sought out the best people, tried to give them a sense of direction, and then let *them* make it happen. The key element in the plan was the search for the person to take command of the station and its local service to the immediate community. My hopes were focused on finding a New Yorker, with or without television experience, but someone who had a New

Yorker's sense of the city's people and its streets and who had the wit and imagination to make the public's channel pulse with the rhythms of the diverse and lively area we served. We were led by the enthusiastic recommendations of several prominent business-men to a young vice president at Harper & Row. John Jay Iselin, they said, was bright and articulate. What's more, he was available.

As a young man, Iselin, the scion of a wealthy South Carolina textile family and a direct descendant of the nation's first chief justice, had passed up textiles and torts—he had an Oxford law degree and a Harvard doctorate—to try his hand at reporting, first on the *Congressional Quarterly,* and later with *Newsweek,* where he rose swiftly to the post of national-affairs editor. Book publish-ing followed.[18] Iselin impressed us with his almost boyish enthu-siasm for new challenges. Satisfied that he also had the requisite energy and imagination, and was—to borrow one of his own fa-vorite metaphors—dialed into New York, we appointed him gen-eral manager of Channel 13. He immediately placed Jack Willis, *The Great American Dream Machine*'s co-executive producer, in charge of public-affairs programming, and Robert Kotlowitz, the recently resigned managing editor of *Harper's,* in charge of cul-tural programming. With a team in place, and Ford's $2 million in hand, the way was open to turn our collective vision into visual reality.

The new team benefited from an early start that Christopher (Kit) Lucas had made before he was replaced as program director by Jack Willis. Lucas had been storing up program ideas all through the long dry spell in WNDT's local programming. The minute the merger was fact, he and producer Fern McBride leapt into action by creating an unconventional and free-spirited local series they called *Free Time.* Their original concept was an open studio—anyone with the desire to be seen and heard would be welcome to drop in—but that gave way to the more practical con-cept of a thrice-weekly, late-night (10:30 P.M. to midnight) live show with a minimum of structure and a maximum of provoca-tion. Abbie Hoffman "moderated" a panel on the press; the con-suls general of India and Pakistan debated the war in Bangladesh; and Tom Hayden and Jane Fonda aired their unpopular views on the Vietnam War. The show's tissue-thin budget produced lots of talk: open-ended discussions by Bronx street gangs, New York cabbies, black film producers, women writers, domestic help, telephone operators, and other denizens of a world rarely glimpsed on the tube. Journalism's avatar of free speech, Nat Hentoff, found *Free Time* a fascinating expression of the power of the First Amendment: "They are not capons in make-up, they are distinct individuals with points of view, even heretical ones."[19]

On one memorable evening, *Free Time* featured the spiritually inspired films of Yoko Ono, including a film consisting only of the movements of a fly on the nipple of a woman's breast. The attention to the film was broken, however, when her husband John Lennon put in a surprise appearance, set up a ladder, and invited the studio audience to join him in "flying" off the top rung. One hapless "bird" sustained a broken arm. The spirit of *Free Time* was a holdover from the turbulent sixties, provoking more than its fair share of controversy and attracting—but surmounting—Fairness Doctrine complaints from the right-wing organization Accuracy in Media. Although it was honored with a local Emmy, the show's off-beat character left the local TV critics puzzled (but not without a tolerant good humor toward the show). The staid *New York Times* noted that "in the generally bland area of television, occasional excursions into the rough and ready are downright necessary."[20] *Variety* agreed: "Stirring things up is a commendable aim.... WNET may become known as the conscience of television here [in New York]."[21]

Iselin's team built on this foundation. By exhuming a seldom-used mobile unit, the station moved out of its studios and into the community, providing a front-row seat at such highly publicized events as the Knapp Commission hearings on police corruption, which the *Christian Science Monitor* praised as "drama of a kind rare in television."[22] Encouraged, we moved into hearings on proposed hikes in commuter rail fares and United Nations Security Council debates. Budget-bare "live" coverage of the Spassky-Fischer championship chess match in Iceland was achieved simply by using minute-by-minute wire reports from Reykjavík to simulate the match in our New York studio. In the fall of 1971, we added

Up Against New York, a show that explored with a sometimes serious, sometimes satiric eye the strategies for surviving the vexations of urban living—mass transit, divorce, air pollution, housing, and sex education. A year after the merger, WNET had begun to project an image as quintessentially New York as Zabar's and the St. Patrick's Day parade.

At the time the brouhaha broke over PBS's removal of Paul Jacobs's FBI segment from *The Great American Dream Machine*, the WNET staff was readying a local program called *Behind the Lines*, a weekly review of the performance of New York's media. Although the series was not due to debut until three weeks later, producer Carey Winfrey advanced the date of the premiere to take advantage of the major media story in his own backyard. He readied a full airing of the PBS dispute in a show that included a screening of Jacobs's disputed report followed by a panel discussion with a group of experts. *Behind the Lines* had been planned as a local show, but PBS president Hartford Gunn wisely arranged for this special edition to be aired on all PBS stations; he hoped it would mute criticism of the network's decision to cut the Jacobs piece from the *Dream Machine*. The opening special gave an auspicious start to a local series that would later go national when Iselin succumbed to the irresistible force that tempts so many producers of successful local shows to seek the greater glory of national exposure. In going network, *Behind the Lines* lost some of its local specificity—it no longer produced shows about the outrageous picture on tonight's *New York Post* or the bad taste of a local news show, for example—that gave the original show its bite. Before ambition lofted *Behind the Lines* out of the ranks of local programs and into national distribution, *Variety* wrote what we longed to hear, that its "production zing and values, the elements of audacity and imagination, are in living-color contrast to the drab and dreary output of the cold coffee pot that WNET was just a few months ago."[23]

Behind the Lines, *Up Against New York*, and *Free Time*—as well as a more conventional *How Do Your Children Grow?*—did light a flame under the pot of local programming and created a visible difference in the image of the New York channel. But it was an audacious venture into local journalism called *The 51st State* that set the programming pot to boiling. No one doubted that nightly news would be part of our revitalized local schedule; formidable forces were pushing us in that direction, including the expectations aroused by my earlier association with KQED's *Newsroom.* Those expectations were fed further by the palpable presence in the wings of Fred Friendly. The patron saint and proselytizer of the newsroom format was waiting impatiently to see how the $2 million Ford grant might be transformed into a local news show. Before the merger, Channel 13 had aired a nightly news program with Mitchell Krause. Although it was well done, the conventional format, I felt, added little to what the other channels were doing. After its cancellation, work was begun on the new show with the certainty that it had to be different.

The 51st State was nothing if not different: it was purposely provocative, unpredictable, irreverent, and probing. Like its title, appropriated from Norman Mailer's pledge in his 1968 mayoral campaign to see the metropolitan area made into the nation's fifty-first state, it was narrowly focused on the people of New York and their immediate environs. In style, it borrowed heavily from *The Great American Dream Machine,* which was not surprising since the executive producer for *The 51st State,* Jack Willis, had been one of the earlier show's creators. In concept, *The 51st State* was seen by Willis as "news from the bottom up," a voice for the disenfranchised, the people in the streets who rarely made it into the evening newscasts. Willis believed that a community station had an opportunity if not the obligation to seek out and tell their story.

Willis reached across the border into Canada for his anchor: the writer, reporter, interviewer, and gentleman farmer Patrick Watson. Six years earlier, Watson had hosted the CBC's *This Hour Has Seven Days,* a roughly similar and equally controversial show that briefly lighted the Canadian skies only to be extinguished by parliamentary and public bickering. Despite his casual dress—he customarily appeared on camera in Levi's and a baggy gray turtleneck—Watson brought a quality of urbanity and distinction to the show, qualities too often lacking in local news anchors. Willis and Watson surrounded themselves with first-rate reporters and seasoned journalists such as Selwyn Raab, Robert Sam Anson, John Parsons, Richard Kotuk, Hal Levenson, and Gary Gilson. To allow time for their stories, *The 51st State* was, in its first season, an open-ended show, its length determined each night by the demands of the news and not by the tyranny of the clock. Continuity and context were important; stories were followed up, not dropped and forgotten.

The 51st State's idiosyncratic approach to news was bound to draw fire, particularly for its perceived lack of objectivity. "We're supposed to be impartial conduits of the news," complained Ted Kavanau, news director of commercial station WNEW, "but they give journalism a bad name."[24] ABC *Evening News* producer Av Westin was even blunter, charging *The 51st State*'s producers with "perverting their obligation to cover the news truthfully."[25] Willis saw it differently, calling the issue of objectivity "a false issue," arguing that the real question was whether it was good or bad journalism. "Are you going out and getting the facts?" he asked his reporters. He thought they were. His argument that a community station has an obligation to treat news differently ("we're basically for the underdog, the person who's not being serviced by the city . . . so in one way and another we're always attacking institutions") was a position not shared by most stations in the system—not even with the added assurance that "we try to rely on our experience as journalists to be as fair as we possibly can."[26]

Willis's views were shared by his editor and anchor, Patrick Watson. Interviewed on a commercial news show, Watson dismissed balance within the body of a program as "an old-fashioned concept that went out of broadcasting—where I live, anyway—a long time ago. You do the best program you can to deal with what you're dealing with at that moment . . . you don't balance out the astronauts with the Flat Earth Society."[27] Watson's views touched off a small firestorm, not with the Flat Earth Society, but with Washington. Outraged over Watson's reported views on "balance," Representative Robert Michel called on Congress to exercise stricter oversight to "get this whole program [of federal support for public television] under control."[28] Predictably, Michel's outburst rattled the Corporation for Public Broadcasting's sensitive antennae, prompting an immediate query from John Macy: "I would like to know from you," he wrote, "whether [Watson's] view represents the philosophy at [WNET]. If it does," he warned, "I believe we must reconsider CPB granting of funds to [WNET]."[29]

The controversy over balance was sharpened on May 11, 1972, the day the Nixon Administration announced that U.S. forces had mined North Vietnam's Haiphong harbor. *The 51st State* preempted the station's entire evening schedule for a marathon "War Watch," a loosely organized show of news and comments whose purpose was to be on the air when the first ship struck the first mine (none did). With a clear purpose of dramatizing the escalation of the unpopular Southeast Asian war, the show presented thirty or more spokespersons. But of those invited to appear and defend the Administration's actions, only one accepted: Senator Robert Dole. Charges of political bias swirled around the heads of the producers the moment the show was off the air. Patrick Watson leaped to the program's defense by arguing that it reflected and articulated "that body of opinion in the country that's concerned and frightened over what's going on in Vietnam." The Administration's views, he pointed out, were available in abundance on other news shows. "It seems silly to try to balance all possibilities in a given program. . . . It's probably impossible. . . . Your credibility as an observer is a lot more reliable."[30]

The controversy over balance in *The 51st State* was significant but diversionary. The main event was the show itself. Night after night, investigative reporters, not waiting as most local shows do for leads in the morning papers or wire service daybooks, ferreted out their own leads. There were stories of squatters evicted from federal housing in Brooklyn's Brownsville section; of a Vietnam veteran brutally beaten by a cop; and of a drug pusher, known to his neighbors and the police, escaping punishment through the good offices of a lenient judge. The reporters' beats went beyond Manhattan and into the entire metropolitan region—Park Slope, the South Bronx, Williamsburg, Newark, and Co-op City. One reporter from *The 51st State*, posing as a drug addict, broke the story of a drug rehabilitation clinic illegally administering methadone without subjecting patients to a medical examination. Tony Batten's inquiry into youth gangs in the South Bronx was praised as "one of the year's most effective examples of local TV journalism."[31] Another producer and reporter, Richard Kotuk, showed "a more sophisticated understanding of school decentralization than anyone else in TV journalism."[32] Across the Hudson, where he seemed in constant trouble with the law, Ron Porambo, an aggressive, contentious reporter, uncovered serious financial irregularities in the administration of Newark mayor Kenneth Gibson. Observed one critic, *The 51st State* "has provided by far the best electronic coverage of the criminal justice system in New York," citing particularly Hal Levenson's report on the grand-jury system.[33]

The season's biggest headlines, however, came from the show's most experienced investigative reporter. Selwyn Raab had been tracking the fate of a young black man, George Whitmore, Jr., who had been convicted earlier of attempted rape and imprisoned. Raab, convinced that the young man was innocent, doggedly pursued leads over the years, always believing that new evidence could be found to win Whitmore's freedom. The effort paid off. Raab uncovered evidence that Whitmore was miles away when the rape occurred. His investigation resulted in freeing Whitmore after "a Dickensian legal nightmare in which police, courts, and prisons had entangled his life for nine long years."[34]

For whatever reason, whether it was the show's energy, its brashness, or simply the novelty of a news show that didn't look, sound, or feel like other news shows, *The 51st State* succeeded. For a time it attracted larger audiences than two of the three competing ten o'clock news programs on the commercial channels. And while it drew fire from some critics, many more sang its praises. Columbia Graduate School of Journalism's Marvin Barrett called *The 51st State* "the liveliest, if not the most professional, operation in town."[35] Nat Hentoff was even more expansive. "This provocatively unpredictable nightly news show," he wrote, "is beginning to present a formidable challenge to print journalists while leaving the other local television news operations a light year behind. The question now is how those of us reporters without a camera are going to keep up with this really new journalism."[36] He need not have worried. *The 51st State* was not destined to herald a new era in television reporting, but it turned out to be an aberrant blip on the unwavering line of establishment journalism. It made a loud noise, but for only a brief time.

After its first season, the rambunctious, free-wheeling show that was the original *The 51st State* began to slide into more conventional patterns, as often happens in the capricious world of television. When it returned for its second season, the show was trimmed to a half-hour, was no longer open-ended, and was shown at the earlier time of 7:30 P.M. Even with a repeat airing at the old 10 P.M. hour, the show lost audience. Other factors worked against its continued success as well. Management, concerned with wooing corporate money for national programming, grew increasingly critical of the show's disregard for the toes it stepped on. An investigative piece on Newark was critical of the Prudential Life Insurance Company at the very time that the company was being solicited for an underwriting grant. The conflict set in motion a classic clash of principles common in public television: Willis was dedicated to giving voice to the disenfranchised, whatever the cost in dollars; Iselin was determined to keep the news show from interfering with the more serious work of fund-raising, whatever the cost in principle. Their disagreements grew daily. After Iselin began to inject himself into the show's editing process, the showdown was inevitable. It came in January 1973, at a breakfast meeting. "You don't like the way I run the staff and take news from the bottom up," said Willis.[37] "That's right," Iselin responded. Willis resigned. Later, Iselin offered an explanation: "When I learned enough about broadcast journalism to realize Jack Willis was not a journalist but an evangelist, I decked the show."[38]

Patrick Watson left the show several weeks later. Though publicly citing "personal reasons"—he commuted weekly from his farm in Ontario by flying his own plane and was wearying of the travel—he told me privately that his resignation was hastened by Iselin's "improper interference" with the show. Jack Willis and Patrick Watson had given the *The 51st State* its energy, its direction, defined its limits, and set its irreverent tone. With their departure. The show lost much of the style and the brash courage that had accounted for its panache and, for many, its popularity. Willis later went on to become president of the Twin Cities public television stations, and Watson to chair the Canadian Broadcasting Corporation.

Rumors that *The 51st State* would not return in the fall of 1973 prompted the formation of a citizens' protest group. Its sentiments were voiced by Jack Newfield in the *Village Voice*: "This will be a worse city to live in," he wrote, "if *The 51st State* goes off the air."[39] The show did return for yet another season. But it returned to a television environment that was no longer hospitable to bold and innovative programming. The creeping forces of caution were at work, both inside and outside the station. Inside, Chairman Hitchcock exercised his oversight with a strong hand and an eye cautiously wary of any programming that failed to fit the weltanschauung of the corporate world he knew best. Nor was Iselin free from responsibility. Late in the spring of 1973, forty irate members of his production staff (many of them from *The 51st State*), who were outraged at what they termed Iselin's "coercive distrust" of the staff, delivered a petition to his Upper East Side townhouse. The message: "We are chilled."[40]

The chill, however, was not limited to Channel 13. Nor was it entirely of Channel 13's making. Colder blasts were blowing off the Potomac. The Nixon White House, crippled by a paranoia that saw the press as its "enemy," was preparing to do battle with the media. It was generally understood that the president viewed the public system as an excrescence on the federal payroll, didn't much care for its "left-leaning ideology," and was prepared to watch it struggle for air while he kept his foot on the oxygen hose. By 1973, the signals were unmistakable: aides in the Nixon White House were laying out battle lines for the Administration's first assault on the public medium. Some in public television's Washington headquarters believed that the president could be "brought around." No price was too high if it kept the federal funds coming. In this environment, *The 51st State* and shows like it became a test of public television's ability to maintain some measure of independence and integrity. But this was not the case for those who thought that peace was possible; they saw boldness and controversy only as an "embarrassment to our friends in Washington." Chairman Hitchcock instructed me to "cooperate more fully" with PBS and the Corporation. Unfortunately, both CPB and PBS had grown gun-shy from peering down the barrels of the White House artillery. Furthermore, PBS lacked the political clout needed to counter a hostile federal bureaucracy, and the Corporation for Public Broadcasting was about to be co-opted and made part of the very forces it was created to protect against.

In time the rules of the game would change. But not before the destructive force in the White House wreaked its havoc on the vulnerable institution of public television, leaving in its wake scars that are visible to this day.

12

HUMPTY-DUMPTY AND
THE NIXON YEARS

"When I use a word," Humpty Dumpty said, *in a rather scornful tone, "it means just what I choose it to mean, nothing more nor less."*

"The question is," said Alice, *"whether you* can *make words mean so many different things."*

"The question is," said Humpty Dumpty, *"which is to be master— that's all."*

Lewis Carroll,
Through the Looking Glass[1]

Richard M. Nixon was not the first occupant of the Oval Office to view the press with unconcealed hostility. Every president since George Washington felt unfairly put upon by an unfriendly press, even the paladin of press freedoms, Thomas Jefferson. The man who once said he preferred a press without a government to a government without a press changed his tune once he was in office and the victim of "unfair" press attacks. "A few prosecutions of the most prominent offenders," Jefferson confessed to a friend, "would have a wholesome effect in restoring the integrity of the presses."[2]

And yet of all those who preceded him into the White House, Nixon was the first to turn personal hostility into public policy and to use his Administration to try to neutralize the critical media. Nixon believed that the press was out to get him. It was unable, he thought, to forgive him for his anti-communist crusades and, particularly, for his relentless pursuit of Alger Hiss. Nixon's paranoia bred a distrust so deep that he created an "enemies list," including reporters, and dealt with the media as with any other subversive elements bent on destroying the republic. Not surprisingly, his suspicions and hostility led Nixon to target the more-or-less freewheeling public-broadcasting system. His attitude was colored by his past difficulties with the "liberal establishment" and by his skewed view of public television as an arm of that establishment. It made little difference that the public medium, unlike the major press and commercial networks, had a minuscule impact on public opinion. More important, the public system, unlike the commercial system, could easily be brought to heel. The Administration had the weapon at hand: its control over public broadcasting's federal subsidy. And Nixon had no scruple about using it.

Nixon's first term had barely begun when his initial salvo against television was launched by Vice President Spiro Agnew in a nationally televised speech from Des Moines. The Administration's stinging rebuke of television charged the medium with being controlled by "a closed fraternity of privileged men" whose views were predominantly "Eastern liberal."[3] Agnew's address was only the tip of the iceberg. Behind closed doors, plans were being laid for further assaults—known to us now only by the revelations of internal memoranda produced by the Freedom of Information Act.

One such meeting presaged the Nixon strategy in dealing with the public system. In November 1969, during the week of the Agnew attack, White House aide Peter Flanigin called together two members of the Corporation board—its chairman, Frank Pace, Jr., and one of its directors, Albert Cole, who had been recently appointed by Nixon. Their purpose—to discuss a plan for a "more geographically and ideologically balanced" public system—produced an agreement to use NET as a production center only "until new facilities are in operation," presumably elsewhere in the country. In the interim, not only would NET's funding not increase, "rather [it] would decrease to zero over the next two or three years." The death warrant for NET, administered by the White House and secretly agreed to by the Corporation ("Pace agrees with these conditions") came at an awkward time for me: I had moved into the presidency of the doomed organization only weeks earlier, unaware that the ground had been sold from under me by the Corporation's willing complicity in the Administration's so-called policy of "geographical and ideological balance."[4]

But greater ironies were to come. The White House plan for achieving "ideological balance" was absurdly simple: do away with NET and place responsibility for production elsewhere, anywhere outside New York City. The Corporation, willing to play the Administration's game to win continued federal support, announced in July 1971 the creation of NPACT, the National Public Affairs Center for Television. By shifting production of public-affairs programming from New York, where it had proved an offense to the Nixon White House, to Washington, where it could be kept under closer scrutiny, the Corporation hoped to placate the enemy and gain a peace. But the effort backfired. NPACT produced a provocation of the first order.

To head the new Washington-based public-affairs production house, NPACT chose James Karayn, a broadcast journalist with a high-decibel personality who had established his credentials by directing news at a Los Angeles commercial station before coming to Washington as a producer and writer for NBC News. In 1965, he became NET's bureau chief in Washington, where he was responsible for most of the public-affairs shows it produced out of the nation's capital. He slipped easily into the other chair when NPACT assumed NET's public-affairs duties, declaring that the new organization would be "courageous, intelligent, witty and shrewd . . . but operate with self-restraint, common sense and fairness."[5] The world of the White House, the public-television establishment, and the profession of journalism could hardly wish for more.

To fulfill Karayn's vision, NPACT needed a "presence" on the screen, an identifiable on-air personality to serve as a counterpart to the familiar and readily identifiable network news anchors. Karayn's first choice, the Canadian-born journalist Robert (Robin) MacNeil, was still relatively unknown in this country despite his extensive experience covering major international stories for the CBC, Reuters, the BBC, and NBC. "I wanted Robin and one superstar," Karayn recalled.[6] After NBC's Edwin Newman turned him down, Karayn turned to Sander Vanocur, another NBC colleague, but one willing to leave the network. "Sandy" Vanocur came to NPACT with fifteen years of experience in broadcast news and a solid reputation as a highly competent, competitive news reporter. Although he had developed a close relationship with John Kennedy during his stint as NBC's White House correspondent, Vanocur was known for his independence of mind and his readiness to speak it when the occasion warranted—as he was quick to demonstrate by speaking out against President Johnson's escalation of the Vietnam War. His somewhat flamboyant manner would be an ideal complement to MacNeil's more reserved on-air style. With the blessings of both Pace and Macy at the Corporation, and Fred Friendly at the Foundation, Karayn announced his choices of Vanocur and MacNeil at news conferences in both Washington and New York in early September 1971.

The announcement fell on the White House like a bombshell. Nixon was livid. In the president's opinion, Vanocur was a "well-known Kennedy sympathizer"; worse, the reporter's aggressive and hostile questioning during the 1960 campaign had weakened the Nixon image and contributed to his defeat.[7] And now Vanocur was back—back at government expense and provided with a platform by NPACT to continue his attacks on the president. On the morning after the announcement, Nixon's staff secretary sent a highly classified memorandum to Flanigan with copies to John Haldeman and Alex Butterfield. The NPACT hirings, said the memo, had "greatly disturbed the President who considered this the last straw." The president requested "that all funds for public broadcasting be cut immediately."[8]

If public television had any question about where the president stood before, it had none now. With characteristic bluntness, he made his position perfectly clear: control it or kill it. But not everyone on the White House staff was eager to join the president in his determination to use public television's funding to punish a single reporter. One of the most influential was a young MIT graduate, Clay T. Whitehead ("Tom" to his friends), Nixon's Director of the Office of Telecommunications Policy (OTP). At the age of thirty-three, Whitehead was one of the youngest appointees ever to head an executive agency. "With his utilitarian horn-rims, conservative suits, and boyishly earnest manner," *Newsweek* observed, he "comes across more like a small-town Jaycee than the 'communications czar' he has been called."⁹ As OTP Director, Whitehead was the president's top adviser and official spokesperson on communications, including public broadcasting.

The president's vengeful move to cut public television's funding struck Whitehead as a politically dangerous policy. Other policy options could better achieve Nixon's aim without the dangerous risks of the president's draconian scheme. Whitehead circulated several options in a memo to the White House staff. The most favored was a proposal to push for a funding bill that would send most of the federal money directly to the stations and prohibit the Corporation from using its share to support public-affairs programming.¹⁰ John Ehrlichman was dubious; a legislative solution would require the cooperation of Congress. "The best alternative," he said, "would be to take over the management and thereby determine what management decisions are going to be made."¹¹ His stratagem would have been readily understood by Justice Oliver Wendell Holmes, who once observed that "the only prize much cared for by the powerful is power."

In the long run, Ehrlichman's strategy of seizing control won out. But this was only the fall of 1971. The Nixon White House had not yet stacked the Corporation board with its own appointees, and it still lacked the means to seize control. So it opted to go with Whitehead's more subtle approach. The general thrust of that policy had already been fixed by Nixon and his close political aides: to neutralize the public medium, eliminating its power to function as an enemy of the Administration. Whitehead felt that since the "entire elimination of Federal support of public television is politically impossible," the most effective course of action was to redirect that support away from CPB and PBS "so as to create a structure which will be dominated by those elements of the public television field which are generally most congenial—namely the local stations."¹² The stations, particularly the smaller, educationally oriented stations, were in Whitehead's judgment the system's most conservative elements, potential allies in reducing the influence of the "liberal" Washington organizations. By playing on their instinctual fears of centralized control, on their shared distrust of the Ford Foundation's role, and on their readiness to annex a larger share of the financial pie, Whitehead hoped to create distrust between the local stations and their national organizations, just as Agnew had sought months earlier to pit the network affiliates against their national news organizations.

The opening salvo in the Administration's divide-and-subdue strategy was loosed upon several hundred surprised public broadcasters on October 20, 1971. Whitehead had been invited to address the annual convention of the NAEB, educational broadcasting's professional association. The broadcasters, of course, hoped that Whitehead would come to the Miami meeting with encouraging news of the Administration's plans for long-range funding. They anticipated at least a grudging pat on the back for having achieved, by dumping NET and creating PBS, the decentralized system the Administration apparently desired. Whitehead's words betrayed expectations on both counts. His pat on the back was brief and barbed: "It would be refreshing for you, I'm sure, to hear a convention speaker dwell on all the good things that public broadcasting has accomplished . . . but government policy making doesn't usually concern itself with good news, it deals with problems, and policy is my topic today." With that, Whitehead plunged headlong into a loose discourse on "policy," striking one rhetorical blow after another at the leadership and direction of public broadcasting. He charged it with betraying the mandate of the Carnegie Commission by creating a national network in the form of PBS, with allowing the network to take control of programming, with measuring successes by the same ratings yardstick that the networks used, and, finally, with turning over control of public-affairs programs to the Ford Foundation.

His final words sounded ominously like a threat: "Do any of you honestly know whether public broadcasting—structured as it is today and moving in the direction it seems to be headed—can ever fulfill the promise envisioned for it or conform to the policy set for it? If it can't, then permanent financing will always be somewhere off in the distant future."[13] The message was clear and unmistakable: conform to what we in the White House want public television to be or be prepared to forgo the Administration's support for continued federal funding. Public broadcasters reacted with disappointment and indignation. The Corporation leaped to the system's defense in a memorandum prepared by Macy's lieutenant, John Witherspoon. The memorandum accused the White House of using funding to pressure the system into acceding to the Administration's demands. "If we yield to that [pressure]," warned Witherspoon, "it will be well known that we can be had."[14]

Most people in the system had no quarrel with Whitehead's basic thesis; they were as wedded to the primacy of the local station (as opposed to centralized program control) as was he. But they were baffled by his charge that public television had abandoned localism when the charge was clearly contradicted by the facts. If the White House felt the system had not moved far enough, or fast enough, let them find the fault within themselves for failing to provide adequate funding. Witherspoon's memo reminded Whitehead that another Nixon stalwart, FCC Chairman Dean Burch, had told this same group of public broadcasters a year earlier that "it ill behooves the Federal government to look askance at public broadcasting when the government has not fulfilled its own promise."[15]

The Nixon Administration was fully aware of the populist appeal of an attack upon centralized power, and it had no shame in using the pulpit of its own highly centralized power to decry this power in those whom it wished to destroy. The Administration's attack was ironically made easier because many in the ranks of the public medium were crusading to save the medium from centralized power. Only three months earlier, at another gathering of public broadcasting executives, Arthur L. Singer, Jr., one of those responsible for the formation of the 1967 Carnegie Commission, used its recommendations to flay public broadcasters for casting their medium in the mold of commercial television. Its national programming, he charged, "is every bit as centralized and in its own way as dehumanized as the network programming of CBS or NBC," and its local stations were mere "branch offices for Washington and New York."[16] His words, startlingly similar to those uttered later in the year by Whitehead, gave a false ring of legitimacy to the White House's spurious concern for the plight of the local stations and further undermined the leadership role of the national organizations.

In his initial attack upon public television, Whitehead had judiciously steered clear of criticizing program content. But in early 1972 he opened a new front, questioning "whether public television, particularly . . . the federally-funded part of public television, should be carrying public affairs and news commentary, and that kind of thing."[17] He repeated his doubts a month later, telling Bill Moyers that federally funded public-affairs programs raised a serious question of principle "because here you're taking the taxpayer's money and using it to express controversial points of view."[18] (His question of principle conveniently ignored the accepted use of taxpayers' money to support the expression of controversial points of view in such publicly supported but less visible institutions as schools, colleges, and public libraries.) The Nixon Administration's opposition to our public-affairs programming stemmed in part from its profound distrust of the Ford Foundation and what it thought was the Foundation's Svengali role in our "anti-Administration" public-affairs programs. That the Foundation had an important hand in our public-affairs programming was clear, but it was a hand that fostered the genre without dictating its content, a conceit that may be too complex for the obsessed to grasp. The Nixon forces were convinced that if the Foundation was paying the piper, the Foundation must be calling the tune.[19]

Given the nature of our programming mission and the White House's sensitivity to criticism, provocation was probably inevitable. We did not, however, deliberately invite it. The decision to treat difficult and ticklish problems at the risk of inviting a torrent of calumny from Washington was our own to make; we didn't need the complicity of the Ford Foundation to get our names on the Administration's "enemies list." But provocation came easily and often to an Administration that measured balance by the congruence of our biases with theirs.

One such provocation was *Banks and the Poor*, broadcast in late 1971. The controversial documentary tripped the White House alarms, sending presidential assistant Peter Flanigin flying to his typewriter to dash off a memo to Albert Cole, Nixon's first appointee to the CPB board. Describing *Banks and the Poor* as "another example of NET activity that is clearly inappropriate for a government supported organization," Flanigin asked Cole to inquire into the extent of NET's present and planned future support from CPB. He cautioned that the inquiry "comes better from you to the board and management of the Corporation than from the White House."[20]

The response of public television's leaders in Washington to the Administration's efforts to bring it to heel showed the limits of its strange hydra-headed leadership. PBS president Hartford Gunn, responsible for what aired nationally, played a defensive game: keep your head down, play it safe, don't make waves. His efforts to block the airing of *Banks and the Poor* was a case in point, and his constituency, the local stations to whom he was accountable, would not have wished it otherwise. Had he wanted to stand up to government, to assert the independence of the public system, he could not have done so without the concurrence of the system's other leader, CPB president John Macy. But Macy, who had spent virtually all of his professional career in government service, and who, rightly or wrongly, felt himself accountable to Congress, had little or no inclination to buck the White House. An amenable man, he aimed to appease the enemy by showing his readiness to cooperate. He demonstrated this strategy of appeasement when he adopted the Administration's "program priorities"; when he accepted Herb Klein's suggestion of Nancy Dickerson as the PBS correspondent to the White House; and when he showed his readiness to meet with Flanigin and Whitehead to supply them with information, including a list of forthcoming public-affairs programming. "You couldn't ask for anyone more compliant than Macy," said OTP attorney Henry Goldberg.[21] The divided and unassertive posture of public television's leadership contrasted sharply with the early experience of the BBC, whose sole leader, Director-General John Reith, his spine stiffened with a morally rigid Calvinism, stood off the Parliament and secured for the public corporation an independence from governmental interference that marked the BBC for decades afterward. A comparable act of self-definition might have spared the American system its years of obeisance to the whims of Washington.

Macy's efforts to play the Administration's game had an ironic aftermath. Whitehead wanted him out. ''To achieve your goals,'' he told the president, ''we must first replace the current CPB management,'' recommending that they begin immediately ''to find five tough-minded [board] appointees who will vote with us to fire John Macy and his top staff and replace them with suitable people.''[22] With Macy out of the way, Whitehead could push ahead with his plan of reform: restructuring the system, reducing the funds and power of CPB, and transferring both the money and the power to the more conservative local stations. ''We cannot get the Congress to eliminate CPB, to reduce funds for public television, or to exclude CPB from public affairs programming,'' he told the president. ''But we can reform the *structure* of public broadcasting to eliminate its worst features.''[23] It was a shrewd strategy, a means of ''defanging'' the system without seeming to be involved.

The Whitehead strategy had another, complementary element that was both diabolical in design and Machiavellian in purpose. It was triggered by NPACT's announcement of the hiring of Sanders Vanocur and Robert MacNeil. Whitehead outlined his plan in a memorandum to White House chief of staff H. R. Haldeman:

After Vanocur and MacNeil were announced in late September, we planted with the trade press the idea that their obvious liberal bias would reflect adversely on public television. . . . We then began to encourage speculation about Vanocur's and MacNeil's salaries. . . . We plan to do two things in the next few weeks to continue to call attention to balance on public television, especially NPACT. We will quietly solicit critical articles regarding Vanocur's salary coming from public funds. . . . We will quietly encourage station managers throughout the country to put pressure on NPACT and CPB to put balance in their programming or risk the possibility of local stations not carrying these programs.[24]

Thus began one of the ugliest episodes in the story of public television, a malicious campaign, cynically managed from the White House, to discredit the public medium and two of its most visible professionals. The purpose of the campaign was clearly and simply to foster suspicion and distrust among the public medium's constituent elements. Sadly, by capturing the headlines it would divert attention from the more serious issues for most of the rest of the year. The White House media managers were fully aware of the effectiveness of the salary issue as a headline grabber. Revelations of the usually close-kept secrets of what the mighty are paid hold an inexplicable fascination for the average citizen. So when it was revealed through press leaks that Sander Vanocur was paid $85,000 a year—twice the salary of a Supreme Court justice, a cabinet officer, or a Congressional representative—there was no dearth of hand-wringers to condemn public television for its excesses. (Robin MacNeil's $65,000 salary made a smaller target only because he was, at that time, a less visible presence.) No mention was made, of course, of the 40 percent pay cut Vanocur took when he moved from NBC to NPACT. Nor was consideration given to the standard pay scales in television's big-buck talent business.

The salary fever spread quickly to Congress, where Rep. Lionel Van Deerlin, member of the House Communications Subcommittee, and himself a former television news commentator, held hearings to probe public television's salary scales. Macy, asked to supply the subcommittee with NPACT's salaries, readily complied. NPACT's chairman, Sid James, was furious that Macy had released the privileged information without NPACT's consent. But his heated protest backfired. The CPB board, unwilling to stand up to Congressional interference, adopted a policy of salary disclosure that led the Corporation to publish the salaries and talent fees of all of its principal performers as well as the salaries of its own executives. (When Macy's annual $65,000 became public knowledge, he quickly volunteered to take a pay cut. But his board, less guided by the Puritan ethic of self-sacrifice, turned him down.) The hearings produced an amendment to the public-television-funding bill that fixed ceilings on public-television salaries paid from federal funds. The bill, however, was subsequently vetoed for reasons unrelated to the salary issue.

The Great Salary Dustup of 1972 had the Administration's intended effect on local stations. Their disaffection with national leadership was fed by a growing resentment over the five-digit salary disclosures, and even more by the whirlwind of criticism they were reaping for the apparent profligacy of one of their number. The greatest harm, however, fell upon NPACT. Karayn and his staff, preoccupied with juggling the politics of public television, barely had time to follow the political campaign of 1972, which, after all, was the primary reason for hiring the two correspondents. When NPACT did focus on the elections, its coverage was inevitably affected by the White House pressures. MacNeil, describing the pressures as "inhibiting but not paralyzing," confessed that it was difficult not to speculate on how one's story would play at the White House.[25] Critics found NPACT's programs in the series *A Public Affair: Election '72* too middle-of-the-road and often bland. The problem was "not that they were bland," explained Vanocur, "but that they weren't more daring." On the positive side, MacNeil thought the pressures made public television more conscious "of the need to be more balanced than we otherwise might have been if that climate hadn't existed."[26] But the climate did exist. And the pressures had their desired effect.

With summer approaching, and with it the two national political conventions, NPACT was forced to scrap its original plans for comprehensive, gavel-to-gavel coverage after the Corporation board cut a whopping 25 percent from its budget. One of Nixon's recent appointees to the board, Hollywood television producer Jack Wrather, explained that "because of the sensitive nature of public-affairs programming, a concentration of this kind of production in one or two stations is undesirable." To which he added, "Further decentralization and diversification would be healthy for the system."[27] Coming from one who had profited from the concentration of commercial production in Hollywood, not only were the words strange, but they also defied the logic of television. Some public-affairs shows, because of their complexity and cost, can only be done by concentrating resources. Political conventions are among them.

When the Democrats met in Miami in July, NPACT's pared-down coverage was a thin daily ninety-minute preview program plus a nightly half-hour summary of the day's events, less distinguished and certainly less informative than the convention coverage available elsewhere on the dial. It was not the vision Karayn had for NPACT. With the Republican convention only a month away, Karayn decided to do the job right and to give the Republicans straightforward, unedited, gavel-to-gavel podium coverage that would be a clear alternative to the networks' restless razzle-dazzle. But his two stars refused to go along, arguing that Karayn's plan gave unfair political advantage to the Republicans with an imbalance that could only lead to charges that NPACT had buckled under to White House pressures.[28] With Vanocur and MacNeil willing to do no more than they had done for the Democrats, Karayn turned to WNET's Bill Moyers for running commentary on the full coverage of the Republican Convention. Though he was unaware of the protests of the two NPACT correspondents, Moyers agreed that the Republicans should get full coverage despite NPACT's error in not giving proper coverage to the Democrats. Moyers brushed aside charges of White House intimidation, explaining that "no one can intimidate you unless you feel intimidatable."[29]

Before the storm over NPACT died down, Karayn added the name of Peter Kaye to his rosters of correspondents. No one challenged Kaye's credentials as a journalist. Skeptics, however, read significance into the fact he had been a Nixon press aide in the 1960 campaign.

The politically charged atmosphere of the early seventies should have warned those of us at NET that the times were hardly propitious for political satire—and certainly not on the public medium. But so eager were we to bring an element of lightness, a laugh or two, to public television's overarching solemnity that we unhesitatingly accepted Woody Allen's offer in late 1971 to produce a special. We didn't even pull back after learning that he intended to use the show to satirize the Nixon White House. Allen approached us after having produced two prime-time specials for the commercial networks, fully expecting the public medium to give him greater artistic license to write and perform the kind of humor for which he is justly celebrated. He was wrong.[30]

The script for the hour-long special was delivered to NET's veteran producer Jack Kuney. Although Kuney found it "deceptively

simple, but funny," his boss, programming vice president Bill Kobin, disagreed. Kobin came to my office a day or so later, script in
hand. "We can't use it." Why not? "Because it's not funny." I
accepted his judgment; the last thing we needed was an unfunny
comedy show. There the matter rested, or so I thought. Three
months later, however, I was more than a little surprised to learn
that we had delivered to PBS a show called *The Politics—and Comedy
of Woody Allen.* Receipt of the show tripped the alarm and bells
began to ring. First, I had a call from WNET's chairman Ethan
Allen Hitchcock. He had just heard from John Macy, who was
"hopping mad" about a show with someone named Allen. Hitchcock had never heard of Woody Allen. When he learned that I
had not seen the show, I was ordered to screen it and call him
back immediately. Even as we talked, a telex message was thrust
into my hand from PBS to its member stations. *The Politics—and
Comedy of Woody Allen,* it said, would not be distributed by PBS as
scheduled. But taking no chances on being labelled "censors"—
as they had been when they killed the FBI segment on the *Dream
Machine*—PBS offered to make the show available to any station
requesting it. There was a hook in the offer: in the opinion of the
PBS legal staff, the Woody Allen show "presents fairness problems
. . . personal attack, equal time and taste problems," a solid guarantee that no public station in the country would risk airing it.[31]
Except, of course, our own WNET.

What I and a brace of our attorneys screened with nervous interest was a mock documentary, *Men of Crisis,* that mimicked the
style of the old *March of Time,* in which authentic news footage was
combined with dramatic elements, a technique Allen later per-
fected in his feature film *Zelig.* The original hour-long script had
been trimmed to the twenty-five-minute "documentary," and the
balance of the hour had been filled by an interview with Allen on
the nature of comedy. *Men of Crisis* managed not only to lampoon
the Nixon White House but to needle both the president's foes
(Humphrey and Wallace) as well as his friends (Agnew, Hoover,
Laird, and Mitchell). Allen himself played the fictional Harvey
Wallinger, high-living confidant and counselor to the president,
whose resemblance to National Security Advisor Henry Kissinger

was more than coincidental. As might be expected, the show included moments of questionable taste. Allen explained that "it is hard to do anything about the Administration that wouldn't be in bad taste."[32]

I withdrew the show after the screening, hoping to find a broader context to make *Men of Crisis* acceptable to the system, perhaps by marrying it with other satirical pieces that took aim with prudent impartiality at a broader range of political icons. But it was too late. Though I rejected Hitchcock's demand to arrange a private screening for WNET's Executive Committee to determine the film's acceptability, he managed a surreptitious screening for himself. He emerged from the screening ashen-faced, his jaws tightly clamped, and hurried back to his law offices where he dashed off a hand-delivered letter to me within the hour. He first reminded me that it had been the hope and purpose of the board never to have to judge a program before broadcast, but, he said, "The Allen program has, in my opinion, now been removed from that category because of the questions inherent in it and which have been raised within the public television system." There followed an ultimatum: "If you, for any reason, desire to release the program in its present form or any modified form for any showing of any kind, you will first advise me, or, should I not be available, two other members of the Executive Committee, in sufficient time in advance of such a release to permit the Executive Committee to be convened and review whatever you propose to be released."[33]

There the Woody Allen caper ended. It was apparent to me that a board committee, and especially one weighted with Nixon partisans, would hardly be willing to allow the show to air and risk the economic reprisals of an irate White House. Jay Iselin made a feint in the direction of airing it, but his flashy backfield manner was no match for the Executive Committee's tight line. Nor were the other PBS stations willing to take the risk; they leaned heavily on the warning words of the PBS lawyers to defend their decision. (PBS was in error in stating that the show would trigger demands for equal time; political satire is exempt from equal-time rules.) Placed beside the political skits on today's *Saturday Night Live*, Allen's satire seems pallid and harmless. But times and tastes change. In 1972, the Nixon White House, clean as a hound's tooth, was on the threshold of an electoral landslide. Watergate was no more than a cloud on the horizon, barely larger than the hand that taped open the door to the Democratic National Committee headquarters. If we were disingenuous in thinking that we could get by the station gatekeepers with a show that might offend our chief sponsor, we did so firmly believing that satire, holding up to view our individual and collective absurdities, has a cleansing effect on the body politic. *The Politics—and Comedy of Woody Allen* may or may not have been the best-suited vehicle for our purpose—Allen has since expressed his own reservations—but its intentions were rooted in an honorable tradition.[34]

Beneath the tensions created by the salary squabble and the Woody Allen episode was concern over how these incidents might play upon public television's quest for the holy grail of long-range funding. Encouraging signals issued from Capitol Hill, but the Administration had its own agenda. Early in 1971, Tom Whitehead sought the help of a former University of Virginia law professor, Antonin Scalia, in drafting the Administration's long-range funding bill. Although Scalia's bill provided for a surprising five-year authorization, which was longer than expected, it also mandated a larger proportion of the federal funds to be allocated to the local stations. Macy immediately denounced it as "a sweeping amendment to the 1967 Act," clearly intended to reduce "the scope and function of the CPB."[35] He was right. It cleverly advanced Whitehead's plan to redirect funds away from CPB and PBS and into the pockets of the more "congenial" local stations. When Whitehead attempted to work out a compromise bill satisfactory to the Corporation, he increasingly came to feel that Macy was the stumbling block to achieving his aim. So in a wily maneuver to remove the obstacle, Whitehead recommended that the president offer his loyalists on the CPB board a trade-off: the Administration would deliver a funding bill acceptable to the Corporation in return for the board's agreement to "replace John Macy as soon as practicable with a nonpolitical professional."[36] The White House, not yet ready to go public with its hostility toward the medium, rejected the stratagem. Whitehead offered another. Blithely assuming that "local stations' support could be bought for about 30 million dollars," Whitehead proposed a two-year bill that offered a boost in the funding limits from $35 to $60 million for the first year. He fully expected that the additional funds would separate the stations from the Corporation and win (or buy) their support for the Administration's original bill.[37]

But events intervened. Nixon exploded and gave an order to "kill the bill" after learning of Vanocur's appointment, and Whitehead, following the White House lead, went to Miami to deliver his "no funds until reform" ultimatum to the public broadcasters. In the long run, the Administration produced a chastening and meager one-year funding bill, cutting back the funding limits to $45 million. Hopes for long-range funding rested with a more amenable Congress. In 1971, Rep. Torbert Macdonald, chairman of the House Communications Subcommittee, took the initiative by introducing a five-year funding bill that, after compromises, reached the floor as a two-year authorization of $65 million the first year and $90 million the second. Although it mandated a sizeable 30 percent of the funds to the stations, Macy, after raising a finger to the political winds, accepted the provision knowing that it would help to win station support for the bill. Whitehead, predictably, testified against it. Fortunately, the bill had strong support in both houses and sailed through with substantial majorities. It was a major victory for the public medium and a cause for celebration.

The jubilation was short-lived. On June 30, 1972, four days after the Senate adopted the Macdonald Bill by an overwhelming 82–1 majority, President Nixon vetoed it.[38] His veto message cited "the serious and widespread concern expressed in Congress and within public broadcasting itself, that an organization, originally intended only to serve the local stations, is becoming instead the center of power and the focal point of control for the entire public broadcasting system."[39] Nixon's words were a cynical replay of Whitehead's obsessive invocation of "localism." Congress, stunned but uncertain that it had the votes to override the veto, made no effort to do so, voting instead to accept the Administration's niggardly single-year funding bill.

News of the veto rocked the system like a temblor; most of us had expected the president to yield to the clearly expressed will of Congress. Only four days before the veto, Tom Whitehead assured Norman Cousins and the members of his National Programming Council that "if the Congress votes [the Macdonald Bill], the President will do nothing to prevent that action moving forward."[40] Only after the release of confidential White House documents did we learn that, on the afternoon that he had assured us of the president's support, Whitehead had been closeted with the president and a group of commercial broadcasters. In the words of one who was present at the meeting, President Nixon "dumped all over public television" in response to the broadcasters' complaints of competition from a growing PBS.[41] Four days after assuring us there would be no veto, Whitehead sent a secret memorandum to the president strongly recommending a veto of the funding bill and warning him that public broadcasters "are seeking funds and independence to create a TV network reflecting their narrow conception of what the public ought to see and hear." This, he told the president, "should not be allowed to happen."[42] It would be an understatement to describe his role in the veto as a model of dissimulation.

For a weary, frustrated, and ailing John Macy, the veto was the last straw. He had fought hard for the funding bill only to see it killed by an Administration he had tried desperately to accommodate. Worse, he felt abandoned by his own friends and allies at a critical time in the life of public television. The CPB board, which might have been expected to protest the veto, sat on its hands, making no comment and refusing even to rebut the implied challenge to its stewardship. Macy called it "shameful." But he was caught in a no-win situation and he knew it. He also knew that Nixon's chances for reelection were virtually assured. The reelection, said Macy privately, would be "the death blow to public broadcasting as I have envisioned it." His health weakened by abdominal surgery, and "convinced that my incompatibility with administration positions would endanger the system," John Macy resigned the presidency of CPB on August 10, 1972.[43] In the weeks that followed, most of the Corporation's top executives followed suit. The Corporation, created by Congress as a "heat shield" to insulate public broadcasting against political interference, had in five short years become the instrument of that interference.

13

THE MAN WHO SAVED
PUBLIC TELEVISION

What is emerging is not public television but government television shaped by politically conscious appointees whose desire to avoid controversy could turn CPB into the Corporation for Public Blandness.

Bill Moyers[1]

The next six months were easily the most crucial in the troubled history of the public medium, threatening to consume forever the hopes of the first Carnegie Commission for an independent voice with "the freedom to create, freedom to innovate, freedom to be heard."[2]

John Macy's resignation from the CPB in August—and Frank Pace's resignation as board chairman a bit earlier—gave the White House the opening it needed to consolidate its control over the public-television system. Although they had sought control earlier, particularly with the appointment in the spring of 1972 of six Nixon loyalists to the Corporation board, the Administration was still shy of its needed majority on the fifteen-member board. Now, with the additional vacancies, the time was ripe for a move. The White House filled one of the vacancies with Thomas B. Curtis, a former Republican congressman from Missouri. In what was a foregone conclusion engineered by the White House, Curtis was elected chairman, succeeding Pace, at the board's first meeting following Macy's resignation. (Whitehead had pushed for the appointment of the politically conservative scholar and author Irving Kristol, but Nixon's friend John Olin had persuaded him to name

Curtis.)[3] That accomplished, Jack Wrather then nominated Henry
Loomis to succeed John Macy in the Corporation presidency.
Loomis, the deputy director of the Voice of America, was the
White House's handpicked candidate for the post. But another
director objected: "We can't be voting for a president that this
board hasn't even met, for God's sake."[4] Whereupon Wrather
rang Loomis at his USIA office, had him rush over to be interviewed briefly by the board, and saw him elected unanimously.
Loomis, like his predecessor, had spent most of his career in government service. But unlike Macy, the new president was independently wealthy. He could look upon government service from
the comfort of his Virginia estate with an air of noblesse oblige.
What he could not look upon, however, was the service he was
now hired to head; because his estate was beyond the range of
WETA / Washington's UHF signal, he boasted of never having
viewed public television ("If innocence is a virtue, I am very vir-
tuous").[5] Moreover, until his appointment he had never heard of
the Corporation for Public Broadcasting ("What the hell is it?"
he was reported to have asked).[6] But with the appointments of
Curtis and Loomis, the White House was now firmly in control of
the Corporation. The stage was set for the next move.

Nixon's November landslide victory over George McGovern in-
tensified Nixon's determination to silence his critics. In the inel-
egant words of Nixon aide John Dean, the goal was "the use of
the available machinery of government to screw our enemies."[7]
Public television, one of those putative "enemies," was involved
in a high-stakes game in which the other player held all the face
cards. Worse, we were up against an adversary whose policies
were informed by a cynicism that overshadowed reason. The Administration's narrowly targeted objective was to rid the public-
television system of the programs they found offensive by the
quickest means possible. Whitehead's strategy of neutralizing the
system by sharing power with the more conservative stations was
abandoned after the presidential veto of the funding bill, giving
way to Ehrlichman's strategy of direct action aimed at bringing
the system under the Administration's thumb. OTP's attorney
Henry Goldberg summed up the Administration's aims: "They

didn't care about structure, didn't care about localism, didn't care about decentralization or insulated funding. They cared about 'them' and 'us.' "[8]

Henry Loomis figured prominently in the White House's plan of action. His announcement immediately after taking office that "cpb intends to exercise control over program judgments" signaled unswerving loyalty to the Administration's aims.[9] The game plan became clear with a telex to the system's producing stations announcing that henceforth all proposals for new programs were to be submitted not to pbs as in previous years, but directly to the Corporation. It was not clear whether Loomis fully understood the limited role that Congress had intended for the Corporation and the crucial fact that it was a nongovernmental entity. His actions gave rise to speculation, both in public-television circles and in the press, that he was embarked on a course to turn public television into a "domestic Voice of America." Less than two months after taking over, he sent Whitehead a 276-page document listing all the staff's program recommendations for the coming season. Attached to the document was a note: "Tom—this is our 'burn before reading document.' No one knows you have it. [signed] HL."[10] His seeming lack of concern for the Corporation's independence, including his frequent contacts with presidential aides and his readiness to consult with them on planning, raised our collective fears and fed our doubts.

One incident in particular fueled those doubts. A month after taking office, Loomis blithely bypassed pbs, the system's established mechanism for distributing programs, and approached the stations directly with a proposal to provide twenty-one hours of live coverage of the Apollo 17 moon flight. The three-day telecast would be funded and produced by the National Aeronautics and Space Administration. pbs reacted with predictable resentment, not only at having its role usurped by the Corporation, but also at what it saw as an ominous precedent, "like letting General Motors underwrite and produce programs for public television on car safety."[11] Luckily, nasa, sensing a system-wide controversy, backed down on its offer to fund the telecast, and consequently the Corporation withdrew its proposal as well. If Loomis imagined that his offer would have been embraced by the PBS stations, he was given a rude shock by the blunt message from KETC, the St. Louis public station: "Get the hell out of programming and stay out."[12]

The Corporation, of course, had no intention of getting out of programming. On the contrary, it was clearly determined to seize control and to eliminate those programs that the Administration found offensive. Any doubts about its resolve were settled on January 10, 1973. That was the day Loomis was directed by his board to produce "at the earliest possible date" a plan to "establish, solely within the Corporation, the staff and resources necessary" to take over from PBS all responsibility for national programming.[13] PBS was to be relegated to the purely technical function of operating the interconnection, the lines used for delivery of programs to the stations. The crucial decisions about which programs were to be delivered—including their funding and production—would henceforth rest with the Corporation, and specifically with the board's Program Committee headed by Jack Wrather, the Hollywood television producer responsible for such television classics as *Lassie, The Lone Ranger,* and *Strike It Rich.*

Reaction to the Corporation's heavy-handed seizure of program control was immediate and harsh. John Macy told a Columbia-Dupont Award audience that "the heat shield [has been] penetrated and video journalism, public style, severely burned."[14] An unidentified public-broadcasting "pioneer" told a *Newsweek* reporter with bleak finality, "I think public television is washed up."[15] The press joined the baleful chorus. Cecil Smith told his *Los Angeles Times* readers that "the long-predicted emasculation of public television has begun,"[16] while in the *New York Daily News,* Kay Gardella led her story on the coup with "the death knell was sounded this week."[17] It was a grim assessment of the present and an even grimmer forecast for the future of a medium that seemed to be perpetually in crisis.

A month after the board resolution that cast the Corporation in the programmer's role, a "partial" list of approved programs was announced. Dropped from consideration—at least for the time being—were public television's principal public-affairs series: *Bill Moyers' Journal*, Elizabeth Drew's *Thirty Minutes With . . .* , WETA's *Washington Week in Review*, and KQED's *World Press Review*. Loomis "explained" the loss of the programs with the rationalization that money spent on public-affairs shows was less "efficient" because the shows become outdated so quickly. Curiously, the sweep of topical programs even removed William Buckley's *Firing Line*, often cited by critics as public television's "token" conservative show. (Rumor had it that Buckley's opposition to Nixon's historic trip to China entitled him to a place on the Administration's "enemies list.")

Only one major public-affairs show was spared, Tony Brown's *Black Journal*, and then only because Brown, a scrappy veteran of broadcasting politics, saw the handwriting on the wall, mobilized his black constituency, and successfully pressured the Corporation to reverse its earlier decision to drop the show. NPACT (by then merged into Washington's WETA) also made the approved list with its proposed series *America '73*. But when the producers learned the conditions of the grant—every program in the series was subject to the Corporation's prior approval—they said "No thanks" and turned the grant down. Of the prime-time topical shows, only WGBH's *The Advocates* survived the purge. The show featured advocates on opposite sides of a topical issue arguing their cases in a courtroom-like setting. The series was so carefully balanced, quipped *Variety*, that "viewers are likely to get two sides of the Adolph Hitler stories and the pros and cons of drug abuse."[18]

Seizure of program control by the Corporation sent shock waves through the system, leaving in its wake, said Robert MacNeil, "sadly disillusioned people" watching "their dream being perverted . . . [and] their ideal of independence made a travesty by Mr. Nixon's appointees."[19] MacNeil's show, *Washington Week in Review*, was a victim of the purge. The pervasive disillusionment left little room for an appreciation of the ironies in the situation: an Administration that said one thing and did another, that preached decentralization and practiced the worst kind of centralized control. When Nixon charged PBS with becoming the "center of power and the focal point of control," as he did in his veto message, he effectively defined "centralization" as control of programming by 150 independent local stations. In this Alice in Wonderland world, "decentralization" came to mean the monolithic control of programming by the Corporation and its White House minions. But inconsistency was no problem for Tom Whitehead; he brushed it aside explaining that "you have to take power in order to disperse it."[20] His logic would have delighted the Red Queen. However, Henry Greenburg, his own general counsel, warned the OTP head that the inconsistency was so apparent "our motives become suspect and the continued restatement of the localism goal is discounted as simply not being credible."[21]

While the Nixon team clothed its purpose in disarming rhetoric, using such felicitous terms as "decentralization" and "localism," its true aims were deceptively simple. Put bluntly by White House aide Jon Rose, it was "to get the left-wing commentators who are cutting us up off public television at once, indeed yesterday if possible."[22] At the time, we could only guess at their aims by their actions; we were not privy to the White House's internal communications. The truth came to light years later with the release of documents under the Freedom of Information Act. But if a clue were needed, the president's outspoken and garrulous speechwriter Patrick Buchanan could be counted on to supply it. Early in 1973, Buchanan appeared on the *Dick Cavett Show.* In the course of defending the Administration's heavy-handed policies toward public television, he told Cavett that the Corporation, with its "new board," had "a new awareness" of the people's interest in "balance." By way of explaining the Administration's concept of balance, he ran down virtually the entire roster of PBS public-affairs shows—among them, *Washington Week in Review, Bill Moyers' Journal,* and *Black Journal*—and charged each one with being "balanced against us."[23] It confirmed what we had guessed. Our differences were not philosophical—Buchanan's remarks had stripped the Administration's policies of any philosophical importance—but tactical. It was simply a matter of "them" against "us."

PBS, powerless to block the co-option of its programming functions by the Corporation, was caught in a power play that consigned it to a purely technical function. The *New York Times* called it "a wholly disowned subsidiary."[24] Tension between the two, always present, grew ugly in early 1973 with the Corporation's move to take over the entire game. Trouble between PBS and the CPB was as predictable as it was inevitable. They were both victims of a byzantine structure that only a committee (in this case, the Carnegie Commission) could have designed: two opposing forces, delicately counterpoised, one with all the money, the other with all the stations, and both with the primal urge to be programmers. Frictions inherent in the structure were compounded by factionalism in the two staffs. Macy and Gunn, in the early days, had been able to maintain a thin veneer of collegiality; many people on their staffs had previously worked together elsewhere. Loomis, however, brought a whole new team to the Corporation, and with each of their positions carved in granite, jealousies raged. The resulting discord exhausted energies and eroded morale; worse, it showed up on the television screen. *Variety* called 1972–73 a "Floppo Season" for public broadcasting and reported that it was "by far the worst yet in the short, troubled history of the network."[25]

PBS did its best to tough it out. The PBS board reaffirmed by resolution its belief that "the Congress never intended for this country to have a centralized broadcasting system."[26] The resolution, hardly more than a rhetorical flourish, was followed by PBS president Hartford Gunn's effort to rally member stations by reminding them that the issue was "first and foremost . . . how you at the stations want the public television system to operate."[27] But the best cards in the game were held by the Corporation—it had the money as well as the backing of the White House—rather than by the paid professionals who managed the stations and made up the board of PBS. Their largely futile efforts to defend themselves were, said one observer, little more than "an elaborate dance of death."[28]

And then, suddenly and miraculously, a shift occurred that in a curious way anticipated the fall of the Nixon Administration. The earliest indications of the shift showed up in the reactions of an audience "aroused over the White House maneuvers to control the medium and . . . over the White House declarations and ac-

tions to squelch news and public affairs on the national PTV network."[29] Letters began to pour into public television's mail rooms.
In the early months of 1973, after Robert MacNeil told his *Washington Week in Review* audience that the show was in jeopardy at the
hands of the White House, his office was swamped with more than
13,000 responses.[30] Local stations experienced a similar outpouring of viewer support, some even reporting an "unprecedented"
response to their fund appeals. Public television, perhaps for the
first time, became aware of a loyal constituency large enough to
make a difference when the chips were down.

But gratifying as it was, viewer support alone could not face
down the powers in the White House. The beleaguered state of
the public system cried out for leadership, for a strong and effective leader with the will to take command and the clout to be heard
in the Oval Office. It was unlikely to come from the ranks of the
system's own leaders; the Public Broadcasting Act of 1967 had
diffused the leadership by spreading it among the many constituent elements of the system, the better to ensure against centralized control. Even the PBS presidency, which certainly held a potential for strong leadership, was kept on a short leash by the
member stations, which feared that an ambitious occupant might
undermine their independence. Leadership of the type and
strength needed could only come from outside the ranks of the
public-television professionals. Fortunately, it did emerge in the
person of Ralph B. Rogers, a blunt-spoken, white-haired, self-
made millionaire from Dallas. Although a native New Englander,
Rogers had made his modest fortune in the Lone Star State in the
concrete construction business. His energies, however, could not
be contained by Texas Industries alone; they were turned to a
variety of civic responsibilities. After rescuing the Dallas Symphony from early retirement, he was drafted by the moribund
KERA / Dallas public-television station to save it as well. With Rogers as board chairman and his young assistant from Texas Industries, Robert Wilson, as general manager, KERA was transformed
into one of the system's brightest and liveliest stations. The Dallas
success story led to Rogers's election to the NET board, where the
transplanted Bostonian first became involved in public television's

national affairs. Shortly thereafter, when the Children's Television Workshop separated from NET, Rogers was invited to become one of its founding directors. His commonsense counsel and business acumen helped CTW launch its earliest ventures into the commercial world of product licensing.

None of these posts, however, positioned Rogers to become "The Man Who Saved Television," the title conferred upon him by a grateful public-television community when he retired in 1976. That episode began with his participation in the push to win Congressional approval for the Macdonald long-range funding bill. In previous years, public broadcasting's own professional association, the NAEB, had taken the lead in lobbying Congress. While the paid staff had been reasonably effective with Congress, public television was not taking advantage of the most effective voices for selling our cause, namely the volunteer community leaders on our local boards. With Fred Friendly's encouragement, I arranged a meeting of the chairpersons of the seven largest stations with the goal of creating a legislative committee. Rogers was the obvious choice to chair it; in addition to his organizing successes in Dallas, his service as finance chairman of George Bush's first successful campaign in Texas for the U.S. Senate gave him credence with the party in power in Washington. The committee of seven met only once. The smaller stations, fearing a conspiracy of the big stations, pressured Rogers to broaden the committee to include each of PBS's stations, large and small. With NAEB's help, Rogers soon convened the lay-leaders of the system's local stations, formed the Governing Board Chairmen's Group, and was elected its leader. The group's first meeting closed in euphoria with the news that Congress had passed the Macdonald Bill by overwhelming majorities. Unfortunately, the euphoria was short-lived. On the following day, President Nixon vetoed the bill, and, with a stroke of the presidential pen, unwittingly endowed the lay-leaders with a renewed mission. Rogers embraced the mission as his personal cause.

To make certain that he had the support of the fractious stations, Rogers convened a series of regional meetings with the local managers, only to find that some of them resisted the move to place the system's fate in the hands of board members, "nonprofessionals" with no experience in broadcasting. Rogers, a diplomat, but one with little patience with parochial attitudes, persuaded the more reluctant among them to accept the leadership of the new group. That done, he asked for and was granted a meeting with the Nixon-dominated Corporation board, a meeting for which the station managers had tried earlier but had been denied. Rogers addressed the key issue. "Freedom of the interconnection," he told them, "is the air we breathe."[31] To secure that freedom for PBS, he asked the Corporation board for two concessions: consultation with the stations before funding programs from federal funds; and access to the interconnection for programs funded with private, nongovernmental dollars. He didn't get the concessions immediately, but the directors were impressed with the man from Dallas. He indulged in no name-calling, placed no blame, and made his case with directness, conviction, and passion. Arrangements were made for further meetings.

Meanwhile, Rogers, with the support of the Ford Foundation, pressed for yet another restructuring of the public-television system, one that would rationalize the way the stations voiced their collective concerns to Washington. Two Washington organizations, PBS and the Educational Television Stations division of the NAEB, both made up entirely of professional broadcasters, had represented public television's interests in the capital prior to the formation of the Rogers group. The Corporation board had seized on the divided leadership as an excuse for not meeting with either, asking rhetorically, "Who do we meet with?" The chairpersons' group added a third element, but one that the Corporation's board could ill afford to ignore, with its unified leadership in the hands of well-placed and influential laypeople. By agreeing to meet with Roger's group and not with the other two, the Corporation sent a clear signal to the system: it was prepared to deal only with its lay leaders.

By March 1973, the professionals' resistance to the new "nonprofessional" leadership began to melt away in the face of an increasingly desperate situation. With only a single dissenting vote they merged their two professional organizations, PBS and ETS / NAEB, into the chairperson's group. They retained the PBS name and restructured the new entity to accommodate two boards, one of elected chairpersons for "policy" and one of elected station chiefs for "management."[32] Rogers, recalling public television's proclivity for infinite subdivision, referred to the three-into-one merger as a "miracle."[33] It would be the last major restructuring of the public-television establishment for more than a decade.

With the merger accomplished, Rogers resumed his efforts to resolve the differences between PBS and the Corporation. His early meetings were with the Corporation's three-person negotiating committee—Thomas Moore, Jack Valenti, and James Killian—but as time passed he turned more and more to board chairman Thomas Curtis, with whom he seemed to have a special chemistry. By early April, the two chairmen reached a compromise: the Corporation would have the final say on how federal funds were to be spent, and the stations would gain some measure of control over scheduling and have access to the interconnection for privately funded programs. Valenti and Killian were prepared to recommend acceptance of the compromise to the full board with the hope that it would "extract the thorns of discontent, disaffection and persistent controversy that have infected public and private views of the current public broadcasting arena."[34] The compromise would be presented at the next board meeting, ominously set for Friday, April 13th.

Rogers, preparing to holiday in Portugal and confident that the fracas was finally at an end, left behind a draft memorandum to go to the stations after the Corporation's expected acceptance of the agreement: "At this point it is important to put aside all the animosities of the past. Let's start a clean sheet."[35] But he and Thomas Curtis had grossly misjudged the board's mood. By a 10–4 majority, it voted to "defer action" on the agreement and turned further negotiations over to a new three-person committee, two of whom were considered "hard-liners."[36] Curtis resigned three days later, angry at what he felt was a betrayal by his friends in the Administration. In parting he charged that the White House had "tampered with" the independent board by making telephone calls to at least four board members on the eve of the board meeting. It was, he said, impossible to defend "the integrity of the board" now that it had been so thoroughly breached.[37]

The Curtis brouhaha gave the White House what it wanted—a defeat of the compromise agreement and the resignation of Curtis (the Administration had soured on him once he showed signs of independence). But Curtis's resignation was also an embarrassment. The press, seizing upon his charges, painted a picture of a White House filled with petty power grabbers whose deeds gave the lie to their pious utterances of support for public television's ideal of localism.

Whether, as Curtis claimed, telephone calls from the White House were actually made is less important than the documented evidence that the White House exerted continual pressure on the board, if not on the eve of the meeting, then at other times. According to memos and notes revealed later, on the day before the crucial April 13 meeting Curtis and Moore were called to Whitehead's office, told of the president's opposition to the compromise agreement, and warned that its adoption could mean another presidential veto of the funding bill. However, the story of the defeat of the agreement is not entirely a tale of furtive White House phone calls and threats of presidential vetoes. Perhaps a more crucial factor was the widespread antipathy toward Curtis among his fellow board members, many of whom felt that he was arrogant and at times insensitive, that he was given to temper tantrums and rigidly autocratic in his conduct of the meetings. The surmise that their hostility played a part in the defeat gained credibility with the board's action at its next meeting. It adopted an agreement almost identical to the one it had rejected four weeks earlier.

Whatever his abrasive qualities had been—he had apparently irritated virtually everyone he worked with except Ralph Rogers—Curtis had shown considerable integrity by staunchly defending the independence of the Corporation board. He was deeply disturbed by the continuing contacts of some of his board members with White House staff, but refused to believe talk about a "Nixon network." Less than two weeks before his stormy resignation, he told the *New York Times* that "President Nixon [has] instructed me to so structure CPB that this and no future administration will be able to make a political arm of it."[38] When the truth of the situation was finally revealed to him, he had no choice but to rescue his tattered integrity by resigning.

The shock of recognition that accompanied the Curtis charges proved to be a turning point, like the moment in an illness when the fever breaks and the healing begins. Nothing hastened the healing faster than the board's choice of James R. Killian, Jr., to succeed Curtis as chairman. Killian was the board's only political independent. Presumably above the fray of partisan politics, he represented the Corporation's best hope of shaking the image of White House control. Fortunately, he also had a good working relationship with the Corporation's chief executive. The two men had worked together before. Henry Loomis had been Killian's assistant at MIT and later had served as his staff director while Killian was science adviser to President Eisenhower. Their easy relationship contrasted sharply with the muted hostility that had kept Loomis and Curtis at each other's throats until the day Curtis resigned.

Before he accepted the position, Killian wisely laid down five conditions. Among them was an end to White House interference and a speedy completion of the agreement with PBS. The board accepted the conditions without argument and then, as if to give Killian his due, approved a draft proposal for a partnership agreement with PBS. The compromise, however, was not fully satisfactory to either party. Particularly objectionable was a provision for a committee to decide which shows would go on the interconnection. This committee of seven—three from the Corporation, three from PBS, and one from the outside—was disparaged by Rogers as the "seven-headed monster." The Corporation, however, did show a new willingness to bend on principle by resuming its funding of Buckley's *Firing Line* and WETA's *Washington Week in Review*. Both shows had been dropped earlier as "inappropriate" to a federally funded medium.

At this crucial juncture, Congress jumped into the action. Rep. Torbert H. Macdonald, the influential chairman of the House

Subcommittee on Communications and Power, knocked heads together by handing Killian and Rogers an ultimatum: cut out the internal bickering and ensure against the future possibility of Administration control, or face a probable freeze on Congressional funding the following year.[39] Six days later, on May 24, 1973, the two men and their negotiating teams emerged from an all-day meeting with an agreement. The seven-point pact "insured public television licensees a crucial measure of control over their national service" by requiring the Corporation to consult with PBS on the shows it proposed to fund; granted PBS access for its privately funded shows; and left the interconnection's scheduling to be jointly administered: PBS was to propose a draft schedule over which the Corporation had final approval. Any differences were to be resolved by the chief executives of the two organizations. Six months of bickering and internal dispute were at an end—for the moment.[40]

The partial return of programming control to PBS and its stations left the Administration's game plan in disarray. "At this point," wrote Henry Goldberg to Tom Whitehead, his boss at OTP, "we are at or near the bottom of the 'slippery slope' we first set upon a year and half ago."[41] The Curtis resignation and its revelations of White House attempts to seize control of programming left Whitehead's cry for "localism" echoing off the walls with a mocking hollowness. It was time for a new strategy. Goldberg suggested calling together the Corporation, PBS, and other station interests "to work out a legislative restructuring of public broadcasting we can all support," but the odds didn't favor it. The three organizations—PBS, OTP, and the Corporation—differed on most things and nowhere more markedly than in their approaches to Congressional funding.

In early 1973, prior to Curtis's resignation, CPB president Henry Loomis had submitted to Congress a cautious budget that requested no more than the previous year's Congressional commitment of $35 million. The Administration's Office of Management and Budget responded with a recommended increase to $45 million and made clear to Loomis that "the President expects each and every official in the Corporation for Public Broadcasting to actively support the budget set forth in this letter."[42] The Corporation rebuked the OMB for treating it as another federal agency. "Your letter," Tom Curtis wrote, "assumes a degree of compliance not consistent with the independence of the board of directors of the Corporation acting in pursuit of the aims and objectives of the Public Broadcasting Act of 1967."[43] The Corporation refused to support the Administration's bill and voted instead to support the levels proposed by Congress, a two-year authorization that would provide $60 million for 1974 and $80 million for 1975. By April, when Senator Pastore convened hearings on the legislation, the Congressional bill had gained virtually unanimous support. The one holdout was the White House mouthpiece Tom Whitehead.

The OTP director's testimony to the Pastore committee had a familiar and altogether unconvincing ring: PBS's distribution of programs "amounted to precisely the kind of federally funded 'fourth network' the Congress sought to avoid," to which he added the threadbare argument that it was "inappropriate and potentially dangerous" to use federal funds for public-affairs programming.[44] Pastore, however, was loaded for bear. He had signalled his feelings earlier by opening the hearings with a reading from the transcript of Buchanan's intemperate and embarrassing "them versus us" remarks on the *Dick Cavett Show*. Now he tore into Whitehead's testimony, accusing the OTP director of praising public broadcasting in one breath and condemning it in the next. "I really think, Mr. Whitehead, that you are against us."[45] Two months later, Whitehead, on firm notice that an "uncooperative" Congress, fed up with tales of Administration interference, would not go along with the White House starve-them-into-submission strategy, suggested that the Administration make a tactical shift. "In exchange for our agreement not to fight a two-year bill," he wrote the president, "I shall seek to have the level of funding reduced to around $100 million for two years." At the same time, by "mildly" opposing the two-year bill, he hoped to create an aura of a false consensus. That, he felt, would increase the Administration's chances of "continuing to have a voice on the future directions of public broadcasting."[46]

But as the Potomac spring slipped into the doldrums of a Washington summer, with it slipped the Administration's chances of influencing the future of public broadcasting. The White House was increasingly on the defensive over what had appeared at first to be a minor burglary in the Watergate office complex. By midsummer of 1973, its credibility had worn tissue thin. Despite Whitehead's opposition to it, the two-year funding bill, its levels reduced by bipartisan compromise from the original $60 and $80 million to $55 and $65 million, sailed through the lower chamber with a lopsided 363 to 14 vote and, with Whitehead's recommendation, was signed by the president on August 6, 1973.

Clearly, the tide was turning against him, and yet Whitehead could still see "hopeful signs of progress." In October, he wrote to the president to report that the Ford Foundation—which "because of McGeorge Bundy and Fred Friendly" was "the largest force behind public affairs shows on public TV"—was phasing out its support to the medium. The Corporation was also reducing budgets for its public-affairs shows. "We have gone about as far as we can go in getting such programs reduced with our old strategy," he told the president, recommending that the emphasis "shift to getting a solid majority on the CPB Board and taking a positive approach to longer range funding for CPB."[47] Patrick Buchanan, still the brawler, took exception to Whitehead's "soft line" tactic and proposed a strategy of his own. "My view is that we should not quit; we should hold their feet to the fire; the President has the power to veto, and we should not hesitate to employ it on public broadcasting if that institution continues to provide cozy sinecures for our less competent journalistic adversaries. If they are going to have public broadcasting, and they are going to overload it against us, why should we approve of any public funding at all. In that event, I would bite the bullet, and keep them at the present level of funding ad infinitum."[48]

But time was running out for the Nixon Administration. By the winter of 1973, the minor disgrace of spring had, with the tendrils of petty crime, corruption, and cover-up that led out from that event, burgeoned into a major scandal that entwined a number of the president's close associates and threatened to reach into

Frieda Hennock, the first woman to serve on the FCC, proved a tough adversary for her six male colleagues who balked at devoting any part of the television spectrum to noncommercial use. Her relentless suasion resulted in the reservation of 245 channels and the start of public television. The FCC commissioners in 1952: *Left to right, back row:* Rosel Hyde, E. M. Webster, Robert Jones, George Sterling; *front row:* Robert T. Bartley, Paul Walker (chairman), and Frieda Hennock. Courtesy of Broadcast Pioneers Library

C. Scott Fletcher, who could sell ideas with the same fervor he once used to sell Studebakers in Australia, did "more than any other person to bring public broadcasting into being and set its course" during the ten years he headed the Ford Foundation's Fund for Adult Education. Reprinted from *Broadcasting Magazine,* September 17, 1973, by Cahners Publishing Company

When money ran out after its first year on the air, KQED was kept alive with a televised auction of donated merchandise. Jonathan Rice (*far right, beside camera*) inaugurated an annual tradition by producing the event every spring for more than two decades (1957). Courtesy of KQED

Not even the comics—read by Mimi London to the amused surprise of managing editor Bill German (*left*) and science editor David Perlman—were overlooked when KQED hastily organized the nightly *Newspaper of the Air* to fill the gap created by a strike of the city's two metropolitan dailies in 1968. Courtesy of KQED

Eleanor Roosevelt was not John F. Kennedy's most enthusiastic fan. But with the urging of producer Henry Morgenthau III (*far right*), she invited the president to be a guest on her NET / WGBH series, *Prospects of Mankind*. The show and its distinguished guests gave early and much-needed national attention to the nascent public medium (1961). Courtesy of Henry Morgenthau III

"It takes courage to depart from the safe and sterile . . . If we don't have that courage, we don't belong in this business." NET president John F. White backed the rhetoric with series like *News in Perspective,* in which *New York Times* Sunday editor Lester Markel challenged (some say badgered) his colleagues Tom Wicker and Max Frankel on the significance of the week's events (1965). *Left to right:* Wicker, White, Markel, Frankel, and WNDT/ New York president John W. Kiermaier. Courtesy of Thirteen / WNET / New York

Their plan was praised by the press as "an imaginative proposal to a very vexatious problem," but Fred W. Friendly (*at microphone*) and Ford Foundation president McGeorge Bundy (*far left*) failed to swing the FCC behind a bold scheme to help fund public TV from the proceeds of a nonprofit satellite system. Courtesy of Ford Foundation Archives / City News Bureau, Inc.

"I believe that educational television has an important future in the United States and throughout the world." Lyndon B. Johnson, having six months earlier made the government a partner in public television by signing the Public Broadcasting Act of 1967, gathered his appointees to the Corporation for Public Broadcasting's first board for the signing of a bill extending its federal funding. *Left to right, front row:* Frank Pace (chairman), President Lyndon Johnson, Oveta Culp Hobby, John D. Rockefeller 3d; *back row:* Joseph Hughes, Michael Gammino, Carl Sanders, Robert Benjamin, Frank Schooley, James Killian, Roscoe Carroll, Jack Valenti, and Saul Haas (1968). Courtesy of LBJ Library

John W. Macy, Jr., the first president of the Corporation for Public
Broadcasting (CPB) (*at right*), feared that his longtime government service
contributed to the misperception that CPB was a government agency. He
joined CPB's first chair, Frank Pace, Jr., to urge Congress to increase federal
funding for public television. Courtesy of City News Bureau, Inc.

Before Fred Rogers donned sweater and tennies to star in
Mister Rogers' Neighborhood, he was the behind-the-scenes pro-
ducer, musician, writer, and puppeteer of *The Children's
Corner,* hosted by Josie Carey (*right*) and produced by WQED /
Pittsburgh for NET (c. 1955). Courtesy of Family
Communications, Inc.

"I have been driven by a sense of obligation since adolescence." Joan
Ganz Cooney changed the face of children's television when
the hugely popular *Sesame Street* debuted on PBS in 1969. The
founder and president of Children's Television Workshop
comes face-to-fur with Grover the Muppet and the hand and
voice behind the Muppet, Frank Oz (c. 1978). Courtesy of
Children's Television Workshop

"I am just not cut out to be a television performer." Bill Moyers's unique talents were wasted on his first series for public television, NET's *This Week*. But the following season *Bill Moyers' Journal* established him as one of the medium's strongest performers (1970). Courtesy of Thirteen / WNET / New York

"Morton's Lemon Cream pie. No lemon. No cream." Marshall Efron played serious fun with vulnerable targets as the consumer's watchful friend on the innovative PBS series *The Great American Dream Machine* (1972). Courtesy of Thirteen / WNET / New York

"It seems silly to balance all the possibilities in a given program . . . you don't balance out the astronauts with the Flat Earth Society." Patrick Watson, rapping with South Bronx street gangs, rattled sensibilities and enlivened issues as host and editor of WNET's nightly news show, *The 51st State.* Courtesy of Thirteen / WNET / New York

Opposite: *"We weren't deceived, but we were misled."* For seven months, Pat Loud (*second from left*) shared her life and her family, including her youngest son, Grant (*far left*), with filmmakers Alan and Susan Raymond (*at right*) for the controversial twelve-part PBS series *An American Family* (1973). Photo from WNET Archives

"Do any of you honestly know whether public broadcasting—structured as it is today and moving in the direction it seems to be headed—can ever fulfill the promise envisioned for it or conform to the policy set for it?" As director of the Office of Telecommunications Policy, Clay T. Whitehead served as point man for the Nixon White House assault on public television (1971). Reprinted from *Broadcasting Magazine,* September 17, 1973, by Cahners Publishing Company

"Nixon vetoed our bill, cut our funding. Now he's given us our best programming."
NPACT president Jim Karayn (*left*) and executive producer Martin Clancy reveled in the outpouring of favorable responses to NPACT's gavel-to-gavel coverage of the Watergate hearings, which PBS was at first reluctant to take on (1973). Photo from National Public Television Archives

Opposite: Hiring Sander Vanocur and Robert MacNeil as principal correspondents for NPACT "greatly disturbed" President Nixon, who saw it as "the last straw" and demanded "that all funds for public television be cut immediately." The NPACT team, *left to right:* Peter Kaye, Sander Vanocur, Elizabeth Drew, and Robert MacNeil (1972). Courtesy of James Karayn

Notwithstanding his conviction that "massive bureaucracies inside the system [are] reversing priorities by dominating rather than supporting programming," independent filmmaker Frederick Wiseman has managed to place more than two dozen distinguished cinema-verité documentaries in the system since he made *High School* (PBL, 1969) more than twenty-five years ago. Courtesy of Zipporah Productions

The *New York Times* called independent filmmaker Ken Burns "the most accomplished documentary maker of his generation" after his *Civil War* series made television history of its own with the highest audience ratings PBS had reached in its twenty-one years (1990). © Cori Wells Braun

After spending five years raising money from forty-four funders to mount his landmark civil rights series *Eyes on the Prize,* independent producer Henry Hampton (shown with members of his staff) concluded that the structure of the public television system discourages risk-taking (1987). Courtesy of Blackside Inc. and Lou Jones (photographer)

the Oval Office. Earlier in the year, many months before the Watergate burglary had become a major scandal and when its political ramifications were still hidden behind a cloak of official secrecy, the Senate had announced plans to investigate the break-in to the Democratic National Headquarters. At least one broadcaster in Washington, Jim Karayn, looked upon the Senate hearings as public television's opportunity to recapture its self-respect.

Karayn's organization, NPACT, had been the White House's principal target. His correspondents had been vilified, his budget slashed, and his programs reduced to bland coverage of the previous year's campaign. So whether or not he had foreseen the ominous implications of the hearings, he did have an eye out for the chance to stage a comeback. He urged PBS president Hartford Gunn to announce the public system's intention of covering the Watergate hearings, but Gunn didn't buy it. "I went twelve weeks in a row, every single day, five days a week, to see Gunn," Karayn said, arguing that PBS's announced intention of covering the controversial hearings would be proof that the public medium was not in the president's pocket—even if the hearings never took place.[49] But if they did take place, daily coverage could put PBS on the map and do for the public network what the broadcast of the Army-McCarthy hearings had done for a young ABC network. Gunn felt the times were not propitious for bold programming moves. Karayn's proposal was tabled. It was still winter, the authorization bill had not yet passed Congress, and public television was still cautiously wary, even fearful, of the Administration's undiminished power to destroy the system's hopes for long-range funding.

By spring, however, PBS felt more confident of its future. The pending CPB-PBS agreement promised an end to a long-festering dispute. And the White House threat appeared to be in decline. Gunn agreed to take a second look at Karayn's proposal. The manner of Gunn's "second look" underscores with disturbing clarity the public system's fainthearted approach to effective leadership and its readiness to substitute consensus for conviction. Gunn put the question of whether the public network should cover the Watergate hearings, arguably the most important congressional hear-

ing of the decade, to a vote of the 237 PBS stations. While the
majority approved, it was by the thinnest of margins: 52 percent
of the stations that responded favored coverage of the hearings.
Some feared a negative reaction locally, allowing their parochial
concerns to blind them to the obligations of national service that
are central to the public medium. "You've finally had it," one
station chief told Karayn. "You've decided to commit professional
hara-kiri."[50]

In mid-April 1973, PBS acted upon its underwhelming mandate
and announced plans to have NPACT cover the Senate Watergate
hearings from their opening on May 17, 1973. The daytime live
broadcasts were to be encapsulated for the evening audience with
excerpts and analysis of the day's events. To anchor the on-air
coverage of the event, NPACT paired its veteran correspondent
Robert MacNeil with a young journalist from Dallas, Jim Lehrer.
Karayn had brought Lehrer to NPACT six months earlier to replace
the departed Sander Vanocur. The MacNeil-Lehrer team produced a dynamic synergy that eventually resulted in public television's first nightly news show.

By any measure, PBS's coverage of the unfolding drama was a
huge success. Day after day, through May and June and into July,
NPACT's cameras focused on a seventy-six-year-old country lawyer
from North Carolina, Senator Sam Ervin—crusty, aphoristic, and
perfectly suited for the television camera. As he and his seven-
member select committee peeled back the layers of chicanery and
deceit that underlay the Watergate case, a nation watched in fas-
cinated disbelief. The daily tales of skulduggery in high places
brought new viewers to the public medium, set new highs in audience ratings, and triggered a renewed outpouring of audience
contributions. "For the first time in its brief history," said Mac-
Neil, "it seemed the entire nation knew what public television
was."[51] More important, the nation saw what it was not. Curtis's
dramatic resignation a month earlier, with its charges of White
House control of the Corporation, had left a bad aftertaste. The
Watergate hearings cleansed the image and gave proof that public
television was no one's official patsy. MacNeil, hoping that the
lesson of the Watergate hearings was not lost on skeptical man-

agers of local stations, cited the coverage as evidence "that public television journalism could be vital, fair, and trenchant when dealing with the most sensitive political material."[52]

The Watergate hearings infused the whole public-television system with a renewed sense of vitality and excitement. Morale, reported the *Wall Street Journal*, had risen "from sulky to exuberant."[53] Karayn, whose NPACT had been down for the count of nine after the Nixon-Whitehead assault on public affairs, gloried in the poetic justice. "Nixon vetoed the funding bill, cut our funding," he exulted. "Now he's given us our best programming. It's sort of like being reborn."[54] NPACT was not alone in its sense of rebirth. *Bill Moyers' Journal*, which like NPACT had been an early casualty of the White House's paranoid fear of free expression, was revived in late October with a grant from the Ford Foundation. The timing was propitious. Moyers's first show on his return, "An Essay on Watergate," was arguably the best that he has ever done. With perception and wit, he looked into that dark moment in our political history and found our weakness and our strength—weakness in ethical values that allowed a president to define his own standards of right and wrong, and strength in the indefinable force that blew the whistle on the process before it was too late. "It was close," he said. "It almost worked. But not quite. Something basic in our traditions held." He wondered aloud why it had taken "so great an affront to decency to make us realize how hard-won rights can be lost simply by taking them for granted." After you've put the myths and folk tales behind you, he cautioned, "believing that what is best about this country doesn't need exaggeration. It needs vigilance."[55]

By late 1973, it was apparent that another act in the irresolute drama of the public medium was ending. "As Watergate sluiced through the press," noted one observer, "the Administration's sense of divine omniscience began to crumble."[56] And with the loss of its crudely fashioned majesty went the force of its assault on the media. Whitehead, the Administration's field general, was never himself implicated in the below-stairs dealings of the president's advisers. Nevertheless, his willingness to play the White

House game of saying one thing while meaning another effectively undermined his credibility with Congress and the public. So long as he had championed the doctrine of "localism," of ceding power to the local stations, even with the cynical aim of giving control of the system to its most conservative elements, he had had the support of many of the public broadcasters. But once he joined with the Administration's policy of centralizing power in the hands of the presidentially appointed party faithful on the CPB board, his deeds gave the lie to his pieties and he lost whatever support he had inside public television. The Administration's stratagem of "centralizing in order to decentralize" just didn't wash.

By this time I was no longer a participant in the events that rocked public broadcasting. Early in 1973, I submitted my resignation to the trustees of Channel 13. My departure from the public medium after twenty years, unpremeditated and mildly acrimonious, offered me a blessed relief from the frustrations and frictions of the office. If in joining the chairman of Channel 13 with the president of NET the Corporation and Ford Foundation had hoped for synergy, they miscalculated. Ethan Allan Hitchcock and I were not meant for each other: our temperaments, backgrounds, and management philosophies were worlds apart, as a series of contretemps—including the Woody Allen caper—demonstrated. The proximate cause of my departure, a dispute over a key staff appointment, threatened to divide authority and force employees to ally themselves with one side or the other. The resolution was as obvious as it was inevitable.[57]

In the spring of 1974, Tom Whitehead announced plans to leave government service "as soon as I can gracefully extricate myself."[58] The White House since Watergate, he said, had become "pretty much an armed camp."[59] Before leaving, he wanted to achieve two things: a report on the future of cable and a long-term funding bill for public television. Whitehead had taken a lot of heat as pointman for the Administration's policies on public television and had even surrendered his reputation as a nonpartisan, but he felt "a strong personal commitment" to carry these policies to their logical conclusion. In early April, he outlined for the president his thoughts on a bill that would authorize funding over a five-year period, starting with $70 million in fiscal 1976 and rising to $100 million in fiscal 1980. A substantial portion of the funds—up to at least half by 1980—would be passed on to the local stations in order "to decentralize program control and minimize the network character of the system."[60] The time was ripe, he reasoned, for capitalizing on the consensus that backed the Administration's plans for restructuring public television. The bill would not preclude the use of federal funds for news and public-affairs programs. "While I share your view," he explained to the president, "that such funds should not be used for this purpose, [the bill] would not pass if we attempted to deal with the problem legislatively." That solution, he suggested, should be left to the cpb board.

The president, however, was not impressed. He did not even heed Whitehead's argument that the long-term bill "would carry the issue of public broadcasting structure and funding through to a new Administration—one that may not be as sympathetic to the role of local stations as we are."[61] Only three weeks away from the House hearings on his impeachment, Richard M. Nixon was far less concerned with future administrations than he was with the survival of his own. He rejected the Whitehead proposal. Incredulous, the otp director fired off a memo to General Alexander Haig, Haldeman's replacement as Nixon's chief of staff. Voicing strong disagreement with the president's apparent intention either to "end" public television or to submit a "very limited" budget proposal, Whitehead asked for an appeal to the president. "Rightly or wrongly," he argued, "the commitment to Federal funding of public broadcasting has been made. For the President to attempt to back away from that commitment now is unwise, unworkable, and quixotic."[62] Whitehead met with Haig and made his arguments, but to no avail. The president rejected the proposal a second time.

Knowing he was not going to get the president to do what he wanted and feeling deeply that the issue was important, Whitehead decided to "go public." On the day after his meeting with

Haig, the story—"Nixon Said to Reject Public TV Funding"—broke on the front page of the *New York Times*. Editorials appeared in the *Washington Post* and the *Wall Street Journal*. The strategy had its intended effect; the Administration gave in to the pressure. "Ron Ziegler stood up and lied through his teeth," Whitehead recalled later, "and said the President had never made a decision."[63] In any case, Nixon decided a month later to approve the proposal for five-year funding and sent it on to Congress. A month after the president's decision, Whitehead appeared before Senator Pastore's subcommittee with a ringing endorsement of the five-year funding bill. "We have created a system; it is a reality. We must now give it a chance to succeed according to the original vision for a truly independent and financially insulated system of public broadcasting."[64] He had won the fight and in the process had won back a small piece of the integrity he had sacrificed in the White House's partisan wars. But from the moment he decided that he had to go public to win his fight, Whitehead knew that he had to resign. On his way back from testifying on Capitol Hill, he stopped by the White House to drop off his resignation. Two days later, President Nixon resigned.

Another era—turbulent, threatening, and altogether irrational—had come to a sudden and unexpected end. Tom Whitehead summed it up: "The separation we have, by and large, between the press and the government kept [the White House] from doing anything very meaningful with the rest of the media; but that separation blurred with public broadcasting and that gave them some levers, which they proceeded to utilize. You put a hammer in front of a little boy and he'll pick it up and pound something. That's what the funding of public television was to the Nixon political people."[65] It was a lesson that would be too easily forgotten.

14

GREAT NOISE. BIG WIND. MUCH DUST. NO RAIN

*There are two ways to operate in a democracy. The safe way is to . . . act
only when there is agreement by everyone in advance. The other is to . . .
find the mainstream . . . and then act on what you decide is best for all.
This way has its risks. . . . If you push the stations into something they
don't want, they'll get rid of you. But this is the course I intend to take.*

Lawrence K. Grossman[1]

The damaging effects of the
Nixon years on the public media were not swept away by the blast
of the chopper blades as the presidential helicopter lifted off the
White House lawn for the last time. Richard Nixon left a legacy,
summed up by one journalist as "a system torn by disputes . . . a
system relying on local stations to produce programs rather than
national production centers . . . weakened public affairs programming . . . and an atmosphere where experimentation and innovation were discouraged."[2]

The more devastating consequences of those years, however,
would surface later. In the months immediately following Nixon's
resignation, an unusual calm settled over the system. The peace
pact signed by Killian and Rogers kept a lid on their rivalries for
the moment. A more effective restraint, however, was the political
pressure to maintain an image of crosstown amity while the Public
Television Finance Act of 1975 made its way through Congress.
With PBS "saved," the man who saved it could now turn his attention to its internal affairs. Ralph Rogers did just that. Rumors had
begun to circulate in early 1975 of growing differences between
Rogers and his chief executive officer, Hartford Gunn. According
to press reports, the two men had had "a serious falling out" over
Gunn's tendency to "ponder the long-range problems . . . and

leave daily decisions to a group of middle managers who generally made mediocre decisions.''[3]

Their differences could come as no surprise to any who knew both men: one was a self-made industrialist whose actions were swift and decisive; the other, a Harvard Business School graduate who acted only after careful planning. Impatient as Rogers may have been with his deliberate style, Gunn's predilection for "pondering long-range problems" nevertheless played an important part in building PBS—and in guiding the development of many other aspects of public television. Gunn's vision for the public medium was a force in shaping it almost from the day in 1957 when an intramural dispute catapulted him into the general manager's chair at WGBH. In the dozen years during which he led the Boston station, Gunn moved it into the front ranks of public television, positioning it as one of the nation's top two public stations. In the course of those years, Gunn created the first interconnected regional network (Eastern Educational Television Network) and goaded NET into adopting higher technical standards, including a major shift into color television. Later, at PBS, he led the planning for the satellite distribution system that is in place today. Gunn was a "systems man," a master planner, somewhat less interested in programs than in perfecting the process that produced them. Nonetheless, he was not Rogers's kind of chief executive.

Rogers knew what he wanted and proposed to get it by creating the position of executive vice president with full responsibility for PBS's day-to-day operations. The board accepted the plan, appointed a search committee, and produced its favored candidate, Robert Wilson, the well-respected general manager of KERA / Dallas. Wilson had been Rogers's assistant at Texas Industries before Rogers brought him to the Dallas station to resurrect the moribund channel. Not surprisingly, the PBS station membership viewed the possibility of a Rogers-Wilson team as a Texas-style takeover—notwithstanding the fact that both men were actually from New England. As opposition mounted, Wilson withdrew his name, resigned from KERA, and left public television for a new career in public relations.

Rogers, disappointed at the outcome but still resolved to

strengthen the PBS management, returned to the board with a revised plan. He proposed to shift Gunn into the newly created post of vice chairman with responsibility for long-range planning and systems development, and then to begin the search for a chief executive to fit the Rogers mold. The search for the new chief executive, however, proved tougher than anticipated. For six months, through the spring and summer of 1975, the search committee advertised for candidates and interviewed likely prospects, but came up empty-handed. Candidates who might otherwise have leapt at the opportunity balked at having to report to two boards—the lay board and the board of professional managers. And because PBS didn't produce, fund, or acquire programming, but simply scheduled what the stations acquired or produced, the post had little or no appeal for program executives with an itch to create or a desire to exercise authority. The PBS president could only play ringmaster—suggesting, persuading, cajoling, or coordinating—and in the long run could do no more than the member stations would permit him to do. It was not the post to attract an activist. Thus, it came as something of a surprise when, in the closing weeks of 1975, the board announced that Lawrence K. Grossman had accepted the PBS presidency.

No small part of the surprise was the fact that Larry Grossman represented everything the stations feared: New York, networks, advertising, and strong, assertive leadership. For some, his selection was nothing less than apostasy. But if the stations thought they could block it, they failed to reckon with Rogers's obduracy. The PBS chairman brushed aside the stations' complaints and saw his man—"a genius because he's advocating things I've been saying for years"[4]—installed in the PBS presidency. Grossman, however, disappointed the hardliners by failing to live up to the stereotype of the Man in the Gray Flannel Suit (even though the advertising trade was in his blood). After graduation from Columbia College and Harvard Law School, he began his broadcasting career in the advertising department of CBS, later moving on to NBC's advertising department as a network vice president. Four years later he left the networks to start up his own advertising and public-relations business. Grossman saw advertising as something more than a marketing tool for products and services; for him it was an opportunity to use the traditional sales techniques of selling toothpaste "for significant social purposes."[5]

The new chief executive was no stranger to public television. Prior to his arrival at PBS, Grossman had for several years consulted with it and the Ford Foundation on techniques to improve the image and fund-raising potential of the public medium, leaving him with few illusions about the nature of his new tasks and the difficulties that would bar their easy accomplishment. The three tasks with the highest priority, he told a reporter, were "programming, programming and programming."[6] But that was more easily said than done. Unlike its commercial counterparts, PBS had a severely limited power to effect change. In the first place, it was hampered by the limits on its programming role, prohibited as it was from either creating or acquiring programs on its own. Other, equally formidable forces lurked in the shadows to hinder whatever changes Grossman might seek: the resistance of his own membership, the rivalry of the Corporation, and the interventions of Congress. He had only one weapon to achieve his ends: the force of persuasion.

One of the toughest problems Grossman faced was the parochialism of his own membership. Although Grossman succeeded in winning over many of the doubters in the stations with his unthreatening manner—a soft-spoken and unhurried self-confidence coupled with an off-handed, shirt-sleeves informality—below the surface of their acceptance lurked a fear of his "network mentality" and the worrisome thought that he secretly planned to turn PBS into something resembling the commercial networks he once served. Their fears were fed by the message of his initial speech. "A distribution system," he told them, using the term favored by PBS to distinguish its service from the lockstep programming of the networks, was "more suitable to the grocery trade than television."[7] And yet despite their fears, he was able later to put his rhetoric in high gear and persuade them to accept a proposal that in some ways moved PBS a bit closer to the networks. The proposal aimed to overcome the random scheduling that placed PBS shows into a helter-skelter, nonuniform pattern across the country, making it virtually impossible to promote the shows nationally. As an advertising man, Grossman was sensitive to the value of program promotion for building audiences, but national promotion was impossible when a show seen in one locality on a particular day and time might be seen elsewhere three days or a week later and at a different hour. The stations were persuaded to accept a "core schedule" and to pledge to run certain key programs, if not at the same hour, at least on the same evening of the week. (NET had made a similar arrangement a decade earlier, and for the same purpose.)

The benefits were immediately apparent: national advertising, made possible by more uniform scheduling, brought new viewers to the medium and resulted in a substantially larger audience for PBS. The principal beneficiaries were the stations. But although most gave full credit for the gains to Grossman's creative leadership, some stations grudgingly accepted the positive results of audience growth and then, in the same breath, condemned Grossman for "centralizing" the system. For these curmudgeonly few, the sanctity of local autonomy superseded the public interest they were created to serve. Grossman made war on what he called their "false dichotomy" by asking stations to "lay aside this divisive, destructive and just plain dumb idea that quality local public television programming is somehow incompatible with quality nationwide programming."[8]

Grossman followed his successful pitch for a "core schedule" with a corollary proposal to have stations dedicate one entire evening's schedule each week to public-affairs programs. Friday was the night chosen. Into it went such regulars as *Wall Street Week* and *Washington Week in Review*, together with a new entry, the *MacNeil/Lehrer Report*, a nightly half-hour of in-depth analysis on one of the day's major news stories. These changes, however, were more cosmetic than substantive; most involved only matters of scheduling. The main body of PBS programming was beyond Grossman's reach—thanks in large measure to a devilishly ingenious device that had been introduced by his predecessor to prevent the Corporation from seizing control of the system's programming. Hartford Gunn's innovation, called the Station Program Cooperative, was deceptively simple in concept but fiendishly complex in execution. By persuading Congress to mandate that some part (ultimately half) of its federal appropriation for public broadcasting go directly to local stations as Community Service Grants, the Corporation's control over programming was minimized. At the same time, stations gained discretionary dollars to invest in the production of national programming. The decision of which national programs would be produced with the stations' dollars was decided by referendum. Each station programmer gave a thumbs-up or thumbs-down to the programs proposed in any given year and agreed to provide their station's share of the production costs for those shows chosen by the majority.[9] The plan was disarmingly democratic, reason enough for its broad appeal to members of Congress.

As a device for piecing together a national schedule, however, the SPC had crippling drawbacks. Stations rarely voted to take risks on new or untried series, preferring to stick with the proven winners. *Wall Street Week* and *Sesame Street* were among the perennial favorites. Regardless of their quality, with the same old shows returning year after year, the PBS schedule lost much of its freshness. Grossman tried to break the pattern by persuading the stations to accept a plan in which PBS would "take a leadership role in deciding what [the] programs should be, when they should be played, how they should be promoted and selected."[10] But the stratagem of a "recommended buy" faltered and was abandoned after only two seasons. Stations were loath to accept "centralized" decision-making.

Grossman's frustrations in effecting change were not confined to his own PBS family of scattered stations. He had problems as well inside the Washington beltway; the network's crosstown nemesis had fanned the coals of institutional rivalry into full flame again. The Corporation for Public Broadcasting had held itself in check while Congress considered the 1975 funding bill, but once the bill was enacted, and long-range funding for five years was thought to be secured (it was later rescinded), the battle over turf and tax dollars resumed. The feud was fed by the Corporation's rankling practice of skimming off 10 percent of each year's federal appropriation to cover its own upkeep. No one complained when appropriations were small. But with the 1976 appropriation topping $130 million, the Corporation pocketed a whopping $13 million. Loomis's insistence on staying with the 10 percent triggered outrage among the station managers, who feared that the Corporation, with its one hundred or more employees, was fast becoming a bloated bureaucracy. (It was wryly observed that the Ford Foundation had managed to dole out far more money to public broadcasting with a staff of only six.)

More problematic than money in the system's internecine rivalries was the thorny issue of program control—the question of who would decide which programs were to be produced. Although the introduction of the Station Program Cooperative shifted much of the control over program selection from the Corporation to the stations, it did not eliminate the Corporation as a player. By 1976, Loomis and company had returned to the programming game with a plan to put the Corporation's funds into "high risk, innovative" programs. Their aim was to provide the national schedule with programs of the sort that the SPC was likely to bypass in its consensus-oriented selection process. The Corporation's largesse, however, was limited to injections of "risk capital" that was available to launch new projects but not to sustain them beyond their first two years. The Corporation reasoned, wrongly as it turned out, that if the shows succeeded then other funders would keep them going.

The Corporation's reentry into the programming process meant that PBS had to settle for a program schedule that was a pastiche of independent and unrelated program choices. Part was controlled by the Corporation, which chose which "innovative" ideas to fund, another part was controlled by industrial corporations, which chose which shows to underwrite, and the final and largest part (40 percent) was controlled by the stations through the laboriously arrived at "democratic" decisions of the SPC. With so many organizations involved, trouble was no less predictable than tomorrow's sunrise.

The frustrations bred by the system's tangle of waste and duplication peaked near the close of Grossman's first year, when he declared that public television "can no longer have two operating organizations on the national level." The system, he said, is "a bureaucratic nightmare,"[11] a "three-legged race in which the partners hobble each other," and in which "we spend so much time quarrelling that we can't do the work we should be doing."[12] Of the many quarrels over programming, the bitterest erupted over the Corporation's unilateral decision to invest $1.2 million of its federal funds offshore in a gigantic BBC project to produce all thirty-six of Shakespeare's plays for television. The Corporation saw the BBC proposal as a prestigious project with rich rewards for future students. PBS, starved for production funds, saw it only as a gross misuse of federal dollars; the money, it said, should have gone into an American production with an American cast. PBS also challenged the investment of federal dollars, supposedly earmarked for "high risk" projects, in a series that was both prestigious and "safe" and thus might easily have attracted corporate dollars.

Grossman's frustrations were further fanned by the Corporation's insistence on limiting the funding of innovative new series to two seasons. Controversy broke out when it refused to fund a third season of *Visions.* A rule is a rule, said the Corporation. "A dumb rule," said Grossman; "every time we start something, it goes off the air."[13] *Visions* was a series of American television plays, at times controversial, which provided a unique service and won the plaudits of critics. But it was a series that by its very nature was unfundable from other sources.

From PBS's perspective, the Corporation's actions began to appear unnecessarily provocative, as though the Corporation was deliberately scuttling the delicately balanced partnership that had been so carefully worked out. When, for example, the Corporation announced plans to establish a $1 million "revolving fund" for documentary production, it pointedly excluded PBS from any voice in the selection of the programs to be funded. "The same guys who wanted to kill off news and public affairs," muttered a frustrated PBS executive, "now want to select it."[14] The final blow came with the Corporation's decision not to continue its annual subsidy to the Station Program Cooperative, which was then struggling into its third tentative year.

By the close of 1976, PBS and its stations had reached the limits of their patience; the time had arrived for a "high noon" shootout. The chosen occasion was a December meeting of the joint Corporation–PBS Partnership Review Committee. The chosen instrument, known later as the "Kansas City Resolution," was a clear message to the Corporation: get out of programming once and for all. Each side leveled charges against the other. PBS backed its charges of wasteful duplication at the Corporation with specific facts and figures. Loomis, however, brushed them aside, explaining that "democracies are always messy bureaucratically compared to dictatorships." The confrontation was headline material for the media tabloids: two large and important organizations on a collision course. But Ralph Rogers and Robert Benjamin (who had replaced James Killian as chairman of the Corporation) were determined to dampen the ardor for a scrap lest the Congress be drawn into the quarrel and resolve the dispute on its own terms. They met beforehand, quietly worked out an agreement, and in the next day's meeting—from which Grossman and Loomis were excluded—each side pledged to rededicate itself "to the fulfillment of the spirit of the 1973 partnership agreement."[15] The "shootout," said a disappointed PBS executive, had proved to be no more than "rhetoric and irresolution," an assessment that was borne out a month later when the specifics of the agreement were still shrouded in a mist of ambiguity. The Corporation agreed to allow PBS staffers "to participate" in the decisions on the CPB-funded documentaries, promised to "work jointly" with PBS in planning new programming, agreed to "explore the possibilities of further assistance" to *Visions*, and said it would "welcome" a corporate underwriter to take over its commitment to the BBC series of Shakespeare plays. *Variety*'s Bill Greeley tallied up the outcome in what he called "the language of the five civilized tribes" of Oklahoma: " 'Great noise. Big Wind. Much dust. No rain.' "[16]

The year 1978 should have been a banner one for public broadcasting. All the portents were positive. Viewership was up and with it the medium's income from public subscription had risen; Congressional funding appeared to be assured by 1975's five-year funding bill; and, with the previous year's inauguration of Jimmy Carter, public broadcasting had a sympathetic ear in the White House for the first time in eight years. Hopes for an even better year were raised by President Carter's request to Congress for a five-year appropriation for the public media. The total of more than a billion dollars was to build what he termed "a truly national system." The prospects for fulfilling public broadcasting's mission had never looked brighter.

Unfortunately, success, even on so modest a scale, has a curiously destabilizing effect on the volatile rival factions of public television. Money means power, and more money means more power. The heady prospect can lead public television's competing forces into apportioning the spoils with the focused self-interest of arbitrageurs. Carter's billion-dollar funding proposal provided a perfect opportunity for discord. The leadership at PBS—Larry Grossman and both the outgoing and incoming chairmen, Ralph Rogers and former FCC chairman Newton Minow—backed the president's bill. But most of their member stations, angered at the president's plan to "devote more resources to high-quality national programming,"[17] rallied to oppose the bill. With 25 percent of the funds earmarked for national production, local stations feared a loss of hegemony over national programming. Mounting the well-worn ramparts of localism, they denounced the Carter proposal as "an attempt to erode public broadcasting's freedom" and a first step toward "government control and domination."[18]

They need not have worried. Not, at least, about the Administration's bill. Carter's legislative proposal faced even tougher opposition in Congress. Several key legislators, far from being concerned about the constraints the proposal placed on the system, felt that the bill didn't go far enough in correcting the system's deficiencies. One Congressional aide noted caustically that "you don't reward a group which has been doing its job poorly, by giving it more money and five years to do it in."[19] Rep. Lionel Van Deerlin, chairman of the House Subcommittee on Communications, together with his counterpart in the Senate, Ernest Hollings, submitted their own legislative proposal that authorized a modest increase in funds but carried some tough conditions clearly aimed at straightening out the system and lowering the decibel level of its internal bickering. Public broadcasters would be required to give more than lip service to equal employment opportunity, to tighten their financial management and accounting practices, and to allow independent producers increased access to station air time. Responsibility for policing these provisions was handed to the Corporation, raising fears that Congress was forcing the Corporation into the role of a government regulatory agency.

Whatever else may be said of its intentions, the 95th Congress was in a mood to take the public-broadcasting system out to the woodshed for a hiding. In the spring of 1978 the House held hearings on the several pending public-broadcasting bills. Corporation and PBS officials tramped up to the hill to testify, only to discover to their astonishment and dismay that for the first time in memory public television found itself on the defensive. The legislators confronted the system's witnesses with a battery of sharply worded questions. They were asked to explain, among other things, the underutilized facilities at local stations, the huge overhead charges levied by some of the system's producing stations, and the generally sloppy financial-accounting practices that were too common throughout the system. Public broadcasters had come to expect this kind of treatment from its naysayers but not from their traditional "friends."

While most of the puzzled witnesses could only mumble "Why us?", one longtime supporter of public broadcasting leapt to its defense. Responding to an invitation from the chairman to share his views with the subcommittee, Fred Friendly fired off a seven-page letter to Rep. Lionel Van Deerlin detailing point-by-point his objections to the pending legislation. "After ten years of a perilous and vulnerable existence," he wrote, "public broadcasting now needs independence from well-intentioned regulation as much as it does long-term financing."[20] In his reply, Van Deerlin challenged Friendly's assertion that public broadcasting might inadvertently be fettered by such "public policy criteria" as open meetings, EEO standards, community advisory boards, and uniform accounting principles. "My view," wrote Van Deerlin, "is the *lack* of such criteria has been responsible for many of the current problems of public broadcasting. The record shows that the waste of human and financial resources in the systems has been outrageous; even to the extent that certain members of our committee have all but given up hope for improvement. While I do not share that hopelessness, I am convinced that some legislative direction is now required."[21] The chairman's snappish response reflected all too accurately Washington's prevailing posture toward the public medium.

Congressional disaffection, or at best its impatience with public television, was apparent in the spate of rules that found their way into the Public Telecommunications Financing Act of 1978: open meetings, community advisory boards, and a call for improvement in its minority hiring practices. Even the good news—more money for public broadcasting—came with a bitter pill: the monies were no longer the exclusive claim of the public television and radio community but were now available to a wider, ill-defined world of "public telecommunications." The bitterest blow, though, was the regressive nature of the funding itself. What had been won in 1975—"long-range funding" in the form of five-year authorizations—was rescinded only three years later. From now on, said Congress, authorizations will be limited to three years, and appropriations to two. The message from the hill was clear: Congress had lost confidence in the system's forward planning, if not its future. The Congressional flip-flop on the five-year authorization forced the unwelcome conclusion that public broadcasting's federal funding was in a precarious position.

The spirit of reform that in 1978 moved Congress to saddle the system with new rules was apparently infectious. Three major efforts to reform and reorder the public broadcasting system were undertaken that year. One was embedded in Rep. Van Deerlin's broader legislative proposal to update the basic statutes governing all U.S. communications. Another was embodied in the work of a second Carnegie Commission, convened to update and correct the errors and oversights contained in the original Carnegie Commission Report of 1967. Both attempts at reform failed. We shall have reason to look at them again later. The third was an internal effort by PBS to reform itself, motivated in part by a mild dissatisfaction with Larry Grossman's leadership. Characteristically, the reform movement produced not one but three separate and competing plans for restructuring PBS. Two of the three—one from PBS's vice chairman Hartford Gunn, and the other from an ad hoc group of station managers—would decentralize PBS still further. Both would eliminate the post of the single chief executive, Grossman's position, and would then subdivide PBS into three autonomous divisions, each with its own program service, its own board, and its own chief executive. Grossman, not to be outdone, or done out, countered with his own plan. His would retain the single chief executive but reduce his authority over programming. Surprisingly, the stations ignored the recommendation of their own board and voted to retain the single chief executive. They did, however, embrace Gunn's plan to subdivide the one program service into three, each with a different objective and each with its own program director. The most positive result of the reorganization was the thinning of the PBS board from an unwieldy fifty members to a slimmer thirty-five and the jettisoning of its role of lobbyist and long-range planner to a newly created organization, the National Association of Public Television Stations.[22]

Despite the effort to eliminate his position, Grossman emerged from the reorganization of PBS with his power and influence strengthened. But even as his leadership inside the PBS organization was strengthened, the leadership position of PBS itself was coming under increasing challenge from its old rival, the Corporation for Public Broadcasting. The man who in the past had given PBS so many problems, Henry Loomis, resigned the presidency of the Corporation in the fall of 1978—under pressure, so he told reporters, from President Carter's appointees on the Corporation board. He was succeeded by the sixty-two-year-old president of the University of Michigan, Robben W. Fleming. A former labor lawyer and arbitrator, Fleming brought to the leadership of the Corporation a "rare brand of intellectual integrity" that allowed him to be both "an idealist and tough-minded pragmatist."[23] Both qualities were evident in his plan to reorganize the Corporation, a controversial design intended to distance it from the unwanted governmental influence that it had experienced under Loomis. The key element of the Fleming plan would remove the politically appointed board from direct involvement in programming. He told those most directly affected—the board of the Corporation itself—"A board cannot and should not try to run the day-to-day affairs of an institution."[24] He may have lacked broadcasting experience, but he clearly understood the ways of nonprofit institutions and the tricky business of their governance.

To further isolate programming from the pressures of politics, Fleming proposed to divide the Corporation staff into two discrete units. One, a "management unit," would be given responsibility for the business, planning, and research functions, including the distribution of funds to the stations. The other, a "program fund," a separate and independent unit with its own director, its own advisory board, and its own budget of $30 million, would deal exclusively with the sensitive area of programming. What appeared to be an audacious break with convention was more probably, in Fleming's view, a practical accommodation to political reality. Fleming knew that both Congress and the second Carnegie Commission were bent on eliminating the CPB with its taint of political influence. Fleming's proposal offered a less drastic way of achieving the same end. Barely noticed, however, was the way a programming role for the Corporation was institutionalized with the creation of the Program Fund. Prior to the Nixon Administration's attempt to use the Corporation to control what was aired on public television, the Corporation had almost no part in programming.

With only minor changes, Fleming's plan went into effect January 1, 1980. A select committee sorted through 250 applicants to find a head for the new Program Fund. Their choice of Lewis Freedman gave a clear signal to PBS and to all concerned that the Corporation's Program Fund would be more than a quasi-foundation doling out money to needy supplicants. Freedman was one of the medium's most experienced and talented producers. His career as an innovative program executive stretched back to television's earliest days with shows like *Play of the Week* and *Camera Three*. He had come to public television first as WNDT / New York's programming chief, and later as director of cultural programs for Friendly's experimental Public Broadcast Laboratory. With the demise of PBL, Freedman had moved to the West Coast and KCET / Los Angeles to launch his award-winning *Hollywood Television Theater*. Only two months into his new post at the Program Fund, Freedman handed the board a five-year blueprint. It called for more programming in American drama, history, government, art, and health. Clearly, he intended to leave his mark on the medium. Few would question that he did just that in the two-and-a-half years he presided over the Program Fund.

In the early months, however, Freedman and the Program Fund were handed the onerous task of implementing a provision of the 1978 funding bill that required the Corporation to devote "a substantial amount" of its federal funds to independent producers—video and film producers unattached to any established production organization. The burgeoning movement of "independents" had grown out of technological advances that produced lightweight and affordable film and video gear. The easy accessibility of equipment encouraged hundreds of individual video- and filmmakers blessed with a good eye, a good idea, and a compelling desire to communicate to enter the market. Commercial networks, with rare exceptions, refuse to air documentaries that they have not themselves produced, leaving the public medium as virtually the sole broadcast outlet for independent work. But that relationship, too, has had its problems. Despite public television's need for the output of independent producers, many station programmers perceive them as a threat, not only because dollars paid to them might otherwise have gone to support the institution's own staff and overhead, but also because the personal style of independent producers' work has been known to challenge public television's rules of journalistic "balance."

During the hearings on the 1978 funding bill, the independents, working through their own Association of Independent Video and Filmmakers, succeeded in winning the concession that required the Corporation to dedicate "a substantial amount" of

its funds to independent production. But the 1978 provision did
not go into effect until two years later. It fell to Freedman to make
it work. At the time, the system already supported several established channels to fund independent production. The most notable among them was WNET's TV Lab, an experimental project
started several years earlier by David Loxton. Although the TV Lab
was very much in need of the Corporation's funds to carry on its
work, Freedman chose to keep the funds in his own hands and to
use them to create the Program Fund's own outlet for independent work. Short pieces of thirty minutes or less, solicited from
independents and juried by a peer panel, were assembled into an
anthology under the generic title of *Matters of Life and Death.* In a
manner characteristic of the fragmented system's bizarre way of
doing business, however, PBS rejected the series for airing. Too
many of the individual pieces, it said, failed to meet the network's
standards. *Matters of Life and Death* ultimately found a means of
national distribution by way of a supplemental satellite feed. Few
stations, however, bothered to air it.

The following year, Freedman replaced the failed series with
another anthology of independent work. *Crisis to Crisis* consisted
of one-hour shows, primarily to accommodate the long-form documentary. But in the curious way that public television has of re-
peating its mistakes—in this case isolating production from distribution—the second series fared little better than the first.
Although *Crisis to Crisis,* unlike the first series, managed to make
it into the PBS schedule, it aired in an out-of-prime-time hour that
virtually guaranteed obscurity. Freedman's lasting contribution to
the public medium would come later.

Fears that the Corporation's reentry into programming might
threaten public television with a return of undue governmental
influence were thoroughly dispelled by a single show aired in the
spring of 1980. The show was *Death of a Princess.*[25] While few critics
would go as far as Richard Goldstein of the *Village Voice*—for
whom it was "public television's finest hour"[26]—none would deny
that the controversial program about a Saudi princess put to the
test PBS's independence and integrity and subjected the system to

the heaviest political and public pressure since the days of Richard
Nixon. Against all expectations, public television held its ground.
Credit for its steadfastness belonged in large measure to PBS president Larry Grossman, who was, said one observer, "about as fraz-
zled as a glass of ice tea."[27]

Death of a Princess was an example of the genre known as "docudrama," neither a conventional true-to-the-facts documentary
nor a wholly fictional drama, but a combination of both. The plot
line, ostensibly based on fact, told the tale of an ill-fated nineteen-
year-old princess of the Saudi Arabian royal family who, after rejecting her family's arranged marriage, fell in love with a classmate
while attending college in Beirut. She entered into an adulterous
relationship with him and made no effort to deny her act. Both
were made to suffer the penalty for adultery prescribed by Islamic
law: public execution, she by a firing squad, he by beheading.

Death of a Princess was a collaborative effort between British Independent Television and WGBH/Boston and was written and
produced by two expatriate South Africans, one an American, the
other British. David Fanning, who cowrote the docudrama, was
also the executive producer of PBS's *World*, the WGBH-produced
series in which the controversial show aired on American television. It was Fanning's friend and collaborator, Anthony Thomas,
a reporter and producer for England's Associated Television, who
first heard the story of the 1977 execution of the princess and
determined to ferret out the details for a conventional documentary. But those with first-hand knowledge of the royal drama were
unwilling to appear on camera, so he opted to use a dramatic
format. Actors, using fictional names, spoke the actual words spoken to him in the interviews. The dramatic plot would be con-
structed on his own frustrating, Rashomon-like search for the
truth.

Under normal circumstances, the program might have aired
without incident, received mixed reviews, and been forgotten. But
in the world of television, nothing raises a program, however commonplace, to the heights of celebrity faster than the shrill cries of
would-be censors, which virtually guarantee the show an audience
many times larger than what the show might otherwise attract or

even deserve. Such was the fate of *Death of a Princess.* The protests began with its airing in Britain a full month before its American airing. The British broadcast triggered a major diplomatic crisis in which King Khalid's planned state visit to London was cancelled, the British ambassador was expelled, and Britain's economic ties to the Arab state were thrown into jeopardy. In the eyes of the Saudis, *Death of a Princess* defamed the royal family and gave an untrue and wholly negative picture of Saudi culture. They were particularly outraged at a scene in which legions of royal princesses, bored with the drabness of their court lives, are shown cruising in their chauffeured limousines along an infamous stretch of desert road in search of anonymous sexual liaisons. Although the British were the first to feel the Saudi wrath, they were not alone. Dutch and Australian broadcasters faced similar Saudi threats, but they aired the show anyway. Only in Sweden, where a group of conservative business leaders bought up and withheld the broadcast rights, did the Saudis succeed in keeping the show off the air.

In the weeks before PBS was due to broadcast the show, the story of the brouhaha in Britain played prominently in the American press. It was an early warning of trouble to come. David Ives, president of WGBH/Boston, the coproduction's American partner, said "I knew we were in for it."[28] But after assuring themselves of the show's accuracy, Ives and the PBS executives decided to stand their ground and braced themselves for the inevitable assault. The onslaught began with a letter from the Saudi ambassador in Washington to the U.S. State Department, protesting the planned PBS airing of the show on grounds that it showed "a completely false picture of the life, religion, customs and traditions of Saudi Arabia." He tactfully explained that he did not wish to infringe upon America's rights of free speech, but "we feel that you and other responsible officials of your government would want to know of our concerns." Acting Secretary of State Warren Christopher forwarded the Saudi ambassador's letter to PBS president Larry Grossman. In addition to underscoring the obvious—that the Saudi government was "deeply offended"—Christopher's cover letter stated that while the U.S. government "cannot and will not attempt to exercise any power of censorship, we ask that appropriate consideration be given to the sensitive religious and cultural issues involved." Grossman interpreted the letter to be a veiled request to dump the show and rejected it. He reminded the State Department that public television believes "that a free society requires open and candid discussion of issues so that an informed public may make rational judgments."[29]

The Saudi protest ignited a chain reaction. Senator Charles Percy of Illinois carried the matter into the Oval Office with an assurance to Jimmy Carter that "if the President made a determination that the showing of the program would not be in the national interest," Congress would probably back him.[30] The worst fears of those opposed to federal subsidy of the media were confirmed when Rep. Clement Zablocki, the chairman of the powerful House Foreign Affairs Committee, threatened to block public television's forward funding. "If [public television] is going to show substandard films," he told the press, "why should we waste the taxpayer's money?"[31]

But the single act that stiffened PBS's will to resist was the placing of newspaper ads in a half-dozen American papers denouncing the film as "a fairy tale." They were placed there by Mobil Oil, a partner in Aramco—the Arabian-American oil venture—and public television's largest program underwriter. (Its investment in one show, *Masterpiece Theater*, added up to $3 million that year.) The Mobil ads called on PBS to review its decision and to "exercise judgment in light of what is the best interest of the United States." Mobil's opposition left PBS no choice: either air the show as planned or suffer the stigma of having bowed to pressure from a major funder. In the end, the sole concession to pressure was a one-hour panel discussion among Arabs and Arabic scholars, aired at the conclusion of the docudrama. Of the countries that aired the show, the United States was the only that felt a need to "explain" it to its audience. The act in itself makes a significant comment on the American perception of public television's responsibility.

Death of a Princess was broadcast on May 12, 1980. The PBS decision to air it won almost universal support from the editorial pages of the nation's press even as it met with mixed reviews from its television critics. One critic, Tom Shales, found it ironic that a "film whose telecast has generated probably the biggest flurry of protest in public TV history . . . is exceeded in its presumptuousness only by its tediousness."[32] A handful of PBS stations declined to go along with the PBS decision to air the show. KUHT / Houston turned it down after the Saudi protest and was taken to court by a disappointed viewer who charged the station with trampling on his First Amendment rights. His argument—that because KUHT had been licensed to a state university it was as an arm of government and therefore specifically prohibited by statute from interfering with free speech—was upheld in the lower courts but reversed on appeal. A similar suit to force the Alabama state network to air the show also was defeated. The only other state network to reject the show, South Carolina ETV, explained that the appointment of its former governor, John West, as ambassador to Saudi Arabia had made the state "more sensitive to relationships with the Saudi Arabian government."[33]

The broadcast of *Death of a Princess* provoked a brief flurry that included a hike in oil prices, although whether this was in retaliation for the program by the Saudis was never proved. The tide of protest calls that swamped the stations prior to the program's airing turned, after its airing, to calls of praise. PBS, exulting briefly in the warm glow of self-righteousness, enjoyed numbers on the Nielsen charts that had not been seen since the broadcast five years earlier of a National Geographic Special, *The Incredible Machine*. Within days, the show that had stirred controversy on three continents was largely forgotten, relegated to the dustbin of yesterday's stale news. Its transience led some to reflect on why so ephemeral a medium can rouse such fears of long-term negative effects. Patrick Buchanan, the oracle of the conservative right, offered his own bitter benediction to the affair. "If there is to be a sequel to . . . *The Death of a Princess*, let us pray that it is *The Death of a Public Broadcasting System*."[34]

Perhaps the most apposite epitaph for *Death of Princess*—if not for our times—was uttered by a disgruntled viewer in San Francisco. "What good is free speech," he asked "if there's no gasoline?"[35]

15

MONUMENTAL DREAMS
ON SHOESTRING
BUDGETS

I really believe the greatest problem public broadcasting faces is itself.
Edward J. Pfister[1]

Ronald Reagan's arrival at the White House in January 1981 was not good news for public broadcasting. The prospect of four years of an Administration that had pledged to shrink the size of government and slash federal spending promised a bleak future for the system's hard-pressed institutions. Fears were rampant among the stations that deep cuts in public television's federal support would leave the system more vulnerable than ever to inflationary pressures. Rising costs had, by the beginning of the 1980s, already left it weak. Nor were funding cuts the public system's only threat from the new Administration. Also at risk was the Corporation's independence as a nongovernmental agency. In preparing the way for the new Republican broom, Reagan's transition team had paid little heed to the independent status of the Corporation for Public Broadcasting, giving it the same once-over they had accorded the established agencies of the federal establishment. Worse, they concluded that it was an "unnecessary layer of bureaucracy," recommended that it be phased out, and voiced strong sentiments against continued federal funding.[2]

Candidate Reagan, on the stump seeking the nation's highest office, had warned public broadcasters to look not to the federal

treasury but to alternative sources of income. Curiously, his threatening rhetoric was partially modulated by reassuring messages
from his aides. Not to worry, they told public broadcasters. Even
if government pulls back on its funding, "they [the public] will
not let public television wither."[3] Public broadcasters, however,
did worry. The White House's Office of Management and Budget
dismissed public broadcasting's contribution to society as "debat-
able," and recommended deep cuts in current and future funding.[4] So despairing were the portents that PBS president Grossman
was moved to declare public broadcasting an "endangered species."[5] Alone among the Cassandra cries within the system was the
optimistic voice of Dr. Michael Kelley, a Carter appointee to the
Corporation board, who felt that the budget cutbacks "could well
cause a creative surge in the public broadcasting industry, paring
away both fat and deadwood."[6] Most, however, felt that Kelley's
optimism was as misplaced as his metaphor.

The view that public broadcasting might benefit from a little
belt-tightening could not be dismissed lightly. The notion had
been born in the Carter years, long before the Reagan forces in-
vaded Washington wielding their budget-cutting axes. The Republican prophets of supply-side economics simply added new lyrics to the previous Administration's familiar cut-the-costs melody.
But those lyrics helped to shape the Reagan Administration's major long-range impact on the public medium. One of the most
visible results was the introduction of the much hated but now
familiar noncommercial "commercials" that grace the spaces between public television's underwritten programs. Reagan, unlike
Nixon, felt no compelling urge to silence the voice of public
broadcasting or to take it over and make it his own. He saw it not
as a threat—it was too irrelevant for that—but only as another
debit to be removed from the government dole. The Reaganomic
solution was to set the system adrift among the forces of the free
marketplace and let its ability to survive prove its value to society.

The president's sink-or-swim policy was preceded by two failed
efforts to apply new and imaginative solutions to public broadcasting's funding problems. Both initiatives had taken place in the
years immediately prior to his election victory. The first was an

effort to update the ten-year-old Carnegie Commission study with a fresh look into the public medium's highly visible problems of structure and finance. Like its 1967 predecessor, the 1977 Carnegie Commission on the Future of Public Broadcasting (Carnegie II) was sponsored by the Carnegie Corporation. The foundation appointed the seventeen-member Commission, funded its work, and published the results of its deliberations eighteen months later.[7]

The Commission found "public broadcasting's financial, organizational and creative structure fundamentally flawed," directing much of its criticism at the Corporation for its inability "to fulfill the need for effective leadership." (The Corporation, it must be remembered, was itself the creature of the earlier Carnegie Commission.) Carnegie II urged that the "flawed" system be replaced with a "fundamentally restructured and reorganized" system that, in their plan, would be erected upon two new private, non-profit entities. The first, a Public Telecommunications Trust, would supplant the Corporation as "the principal leadership, planning, and evaluation agency." Although the Trust's functions would be similar to those of the Corporation, its directors would be selected by a wholly different method to protect it from political control. In addition, it would have no role in programming. Programming would be left to the other new entity, the Program Services Endowment, which would serve as a semi-autonomous unit under the wing of the Trust. The Program Services Endowment would have "the sole mission of underwriting a broad range of television and radio productions, program services, and related research." PBS's probable fate in the proposed reshuffling was not immediately clear. It certainly received no reassurance from Carnegie II's chairman, William J. McGill, who in a later reference to the network called it "a logical monstrosity" with too many voices trying to be part of the decision-making process. And although the Commission's recommendations said that PBS hadn't been "very effective in its present form," Carnegie II chose to leave it with limited responsibility for operating the interconnection. Carnegie II's recommendations on funding were less revolutionary. The report called for substantially higher levels of federal support from general tax revenues, which were to be partially offset by a "spectrum fee" levied on all users of the "public airwaves." The report underscored the value of politically free, locally generated revenues and proposed to link them with a matching formula to federal funds in order to stimulate local fund-raising.

In the long run, Carnegie II failed to generate the interest and enthusiasm of the original Commission study; response to the report and its recommendations was muted. Even those who praised the Commission's efforts doubted the political feasibility of its recommendations. The proposed spectrum fee would unquestionably run into stiff opposition from the group hardest hit, the commercial broadcasters, whose powerful Congressional lobby could block efforts at reform and whose attitude was signaled by *Broadcasting*'s sour assessment of Carnegie II: "The worst features of the existing system would be preserved, if by other names, at three times the existing expense."[8] After a brief but futile effort to incorporate the recommendations into legislation, Carnegie II's report was shelved and forgotten.

The other reform effort, mounted at about the same time by California congressman Lionel Van Deerlin, embraced all of broadcasting, not just the public sector. Rep. Van Deerlin's proposed legislation sought nothing less than a total rewrite and updating of the creaky and overburdened Communications Act of 1934, the basic statute regulating electronic communications. His bill included sweeping changes in both the public and the private media. Like Carnegie II, it would abolish the Corporation and divide its function between two new agencies. The Public Telecommunications Programming Endowment, a private corporation whose nine directors would be appointed by the president, was to be concerned exclusively with program funding. Half of its funds would go to stations to meet direct program costs; the other half would be parceled out in individual grants to a broad range of applicants, including applicants outside public broadcasting. On the other hand, all nonprogramming funds—monies for the planning, construction, and operation of broadcasting facilities— would be doled out by an agency of government, the National Telecommunications Agency. Because the federal agency would hold all recipients to governmentally imposed restrictions on what they could and could not do with operations funded from this source, the Van Deerlin bill fell far short of protecting public broadcasting from political and governmental interference.[9]

Van Deerlin hoped to use the promise of widespread deregulation of the industry to court support for his rewrite bill among commercial broadcasters. His price for deregulation was to be the commercial broadcasters' acceptance of a spectrum fee levied on all broadcasting (a fee much like the one proposed by Carnegie II), a part of which would go to meet public broadcasting's needs. Unfortunately, Van Deerlin's ambition exceeded the limits of what was politically feasible (as one wry observer noted, it was the congressman's genius to include something in his sweeping bill for everyone to hate). Efforts to win over the opposition resulted in a highly modified piece of legislation. But the negotiating parties were unable to resolve their conflicting interests and the bill died an unexpected death in the summer of 1979.

When the Reagan Administration turned its attention to public television, it was far less interested in reforming the system than with getting it "off the government's back." The focus of its interest was turned upon "funding options"—the search for alternative modes of financing public television. The Van Deerlin bill had been dead less than two years when, with the Administration's urging, Congress created a Temporary Commission on Alternative Financing. The TCAF was charged with "exploring financing options to maintain, enhance and expand public broadcast services to the American people."[10] One of the options authorized an eighteen-month experiment in which a limited number of public stations could sell and air commercial announcements. Of the nine stations that took part in the experiment, most—using varying types of commercial messages—experienced a rise in income with little or no negative reaction from their viewers. At the conclusion of the study, however, the TCAF rejected commercials as the answer to public television's needs. Their potential disadvantages—the probable end of federal funding, a predictable drop in viewer support, and the loss of concessions from unions and copyright holders—outweighed the uncertain income benefits of paid advertising. Moreover, some public stations, among them the state-owned networks, were barred by their licensing authorities from airing commercials. The TCAF concluded that the only practical solution to the funding problem was more money from more sources, but the principal source would continue to be the federal government. The Reagan stratagem to cut the system loose from the federal purse came to naught.

The TCAF study did, however, effect a major change in public television funding. Its recommendation of "broadened guidelines" for the on-air credits for public television's corporate underwriters resulted six months later in a relaxing of the FCC rules. Under the new rules, PBS shows are permitted to credit their underwriters with "specific brand or trade names" and "value-neutral" listings of product lines and services. With a light foot on the brake, however, the FCC barred the common commercial practice of making claims that certain products and services are "best" or "leading" or the showing of sleek new automobiles "in motion." To preserve the credibility of its factual programs PBS added its own restriction: corporate underwriters who might have a stake in the program's content are unacceptable. The resulting noncommercial commercials entered the system under the euphemism "enhanced underwriting."[11]

The liberalized rules on corporate underwriting were not yet in place when public television's first nightly news show started: all during its first year, the *MacNeil/Lehrer NewsHour*[12] could do little more than acknowledge AT&T's underwriting grant of ten million dollars with what amounted to a quick and courteous nod since PBS and FCC rules limited underwriting credits to the corporate name of the donor. But in September 1983, Robert MacNeil and Jim Lehrer managed, even without the advantages of the relaxed rules, to create and fund television's first prime-time, hour-long news show. It was a rare instance of public television acting first. For years, the three commercial networks have been working to expand their evening newscasts to a full hour, but their plans have always met with resistance from affiliates unwilling to yield the extra half-hour from their local time. Although PBS succeeded where the networks have so far failed, it would be a mistake to conclude that it did so without meeting some of the same kind of resistance.

When PBS president Larry Grossman first proposed the idea of an hour-long news show, he may have done so believing his member stations would leap at the chance to be first with what he, and both Robin MacNeil and Jim Lehrer, felt was a much-needed service that only the public system could provide. The PBS stations were, at the time, airing the nightly half-hour *MacNeil/Lehrer Report*, a single-topic news analysis show with the eponymous anchors in New York and Washington. Grossman reasoned that more would be better. MacNeil and Lehrer agreed. But the stations, they soon learned, were not so eager. They could be just as resistant to the idea as their commercial counterparts, although for different reasons. For many, it was the money. The stations had been asked to provide approximately one-quarter of the show's $21 million budget, a considerable increase over what they were putting up for its predecessor, the half-hour *MacNeil/Lehrer Report*. More important, they were perfectly satisfied to remain with the half-hour show, not only because it was less costly, but because its thrust—"look at the network news then come to us for an explanation of the major story of the day"—was a much stronger rationale than a "cheap and ineffectual" attempt to imitate what the networks were already doing reasonably well. The *MacNeil/Lehrer* team quickly mounted an all-out campaign. Their pitch to promote the hour-long show was laced with an oblique threat to move elsewhere with the seven-year-old *MacNeil/Lehrer Report* if the PBS stations rejected the expanded version. In the long run, however, it was not the threat but public television's possible loss of AT&T's $10 million underwriting grant, and its additional $2 million in promotion money, that broke the resistance to the hour-long version.

The *MacNeil/Lehrer NewsHour* opened to mixed notices. Professional journalists, for the most part, found the new format thoughtful and thorough, "a better program than its predecessor, not an unqualified smash, but livelier, just as responsible, and infinitely more valuable."[13] A few, however, found it boring, slow-paced, too "talky," a bit like spinach ("good for you but a bit

boring if you indulge it too often").[14] The show's "balance"—
it was as meticulously balanced as a bookkeeper's checkbook—
was a virtue that did not go unappreciated by a system as vulnerable to charges of liberal bias as public television. Liberals, however, challenged what they claimed was only its appearance of balance, noting that the show seemed "always to side with the
powerful while pretending to be 'objective and dispassionate as
possible.' "[15] Audience response to the show's first season was disappointing, with ratings that were only slightly higher than for the
half-hour *Report*. Station programmers, aware of the show's failure
to deliver larger numbers and bristling under the burden of its
increased costs, were ready to deny it a second year until they were
swayed by pleas to allow it more time to build an audience. Ultimately, of course, it was to find an audience and a permanent
place on the PBS schedule.[16] But the dissident voices were not
immediately muted. Two years after the *NewsHour*'s debut, a handful of rogue stations, still fixed on a half-hour news show, made a
collective effort to produce their own, ostensibly to supplant *Mac-
Neil/Lehrer*. The plot failed, but it was evidence of the thin line
that separates democracy from anarchy in the public system.

Six months after engineering the *NewsHour* debut, Larry Grossman resigned the presidency of PBS. NBC president Grant Tinker
had recruited him to head that network's news division. It was,
Grossman told his PBS colleagues, "the only job that I would leave
here for."[17] His success in bringing the nightly news show to the
public network was a fitting coda to his seven sometimes frustrating years at the helm of PBS. The rancor and distrust that had
greeted his arrival in 1976 were largely forgotten by the time of
his departure in February 1984. Most stations granted him high
marks for strong leadership, particularly for his willingness to
speak out on issues of mutual concern. His initiatives had brought
new audiences to the public medium, and he could well afford to
ignore the cavils of a few unreconstructed holdouts who complained that he had used increased centralization to accomplish
it. One press critic, praising Grossman for helping to make PBS
"look more like network TV," may not have realized that a net-

work was precisely what most station executives and members of Congress did not want.[18]

The committee to find Grossman's successor was headed by PBS board chairman Dallin Oakes. In addition to serving on the Utah Supreme Court, Oakes was a prominent leader in the Church of Jesus Christ of Latter-Day Saints. The committee's decision to fill the presidential post with a broadcaster from Utah who was also a Mormon might have raised questions. That it did not was a tribute to Bruce Christensen, who was not only the unanimous selection of the PBS board but also the favored candidate of the member stations. Christensen had managed the public stations at Brigham Young University and later at the University of Utah. The PBS stations saw him as one of their own, an insider who was quiet and circumspect in manner and an effective spokesperson for their cause. In the two years prior to coming to PBS, he had headed the National Association of Public Television Stations, and in that capacity had been public television's principal lobbyist in Washington.

Christensen's manner contrasted sharply with that of his predecessor. Christensen saw PBS not as a network but as "a local communications cooperative." His much more muted notion of leadership was best indicated by the plaque on his desk: "Where did they go? I must hasten to find them—for I am their leader." Christensen's first task was to help PBS regain the momentum it had lost with the drop in federal funding. "Dreams and aspirations . . . have largely been put on hold," he told his membership. "It is time to take some of those dreams off the shelf and make them reality."[19]

By the luck of good timing, several of the system's headiest dreams had become reality before the full force of the Reagan budget-cutting axe slowed the public medium's forward momentum. In the fall of 1983, *Vietnam: A Television History* appeared to remind viewers that public television had not lost touch with its roots. Richard Ellison's thirteen-hour chronicle of the first war that America had ever lost was praised by *Newsweek* as "television at its most riveting and powerful,"[20] and by the *Washington Post* as "an extraordinary film record."[21] The series was also honored by

the television industry with its top journalism awards. Fox Butterfield, who covered the war in Vietnam, called the series "meticulously researched and carefully balanced."[22] But none of this saved
the series from charges of "serious errors and distortions" by Accuracy in Media, the self-appointed media watchdog of the conservative right. AIM's attack was not of the usual shoot-and-duck
variety. The group backed its charges with an hour-long documentary produced by AIM and narrated by Charlton Heston. Funding for the documentary had come from the National Endowment
for the Humanities, whose director, William Bennett, had given
the money without the customary consultation with his staff. AIM
invited PBS to preview the completed documentary at a special
screening in the Reagan White House, an obvious tactic to apply
political pressure for its airing. Although PBS declined the White
House invitation, it did agree to air the AIM film. The network's
news and public-affairs chief, Barry Chase, eager to demonstrate
public television's readiness to air challenges to its own shows, felt
he had found in the AIM film a model for a television version of
newspaper's op-ed page. The op-ed notion, however, died a quick
death when the producer of *Vietnam: A Television History* refused
to participate. They saw the exercise as a charade and bitterly condemned PBS for its cravenness in not standing up for its own show.
The Vietnam series, they pointed out, had in every respect met
PBS's own journalistic standards. The press generally sided with
the producer's view. AIM, undaunted, persisted in its attacks upon
the series and returned to PBS several months later with yet another documentary challenging the accuracy of the Vietnam series. This time, however, PBS turned it down.

The Vietnam affair was a reminder of the mine-strewn path that
public television walks when it attempts to deal with controversy
and helps to explain why the system is constantly in search of
attack-proof formats for dealing with it. What may be the most
innovative answer to that search was supplied in 1983 by Fred
Friendly. The veteran producer of Ed Murrow's *See It Now* was no
stranger to television's efforts to deal with issues on which opinions divided and passions ran high. His idea for a format that later
would become Columbia University's Seminars on the Media and

Society was more than a means of juggling a hot issue without the danger of first degree burns. It was a rare melding of substance and entertainment. Although it seems perfectly suited to television, it was created originally for a different purpose. Before his retirement from the Ford Foundation, Friendly and his assistant Stuart Sucherman had worked together on a Foundation project to narrow the divide separating the press and the judiciary. In search of a nonthreatening framework in which to bring them closer together, they hit upon a solution that was simplicity itself: leaders from both professions were brought face-to-face around a horseshoe-shaped table, presented with a hypothetical situation, and forced to respond to the insistent questioning of a highly skilled law professor. The situation created by this technique, says Friendly, becomes "so agonizing that they can escape only by thinking."

It did not escape the notice of Friendly and Sucherman, after they had used the format in 150 private Foundation-sponsored seminars, that the technique embraced all the elements of good television: the celebrity of big-name panelists; the drama of sharp, provocative questioning; and the wit and humor of the players' spontaneous responses. "Theater of information," one critic called it. In 1981, Friendly brought the format to Columbia University, adapted it to television, and with Stuart Sucherman's assistance and a Ford Foundation grant formed The Media and Society Seminars—some of which were made into specials for PBS. The early roundtables were focused on media issues, but in 1983 Friendly used the format to breathe life into the United States Constitution. The result, *The Constitution: That Delicate Balance*, reached millions of adults, many of whom happened upon the thirteen-week series, stayed with it, and found to their surprise that a show could be entertaining without sacrificing its educational values. In the years since, Friendly has used the much-copied seminar format to deal with a broad and challenging range of public-policy issues, all fraught with the now-legendary agony of controversy from which the only escape is thinking.

The early 1980s saw the rise of another important innovation. Although its roots were political, the outcome resulted in a spate of new series in the PBS prime-time schedule. The initiative for change came from Lewis Freedman. As the first director of the Corporation's Program Fund, and a highly imaginative producer of Emmy Award–winning television drama, Freedman had hoped to use the office and the power of the Corporation's funds to initiate a new era of programming. He quickly discovered the limits on the power of the Corporation to initiate programming changes. That power rested for the most part with individual producing stations. Freedman had long since learned the difficulties of working through individual stations toward a concerted goal. In the early 1970s, with the support of KCET / Los Angeles, Freedman undertook to supply PBS with a much-needed drama series. The result was *Hollywood Television Theater.* WNET / New York also wanted to do a major drama series for the network, and they produced *Theater in America.* The predictable result was competition between the two stations for limited production dollars, performance rights, and talent. Efforts to combine the two series and end the competition fell on the sword of local pride. The experience was a lesson to Freedman in the absurd wastefulness of interstation competition.

In the waning months of his tenure at the Program Fund, Freedman hit upon a stratagem to overcome the system's built-in barriers to concerted action. He called it a "consortium" (while mischievously claiming he didn't know the meaning of the word). Instead of following the conventional pattern of funding a new series by awarding the grant to a single producing station, Freedman created a working party of several producing stations, any one, or all, of which might otherwise be competitors for the same funds. One of the consortium partners was designated as the "lead" station—in effect, the producer of the series—while the others were cast in consultative roles as the consortium's board of directors. It was a Machiavellian stratagem, but it worked. And because it resulted in the addition of several new series to the PBS schedule, it may well have been the decade's most significant contribution to public television programming.

Given Freedman's obsession with seeing a sustained drama series on the public medium, specifically one drawing on the creativity of American writers, it was no surprise that American Playhouse would be the first consortium established. In fact, it resulted from a confluence of interests: Freedman had been approached by former Ford Foundation executive David M. Davis with a proposal for a drama series jointly produced with the New York and Los Angeles stations. (Davis's interest in drama began at Ford where he engineered funding for several earlier PBS drama series.) Freedman, foreseeing interstation rivalries with two stations, urged a broader participation and encouraged Davis to create the first four-station consortium with himself as executive director, Lindsay Law as executive producer, and WNET / New York as lead station. (American Playhouse separated from the station six months later to become an independent corporate entity, a decision that would figure in its freedom to shape its own destiny years later.) Each season for the next decade, Davis and Law read through thousands of scripts submitted by writers, agents, and producers; chose twenty to twenty-four that met their needs; and either funded, co-produced, or bought the finished films from independent producers.[23] Davis and Law shrewdly stretched their limited dollars (from the Program Fund, the Station Program Cooperative, the National Endowment for the Arts, and corporate underwriters) by an occasional deal to share production costs and first performance rights with theatrical distributors. Thus, several American Playhouse productions—*El Norte, Smooth Talk, Testament, The Thin Blue Line, Stand and Deliver*—were seen first in theaters before they appeared in the PBS schedule.

For twelve successful years, *American Playhouse* was television's sole source of original, regularly scheduled American drama. According to director Gregory Nava (*El Norte*), it "opened the floodgates for a lot of projects that would otherwise never happen."[24] For *New York Times* critic John O'Connor, *American Playhouse* was "a rare and wondrous thing" in a business "obsessed with bottom lines and ridden with tired formulas."[25] In 1994, however, PBS began to draw the curtain on original American drama. The system was falling into the thrall of the bean counters; its priorities were shifting to shows with broader appeal. PBS promised two more years of partial funding, and then no more. American Playhouse responded by spinning off a for-profit subsidiary, Playhouse Pictures, and signing a partnership with Samuel Goldwyn Company for the production of fifteen independently produced theatrical films the first year. PBS will presumably benefit by having the right to air the films after their theatrical and home video release, a waiting period that could be as long as eighteen months to three years. However parsed, the decision to cut back on *American Playhouse*'s support is a blow to original drama—already an endangered species, and not just in the United States—and a retreat from public television's commitment to do what others cannot or will not do.

The original success of the American Playhouse consortium encouraged Freedman to create three others: *Frontline, Great Performances,* and *Wonderworks. Frontline* filled the need for a weekly documentary series that had been absent from the PBS schedule since the late sixties when NET *Journal* fell victim to the NET-WNDT merger. Freedman found the needed framework for his documentary consortium at WGBH / Boston where David Fanning had demonstrated a firm grip on the nonfiction form with *World,* the irregularly scheduled series in which the provocative *Death of a Princess* had appeared. *Frontline,* with Fanning as the executive producer and WGBH as the lead station, entered the PBS weekly schedule in the fall of 1982. Although its startup was uneven, it has at times provided a forceful reminder of E. B. White's prescriptive injunction to the public medium to "restate and clarify the social dilemma and the political pickle."[26]

Shortly after the formation of the *Frontline* consortium, Freedman encouraged WNET / New York to form a consortium for its *Great Performances* series, bringing the counsel of four new production partners to the station's anthology of virtuoso drama, music, and dance performances. With the money then remaining in the Program Fund budget, he set out to form a final consortium. This consortium was to produce children's programming. But a number of stations objected, arguing that in times of tight money, production funds would be wasted on children's shows because they do not attract viewer donations. (They were wrong.) However, his own board was pushing him at the same time to aim for the vaguely defined area of "family" programming. Freedman effected a compromise by forming a consortium around WQED / Pittsburgh for the production of *Wonderworks*, a family-oriented series of independently produced dramas that had broad appeal for both children and adults.

Before the last of his consortia was up and running, Freedman, ground down by the frictions and frustrations of the atomized system, resigned the directorship of the Corporation's Program Fund. He was succeeded by Ron Hull. Just as Freedman had reflected the urbanity of his upbringing on Manhattan's Upper East Side, Hull exuded the openness and ebullience of his native Nebraska, where for fifteen years he had presided over the programming of that state's network of public stations. In the long run, however, their contrasting styles proved less important than the timing of the turnover. The long-feared Reagan year of reckoning arrived in 1982. Congress, under White House pressure, had rescinded $35 million of 1983's $172 million appropriation, dropping public television's federal funding to its lowest level in four years (or the lowest level in ten years if measured in constant dollars). "The sadness begins," said the Corporation's president.[27] The budget cleaver of Reaganomics had seriously undermined public television's localism. Stations, caught in the dual squeeze of rising inflation and lowered appropriations, were forced to trim or eliminate local programming. Further, those stations most dependent on federal funds faced the prospect of being eliminated altogether. Although it was hardly unexpected—the White House, after all, had been trying since 1980 to reduce public broadcasting's federal support—it was a bitter pill nonetheless.

The cutback in federal funds was equally devastating to PBS's plans for national programming. Its hopes for a bright opening to the 1983 season faded as funding dried up. New program series, normally in the production "pipeline" for future release, were languishing for lack of production money, their costs rising daily as inflation drove their budgets up. *The Brain*, one of several prestigious program series that were originally scheduled to kick off the 1983 PBS season, provides a typical example of the way repeated delays in funding can boost production costs unnecessarily. WNET's eight-hour science series had been budgeted at $5 million, a difficult nut to crack under the best of circumstances. When 1982's funding crisis broke, the series had been languishing on the drawing boards for almost four years while the station solicited production funds. A $200,000 grant from the National Science Foundation had lifted the project out of the idea stage into a tentative kind of reality, but it was not yet enough money to produce a single one of the eight projected episodes. The weeks of fruitless searching turned into months and resulted in the loss of the BBC as a coproduction partner. During these long months of unproductive effort, the project's costs for planning, preparing proposals, and knocking on doors ticked on like the meter of a taxi stuck in traffic.

The Brain's first major break had come in 1981 with the announcement that Walter Annenberg, the wealthy publisher of *TV Guide*, was giving the Corporation $150 million over fifteen years to subsidize the production of programs for adult education. When the queue formed for the initial round of Annenberg / CPB production grants, *The Brain* was at the head of the line and received a $2 million grant. The first burst of elation over the blessings of Annenberg died quickly when the producers realized they were caught in public television's classic double bind: having money enough to start but not enough to finish. By 1982, and still $2 million short of its production budget, *The Brain* had not only made a commitment to PBS to meet a 1984 air date, it had accepted both the Annenberg and the National Science Foundation grants on the condition the money would be spent for the production of one or more of the eight shows. The staff had no other choice but to risk moving ahead in the hope that the balance of the funds could be found before production was finished. The gamble doesn't always pay off, but this time it did. The grant that closed the gap arrived only days before the first show aired.

The completed series walked away with virtually every major television award the industry offers. But its success masked the price that public television had paid for the long delays in getting it produced. The piecemeal funding and the corrosive effects of inflation over the course of its delayed production had added an estimated half-million dollars to its costs. *The Brain*, whose experience is all too common, was but one of public television's many "big ticket" productions.

If the baleful effects of the 1982 rollback on public television's programming were not immediately apparent to viewers, they were certainly visible to the television critics. Tom Shales, grumbling over the thinness of the season's schedule, called 1983 "one of the dullest and dreariest years since [PBS] began."[28] In fact, large portions of the 1983 schedule had been around for more than ten years, including such perennials as *Masterpiece Theater, Nova, National Geographic Specials, Wall Street Week, Washington Week in Review,* and *Great Performances.*[29] The continued presence of these programs signified a commendable tendency to stick with winners, but it also lessened the opportunities for innovative and fresh programming to brighten the new season.

The 1984 season fared somewhat better. By then, PBS had two high-visibility "blockbusters," *The Brain* and *Heritage: Civilization and the Jews*, to launch the new lineup. The seeds not sown in 1982 had a significant effect in 1985, however: that season was a disaster. Because the budget cutbacks had dried up the production pipeline for the previous two years, no new projects had been launched with which to energize the 1985 season. PBS was reduced to rerunning *The Brain*, acquiring more shows from abroad, and serving up old shows in new dress. *Heritage: Civilization and the Jews* was repackaged with the addition of interviews by Bill Moyers and given a new title. And the BBC's distinguished productions of Shakespeare's plays returned, but this time they were conveniently broken down into bite-sized, hour-long segments "hosted" by Walter Matthau. The truncated version was billed in newspaper ads as a more convenient way to watch Shakespeare in these busy times. One wonders what still busier times might have produced.

Nor did the "sadness" go away at the end of 1984. The electorate had returned to the White House for a second term the man who had, with dismaying consistency, ordered cuts in the public medium's federal funding. Bruce Christensen, only six months in the PBS presidency, tried valiantly to put a happy face on the situation by reporting that President Reagan "likes public television very much." The only difference we have with him, he said, "is in the manner of funding."[30] But it was to prove a big difference, even to Christensen. "How," he later asked rhetorically, "do you build the monumental dreams on shoestring budgets?"[31]

Monumental dreams, of course, are built on more than fat budgets. They need the vision, the inspiration, and the daring of imaginative and courageous leadership. America's public television not only has lacked that leadership but also may not wish it. Certainly public television cannot expect to get it from the White House if past experience is any measure. The role of the president of the United States in providing public television with leadership began only in 1967; before the passage of the Public Broadcasting Act that year the system relied largely upon a small group of distinguished citizens who composed the self-perpetuating board of NET. With the passage of the Public Broadcasting Act, Congress clearly intended to place the system's leadership in the hands of the Corporation for Public Broadcasting. According to the Act, leadership is to be exercised through the Corporation's governing board, whose fifteen members (reduced to ten in 1981) are appointed for limited terms by the president (with the advice and consent of the Senate). Congress called for the board nominees to be drawn from persons "eminent in such fields as education, cultural and civic affairs, or the arts, including radio and television." President Johnson's appointees to the Corporation's original board generally met the criteria of "eminence" as defined by the *American Heritage Dictionary* ("towering above others, prominent").[32] But the process—and the quality of the board—has been in decline ever since. Successive presidents have with dismaying consistency used board appointments to pay off small political favors, thereby demeaning the appointment process and diminishing the importance and stature of the institution of public broadcasting it is designed to serve.

The appointments have, at times, been so blatantly political as to backfire on the presidents who made them. President Nixon, on his last official day in office, sent to the Senate for confirmation the name of the millionaire brewer Joseph Coors. The Senate, sensing a possible conflict of interest, set the Coors nomination for hearing only to discover that the politically conservative Coors was building his own syndicated television news service with which to "balance" the "left-wing bias" of the network news divisions. The Senators postponed action on the Coors nomination only to find it before them once again when President Ford resubmitted his name. This time the Senate did not hesitate to act, but only because the nominee had made it easier by his own actions. While awaiting confirmation, Coors was approached by a mortician friend who asked him to intervene with the Corporation to block the scheduled showing of a PBS documentary based on Jessica Mitford's *The American Way of Death*. Coors shot off a letter to Corporation president Henry Loomis. "I am not yet familiar enough with the interconnection between PBS and CPB to know whether you can do anything about this," he wrote, "but it is the type of thing which I will be very interested in watching closely if I ever become confirmed on your fine board."[33] His nomination was tabled and died.

Those who thought that a Democrat in the White House would make a difference were forced to reconcile the notion with President Carter's nomination of Irby Turner, Jr., of Belzoni, Mississippi. Whatever Turner's claim to eminence—it may have been service on the board of his state's public-television network—his appointment was stopped dead by revelations that he had served on that board during the time it was refusing to air NET's programming for black audiences. With the additional evidence that Turner had opposed school integration by providing land on which to build private schools, his opponents had all the leverage they needed to have his confirmation tabled.

President Reagan's appointments were even more politically motivated. One of his nominees was Helen Marie Taylor of Richmond, Virginia, a loyal party member active in her state's politically conservative organizations. However, when the Senate learned that she not only held memberships in racially exclusive clubs but also was involved with a foundation formed to circumvent the state's school desegregation order, her nomination was relegated to the let's-decide-this-later limbo. By delaying the nomination instead of turning it down, the Senate sought to avoid a fight with the White House. But although only six months remained in the unfilled term, Reagan was determined to fill it, if not with the embattled Taylor, then with another nominee. Using the presidential power to fill government posts without Senate approval during Congressional recesses, Reagan named William Lee Hanley, Jr., to the board. Hanley, an industrialist in the brick and petroleum businesses, had coordinated the Reagan-Bush campaign in Connecticut. Several days after his appointment, Hanley showed up for his first board meeting only to be denied a seat at the table by the board majority. Recess appointments, they declared, do not apply to nongovernmental agencies. The White House, miffed at the rejection and eager to establish the president's interim power, took the Corporation to court. Before the issue could be adjudicated, however, an unexpected resignation on the board created another vacancy and Reagan promptly filled it with the Hanley nomination. This time he took care to have the nominee confirmed by the Senate.

The quality of leadership that public television has received from the Corporation has been influenced not only by presidential appointments, but also by those whom the board has itself chosen to be chair. The outcome has, at best, been mixed. Its first chair, Frank Pace, Jr., the former Secretary of the Army, was not elected in the usual manner but was appointed by President Johnson. When he resigned at the height of the Nixon effort to co-opt the board, his successor was the former congressman from Missouri, Thomas B. Curtis. Although he had been the White House's own choice, Curtis resigned in anger in May 1973—betrayed, so he thought, by the people who had put him there. The board turned to its only independent, James R. Killian, Jr., the president of MIT. But Killian remained only eighteen months, and was replaced by the board's vice chairman, Robert Benjamin, a lawyer and chairman of United Artists. Benjamin, a forceful but gentlemanly negotiator, had attempted to bring the Corporation and PBS closer together, but with very little success after two years, he too resigned "to speak up as an individual about the issues which divided the two organizations."[34]

The choice of W. Allen Wallis to succeed Benjamin surprised most veteran board watchers. Wallis, who was the chancellor of the University of Rochester, had racked up a record of poor attendance and less-than-enthusiastic participation in the board's business prior to his election. But with the board clearly divided along ideological lines, he emerged as the only compromise candidate. His resignation eighteen months later was no less a surprise, although more by its manner than by its substance. The board had just decided to break for lunch at its 1978 midsummer meeting when Wallis, who was conducting the meeting, rose from his chair, abruptly announced his resignation from both the board and his position as presiding officer, and without apology walked out, caught a plane, and shuffled off to another appointment. He cited "personal" reasons for his resignation, but insiders were quick to point to the severe frustrations that Wallis had suffered over the Corporation's uncertain future. The chairman was particularly irked over Reagan's delays in filling board vacancies. After his departure, and left with barely half its normal complement, the board elected Lillie Herndon, former head of the National Congress of Parents and Teachers. Herndon was the first in a succession of women to occupy the CPB chair, including Sharon Percy Rockefeller; Sonia Landau, former chair of the New York State Women for Reagan-Bush campaign; and Sheila Tate, Nancy Reagan's former press secretary.

Of this number, only Sonia Landau would find herself the center of almost unrelieved controversy and the target of press attention for her occasional theatrics. The former teacher, media consultant, and party loyalist was named to the board by President Reagan shortly after his 1980 election victory. Her appointment coincided—significantly, as it turned out—with Edward J. Pfister's arrival at the Corporation to fill the presidential office vacated by the departed Robben Fleming. Pfister had been the president of KERA / Dallas and thus was the first professional broadcaster to fill the chief executive's post. His years of service with public television taught him all he needed to know about the system's divided loyalties, political intrigues, and parochial cabals. The knowledge made him all the more determined to bring "an end to the antagonism and bickering" that had drained the system's energies and credibility.[35] But even as he voiced these aims, the stage was being set for Sonia Landau to make their realization impossible, if not forever, at least for him.

Three years after she joined the board, its new Republican majority elected Landau chair. In a very close vote, she had managed to unseat the three-term incumbent, Sharon Percy Rockefeller. Rockefeller's departing words, an urgent plea "to keep CPB nonpartisan and apolitical in every way," anticipated the difficulties ahead. Landau's critics had questioned the propriety of her participation in the 1983 Reagan-Bush reelection campaign while serving as the Corporation's "nonpartisan" presiding officer. Nor was politics the only area in which she gave the impression of a conflict of interest. At the time, Landau's husband, John Corry, was the television critic for the *New York Times*. Among the shows he reviewed were those funded by the Corporation.

Landau had been in the chair just six months when the first crisis erupted. The board's spring meeting, held that year in San Francisco, had been an otherwise drearily routine session until late in the meeting when Landau unexpectedly launched an attack on Pfister's plan to lead a Corporation-sponsored delegation of public broadcasters to Moscow. The purpose of the mission was the possible exchange of programming with Soviet television. Landau was shocked to find "that an institution that operates on federal money is dealing with the Soviet government." The serio-comic implications that the Corporation might be guilty of trading with the enemy hung unanswered in the stunned silence. She shifted her line of attack, arguing that the Corporation's responsibility to act as a "heat shield" to protect public television from the undue influence of Congress and the White House meant also that "we shouldn't be influenced by the Kremlin." In one bold, perverse stroke the heat shield had become a sword.[36]

The board's discussion was tense, emotional, and full of the barely contained anger of partisans divided along familiar and predictable lines. Reagan's good friend from his radio days, media consultant Harry O'Connor, supported Landau's thesis, arguing that the Corporation's money was still to be treated as government funds. And although these dollars were not actually paying for the Moscow trip, William Hanley worried that it might "appear" otherwise to Congress and thereby jeopardize future funding. Richard Brookhiser, editor of the conservative *National Review*, didn't care whether the dollars were "federal" or private; his concern was their possible use to buy Soviet programs. It will be "just disastrous," he warned, if we "open the door to Soviet ideas on history." Kenneth Towery, a journalist and a former aide to Texas senator Tower, offered the mildly heretical notion that the Corporation was not, "in fact, a private corporation," to which he added the unhelpful suggestion that the buying and selling of television programs was better left to the U.S. Information Agency.

The "liberal" minority on the board was dumbstruck by what it called "the Cold War reasoning." Lillie Herndon, a fifteen-year veteran on the board and its former presiding officer, charged the Reagan majority with "rewriting the Carnegie Commission language." She reminded her colleagues that Congress established the Corporation not as a federal entity but as an independent, private corporation. We have "worked years to establish that," she said. "If the stations buy inappropriate programming, that's their responsibility. It's not our responsibility to dictate to the stations what they can buy."

Landau, however, was not to be dislodged from her opposition to the Corporation's participation. It was "fine" with her, she told the board, if the PBS people wanted to sponsor the trip (they eventually did), but, she said, "I don't think I want CPB, when I am the custodian of that federal money, to be sending a CPB party there." Her board resolution withdrawing the Corporation's sponsorship of the trip was adopted by a 6–4 vote. Because he had approved Corporation sponsorship of the trade mission, had agreed to lead the delegation, and thought it was "probably the single most important issue" that had arisen during his presidency, Ed Pfister read the board's decision as a repudiation of his leadership. Following the vote, and after what he termed his "twelve agonizing hours," Pfister decided he "could not represent that kind of thinking" and resigned the presidency of the Corporation. It happened that his decision fell on the day that he was due to address a meeting of the chief executives of the system's stations, who were also holding their annual meeting in San Francisco. The station chiefs, stunned by news of the sudden turn of events, greeted his entrance with a standing ovation. In his address, Pfister warned them that the Corporation's decision meant "more of the obligation to safeguard independence falls squarely on their shoulders." The managers were brought to their feet once again in a wave of emotion that, said an observer, engulfed even those who never before thought themselves members of the Pfister fan club. He had become for the moment their martyr.[37]

The search for his successor would, it was hoped, give some clue to the board's future course. But after eight months dragged by and the board named Martin Rubenstein to the post, the system was still at sea about its future course. Rubenstein, a man with no discernible ideological bent, was a professional broadcaster with twenty-three years of experience in commercial radio and television. For the previous five years, he had been the president of the Mutual Broadcasting System radio network. The board appeared to be placing its bet on experience rather than ideology. But appearances can deceive. Barely ten months after he was hired, the board's conservative majority voted in private session to sack Rubenstein for having "usurped board authority." Failure to explain the charge led to speculation that the four directors were angered because Rubenstein had, without board approval, hired a business manager to unknot the tangled mess in which he had found the Corporation's contracts. His action had reduced the authority of the Corporation's vice president and treasurer, Donald Ledwig, who had come to the Corporation from a twenty-five-year career as a naval officer. Ledwig was the favorite of the Reagan-appointed conservatives who had wanted him as Pfister's successor, not Rubenstein (but at the time they lacked the votes). It came as no surprise therefore when the board named Ledwig president of the Corporation following the Rubenstein sack in July 1988. Ledwig remained in the post for three years and after his resignation was replaced in the summer of 1992 by Richard W. Carlson, who had been the U.S. Ambassador to the Republic of Seychelles and was a former director of the Voice of America. Carlson is the seventh to head the Corporation in its twenty-five-year history.

The uneven history of the Corporation's leadership, both of its appointed board and elected chairs, seems not to have hindered the institution's ability to handle its routine business. The competence of its leadership has, in that respect, been adequately demonstrated. The record of the past twenty-five years does, however, underscore the failure of the White House to bring to the medium's designated "leadership" organization those men and women with not only a clear vision of the role—and the vital importance—of public television in the economic, political, and cultural life of the nation, but also the strength of character and conviction to defend it against those who would seek to control it for selfish or ideological purposes.

16

LET THE
REVOLUTION BEGIN

*Rightly or wrongly, public broadcasting in this country emits the tones
of a culture in exile.*

Michael Tracey[1]

By the close of the 1980s, public
television was once more mired in crisis. Without the visionary
leadership to plot a future course and to articulate a unified rationale for the public medium, the system presented an image of
disunity and uncertainty. It was like a feudal society whose energies were directed toward internal battles rather than outward in
a concerted effort to resolve its role in a changing media environment. If the system's disparate elements shared anything, it was a
feeling that fundamental change was needed. But there was little
or no agreement on the direction the changes might take.

In the meantime, there were signs in Congress of a growing
impatience with the system's inability or unwillingness to solve its
own problems. Late in 1987, when the House scheduled hearings
on a bill to reauthorize public television's future funding, it was
immediately apparent that Congress was strongly disposed to take
matters in its own hands and do for public television what it had
so far failed to do for itself. Congress's concerns were evident in
the tenor of the opening remarks of House subcommittee chairman Rep. Edward Markey, who likened public broadcasting to the
bright child with outstanding potential "but who consistently
brings home Bs and Cs." It has not, he added ruefully, "fully

realized the hopes and expectations of 20 years ago."[2] For the first time in memory, the once-favored though not always pampered offspring of the legislative process found itself on the defensive. As witness after witness presented public television's case to the subcommittee, Chairman Markey seemed to take a perverse pleasure in asking each witness to comment on an offhand remark by Larry Grossman. The former PBS president had said that "when the history of American television is written, public TV will be largely a footnote, a sidebar, an afterthought."[3] True? asked Markey. The witnesses, knowing that Congress was unlikely to squander tax dollars on historical footnotes, were unanimous in denying the validity of Grossman's prophesy.

In their own counsels the witnesses were more candid. An increasing number of PBS stations had begun to complain about the system's inability to act quickly and effectively in a fast-moving field. And given a cluttered media environment, they were increasingly unhappy about the absence in the PBS schedule of those qualities that would set the public medium apart from the programming on the other channels. For more than a decade, the principal source of PBS prime-time programming had been the Station Program Cooperative. But the SPC had fallen into a "static state," returning the same tired shows to the PBS schedule year after year and in the process closing out new and innovative ideas.

According to PBS president Bruce Christensen, 1988 was "probably the most uncertain time we've had in public broadcasting in the past 10 years."[4] The chorus of self-reproach by the system's insiders was swelled by the voices of concerned outsiders—among them, Stephen White, principal author of the 1967 Carnegie Commission report on which that year's landmark Public Broadcasting Act had been fashioned. "For all its growth—and occasional brilliance—the system," White observed, "appears to be going nowhere in particular." Because, he added, "it appears heavily committed to the pattern established when it was first created as educational television," the system "lacks initiative and a creative spirit."[5]

The concerns expressed by its critics raised the prickly question of whether the clumsy structure of public television could tolerate, much less initiate, change. The need was clear. "There's a general sense," observed Bruce Christensen in the spring of 1988, "of 'Where are we going and why, and how do we get control of our destiny?' "[6] But the difficulties of getting there were also clear, at least to Sharon Rockefeller. The former chair of the Corporation board wondered whether public television's leadership could "fix things that need to be fixed without worrying about turfs, and zones of power, and without undue hostility."[7] It was a perennial question inside the divided system. Congress's next move, and the system's response to it, provided a partial answer.

Out of its 1988 hearings, the Senate's key subcommittee had drafted a plan that would drastically reduce the power of the Corporation by increasing the power of the individual stations. The plan would remove the bulk of the Corporation's programming funds, monies the Corporation had been using to partially fund major national series such as *Sesame Street, MacNeil/Lehrer News-Hour,* and *American Playhouse,* and leave it with a much smaller fund to finance innovative and minority programming. The larger part of the original fund would be divided among the stations but earmarked specifically for national programming. How PBS would aggregate these funds to support production of national programming was to be left to PBS and the stations.

As frequently happens when Congress attempts to solve public television's problems, the cure was worse than the disease and served only to launch new intramural brawls within the system's divided ranks. Not surprisingly, the Corporation, for whom the plan meant the loss of power and prestige, was adamantly opposed. So, too, were hundreds of independent producers, some of whom had benefited from the Corporation's policy of openly competitive grants. On the other hand, PBS and most of its stations, always ready to kick dirt on the Corporation's coffin, welcomed the Senate's plan. In the political wars of public television, any plan that took from the Corporation and gave to the stations seemed a good thing in itself. If anyone had concerns about the more relevant and immediate problem of the plan's probable effects upon national programming, few voiced them. Richard Moore, chief of the Minneapolis–St. Paul station and a veteran program producer, was virtually alone in pointing to the self-destructive nature of a proposal that would remove the Corporation's program funds without an alternate plan in place for producing, or even sustaining, the system's first-rate national programming. It was another instance of mixing politics and programming and coming up with answers that served neither.

The Senate plan was dropped, but not before the system was brought to the realization that if control of its destiny was not to be relinquished to Congress, public broadcasters had better find their own solutions—and soon. PBS acted first. In the summer of 1988, the network sought the approval of its membership for a radical reordering of the way national programming decisions were made and funded. With public television's audience share eroding, PBS feared for the system's "potential obsolescence" unless steps were taken to strengthen and improve its program offerings. Remarkably, the plan that the network had asked its members to accept was a reversal of public television's long-term trend toward greater decentralization of authority over national programming. The trend had begun twenty years earlier, at the time PBS was created, and had become somewhat of an obsession in the years since. To break down the monolithic authority that NET had exercised over national programming, the stations had placed in their own hands the power to decide which national programs would be produced, leaving PBS with the far more limited role of deciding which of the programs produced would be scheduled for national distribution. The process had proven less than satisfactory, prompting the PBS board to come up with the new plan under which more decisions about national programming would be made by PBS, fewer by the stations.

New York and Boston, the two public stations that had for years dominated the production of national programs, were both opposed to granting PBS the additional powers. WNET / New York's president, William Baker, felt strongly that stations should retain their voice in shaping the schedule, rather than turning the decisions over to a single individual as commercial television does. (Before coming to WNET, Baker had been a commercial-television executive.) "The whole world, even the Soviet Union, is going from a command economy to a democratic one," he argued, "and we're going the opposite way."[8] In fact, considerations of the economy may have been much on Baker's mind. As the system's major producer of prime-time programming, WNET had then, as it does today, the power to initiate the production of shows of its own choosing and therefore had the most to lose if those decisions were made for it by someone else. The objections of WGBH / Boston's president, Henry Becton, were more oblique. He wanted the decisions of the PBS program executive ratified by a two-thirds vote of the stations as a kind of insurance against decisions made by an unpopular or incompetent program executive. Notwithstanding the objections of the two giants, the stations bought the PBS board's plan. In a debate conspicuously free of the usual rhetoric of local chauvinism, the stations agreed for the first time since PBS was founded to cede some of their power over national programming to a central authority.[9] Their decision was a measure of shared concern over the future of the public medium as it moved into the uncertain nineties. But their collective action carried with it a sense of new beginnings, summed up by one exultant program executive in a shout of "Let the revolution begin!"

Revolutions, however, are not fought and won on words alone. Without the funds to carry out its proposed new programming mission, PBS was a paper tiger, unable to affect in any significant way the character and content of its national program service. Congress had long since put control of the federal funds in the Corporation's hands and even then had mandated that the bulk of these dollars be divided up among the stations for the station's own discretionary use. PBS had access to very little money of its own, only what its stations were willing to provide in dues and assessments. Ironically, the plan to centralize program planning had been prompted by the Senate's threat to pass even more of the federal funds directly to the stations. Having dropped that plan after stirring the system into frantic action, the Senate and the House reached a compromise on the future funding of national programming. The legislators directed the Corporation to return by the end of January 1990 with a new plan for the management of its national program funds. If the Corporation failed to reach agreement with the system's other elements, Congress would step in and impose its own solution.

"Summitry" has rarely been used in public television for the resolution of internal differences. But this time, under Congress's watchful and impatient eye, the chief executives of public television's three major national organizations—the Corporation, PBS, and the Association of America's Public Television Stations—huddled and emerged with a plan the Corporation could take to Congress in time for the January deadline. There were few if any surprises. To give PBS a modest start on its programming fund, the Corporation agreed to share half of its program dollars, about $23 million, with the network. But as it happened, these were the dollars the Corporation had been using to support, in part or in whole, several of the system's major prime-time series. Before PBS could invest the funds in *new* programs, it would first have to cut back on the budgets or cancel the production of such PBS mainstays as *Frontline, Great Performances, American Playhouse,* and *Mac-Neil/Lehrer.* But even if PBS chose to take this unlikely course, the amount of Corporation dollars freed for the production of new programming would be insufficient to permit PBS to make the desired changes in its schedule. Knowing that, the Corporation wisely made its contribution contingent upon the willingness of the local stations to turn over to PBS the funds they annually invested in the now defunct Station Program Cooperative. The transfer gave PBS almost four-fifths of the $100 million it needed to put its plan into effect.

The Corporation's plan was still being negotiated when PBS, anticipating its acceptance by Congress, announced in October 1989 that it had appointed Jennifer Lawson to the newly created post of Executive Vice President of National Programming and Promotion. Ironically, PBS had reached into the ranks of its crosstown rival to recruit the new executive. Lawson had only four months earlier been made director of the Corporation for Public Broadcasting's Program Fund. Although she brought limited programming experience to her new task, Lawson was a popular choice with the stations. They saw her as an intelligent, articulate, and politically astute leader, a programmer who would move with

due caution so as not to rock the boat. In the 1960s, at the height
of the civil rights movement, Lawson had dropped out of the Tus-
kegee Institute to join the Student's Nonviolent Coordinating
Committee. She later earned a graduate degree in film from Columbia University and taught film at Brooklyn College. Before administering program grants at the Corporation, Lawson had performed a similar function as director of the Film Fund, a small
agency that helped to fund the work of independent producers.

The stations were quick to dub her the "program czarina," an
unintended irony since her ability to act more decisively and
swiftly than her predecessors had been carefully moderated by the
cautions of a medium that has little tolerance for strong, independent action. Her programming decisions were subject to oversight by a special seventeen-member Program Policy Board that
included representatives from the Corporation, the community of
independent and minority producers, and the PBS stations. None
of these participants could be called disinterested; most represented interests with a financial—and a sometimes conflicting—
stake in the outcome. Fears that the "program czarina" might go
too far too fast were met with PBS president Christensen's calm
assurances that Lawson's decisions "will have to be ratified in
some way by the stations." If Lawson's mock-royal title served no
other purpose, however, it suggested the degree of authority the
stations felt they were relinquishing into the "program czarina's"
hands.

Lawson saw her appointment as a mandate to shake up public
television's national schedule and to make its programming more
accessible, more relevant, and more immediate. "I will have
failed," she told the press, "if, three years from now . . . what you
see is virtually the same."[10] In a memorandum to her station constituency, she summed up her seven-point prescription for the
newly named National Program Service. Primary emphasis was to
be placed upon "the creation of a distinctive, culturally diverse
variety service demonstrating leadership in children's programming and increasing the visibility of public television's public service and educational role." The prescription's key word was *mul-
ticulturalism*, the fashionable term of the 1990s, which Lawson

defined as "our commitment to *cultural diversity*"—the wish to make certain that all PBS programs "accurately reflect and serve our society in all its diversity." If the goal had ring of old coinage—cultural diversity has been a strong element in public television's programming for more than forty years—the emphasis was new: Lawson would have every show proposed for the National Program Service vetted for multicultural content.[11]

Of Lawson's programming goals, the pledge to make PBS a leader in children's programming was the most accessible. *Mister Rogers* and *Sesame Street* had long been staples in the viewing menu of preschoolers, and with the demise of CBS-TV's *Captain Kangaroo*, commercial television's last daily show for children, PBS moved into a leadership position. Young viewers had few alternatives other than the commercial networks' Saturday morning cartoons. But the picture changed radically when cable and home video entered the media mix. The newer technologies offered many more tantalizing options to the young viewer. Although not always of the sort that parents cheer, the explosion of available choices—coupled, some would argue, with a change in the way audience size is measured—resulted in a steady decline in audiences for PBS's children's shows. Lawson reversed the trend by bunching the shows for preschoolers into an easily recognizable block and adding several newcomers to their number. One of the additions, *Shining Time Station*, is a BBC production from the early 1980s that PBS has modified for American audiences. The moderately paced show is a mix of fantasy and storytelling featuring an animated railroad train that talks and an eighteen-inch-high conductor played by stand-up comic George Carlin (in the original British version, Ringo Starr). Lawson's other additions to the children's schedule drew upon home videos that had already made their mark in the marketplace. These series came to television with carefully laid plans to profit from the merchandising of their licensed products. Shari Lewis's *Lamb Chop's Play-Along* first appeared on NBC television in the early 1960s; the parents of today's preschool viewers might have themselves been among its young viewers. Its 1991 reincarnation on PBS, however, has been somewhat overshadowed by another visitor from home video, a round, bouncy purple dinosaur named Barney. The star of *Barney & Friends* was first introduced to the PBS audience in 1992 and, defying conventional wisdom, became an immediate hit with its target audience of preschoolers. PBS, unaware of the show's smashing success with two- and three-year-olds, cancelled *Barney*'s second season when the first was barely under way. Word of the cancellation triggered a storm of protest from station programmers. *Barney* was rescued and restored to the schedule. The show, described by Dr. Keith Mielke, a specialist in children's television, as "a slowed-down *Mister Rogers* for a stressed-out generation," has, if nothing else, proved to be a powerful ally for the local stations' fundraising departments.

Early in her tenure at the top PBS programming spot, Lawson startled the system's more conservative programmers by promising comedy, drama with continuing characters, and a game show. To the system's retrograde purists, Lawson's vision sounded frighteningly like a sell-out to the numbers game. While comedy and drama have remained largely beyond the system's reach, Lawson did introduce the game-show format with the debut in 1991 of *Where in the World Is Carmen Sandiego?* The show, targeted for audiences in the six- to eleven-year-old range, brings geography to life by challenging its young participants to correctly answer questions of place and culture in a global game of pursuit.

None of Lawson's seven goals for the nineties was more likely to fall on the sword of its own ambiguity than the pledge to provide PBS with a "unique" and "distinctive" service, programming that will set public television "apart from other broadcasters or cable services."[12] Public television's path to a "distinctive" service was fairly clear in the pre-cable years when "other broadcasters" meant the three commercial networks. But with today's easy access to a mind-numbing range of cable networks, many tailored for specific niche audiences, claims to uniqueness are cast in a different light. Lawson's efforts to carve out a distinctive role for the public medium have thus far been largely unavailing. Consensus programming, not risk taking, continues to dominate the network's choices.

The start was hopeful. Soon after Lawson took over, PBS introduced an irreverent and idiosyncratic monthly magazine of the popular arts called *Edge*. The show was eclectic in content and wildly unconventional in method, melding, said one satisfied critic, "the softness of CBS's *Sunday Morning* and the hip attitude of the *Village Voice*."[13] Lawson cancelled *Edge* after only six shows. "It had limited appeal to a general audience," she explained, not realizing the same judgment might easily be made of most PBS series. Her criticism that it failed to "realize its potential" (a virtual impossibility with only six quixotically scheduled monthly airings) told less about the real reasons behind its demise than the assertion that *Edge* had been "too inside," a code word for a New York brand of know-it-all sophistication that is reviled in much of the country and feared by most station programmers.[14]

On the other hand, the 1994 miniseries *Tales of the City*, unlike *Edge*, not only appealed to a general audience, it set a new ratings record for a PBS drama. The dramatization of Armistead Maupin's stories of life in San Francisco in the 1970s, a coproduction of *American Playhouse* and Britain's Channel 4, met the Lawson criterion for uniqueness—the sort of program you would not expect to find on commercial television. But when PBS was asked to participate in the production of a sequel, *More Tales of the City*, the network declined in what John Carman of the *San Francisco Chronicle* called "either a case of rank stupidity or cringing cowardice."[15] PBS's explanation—"We don't follow the commercial television model, where a ratings success immediately spawns sequels and spin-offs"[16]—was greeted skeptically by critics who noted the presence of *Prime Suspect 3* on the upcoming PBS schedule, the *second* sequel to a popular British crime series.

Politics, not a disdain for sequels, killed *More Tales of the City*. The unconventionality of the original, particularly its uncritical treatment of homosexuality and drugs, stirred legislators in Georgia and Oklahoma to threaten cutbacks in the funding for the state public systems.[17] And members of Congress received a twelve-minute videotape from the Rev. Donald Wildmon's American Family Association highlighting the series' fleeting nudity, profanity, and pot smoking. PBS's experience with *Tales of the City* demonstrates the problems that lie in the path of the system's hopes for a unique image for the public medium. Individuality and consensus are antithetical terms.

Lawson acquired a new boss in 1944 when Ervin S. Duggan succeeded Christensen as PBS president. A year later, after Duggan downgraded her position by interposing a level of programming authority above her, she resigned, but not before taking the heat for rejecting a series on human rights, hosted by Charlayne Hunter-Gault of the *MacNeil/Lehrer NewsHour*. In the case of *Rights and Wrongs*, the reasoning given for turning down the series became more important than the decision itself. In a letter to the producers, Lawson explained that "human rights is not a sufficient organizing principle for a television series."[18] Thirty-two members of Congress's Black Caucus disagreed. "We are at a loss to understand your rejection of a balanced and responsible program," they wrote the PBS president.[19] In his response, Duggan described PBS's rejection as a routine program decision based on the "fierce" competition for airtime. While PBS has rejected *Rights and Wrongs* for the network, forty PBS stations individually agreed to air it, some in prime time.

Lawson had a corollary objective, the goal of "eliminating programs that might blur the [public medium's] identity."[20] But unblurring public television's individuality is an unlikely prospect with PBS stations filling their schedules with reruns of such commercial warhorses as *The Lawrence Welk Show* and *Leave It to Beaver* in order to build their audiences. Nor does the airing of tired features from the 1940s and 1950s under the celluloid-thin guise of "movie classics" help to set the public medium apart from the movie-laden channels around it. These breaches of image building are committed by the stations and are beyond the control of PBS. But others are not. The 1993 salvaging of commercial television's failed series *I'll Fly Away* was commendable, opening the public medium as it did to a genre that could leaven the schedule's unrelieved absorption with cosmic concerns. But it did nothing to establish the uniqueness of the public medium. On the contrary, it, like PBS's earlier rescue effort with *The Paperchase*, places the public medium in the role of a safety net for commercial television's castoffs, albeit their castoffs of quality.

One of the most conspicuous instances of image blurring occurred during the joint NBC-PBS coverage of the 1992 national
political conventions, when the nightly sight of NBC's signature
anchor Tom Brokaw on the public channel one moment and on
his own network the next effectively narrowed the perceptual distance between the public and private networks. The consequences
of the joint coverage were all the more unfortunate for having
been avoidable. In the course of the 1992 election year, PBS let
slip a rare opportunity to present to the public an image of a
public service unique to the public medium. Two years of talks
and planning ended with PBS's rejection of a $5 million offer from
the Markle Foundation to partially fund a comprehensive 1992
Election Project called "The Voters' Channel." The Foundation,
whose initiative resulted from its twenty-year study of television's
role in political campaigns, proposed an approach to the 1992
political year unparalleled in its concern for addressing more directly and thoroughly the needs of voters. When after protracted
discussions Markle was unable to get a commitment from Lawson
and PBS, the Foundation withdrew its offer, citing the public system's "lack of cohesive response to national problems and opportunities."[21] Markle turned in frustration to commercial cable,
granting $3.5 million to CNN to perform in part the services hoped
for from the public medium. The disappointing outcome served
only to further blur the distinction between the public medium
and cable.

If Lawson has fallen short of her pledge to make the public
medium distinctive, she did demonstrate the efficacy of centralized control over the network schedule. During the war in the
Persian Gulf she led the way to a tighter, tougher schedule not
only by encouraging (with the help of the *MacNeil/Lehrer
NewsHour* team) a fast response to breaking stories, but also by
clearing time in the PBS schedule for continuing news specials and
background reports. For the first time in memory, viewers tuned
to the public network were plugged into the world beyond the
tube, comfortable in the knowledge that Armageddon would not
slip by unremarked by PBS while they were absorbed in *Masterpiece
Theater.* The public system's ability to perform more like a real-

time network and less like a preprogrammed movie channel must
be accounted one of the major gains from centralizing programming under a single executive.

Lawson's programming strategies were intended to meet the
challenges of "a complex and changing media environment . . .
where most viewers have a wide range of viewing and other leisure
options."[22] Added options translate to fewer viewers for public
television. And while public television's decline in average audience size has been small, the downward trend is worrisome. Public
broadcasters fear that shrinking audiences will give legislators pre-
disposed to dumping the publicly supported medium, and who
often have little or no understanding of its national purpose, the
excuse they need. Those fears have been around since the early
1970s, when much of Washington was in the thrall of "emerging
technologies" and the press, trumpeting the coming age of "media abundance," called into question the very need for the public
medium. "Taxpayer-supported television is an idea whose time
has come and gone," conservative columnist William Safire told
his readers. He assured them that promising new technologies
could, for a price, satisfy the demand for "psychic nourishment
demanded by the culturally hungry."[23] If the requiem was premature, the threat was real.

Advancing technology has been both a bane and a benefit to
public television. The advent of cable virtually wiped out public
television's UHF handicap; the "unhappy frequencies" were given
parity with the conventional VHF channels. PBS, in significant ways,
has pioneered the use of the newer technologies. It was the first
national network to distribute its programs by satellite, the first to
televise in stereo sound, and the first to develop and use Closed
Captioning for the hearing handicapped and Descriptive Video
Service for the blind. But keeping up with advancing technology
on thin capital budgets has strained the medium's resources. Satellites, essential to the PBS distribution system, do not last forever.
When their time is up, PBS and the Corporation must scramble to
fund their replacement. Moreover, each new technological development is followed by newer developments, making last year's in-
vestments obsolete and demanding more capital for next year's

purchases. High-definition television (HDTV) is only the most recent claim upon future funds. Chicago's WTTW has put its toe in the stream with the system's first experiments, but only after borrowing the equipment from a manufacturer. Readying the entire system for high-definition television—and that means replacing much of the present capital equipment—will be an enormous and expensive undertaking, and it is unclear how it will be funded.

These advancing technologies have awakened public broadcasters to a realization that public television's place in the media scene can no longer be taken for granted. Hartford Gunn was one of the first to recognize public television's need for a course correction. In the late seventies, while he was vice chairman of PBS, Gunn undertook a long-range planning project in which he concluded that the public system had three options with respect to the new technologies: "Fight 'em, forget 'em, or join 'em."[24] Gunn favored the latter, urging public television to seek out advantageous relationships with the exploiters of cable, satellites, teletext, video recordings, and the rest. Two years after the Gunn study, three holdover members from the second Carnegie Commission staff stayed on to conduct an ancillary study on public television's interface with the new technologies. Their report, *Keeping PACE with the New Television,* urged public broadcasters to undertake "a new national nonprofit pay cable network for the Performing Arts, Culture and Entertainment" (hence the acronym PACE) by entering into a pact with major cultural institutions.[25] The recommended strategy was to pin down for the public medium the considerable cultural resources of these institutions before cable captured them, as it was then threatening to do. Larry Grossman, the PBS president at the time, embraced the idea and, with an advertising man's feel for the quotable copy line, called it "The Grand Alliance" (reduced later to PBS's alphabetic proportions as PSN, the Public Subscriber Network).[26] Grossman set out to sell the stations and the nation's cultural institutions on the idea only to find that neither the arts institutions nor the PBS stations displayed a willingness to provide the risk capital needed to get the pay cable network launched. The "Grand Alliance" dropped of its own weight.

In the years since, the influence of cable has continued to spread. By 1991, six of every ten homes were connected to a cable system. Technology has devised new techniques for multiplying the number of available channels so that the promise of a future with five hundred channels is no longer a science-fiction fantasy. Cable networks, popping up like crabgrass, have filled the channels with programming, much of it recycled from old inventories and most of it targeted for "niche" audiences. Cable networks now serve programming areas that once had been virtually the exclusive province of public television—science, nature, travel, documentaries, culture, and children's programs—with obvious implications for the future of the public medium. Nor are the other broadcast media spared the implications of cable's growth. And yet this same onward surge of technological change may well make cable obsolete, too. Whatever the shape of the newer technologies, the trend is clearly toward a multiplicity of home-delivered communication services that promise to smother the unwary viewer in a tidal wave of images and information. Public television, lacking a well-defined sense of mission, may find itself floundering to demonstrate how it can do what it does any better than the legions of competing technologies and why what it does cannot be effectively performed in the free marketplace.

Public broadcasters are not alone in having a stake in the outcome. The nation as a whole has a collective concern for the possible effects of a media environment that promises to replace the shared experience of network television with hundreds of channels addressing as many narrow interests and further fragmenting the polity into cells of specialized concerns. At risk is some part of the social glue that binds us into a cohesive society. Of equal concern is the danger that the exotic technology of the future will further widen the gap between the information deprived—those who can ill-afford the escalating costs of the newer delivery systems (including cable)—and the information privileged, those who can. In a world of media abundance that offers a wealth of choices for those who can afford them, public television becomes the analog of the public library, a universally available resource open to all regardless of means or place of residence. In this context, the "public" in public television takes on a deeper meaning.

Held in thrall to awesome new technologies, we tend to close our minds to the more important issue: the quality and diversity of messages these technologies make available. Television, cable, satellites, fiber optics, and so forth are nothing more than modes of transmission, the technology by which messages are delivered. They are not the messages, and transmissions without messages are meaningless. To argue that social benefit will derive from multiplying the number of television stations, or adding new networks, or upping the capacity of cable to five hundred or more channels, is mere sophistry unless consideration is given to the nature of the messages they transmit. It follows that the prospect of hundreds of new television channels cannot guarantee hundreds of new choices. Even today, with far fewer channels available, the common complaint is "there's nothing on worth watching." The reason lies partly in cable's penchant for feeding upon the past, consuming the cast-off contents of yesterday's television and raiding the larder of Hollywood's glory years. Profitability in a competitive market is too easily achieved by minimizing original production. In the much more highly competitive environment of the multichannel future, the prospects for a rich supply of original production are, if anything, even less promising. Viewers, grazing through hundreds of channels, may be hard pressed to find one to nourish the mind and spirit—unless, of course, the medium least affected by the competitive pressures of the marketplace, the public medium, is there to fill the void.

The explosion in technology, and the exotic new delivery systems that result, need not be a threat to public television. It can and should be an opportunity, even a responsibility. Lawson's plan for PBS's future was pointed in that direction—toward the creation and production of original material as a way of defining the public system. So long as the public medium stays in the shorter queue of those who create and not in the longer queue of those who rely upon the past, its future role in the overcrowded world of telecommunications will grow more certain.

17

THE INDIE'S SIX MILLION

*The one great thing we've done has been to allow the possibility that an
artist can fail. . . . It's a luxury you very seldom have in television. And
sometimes, if you know you have the right to fail, you succeed in your
experiments beyond your wildest imagination.*

David Loxton[1]

Hit series are rare in a medium
that eschews audience ratings. PBS, however, came dangerously
close to having a "hit" on its hands—the term is relative—with
Ken Burns's historical documentary series *The Civil War*. The
eleven hours, first broadcast over five successive nights in September 1990, set public television's all-time record for audience size.
On each of the nights it aired, the series reached on average of
14 million homes, climbing the numbers charts with an unprecedented 13 percent share of all homes using television. *The Civil
War* was so compelling that viewers reordered their lives to catch
successive episodes. In addition to its popular success on television, the series captured every available award and produced a
companion book that enjoyed huge sales.

Critics lavished words of praise upon the show of a kind rarely
visited upon documentaries: "a masterful, compelling achievement," said one, while to another it was "a kind of video miracle."
The *New York Times* named Ken Burns "the most accomplished
documentary maker of his generation."[2] By common consent, *The
Civil War* was one of public television's finest hours. What was little
remarked upon at the time, however, was the fact that public television's greatest programming success was not, as one might ex-

pect, produced by the system's complex bureaucracy and its billion dollar kitty. *The Civil War* was a product of the community of
independent producers working outside the system, making the
kinds of shows they most want to make, struggling to find the
dollars to fund them, and hoping that the finished product will
find its audience through acceptance on the public-television
system.

Ken Burns is only one of the thousands of creative people who
work outside the system. Very few, however, have had his success
as an independent entrepreneur. He has not only demonstrated
the skills of a highly creative television producer but also shown
equal skill at the frustrating craft of raising production funds. He
has long since learned what every independent ultimately comes
to know: that creativity alone is meaningless without the patience
and skills to find the dollars to make it happen. Burns sought out
and signed General Motors as principal funder for his Civil War
series, although others were also involved. Significantly, the
source of the modest initial grant that launched the project and
gave Burns the encouragement to endure came from a local PBS
station, WETA-TV, in the nation's capital.

Most independent producers encounter great difficulty in funding their projects, however airworthy they may later prove to be.
Henry Hampton, whose 1987 story of the civil rights movement,
Eyes on the Prize, won the plaudits of critics and the gratitude of a
large PBS audience, had to struggle for six years before he was able
to put together no fewer than forty-four underwriters to meet the
project's production costs of $2.5 million for the first six shows.
Stories of creative years wasted in the frustrating search for production money are legion in the ranks of those who work outside
the system.

Independent producers were, until recent years, largely an
American phenomenon. They were in a sense a product of the
mid-sixties when the development of lightweight, relatively inexpensive video equipment made it possible for anyone with a camera, a cause, and a good eye to become a program producer. Many
did. But while independently produced work frequently brought
a needed vitality to public television, independents have not always

been welcomed by the establishment, particularly by local stations. Most stations, eager to keep program production in-house in order to skim off the overhead costs for station upkeep, see the independents as outside competitors, not collaborators. But even with their problems of access, America's independent producers have fared much better than independent producers in many other countries where state-run television systems have kept all major production in-house. In Britain, where the BBC has historically produced virtually all of its own programs, the broadcaster has now been required by government edict to turn to independent producers for at least 25 percent of its programming.

Although their access to the PBS system was limited, the independents felt crowded out of public-television funding by the system's organized elements. Most independent producers could not compete on an equal footing with producing stations armed with institutional political clout and a large cadre of fund-raisers. Nor did their problems end there. Even after they had successfully raised the funds and completed the production, independents faced the often frustrating problem of gaining access to airtime. The commercial networks have never, with rare exceptions, been willing to air nonfiction work produced by outsiders; instead they have relied exclusively on their own staff journalists for documentaries on current issues. As a consequence, public television had been for many years the only outlet open to independents. And although the growth of cable in recent years has added opportunities for the airing of independent work, those opportunities are also severely limited by the small amount of original production most cable networks can afford. So independents continue to knock on the doors of public television. But the doors, while cautiously welcoming to independent production, continue to be tended by the independents' natural competitor—the system's many local stations. The resulting competition has created enduring and unresolved tension between the two parties.

Historically, independent production has for many years played an important role in the development of the public medium— notwithstanding the system's inborn resistance to outside work. In the years before 1969, when NET was the sole producer of national programming, the network regularly commissioned independent work. Its weekly magazine program, *The Great American Dream Machine*, was a notable example of a public-television series that welcomed outside contributions. Nor should it be forgotten that the Public Broadcast Laboratory, the Ford Foundation's experiment in the late sixties with live television, was the first to air a television documentary by the doyen of independent producers, Fred Wiseman.

But it was not until the early 1970s that independent production came into its own on the public network. Much of its vitality during the seventies can be credited to the almost obsessive interest of a young WNET producer, David Loxton. As the founder of WNET's Television Laboratory, Loxton became independent production's strongest ally inside the walls of the public-television establishment. British by birth and educated at Trinity College in Dublin, Loxton was not himself a documentarian but rather a drama producer whose creative energies impelled him to explore new paths. Those energies brought him to my office soon after the NET-WNET merger to seek approval for a plan to create a workshop where creative artists could freely explore the aesthetic dimensions of the electronic medium. He was aware that a similar workshop had been created at KQED/San Francisco during my tenure there and that WGBH/Boston had also instituted an experimental program. My enthusiasm for Loxton's proposal was tempered only by the perceived difficulties of funding such a project. Loxton, however, permitted no doubts. He proceeded to raise the funds on his own by tapping the Rockefeller Foundation for seed money. The WNET TV Lab opened with a group of artists in residence working in a small, fully equipped studio near the United Nations dedicated solely to their electronic explorations. The TV Lab was to become a free-wheeling and semi-autonomous arm of the Channel 13 establishment that was remote from the parent body's doctrinal ways and that offered a refuge for artists whose talents were beyond the pale of conventional television. Among those who found in the TV Lab an opportunity to experiment with the visual medium were such irrepressible video artists as Nam June Paik, Ed Emshwiller, and Bill Viola.

In 1973, two years after its founding, Loxton was approached by a collective of young video artists equipped with handheld video cameras and calling themselves Top Value Television (TVTV). The collective planned to travel to the Houston Astrodome to document a gathering of the followers of the guru Maharaj-ji, a tubby little boy from Long Island who called himself "Lord of the Universe." Hundreds of the guru's worshippers had promised to raise the Astrodome off the surface of the earth with only the strength of their faith. Loxton, sensing the occasion was a fitting subject for the youthful skepticism of guerrilla TV, gave it the Lab's support. Thanks to the use of a Lab-developed device called a time-base corrector, the resulting video documentary, *Lord of the Universe*, was the first show to be shot in small-format video that received a national airing. It was also an encouragement to further risk-taking. Six months after *Lord of the Universe*, the Lab edited eighty hours of video, much of it unusable, that Jon Alpert and Keiko Tsuno brought back from Castro's Cuba. It was their very first attempt at producing a video documentary. The result, *Cuba: The People*, was the first of several PBS documentaries that were subsequently made by the Alpert-Tsuno team, and was a prelude to Jon Alpert's audacious, behind-the-lines career as a freelance reporter for NBC News. *Lord of the Universe* and *Cuba: The People* were the start of the TV Lab's ten-year affair with the independently produced documentary, a supportive relationship that was responsible for what many believe was the period of the independents' strongest sustained presence on the public medium.

Loxton formalized the relationship in 1977 by creating the Independent Documentary Fund. The IDF had all the accoutrements of public television's money-dispensing machinery: funds from the usual sources (Ford Foundation and the National Endowment for the Arts), peer-paneling, and the oversight of an executive editor, Loxton himself. But Loxton and his right hand, Katherine Kline, managed to tease, cajole, and encourage into being some of the public medium's best documentary work. Shows from the Independent Documentary Fund ranged from Jack Willis's Emmy-award winning *Paul Jacobs and the Nuclear Gang*, the first show of the IDF's first season, to Richard Schmiechen and Robert

Epstein's Oscar-award winner *The Times of Harvey Milk*, the final show of the final season. By 1984, however, the TV Lab, and with it the Independent Documentary Fund, was in trouble. Loxton had lost an important part of the Lab's funding when Lewis Freedman, then heading the Program Fund, decided not to renew the Corporation's support but to embark on an independent documentary project of his own. (The result was the ill-fated *Matters of Life and Death.*) Lacking the funds to match the offer of continued support from the National Endowment for the Arts, the Independent Documentary Fund closed its doors, and with it, WNET's experimental TV Lab. The Independent Documentary Fund had lasted seven years, ultimately falling victim to public television's anarchical competitiveness and the absence of any rational centralized planning. Loxton reluctantly returned to his first love, producing drama.

The Independent Documentary Fund served a handful of producers well, in part because it provided a close and mutually supportive relationship between the independent producer and the institution on whose air it was intended to be seen. Loxton was able, without interfering with content, to assist the producer in shaping a product that would meet the standards of the sponsoring station and could be aired without the customary PBS-producer battles. A far larger number of independent producers, however, did not feel well served by the Independent Documentary Fund, if only because too few were involved. Many also clung to an ideal of independence that precluded the involvement of PBS or station collaboration in their efforts. For this group there was only one answer: a slice of public television's federal funding pie dedicated solely to independent production. The professional association to which they belonged, by mounting a vigorous lobbying effort, persuaded Congress to write a provision into its 1978 bill for public-television funding directing the Corporation to reserve "a substantial amount" of its programming funds for distribution to independent producers.[3] The questions of what the legislators meant by "substantial" and of how the dedicated dollars would be distributed sparked an internal debate that continued without resolution for years afterward. Congress set 1980 as the deadline for compliance.

Complying with the Congressional mandate fell to Lewis Freedman, who had just arrived at the Corporation in 1980 to direct the newly formed Program Fund. His plan for meeting the Congressional mandate for independent production was, as we have seen, to micromanage the funds himself by creating *Matters of Life and Death* and *Crisis to Crisis*, rather than to create an independent agency or to turn the money over to the Independent Documentary Fund. When the two Corporation-produced series failed to meet the standards of PBS, much less the demands of the independents, Freedman turned his energies to the creation of the station consortia described earlier. He fully expected that one of these consortia, specifically the group at WGBH / Boston led by executive producer David Fanning, would be the instrument for fulfilling the Congressional mandate. Fanning had promised to use independent producers for his *Frontline* documentaries. The association of independent producers, however, was not pleased at the prospect and seized the opportunity to denounce Freedman's plan as a ruse to subvert the intent of Congress. The battle raged over the intent of Congress and the definition of "independent." The association of independents held that those who worked for *Frontline* were not "independent" but "freelance" producers. The distinction, they argued, was clear and crucial: independents speak with their own voice, free of outside editorial control, unlike freelancers, whose ideas are subject to the editorial standards of the series they are working for. The latter is not independent work but "work for hire."

By the time *Frontline* debuted in January 1983, Freedman had left the Program Fund. Its new director, Ron Hull, had devised a different approach for meeting the mandate. He called it the Open Solicitation Fund. Its modest sum of $5 million in production money was made available to all comers on a competitive basis. Peer panels, made up of independent producers and station programmers, reviewed the applications and recommended which proposals should be funded. Predictably, the flood of applications far exceeded the available funds. Tough as that was, the independents had a more serious complaint. Because the fund was open to everyone, including stations large and small, the independents felt at a disadvantage. Moreover, even when they were successful in the competitive funding game, the independents had no assurance—as they had with the Independent Documentary Fund—that their show would be accepted into the PBS schedule.

Over the years of independent production, starting from 1967, one documentary producer who is more formidably independent than most has successfully managed to surmount these barriers and beat the frustrating rules of the funding game. With enviable regularity, Frederick Wiseman has managed each year for more than twenty years to place one of his cinema-verité films into public television's schedule. *High School*, "a searing portrait of an institution that takes warm breathing teenagers and tries to turn them into forty-year-old mental eunuchs," was the first.[4] It was commissioned by the Ford Foundation's experimental Public Broadcast Laboratory. NET commissioned the second, *Law and Order*, a powerful and, for the 1960s, a surprisingly sympathetic look at the Kansas City police. *Law and Order*'s impact prompted the Ford Foundation to offer NET an ostensibly "unrestricted" grant whose unspoken purpose was not difficult to mistake: more Wiseman commissions, one each year for the next five years. When the Ford grant ran out five years later, WNET / New York picked up the tab for an additional five years. Over the years, Wiseman's cinematic probes into the country's social institutions—always provocative and frequently controversial—have ranged over the full spectrum of American life: an inner-city emergency hospital (*Hospital*), an army training camp (*Basic Training*), a Benedictine monastery (*Essene*), a courtroom (*Juvenile Court*), a research laboratory (*Primate*), a New York welfare office (*Welfare*), a meat packing plant (*Meat*), an American "colonial" outpost (*Canal Zone*), a modelling agency (*Model*), a luxury department store (*The Store*), and a Long Island race track (*Race Track*). As the Wiseman oeuvre grew in stature, each work seemed to grow longer than the last. A four-part series shot in the Alabama School for the Deaf and Blind ran more than nine hours. And 1989's *Near Death* chronicled six tension-filled hours in the intensive-care facility of a Massachusetts hospital.

Wiseman's work makes pussycats of the media's toughest critics. Pauline Kael called him "probably the most sophisticated intelligence to enter the documentary field in recent years."[5] Even Tom Shales, whose stiletto tongue has savaged the best, praised Wiseman as a "brilliant documentary film maker" whose style is "so distinctive and refined that no matter how he is imitated by others, he remains its undisputed master."[6]

Wiseman has learned, however, that golden words of praise are about as bankable as three-dollar bills. After WNET's five-year subsidy ran its course, the veteran filmmaker had no choice but to join the other independents in the chancy game of grantsmanship. Luckily, the Fellows Program of the John D. and Catherine T. MacArthur Foundation—the so-called "genius award"— helped to partially subsidize some of his more recent films. That aside, the search for funding has twice taken him, hat-in-hand, to the Corporation's Program Fund. He was turned down both times. Although he ultimately received a small grant from the Corporation—the Program Fund's director overrode the recommendation of the peer panels—Wiseman found the process so frustrating that he sought and was granted a hearing before the Corporation's board. In a blast at the Corporation's system for funding programs, he warned that "massive bureaucracies inside the system were reversing priorities by dominating rather than supporting programming." His particular scorn was saved for the Program Fund's peer panels: playing "king and queen for a day," the panels were making "random, unplanned and indefensible programming decisions."[7] If the Corporation board was unmoved, Wiseman's words nonetheless echoed the sentiments of hundreds of equally frustrated independents who had battered their heads against the bureaucracy. (Wiseman, once asked why he hadn't turned his relentless camera eye on the institution of American public television, replied "Don't think it hasn't occurred to me.")

Wiseman's frustrations symbolized the dilemma of all independents' efforts to deal with the system, yet he played little or no part in their organized campaign to legislate relief from bureaucratic neglect. In fact, he opposed their legislative remedy—a separately administered fund for independent production—by arguing that "another fund simply fragments the system even more."[8] But for most, a separate fund, "democratically" administered by the producers themselves, has long been a dream and a legislative goal. The independents' 1978 triumph in persuading Congress to mandate a "substantial amount" of the Corporation's program funds to independent production was probably more beneficial to the producing stations—thanks to the Corporation's institution of station consortia—than it was to the independents who engineered it.

Their frustration at the Corporation's failure to meet their demands—and gall at its duplicity in attempting to meet the Congressional mandate by calling freelance work independent production—led the independent producers to mobilize an all-out lobbying effort to get the production funds in their own hands. Their several disparate groups were joined in a loose alliance as the National Coalition of Independent Broadcasting Producers, co-chaired by the heads of the two largest groups, Lawrence Sapadin of the New York–based Association of Independent Video and Filmmakers and Lawrence Daressa of the West Coast–based Association of California Independent Public Television Producers. At every Congressional hearing on public television's triennial forward funding, Sapadin and Daressa urged Congress to issue more explicit directives to the Corporation. A 1984 directive ordering the Corporation to negotiate with the National Coalition produced more meetings but no resolution. By 1987, the coalition had grown impatient with the lack of progress and proposed its own solution: a National Independent Programming Service, described by Daressa as a "laboratory" where independent producers and public broadcasters could work together to "explore ways to bring unfamiliar voices, unconventional styles, and innovation to a medium characterized by homogenized perspectives and numbing habit."[9] The National Coalition asked for half of all the Corporation's programming funds to support the proposed programming service.

To no one's surprise, the public broadcasters, bridling at what they deemed the hubris if not the greed of the independents, turned the proposal down. Congress, however, was determined to give independent producers the money and muscle to make their own mark on public television. The chosen instrument was the 1988 public-television funding bill into which they wrote a provision directing the Corporation to provide $6 million a year for three years to support an Independent Production Service. For the first time, independent producers had what they had struggled for years to get: money to make programs and access to the public stations to get them seen. Or so they thought.

Nothing happened for almost a year while the Corporation and coalition wrangled over details. The Corporation, steadfastly unwilling to relinquish its say in how the funds would be spent, was prodded into coming to terms with the National Coalition only by the intervention of a congressman who threatened the Corporation's future funding. The settlement in 1989 of differences between the Corporation and the National Coalition paved the way for the creation of yet another public-broadcasting agency, the Independent Television Service (ITVS).[10] Two more years would go by before ITVS issued its first call for program proposals. The result was a flood of more than two thousand applications, of which only twenty-six could be funded (an added thirteen programs could be funded from an equal number of applications the second year). But contrary to expectations, those shows that made it to completion—and not all of them did—found the doors at PBS closed to them. The network had little apparent interest in accommodating the random stand-alone pieces that the open call produced. To avoid wasting the $6 million on shows that might never be seen, ITVS changed its approach, commissioning intermediary production groups to pull together independently produced segments into a cohesive series of shows that might be acceptable to PBS. Still, it was not until the 1992–93 season—five years after the Congressional action and two years after the first grants—that the first ITVS-funded show made its way into the PBS schedule.

Not surprisingly, this first ITVS show found a place in the national schedule as an episode in the PBS series *P.O.V.* (Point of View). Since 1988, *P.O.V.* has each season presented ten to twelve independently produced—and frequently provocative—documentaries. The seed for *P.O.V.* was planted by Marc Weiss, an independent producer. His vision of a public-television outlet for the work of independent documentarians led him first to David Fanning at *Frontline*, who encouraged him to talk with David Davis, the founder and chairman of *American Playhouse.* Davis, both a sympathetic ear and an experienced organizer, used his *American Playhouse* four-station consortium to respond to Weiss's idea. The result was a second corporate entity, The American Documentary, Inc., which was chaired by Davis and which employed Marc Weiss as executive producer. By using the point-of-view label as a caveat—be warned: the following program may be injurious to firmly held beliefs—the consortium persuaded PBS to accept the series. Both parties were fully aware that some shows in *P.O.V.* would almost certainly present the more skittish stations with "problems."

In the beginning, *P.O.V.* moved carefully, eager to build a bond of confidence with the stations. The premiere season raised very few hackles and included films on regional dialects, the survivalist movement, living with AIDS, sexism, and Americans who fought in the Spanish Civil War; Errol Morris's early film on pet cemeteries; and two award-winning films, *Best Boy* and *Las Madres: The Mothers of Plaza de Mayo.* The second season's themes were bolder, leading off with *Who Killed Vincent Chin?* The tough investigative documentary, directed by Christine Choy and Renee Tajima, raised serious and disturbing questions about the American justice system and was later nominated for an Academy Award. By 1991 and its third season, *P.O.V.* began to demonstrate a talent for upsetting the domestic tranquillity of the public medium. Peter Adair's *Absolutely Positive* captured the irreverent and bluntly candid observations of eleven HIV-positive men and women, condemned by the deadly virus to face their own mortality. Later, *Maria's Story* painted a vivid video portrait of a Salvadoran peasant woman—a wife and mother of three—turned charismatic guerrilla leader. Both films raised the mercury in the political thermometer. Neither, however, quite matched the explosive reaction provoked by a third film, *Tongues Untied*, Marlon Riggs' angry, funny, erotic, and poetic examination of what it means to be both black and gay.

Tongues Untied was partially funded by the National Endowment for the Arts, cause enough for it to be targeted for attack from the political right for the Endowment's use of tax dollars to support what, in the minds of the moral guardians, was "obscene" art. The Endowment's severest critic, Senator Jesse Helms, wasted no time in tarring *Tongues Untied* with the same brush, charging that it "blatantly promoted homosexuality as an acceptable life style."[11] Riggs' film quickly became another weapon in the political crusade of Congressional conservatives to purge public television of its purported "liberal bias." They used his film to justify punitive amendments to a 1992 bill authorizing $1.1 billion for public television's forward (1994–96) funding. Because the amendments were unacceptable to the Democratic majority, the political right effectively blocked the bill's passage and in the process put the future of the system at risk. Conservatives, then and now, have a radically different vision of public television's future, a vision that advocates not only substantial changes but nothing less than its privatization.

The charges of "left leaning" and "liberal bias" that were prompted by *P.O.V.*'s more provocative shows have had a long history. Similar charges have swirled around the public medium since its birth more than forty years ago. Public television has evidenced no more "liberal bias" than other media, but then conservatives are willing to believe that most mass media are biased against them. Because it is supported in part by tax dollars, however, public television is more vulnerable to their attacks and therefore has provided a more fruitful target for their efforts.

Congress, perhaps without intending to, provided the radical right with the weapon to pursue their attacks on public television by imbedding into the Public Broadcasting Act of 1967 a provision directing the Corporation to facilitate the development of programs of high quality "with strict adherence to objectivity and balance in all programs or series of programs of a controversial nature."[12] As reasonable as the requirement at first appears—who would deny the virtue of "balance" and "objectivity" in the practice of journalism?—it is a subtle trap for public television. Not only does it impose on the public medium a stricter standard than is demanded of the far more influential private medium, it saddles the nongovernmental Corporation for Public Broadcasting with a regulatory function that belongs with government. More damaging than either of these, however, is the ambiguity of the standard itself and the way in which it can be used by those who take issue with broadcasts they find personally offensive.

Scholars and journalists have wrestled with the concept of objectivity since early in this century when changes in the economics of publishing and competition to build readership encouraged a definition of news that emphasized the gathering and reporting of "facts." Opinion was relegated to signed political columns. In her seminal work on news and its relation to reality, sociologist Gaye Tuchman notes that historically "facticity connoted professional neutrality and objectivity." However, she and others have challenged the notion that something called objective truth can be strictly defined. Reporting the news, she says, is "an artful accomplishment attuned to specific understandings of reality." And because those understandings act to "legitimate the status quo," they tend to "limit the access of radical views to news consumers."[13]

Journalists have made similar arguments. Tom Wicker of the *New York Times* argues that so-called objective reporting "almost always favors Establishment positions and exists not least to avoid offense to them."[14] Russell Baker sees it as a restraint on truth. "No matter how dull, stupid, unfair, vicious, or mendacious they might be," Baker writes, "the utterances of the great were reported deadpan, with nary a hint that the speaker might be a bore, a dunce, a brute, or a habitual liar."[15] The consequence, says Brit Hume, is a "mindless neutrality" of the sort that demagogues before and beyond Senator Joseph McCarthy have exploited to the fullest. Dismissing the cult of objectivity as "something of a hoax," political scientist Eric Alterman warns that it "narrows the spectrum of allowable interpretations and restricts the possibilities of thoughtful contextual analyses'' and thus results in ''the intellectual impoverishment of our political dialogue.''[16]

Important as the ideological arguments are to those who cherish robust political debate, the greater danger in the mandate requiring ''strict adherence'' to objectivity is the way it drives public television to blandness. If, as Tuchman and others argue, objective truth defies definition, public television is hostage to an inexact and undefinable standard. In the hands of those who hold the purse strings, objectivity, self-defined, is a ready weapon for intimidating the medium and curbing its occasional temptations to boldness. It is one thing to encourage objectivity as an ideal to be strived for; it is quite another to apply it as an absolute measure of performance.

Similarly, the statutory requirement for ''strict adherence to . . . balance'' in programs of controversy is in its ambiguity an irrelevancy—and like the requirement of objectivity a potential weapon in the hands of politicians bent on neutering the medium. To begin with, even those who accept the standard cannot agree on its meaning. PBS claims it means balancing the program schedule but not individual programs within the schedule. Conservatives, however, want each program carefully balanced. Their differences are pointless. However balance is applied, it implies a specious form of reasoning known to semanticists as ''two-valued orientation'': every issue has only two sides, and each side merits equal weight. The real world is not so easily ordered nor are its issues so neatly divided. By common consent, it is patently absurd to demand a balanced treatment of racism, the shape of the Earth, or the Holocaust. Yet as we move across the spectrum of issues on which we differ, there is a point at which concordance ends and the need for balanced treatment begins. Where that point is will depend upon who is making the call. Balance, as every student of elementary physics learns, varies with the positioning of the fulcrum. The political fulcrum in this country has moved far to the right since the Reagan and Bush years—so much so that political equilibrium has been achieved by balancing the conservative right with the forces of the moderate middle—that the liberal left has practically disappeared from the screen: A survey by the City University of New York found less than 0.5 percent of the program hours on PBS were devoted to working people. The percentage would have been even less had the survey not counted the downstairs servants on the PBS series *Upstairs/Downstairs*.[17] And this was at a time when the conservative right was protesting its lack of access to the public system.

If balance has any relevance to public television's treatment of controversy, it lies in a very much broader context: the medium cannot permit itself to be used as the mouthpiece for any single political faction or ideology. While remaining determinedly nonpartisan, it must not fear to make room for the widest possible range of thought and opinion, for if it fails to do so, no one else will and the nation will be the poorer for it. To serve its audience in the robust spirit of free inquiry, public television must be freed from the specious notion that its programming can or should be weighed only in the balance of partisan politics. In this narrow sense, balance is father to bland and neutral programming of the sort that serves the viewer poorly and undermines the medium's potential for demystifying the public agenda.

Dismissing balance and objectivity as inappropriate for treating controversy does not strip public television of the standards needed to preserve its neutrality and protect its integrity. PBS, with the help of a panel of distinguished professionals, codified its own standards of journalistic practice as early as 1971. The rules, designed to ensure the impartial treatment of controversial issues by its program producers, were reviewed and updated in 1987. But even before PBS promulgated its own standards, public television was already subject to the unambiguous criteria of fairness and accuracy imposed by the Federal Communications Commission on all broadcasters. Fairness and accuracy, both more susceptible to objective measurement than Congress's ambiguous standards, are quite sufficient to shield the system from misuse or abuse of its public franchise. Accuracy is subject to audit: facts can be checked, challenged, and substantiated. In addition, the broadcaster is obligated to play fair—to the facts and to the viewer. Competing points of view or different interpretations of the given facts must be acknowledged; the viewer must not be misled into thinking the whole truth lies with the single presentation. The regulatory standards of the FCC, together with those imposed by PBS upon itself, are fully adequate to protect the public. Congress has no need to submit to right-wing pressures and hobble public television with additional rules whose very ambiguity is an invitation to control.

Ironically, the primary target of Congressional concern with public television's journalistic practices is most often the work of independent producers—ironic because Congress has consistently championed the cause of the "indies" only to be surprised when their work reveals an independence of thought. Right-wing critics are particularly outraged at documentaries that challenge establishment values; they lump them under the pejorative label of "left-leaning" and demand that public television balance them with more documentaries that lean to the right. Critics overlook the fact that social and political documentaries have a built-in tilt: it is the nature of the form to turn a critical eye on the status quo and expose injustice, hypocrisy, social inequality, malfeasance, and ineptitude in office—the sins and faults of an imperfect society. In addition, the people who make social documentaries, as critic Marvin Kitman reminds us, are rarely part of the Establishment. "The idea of making films is itself a dissenting profession," which, he points out, may help explain why conservatives become lawyers and doctors and not documentarians.[18]

The most convincing argument for the continued support of independent producers may in fact be this penchant to bite the hand that feeds them. The nation needs free spirits willing to speak with committed concern through unfettered discussion. If they are to be heard, the public medium is their best, and perhaps their only, hope.

18

INTIMATIONS
OF EXCELLENCE

*Noncommercial television should address itself to the ideal of excellence,
not the idea of acceptability—which is what keeps commercial television
from climbing the staircase. I think television should be the visual
counterpart of the literary essay, should arouse our dreams, satisfy our
hunger for beauty, take us on journeys, enable us to participate in events,
present great drama and music, explore the sea and the sky and the wood
and the hills.*

E. B. White[1]

Much can be learned about pub-
lic television from those who do not watch. For more than a dozen
years, I taught an undergraduate course in public television at
Brooklyn College. At our very first meeting, I asked how many in
the class of thirty had watched WNET / Channel 13. Only one hand
was raised. I urged the others to explain why they had never
watched. Their replies were simple and direct: public television
was for rich people. (I was curious to know why, under the circumstances, they had enrolled in this particular course, only to discover to my dismay that it was because they couldn't get into the
courses they really wanted!)

Clearly, without ever having tried it, the students "knew" public
television's programming was elitist. They wouldn't have used that
word, but that was what they meant by "rich people." They also
assumed that it was intended only for the "educated" with whom,
even as college students, they did not identify. Whatever else
might be said of the public medium, they were certain of one
thing: it was not fun, and in their young minds, that is what television is all about. I assigned them to watch any one of the local
public channels during the semester and to report their reactions
regularly. Several of the more skeptical students happened on a
few programs that they, to their almost embarrassed surprise, en-

joyed. But not even these minor epiphanies rid them of their pre-
conceptions about public television. Because they enjoyed the
shows, the shows "really belonged on commercial TV." The division between public and private was the difference between hard
work and simple pleasures.

Many of my students were the children of immigrant parents,
so it would be easy to conclude that they were not typical of their
age group. Yet they were not alone in drawing a picture of public
television in colors of dull gray; public television's own studies
have revealed a similar reaction by the viewing public at large.
The American perception of public television as "dry, static, too
educational and requiring too much mental effort" also explains
why no more than a tiny portion of the total available television
audience—on average, barely more than 2 percent of television
homes nationally—turns to PBS for its prime-time shows on any
given night.[2] Nor should we be surprised. "You Americans," Huw
Wheldon once teased me, "have a very strange way of treating
television. You have seven channels in New York [in pre-cable days
that was the range of available television], six are fun and the
seventh is good for you." He didn't have to explain which was
which. Wheldon, then the managing director of BBC Television,
pointed out that public television was regarded quite differently
in his own country, where the BBC was among other things the
principal producer of comedy programs.

The failure of the American public system to serve a larger proportion of the television audience makes the United States unique
among the industrial democracies. The public-broadcasting systems in many European countries and Japan, even those facing
competition from private channels, manage to attract as many as
half the homes with television during the prime-time hours. It is
true, of course, that some European public broadcasters face
fewer competing channels, most are far better financed per capita
and spend a greater proportion of their funds on programming
(and less on institutional overhead), and all were well established
prior to the time their governments permitted the entry of private
television. But these differences do not fully account for the comparative weakness of American public television.

From the day the Federal Communications Commission reserved 12 percent of the available television channels for education, America's public television system has been thought of—by
the Commission, the Congress, and by those inside the system—
as a minor appendage to the dominant commercial system. Unlike
European public-television systems, which placed themselves
firmly in the mainstream of their countries' broadcast media, ours
was narrowly pegged as an "alternate" to mainstream television
and limited to serving those "unserved needs" and "unserved
audiences" that the country's market-driven television found unprofitable. The rationale was based on the simplistic notion that
the "alternate" medium should do what commercial television
could not or would not do. The line defining what each should
do was drawn according to program genre: since the commercial
medium reached majority audiences with news, sports, and entertainment, the public medium confined itself to serving minority
audiences with the genres that remained. For the most part, this
translated to adult education, serious drama, children's programs,
high culture, and science. (So eagerly did PBS leap into natural
science that a wag dubbed it public television's "F Factor"—furs,
feathers, and fins.) By serving only minority audiences with specialized tastes—whether cultural elites or illiterate immigrants—
public television has placed itself on the outer margins of the
mainstream media. Its position as an add-on brings into question
not only the legitimacy of its claim upon the public treasury, but
also its claim to call itself "public."

In search of more certain ground, many in public broadcasting
are leading a retreat to the secure redoubt of education—the narrow purpose upon which it made its original claim for the channel
reservations. It makes little difference whether the call for a return
to this earlier purpose reflects the studied convictions of the local
station chiefs, many of whom came from or are linked to the academic community, or whether it is a cynical maneuver to present
to Congress the only face that most legislators readily understand
and are willing to support. In either case it is regressive and the
wrong way to go. Technology's rapid development of alternative
delivery systems, coupled with the limitations and inflexibility of

the broadcast medium—not to say the snail-like pace of the schools in adapting to the television medium—cast a limited future for public television in a field already crowded with well-heeled players.

In their perceptive survey of "The Condition of Public Television in the United States and Elsewhere," the two authors, Willard D. Rowland, Jr., and Michael Tracey, fear that the "plausibility and rhetorical force" have gone out of public television's "claim to fame" as an alternate service that offers programming the commercial system does not offer. They warn that by "seeking pastures elsewhere where the enemy does not roam, or for which the enemy has no desire" the public medium is pursuing a course that "has been the strategy of every social species which has disappeared from the face of the earth." If public broadcasting is to have a future, those who shape its purpose must abandon the sacred canon that "popularity" and "quality" are mutually exclusive. They must cease to define diversity by enumerating the program genres acquired by default from cable and commercial television. True diversity can only result from a program service that is *comprehensive* and of a standard and quality that sets it apart from the product of market-driven television. From this perspective, Rowland and Tracey conclude, "the nature of public broadcasting would be that any program offered, whatever the genre, should be the best of its kind, the best it can be."[3]

Largely unnoticed in the arguments about public television's role in serving unmet needs is the enormous unfilled gap in programs of quality—by which is meant not technical quality (we are the masters at that art), but quality of content. The commercial media, under economic pressure to maximize audiences for all shows in whatever category, stamp their programming out of a common matrix—noncontroversial, consensual, largely conventional in both form and substance, and tailored to meet the conditioned expectations in 90 million television homes. Excluded are the risk-taking ventures that create new art. Judging a program's worth by its rank on the ratings chart produces viewer options that are severely proscribed by the need for instant success. Long before the networks dumped their regular prime-time cultural and documentary programs and turned to an almost solid diet of sitcoms and action-adventure shows, broadcasting's pre-eminent historian Erik Barnouw warned that the commercial media could be neither reoriented nor regulated into fulfilling a broader public interest. Because the industry's economic drives have always won out, "the need for a supplementary system based on other motives is paramount and crucial."[4] Les Brown, taking account of the country's media experience since the Barnouw prophesy, wisely observes that a supplementary system is "not just ordinary television without advertisements," but rather "a separate species of the medium, different in spirit from the commercial and pay forms of television, different in aspiration, different in its regard for the viewer, and different in motivation." Commercial television, he notes, "exists to make money one way or another, but noncommercial television exists to make television."[5]

If it seems somewhat heretical to argue that public television's programming should cover the widest range of program choices, it is only because Americans, accustomed to finding their leisure viewing elsewhere on the television dial, have relegated the public medium to a minor role. Unfortunately, those inside public broadcasting have willingly acquiesced, comfortable in their sinecures and lacking a broader vision of their medium's potential. Yet these same public broadcasters are fond of quoting E. B. White's now-famous letter to the Carnegie Commission. When he wrote that "noncommercial television should address itself to the ideal of excellence," he clearly intended that the ideal transcend the cramped vision of those for whom pop culture lies beyond the pale. Public television, he reminds us, should be "our Lyceum, our Chautauqua, our Minsky's, and our Camelot," allusions that are rich in metaphorical meanings and underscore the catholicity of White's conception of excellence.[6] Not just the upscale culture of the Lyceum and Chautauqua, but the baggy-pants humor of Minsky's burlesque—the inspiration for a generation of comic talents whose outrageous pie-in-the-face humor poked fun at fatuity and regularly booted pretense in the seat of the pants. Clearly, for White, excellence is a standard rather than a genre. *Live from Lincoln Center* and *Great Performances* are models of excellence. But so, too, are M*A*S*H, the films of Buster Keaton, and the Super Bowl. "Standards should refer to the quality of programmes across a whole range of broadcasting," noted a British study. "A 'highbrow' program may be of poor quality, whatever its own professions . . . so may a current affairs programme . . . while a comedy or a sports programme may be each in their own ways of very high quality."[7]

Those who argue that excellence is too subjective and insubstantial a standard on which to structure a mission for public television must deal with Huw Wheldon. In his years as a BBC program executive, Wheldon had frequent need to make judgment calls on program quality, and he airily dismisses those who say one man's excellence is another man's trash. ("On the whole, I think most good programmes are recognized as such by people who are disposed toward that subject.") If, for example, you don't like opera or football, your views on whether either was well done "may be interesting but irrelevant." On the other hand, people who take these things seriously "will generally be in accord when they're talking about the very good and the very bad."[8] Historian Barbara Tuchman, who took these matters seriously, wrote that excellence is more than reaching for the highest standard—it is an "honesty of purpose as against catering to cheap and sensational sentiment." She noted that the latter is an increasing presence in "our mass-mediated lives," and blamed it for contributing to the decline in the level of quality in recent years. This "foolery," she wrote, is destined to leave its mark on future generations. How, she asked, will the young "become acquainted with quality if they are not exposed to it?"[9] The young, for whom the ubiquitous television tube is the leisure activity of choice, must be given the opportunity of knowing television of a different sort, of experiencing the intelligence, wit, and invention of which it is capable when it is not driven downscale by competitive forces in the marketplace.

No area of television programming cries out more insistently for quality than the treatment of news and current affairs. Once-proud standards have sunk to new lows in recent years as com-

mercial television's news programs, faced with increased competition for audience numbers, have fought each other with the tools
of tabloidism for their share of the American audience. Warning
signs, however, were raised years before the present decline. One
such admonition came from John Birt, then head of current affairs for London Weekend Television. Birt, who in recent years
has acceded to the post of director-general of the BBC, advanced
a provocative idea in the columns of the *Times* of London—that
news is biased, not against any party or point of view, but against
understanding. "The typically atomized presentation of events and
issues," he asserted, "systematically misrepresents the world and
its difficulties, thereby making it more difficult than it otherwise
would be for society to solve its problems." To know is not enough;
to act intelligently as political creatures we must also understand
what we know and be able to place factual information in a meaningful context where ideas can gestate and convictions form.[10]

Birt's provocation illuminates a critical weakness in the quality
of television news. At its best, it keeps us informed. But watching
even the best TV news on commercial television, says media critic
William A. Henry III, "is more likely to add to a viewer's store of
unassimilated facts than to enhance . . . perception and understanding."[11] Worse, when the facts themselves go unassimilated,
graver questions are raised about the ability of the electorate to
participate in democratic self-government. A 1993 survey of Ivy
League undergraduates revealed that half could not name their
home-state senators, a third could not identify British Prime Minister John Major, 23 percent did not know that the Supreme Court
has nine justices, and 18 percent could not name a single one of
them. Fewer than half watched television news. In a similar survey
in the late eighties, at a time when events in Central America led
off every day's newscast, half of those surveyed did not know if
U.S. policy supported the government of Nicaragua or El Salva-
dor.

The inadequacy of television as an information source is not
new, or newly discovered. More than thirty years ago, Edward R.
Murrow predicted that historians a century hence, looking at the
record left by the three networks, would discover "evidence of

decadence, escapism, and insulation from the realities of the world in which we live." America's foremost broadcast journalist feared for the future of the republic. "Unless we get up off our fat surpluses and recognize that television in the main is being used to distract, delude, amuse, and insulate us, then television and those who finance it, those who look at it and those who work at it, may see a totally different picture too late."[12] A more recent polemic on the inanities and inadequacies of television news, Neil Postman's *Amusing Ourselves to Death* concludes "that Americans are quite likely the least well-informed people in the Western world."[13]

If Postman is right—and he is not alone in postulating the paradox of a poorly informed America in the midst of a media-saturated environment—the ideal of a self-governing society is at risk unless attention is given to how to meet the need for a reasonably informed electorate. The commercial media are a poor bet to meet that need. Many years ago, long before the Reagan Administration's orgy of deregulation, broadcasters were held to a public-service standard. Although it was indifferently enforced by a lax FCC, it asserted a principle: those who profit from the use of the publicly owned broadcast frequencies are obligated to return a benefit to the public in the form of service. In television's infancy, one such public service was the airing of news shows that, in those early years, were unprofitable. Broadcasters made up the loss with profits from the more marketable shows. But then the unexpected financial success of *60 Minutes* changed news shows forever. News itself became a marketable commodity. Television news departments found themselves under competitive pressures to be Number One so they could charge advertisers the highest rates for their commercials. News shows began to mix generous dollops of entertainment and sensationalism with otherwise serious news. The three national networks, once the lustrous citadel of serious broadcast journalism, lost much of that luster in a frenzy of cost-cutting and competitive zeal that has produced a spate of "reality-based" or "actuality" shows in prime-time. These shows mix news, sensationalism, and entertainment in a heady brew that bears a dismaying resemblance to the quality of journalism encountered at supermarket checkout counters. In the words of Sydney Alexander, "The need to excite gets in the way of the need to inform."[14]

Nor has cable done much better. The Cable News Network, still unavailable to a third of the nation, follows the network pattern of news snippets interrupted by nonrelevant commercial messages. Largely missing is the contextual background, the critical analysis, the extended and continual coverage needed to give meaning and significance to the events on the screen. A pair of British researchers offer another, more subtle reason why cable cannot answer democracy's need for an informed public. In the course of studying the possible effects of privatizing British television, they concluded that whenever access to information for citizenship depends on purchasing power, "substantial inequalities are generated that undermine the nominal universality of citizenship." Moreover, by addressing people predominantly as consumers, as with all market-driven media, cable "marginalizes or displaces other identities, in particular the identity of citizen." The viewer, they concluded, is denied the essentials of citizenship: access to the broadest possible range of information, interpretation, and debate on areas that involve political choices.[15]

Studies of the situation in our own country give cause for concern. A 1990 survey by the Times Mirror Center for the People and the Press found that the younger generation (18–29 years of age) "knows less, cares less, votes less and is less critical of its leaders and institutions than young people in the past." The study concluded that the generational indifference to politics, to government, even to news of the outside world, has had a baleful effect on American politics and society, and lay part of the blame upon "the rise of television." In a similar vein, People for the American Way, concluding that "America's youth are alarmingly ill-prepared to keep democracy alive in the 1990's and beyond," called the situation a "citizenship crisis."[16]

MIT's Sydney Alexander parsed the problem with the studied efficiency of a professor of economics and management and offered his own analysis. "If it is the function of the American news media to make headlines, some other agency is required to make for understanding." His suggested solution: public television. "The achievement of deeper understanding on the part of the viewer" will, he feels, provide the public medium with its greatest challenge.[17] PBS has responded in part to the challenge with the *MacNeil/Lehrer NewsHour,* network television's first (and thus far only) hour-long prime-time news show. (Before crediting the PBS system with the collective wisdom and courage to meet the challenge, however, it must be remembered that Robert MacNeil and Jim Lehrer met a cool reception from the local stations opposed to the hour-long version.) The *MacNeil/Lehrer NewsHour* has given credible evidence of what can result when issues are given time and space to develop. However, the program's tendency to cautiously balance every purported fact with a contradictory and cancelling fact or to play rhetorical ping-pong ("You heard what he said, now how do you respond?") risks leaving those who lack the expertise to sort fact from nonfact more confused than enlightened.[18]

Needed in today's complex world of mass-mediated information is an ongoing analysis of the issues by those who are most informed and least involved: the experienced journalists who cover the day-by-day developments. On the occasions when its knowledgeable reporters feel free to speak their minds, *Washington Week in Review* serves this end. We begin to understand what we may already know. For a still better example, we must turn to National Public Radio's daily and weekend news shows *Morning Edition* and *All Things Considered.* Both programs, including their weekend editions, have won the ungrudging praise of news professionals both in and out of the commercial media, many of whom rate them as broadcast journalism's "finest." The high quality and extensiveness of the shows' factual reporting—much of it, incidentally, by first-rate women reporters—provides a model that public television could profitably emulate. But the shows have an even greater value in their use of incisive analysis and commentary to lend context and dimension to their factual reporting. When it works, the listener comes away with the feeling that the dots have been joined to form a template for understanding and a basis for those convictions that give rise to citizen action.

Programs like *All Things Considered* and *Morning Edition* hold out the greatest promise for fulfilling E. B. White's charge to the public media "to clarify the social dilemma and the political pickle." At the same time, it must be noted that only in America would shows of this quality be unknown or unavailable to large segments of the national audience, distributed as they are in a jerrybuilt system of public radio that, like its television counterpart, consists of a loose confederation of autonomous, under-funded, locally controlled stations, some weak, some strong. It is an absurd failure of public policy that public radio, if only for its informational programming, was not made universally available, as it is in most democratic countries, on a network of powerful transmitters that blanket the nation. As it is, its availability is subject to the whims and uneven resources of local initiative.

Television's traditional vehicle for clarifying the social dilemma has for many years been the long-form documentary, which attempts—commonly, in an hour or more—to explore and enlarge upon a single issue. This neglected and much-maligned form has all but disappeared from prime-time television in recent years, having been given the boot by network number crunchers who believe the public interest is defined by whatever interests the public. In the new age of eight-minute attention spans, the long-form documentary is a dinosaur. Its disappearance from prime-time network television left an information void not filled by news magazines modeled on the success of *60 Minutes*, or worse, by the episodic "special reports" shoehorned into the daily newscast. The compression of what needs to be known into eight-minute features or ten-second sound bites may be the friend of the news producer, but it is the enemy of understanding.

Almost by default, public television remains the last refuge for the long-form documentary. The nonfiction form has been a staple in the schedule of the noncommercial medium from its founding. It dominates today's PBS schedules, treating science, medicine, history, art, travel, and even the star-filled world of entertainment—although the last named tends to appear only during intensive fund-raising drives. But save for an occasional award and the gratitude of their fans, most documentaries pass unremarked. Not, however, the documentary that seeks to clarify sensitive sociopolitical issues on which honest persons honestly disagree. This sometimes incendiary form finds a home in the PBS schedule in such series as *Frontline* and *P.O.V.* The former, when it isn't reaching for the numbers with frivolous topics or jousting with padded lances, gives a good account of how the form can be put to effective use, as it has with such outstanding episodes as "The Betrayal of Democracy," "To the Brink of War," and "The Battle for Eastern Airlines."

Bill Moyers, public television's ubiquitous presence, has practiced a variant on the conventional documentary form. His personal essays, growing from the original PBS series *Bill Moyers' Journal,* have treated a wide range of political and social issues with great effect. Moyers does more than observe with a critical eye and analyze with a keen intelligence. He applies a moral and ethical yardstick to the issue or event, taking its measure in terms of human values. Television critic William Henry III called Moyers "the quintessential reporter-as-performer . . . thoughtful, compassionate, independent but not iconoclastic . . . an unabashed moralist."[19] These qualities hold up well in a medium that prizes personality and abjures abstraction. They are singular in public television, a medium that steadfastly strives to keep an objective distance between the issue and the person who reports on it. But like Edward R. Murrow, with whom he is often compared, Moyers has the wit and skill to transform an abstraction into a personal statement: we care because he cares. Eric Alterman believes that Moyers's "almost superhuman feat of delving into intricate social and intellectual questions while managing to avoid virtually all of the theatricality and reductiveness that characterizes the rest of television's public discourse" demonstrates "that the medium does have the capacity to stimulate debate without giving heed to the twin shibboleths of objectivity and infotainment."[20]

At their best, documentaries on social and political issues challenge conventional thinking, forcing us to reflect upon and reexamine the premises upon which we act. This is profoundly disturbing to those who believe a publicly funded medium should steer around the mine-strewn fields of controversy, reinforcing rather than attacking society's prevalent values. In his study of "Public Television and the 'Ought' of Public Policy," Sydney Alexander argues that while popular art has its place on the tube—"to confirm and validate values"—high art should be there "to disturb, challenge and transform values." It is a process, he argues, "that upsets the viewer to his advantage."[21] Public television has a place for programs that confirm and validate prevalent values; most of its airtime is devoted to that end. But there is also a place for documentaries that challenge those values. Jeremy Isaacs sees it as a "need to see and hear on radio and television how life looks to all sorts and conditions of men and women, of all sorts of opinion; contented, discontented; favoring the status quo, gradual change, or even revolution; men and women who wish to preserve society as it is now, and also those who want to change it, reform it, alter it altogether."[22] Isaacs applied his prescription to the shaping of Britain's unique Channel 4 with results that could serve well as a model for public television in the United States. In America's intellectually cramped environment, however, to apply the Isaacs formula to PBS would trip alarm bells in Congress, notwithstanding that the prescription speaks to the precious freedoms protected by the First Amendment or that it is the embodiment of the marketplace of ideas on which those freedoms rest. "Every idea," wrote Justice Oliver Wendell Holmes, "is an incitement. It offers itself for belief and if believed is acted on unless some other belief outweighs it or some failure of energy stifles the movement at its birth."[23]

The question of whether controversy is compatible with the purposes of the public medium must be answered with another question: if not public television, then who? Robust debate and free and uninhibited discourse, essential in a self-governing democracy, cannot be addressed adequately by media almost wholly in the service of commerce. Public broadcasting's freedom from the economic restraints that keep the commercial medium bland and submissive makes it imperative that it do what needs to be done. Pouring out a Niagara-like flood of information, though, however valid and varied, is not enough. Daniel J. Boorstin has warned that information, ephemeral and transient, is constantly driven out by

chalkdust still clings to its skirts, a legacy from its earlier incarnation as educational television. Too many of its prime-time series—those gaseous explorations of cosmic abstractions in pursuit of corporate underwriters or tedious illustrated lectures rationalized as adult education—sound more like graduate seminars than the fare that might attract us to television at the end of a trying day. If it is to be more than a peripheral phenomenon wasting away on the edge of the mainstream, public television must reach out for a more comprehensive approach to programming, discard its earnest "good for you" image, and lighten up without yielding an inch of ground to its primary mission of high-quality programming. "A service that offered Shakespeare, wildlife documentaries and penetrating interviews . . . would not be a 'good' service," say the British, "even if each program were of prize-winning quality." Excellence as a discrete purpose for public television must embrace the notion of variety as well. "Quality programming does not pre-judge audiences by presumed height of brow."[26] Public television needs the lighthearted and entertaining as well as the earnestly significant and the resolutely educational.

The primary reason for offering varied television fare on public stations, as I've mentioned, is the need to seek broader viewership. The prospective viewers' expectations of unrelieved seriousness must be confounded by programs that deliver some of the pleasures of the commercial media without its insubstantiality. By interleaving lighter shows among the documentaries, dramas, and concerts, public television would attract substantial numbers, many for the first time, with the probability that some would remain for the serious program to follow. Britain's public channels have pursued this comprehensive programming policy from the start; Huw Wheldon called it "education by stealth." That it has had its desired effect can be demonstrated by the fact that the BBC's two channels attract a far larger proportion of the available audience than does PBS. For more than fifty years, BBC television has fulfilled, often with distinction, its Parliamentary order to give the United Kingdom a high-quality educational and informational service. But it has also, without loss to its serious purpose, created the best of British television comedy, setting standards of quality with shows like *That Was the Week That Was, Monty Python's Flying Circus,* and *Fawlty Towers.* Our own public system, by contrast, has not created a single comedy show in its forty years of existence.

Broadening the spectrum of program types is not a deviation from public television's informational and educational purpose but an additional means toward the same end. "Art," Alexander reminds us, "transforms us as it entertains ... enhances our experience ... helps to make us what we are."[27] Network entertainment at it best—and at its best it is art—has offered glimpses of television's power to enhance the human experience. Some found it in the comedy/drama of M*A*S*H, *The Mary Tyler Moore Show,* or *The Days and Nights of Molly Dodd.* Others found it in the more serious serial dramas: *Thirtysomething* or today's *Northern Exposure.* What these programs share, other than intelligent writing and skillfully crafted production, is a connectedness, an insight into our own idiosyncratic behavior and sometimes troubled feelings. That entertainment—when it is art—can also provide insights into our revered institutions was cleverly demonstrated by the BBC's comedy/satire *Yes, Minister.* Imported into America by public television, it provoked laughter primarily for its wit and humor. But for British viewers it was a pointed satire that offered an engaging insight into the foibles of parliamentary government. PBS should do as much for Congress.

There is another, perhaps stronger rationale for broadening public television's range of program choices: to set a standard of quality against which all other television might be measured. Those who would keep the public medium marginalized will be quick to cite the countless hours of light entertainment already available from commercial television and cable. Public television's mission is not to add to the volume but to the *quality,* not by importing from abroad, and not by appropriating "quality" commercial shows that lose out in the competitive drive for audience, but by creating new art, new ideas, new and different programs. Writers, actors, singers, dancers, satirists, and comics—those who are "driven by their own compulsions to the production of great art"—must be given "the opportunity to do what they feel compelled to do."[28] Professor Alexander points out that "even in entertainment programs, especially in entertainment programs, there are potentialities which are unrealized in commercial television, that must remain unrealized so long as it is commercial." The commercial media could do better but doesn't because "the producers are not letting the best artists follow their own standards of what makes good art." In this genre, as in all others, public television's overarching aim must be excellence, a standard of quality against which to gauge all other television. In the absence of such a measure and lacking a higher standard, audiences come to accept what they know, satisfied that it is the best there is. Giving the lie to that inference could be a service to the viewers and to the profession of broadcasting.

The alternative is to surrender ourselves to mediocrity, trivialization, and blandness in a medium that more than any other dominates our lives and fills our leisure hours. We are at risk. "The contest between education and TV—between argument and conviction by spectacle," says social critic Robert Hughes, "has been won by television, a medium now more debased in America than ever before."[29] Neil Postman warns us that we are "amusing ourselves to death," losing touch with a world that is trivialized and decontextualized by the ubiquitous tube. Our cultural landscape should have room for something more: a medium with respect for the intelligence of its viewers, willing to address its audience not just as consumers but as sentient human beings; a medium dedicated to offering the best because it is the best and not simply because it reaches the largest numbers inside the advertiser's demographic target.

In 1992, concerned that countries hell-bent on privatizing television might ignore these distinctions, Japan's Hoso Bunka Foundation commissioned a survey of the world's public-television systems. Willard D. Rowland, Jr., and Michael Tracey, engaged to conduct the survey and report the results, were themselves surprised at the conclusions they were compelled to arrive at on the basis of the evidence they gathered.

Whatever the objective difficulties which face public broadcasting, its canon must be constantly asserted: that it sets its face against the mediocre and the debased; that it asserts the necessity to nurture quality in the life of the public mind by insuring that the population of the polity can be properly informed, properly educated and provided with a sense of coherence and belonging; that it sees itself, the national public broadcaster, as one of, if not *the* most powerful centripetal forces in societies with dangerous centrifugal tendencies. The social forces which so challenge the public broadcaster also provide the most powerful argument for his or her existence; that the modern, democratic nation state *needs* a national broadcasting service, because it needs a quality of life, it needs coherence, it needs to let fly what Lincoln referred to as "the better angels of our nature" and quarantine the impulse to division, degradation and domination.[30]

Public television has a life, a purpose, and a place in the profligate mix of American media. What is needed is the vision to see it and the will to make it happen.

EPILOGUE:
PAST IMPERFECT,
FUTURE IMPERATIVE

When we decide that an investment in "a civilized voice in a civilized community" is worth more than an investment in cold war, we shall find that the financial problem is largely one of shifting our priorities.

Erik Barnouw[1]

For more than forty years, public television has occupied the center of my professional life, sitting like a huge and generally friendly beast in my living space, impossible to ignore and fascinating to observe. The opportunity was given me over the course of this time to observe the beast from several vantage points: as a witness to its birth and an active player in the first two decades of its development, as a sometime performer, as a teacher blessedly removed from its blinkered politics, and, with the task at hand, as a chronicler of its traumas and occasional triumphs. None of these perspectives has altered my early conviction about its potential or lessened my desire to see its promise realized. And yet, in more dispassionate moments, it strikes me that four decades is an uncommonly long time to be wedded to a single cause, particularly a cause that has somehow failed to capture the imagination and ignite the concern of most Americans. It is reasonable, therefore, to ask why I—or anyone, for that matter—would engage in an uphill struggle to see it persevere and grow.

Perhaps the perversity of spirit that sustains my interest has its roots in a vision born during television's infancy, a time when the medium was still moderately malleable and everything seemed possible. We who fell, stumbled, or were pushed into the medium, idealists all, envisioned a television that was something more than a home-delivered electronic billboard hawking products we could comfortably do without or a legal narcotic blocking out the pain and pressures of the real world. The television we imagined would make reality palatable, even pleasurable. It would provide a helpful context for living by opening the mind to yet unexamined textures, deepening faith in the human potential, and provoking a laughter of recognition at the absurdities of our own narrow vision. Unfortunately, our hopes for another kind of television, separate but equal, fell victim to broadcast policies that have long given primacy to the world of commercial profit. Accordingly, television, publicly held for the benefit of the polity, was marginalized as a weak alternative and shunted to the sidelines, there to serve the indeterminate needs of education. Many of us who tended that early vision and who labored to make it real feel let down because we know that for all of its minor triumphs today's system is a pale shadow of what ought to be.

Perhaps shadow is an apt metaphor in another sense: it describes public television's apparent insubstantiality. The public system is increasingly at risk of disappearing from our screens. Lost as it is in the jungle of new technologies and fearful of being devoured by the newer media, its sole preoccupation is survival. And not without reason: the newer media, looking for new income streams to tap, have targeted "niche" audiences, the once exclusive terrain of public television and the principal rationale for its marginalized existence. Undecided about its own place in the scheme of things, the public system wavers between battling the newer media on their own ground and by their own rules or surrendering the field and retreating to the safe haven of educational fare that is even more narrowly defined.

Those who ponder why I and others cling to a notion of television whose time, according to realists, has come and passed need only pick up their remote and surf the channels. There they will find the early harvest of the Age of Abundant Communication:

endless hours of vacuous fare, decontextualized and lacking a moral compass, artlessly trivializing life and the human condition. Not for the first time has the reality fallen short of the promise; we heard in the twenties about radio, in the fifties about television, and are hearing it again with only the vocabulary changed. This time the seducers are interactivity and the information superhighway. Television for quality, not profit, which could and should counter the featherweight fare of common-denominator television, has by official governmental policy been marginalized and denied a fair chance by those for whom the airwaves are, first and foremost, the province of commerce. Sadly, the policy has the acquiescence of a compliant and leaderless public-television establishment.

The situation calls to mind the immediate postwar years when, with the promise of a bright new age of transportation, trolleys and trains were overrun by the speed and flexibility of air travel and buses. Tracks were ripped up, Penn Station was torn down, and rights-of-way were converted to bicycle paths. Today, the dream of a future without such "anachronistic" modes of travel is becoming a nightmare of urban gridlock, jammed highways, and crowded skies. Talk of returning trolleys to the streets and trains to the heavily travelled urban corridors no longer provokes derisive laughter. In our haste to get ahead of advancing technologies, we abandoned a past we now seek to revive.

It is not difficult to see that today's video technology is driving us toward a time when the proliferation of channels will intensify competition and only the profitable will survive. The most likely survivors are pay-per-view cable, "infotainment," and programming whose primary aim will be consumerism in one form or another. The inevitable loss of program quality, integrity, and standards of taste will renew our appetite for substance. If in our lack of vision we allow the public medium to wither, we shall find ourselves—ten, twelve, or fifteen years hence—attempting to breathe life back into what was once regarded as a marginal additive to the laugh tracks of the commercial medium.

So what is to be done?

Certainly not another study. These exercises in self-reform, conducted with the regularity of a tribal rite, have done little to advance the cause of a strong and viable public system. Only the first of the three major studies—the Carnegie Commission on Educational Television—had an appreciable effect on the system by restructuring it in dubious ways and by dumping the stultifying educational television label. The study's most important contribution, the recommendation of a dedicated tax to provide public television with a funding source well removed from the influence of politics, was turned aside by Congress. Ten years later, Carnegie II was launched to rectify the errors of the first study, but with no Johnson White House to move the recommendations into legislation, the report was filed and forgotten. The most recent study, conducted under the auspices of the Twentieth Century Fund, released its report, *Quality Time?*, in the summer of 1993. (The title, said one critic, could be understood "as either plaintive or sardonic.")[2] Its recommendation for "major structural changes ... if public television is to provide a high-quality alternative to commercial broadcasting"[3] was ignored in equal measure by the press, the Congress, and the public-television establishment. All of which lends credence to Tom Shales's observation that if the time and energy devoted to studies were channeled instead into programming, "we would be riveted to our public TV stations, where triumph would follow masterpieces night after night."[4]

All three public-television studies suffer from a common flaw: each treats the public medium as a genus apart—distinct from other video forms—and not simply as another species of the same thing. It is all television. No matter how the images enter the home—by broadcast, cable, or satellite—they show up on the same screen, sharing the same pixels, separated one from the other by no more than a click of a remote control. The absurdity of studying the public medium as an isolated phenomenon can be likened to analyzing male-female relationships by researching one sex and not the other. We do not need another study of public television. What is needed is both a comprehensive study of the entire spectrum of interrelated electronic mass media and a public-policy debate on its future. Other countries show their concern for the social and political impact of television, radio, and cable by periodically reviewing the effectiveness of their broadcast policies.

Most important, they treat private and public communications together, acknowledging their interrelatedness, and define the roles each has to play in meeting the needs of their societies. We are alone among the Western democracies in our failure to chart such a course—we rely instead on a sixty-year-old regulatory statute enacted during the New Deal, when television, cable, and satellites were the stuff of science fiction.

Given the medium's sometimes baleful influence upon our lives, our children, and our political institutions, our unwillingness to debate and adopt a comprehensive public policy is incomprehensible. To some, it is irresponsible. Our curious posture stems from an eighteenth-century libertarianism that believed an enlightened private industry would best serve the public interest. Couple that with Constitutional prohibitions against governmental restraints on the exercise of free speech and a systemic fear of letting the government muck about in the media, and you have the rationale for our unwillingness to regulate. For the most part, private interests have been permitted both to define and to care for the public interest, a policy that peaked in the Reagan years when broadcasting's "public interest" requirement was abandoned and restraints on multiple media ownership were loosened. The cry of the Republican majority in the 104th Congress for the "privatization" of public television only carries that ideology to an absurd finale.

America's let-the-market-prevail approach contrasts sharply with the approaches of those industrial democracies whose broadcasting organizations are treated as cultural institutions—a part of that sector of society "responsible for generating and disseminating its linguistic, literary, spiritual, aesthetic, and ethnic wealth."[5] (Curiously, America once came close to treating broadcasting as a cultural institution, but it was in Japan, during the Allied Occupation, when General Douglas MacArthur used Japanese radio [NHK] to advance the social and political aims of his command. According to Rowland and Tracey, it was a "testament to the belief in broadcasting as a primarily *social*, not economic process" and represented "some of the clearest thinking about the nature of broadcasting and its relationship to society.")[6] Here at home, an interesting anomaly exists between our treatment of the medium and our treatment of schools and libraries. So essential are the latter to a self-governing and productive society that we provide for them at public expense, unwilling to leave them entirely to the vagaries of the market forces. And yet, as every parent knows, the authority of the classroom and library are increasingly eclipsed by the influence of the ubiquitous tube, leaving many to wonder how we can have any less concern for television's role in the education of the young.

The first step toward a more concerned policy is a return to the concept of broadcasting as a public trust. Those who control the images on our screens create a social environment no less important to our health and welfare than clean air and water. We hold industry responsible for not polluting the one; broadcasters should be held responsible for not polluting the other. Good corporate citizenship implies—if, indeed, it does not demand—as much concern for the public interest as it does for what interests the public. But, important as this is, we must at the same time recognize the limitations on what might be demanded of a medium whose success is measured in profit margins. And thus the need for a second corrective measure: a fully integrated and adequately funded system of public television.

Unfortunately, our national need cannot be met by fine tuning the system now in place, a system whose fragmented and multipurposed structure makes it hopelessly resistant to reform. Public television must be reinvented. The idea is not new; press critics have lamented for years that "the whole rickety, grotesque structure of public television [is] in need of drastic reform" (Neil Hickey, *TV Guide*)[7] and "should be taken apart from top to bottom and put back together someplace else" (Tom Shales, *Washington Post*).[8] Its "top-heavy, expensive and stifling bureaucracy," said one of its own leaders, virtually guarantees "that it will remain mired in second-class status."[9]

Predictably, calls for reform bounce off the institutional walls of the public system, a structure made up of more than one hundred autonomous entities with a stake in keeping the system as it is. What is more, the true believers enjoy the support of a Congress that, for reasons of its own, favors a fragmented and marginalized system. The situation prompted Eli N. Evans, the president of the Revlon Foundation and the only person to take part in all three major studies of public television, to advocate a radical break with the past. In an impassioned postscript to the Twentieth Century Fund Task Force report, Evans argued that if we are to "build a new system of telecommunications, with a new definition of the public interest," we must "sweep away this history and create a new national entity that will lead the system into a new world."[10]

Architectural blueprints for the "new national entity" are not in short supply; all who have thought seriously about it have ideas if not a plan. You will not, however, find the ultimate blueprint in these pages. I am secure in the knowledge that a nation with the planning skills to harness nuclear energy or to loft a person onto the lunar surface is well able to meet the challenge of reordering public television without help from this quarter. I will, however, indulge the reader's patience long enough to propose those several elements that, in my judgment, must be taken into account in the ultimate plan if the system is be truly effective.

The first is the creation of the "new national entity" in which to centralize the functions of public television. A *single national institution* is needed to replace the current bureaucratic nightmare of competing entities and overlapping functions, which are grossly wasteful of human, financial, and technical resources, sap creative energy, blur the lines of responsibility, and divert the medium's attention from its principal mission of providing quality programming. Lynne Cheney, former director of the Humanities Endowment, summed it up with the observation that "to talk about a 'public system,' is to verge on oxymoron."[11] Opponents inside public television fear a single national institution would dominate the system. But domination in their sense also means giving much-needed leadership to a system that is currently handicapped by too many arms and no head. Size and solidity count, too. Only big institutions, as the BBC has demonstrated for more than fifty years, can stand up to big government. And only institutions with the political muscle to stay the intrusive hand of government have a chance at sustaining an independent voice. A governing board, preferably small, but determinedly nonpolitical as well as nongovernmental, will be needed to secure the independence of the national entity. Because the board will shape the destiny of one of the nation's most influential educational and cultural institutions, its members must have national reputations in the arts, humanities, sciences, professions, and public affairs, and they must be willing to serve the national interest as individuals and not as representatives of a constituency, whether local, professional, or political.

An early goal of the national trust must be *universal coverage.* Public television loses meaning unless it is easily available to every home, and on an equal basis with commercial television. Other countries take the obligation to provide universal coverage for granted, but the FCC has left the reach and coverage of the American system entirely to chance and local initiative. The result is a patchwork of stations, some strong, some weak, with coverage that is at best spotty. While certain areas are underserved with poor reception or no reception at all, others are overserved with two or more competing public stations airing the same or similar programs and vying with each other for the loyalty and support of virtually the same audience. The barriers to universal coverage are largely political; technology is at hand for rationalizing the system and for bringing the signal of public television into every home.

One logical step is to utilize the overlapping stations as the foundation for a *second network.* Public television needs more than one network. A single network—as PBS has amply demonstrated—cannot provide the full range of program services; the effort to do so only results in a composite that is neither entirely public nor fully educational. Most European nations and Japan have at least two, some have three. A second American network would permit a schedule of programs with more limited appeal, programs targeted at specialized audiences (for example, instructional television for school use), and experimental, high-risk offerings that push forward the frontiers of the medium. Consideration should be given to administering the two networks as separate entities, one with a large centralized production staff, the other with no production staff but with a group of highly skilled editors to commission work from independent sources. A useful model for this approach, dubbed "electronic publishing," exists in Britain's Channel 4. With two national networks, it is essential that each network have separate station outlets in each community, giving the viewer the choice of which to view. PBS once planned for three national program services, but all three services fed into the single PBS outlet in each community. The station, not the audience, would have chosen which of the three would be seen at any given time.

Public television has but a single function: to fill the nation's television screens with a program service that is comprehensive, diverse, and of the highest quality. Everything else is peripheral and should either support or extend the benefits of the program service. Of the three criteria, none is more important than a programming service that is *comprehensive*. It must include all genres of television programming and be capable of competing with commercial television for its audience—but on grounds of superior quality. Because PBS was created as an "alternative" to mainstream television, it has been exiled into the ghetto of high-minded "educational" fare with a prime-time schedule that appears to have risen straight off the pages of a college course catalogue. Despite the excellence of many of its programs, the network's appeal is necessarily limited to a fraction of the public it is mandated to serve. By contrast, Britain's public television is mainstream, competing head-to-head with the commercial channels by offering programming "from the mildly diverting to the intensely demanding." Film director David Puttnam points out that because neither public nor private television in Britain has "operated on the basis of filling the gaps left by the other," the "out-and-out winner" is the British audience.[12]

Public television's other goal, a service defined by high quality, is best met by programming produced for a national audience. Even now, it is PBS's national programming—*Nova* and *Nature*, *Barney* and *Sesame Street*, *MacNeil/Lehrer NewsHour* and *Wall Street Week*—that defines public television for the average viewer. Logic would argue for dedicating the bulk of public television's funding to this purpose. PBS's fragmented system, however, defies logic: a whopping 75 percent of the medium's federal funding is divided among the 345 autonomous stations, primarily to buoy up the system's byzantine structure rather than to support its key national program service. The erratic means of funding national programming drew close scrutiny from the Twentieth Century Fund Task Force. Its report recommended channelling the medium's federal funds entirely into national production, leaving stations to support themselves out of local resources. The recommendation— the Task Force's most significant contribution to public television's future planning—was given little serious consideration by the powerful bloc of station executives. More recently, the man who in 1993 succeeded Bruce Christensen as president of PBS— former FCC Commissioner Ervin S. Duggan—put the problem squarely in front of those station executives by reminding his members that, against the total funding of public television, the PBS stations collectively spend only seven percent on national programming. "We must find a way," he urged, "to liberate more funds for high-quality, original, compelling national programming."[13]

Even so, channelling more funds into national programming is not in itself the answer. More money will not produce a comprehensive, diverse, and high-quality program service without major changes in the way the system's programs are made. Programming and production decisions must be the responsibility of a single national agency—as they are in every other major broadcasting organization, public or private. Since the creation of PBS, this responsibility has been the exclusive province of the stations. Decentralization of production was aimed at satisfying Congress's call for "programs of high quality, obtained from diverse sources," but the programs that resulted too often failed to provide either diversity or high quality. Fewer than eleven stations are responsible for the bulk of the national schedule, and only two—New York's WNET and Boston's WGBH—account for most of it. Production stations, eager to get their program ideas funded, produced, and into the PBS schedule, inevitably pass through the same corporate and foundation doors in search of production money. Precious dollars are wasted duplicating effort. Worse, the competition to market a program idea that fits the interests of the funding agency—generally, science series, business-related shows, and high-visibility cultural programs—cramps the range of prime-time programming and sacrifices the very qualities that help to define the public medium: variety, boldness, innovation, controversy, high-quality entertainment, and, to a lesser extent, programming for children. It is not by chance that PBS's most attractive popular entertainment programs—which turn up in the schedule only during the periodic drives for viewer donations—are produced or acquired with the system's own program funds.

For reasons not easily divined, centralizing programming decisions, by focusing the creative energies of its producers, results in a benefit that is more than the sum of its parts. The phenomenon can be seen in organizations like Britain's BBC or Brazil's TV Globo, where large numbers of creative people, gathered together under one roof, develop a synergy with unusual creative force—as witnessed by the fact that both organizations turn out much of the world's most imaginative and boldly innovative television. Richard Moore, who spent four decades in American public television, both as a creative producer and a station CEO, believes that exceptional talent seems to thrive best in an environment in which tough decisions are made by a single governing intelligence. Only highly centralized organizations, he concludes, "seem capable of establishing an environment in which individual judgment and creativity can flourish."[14] Public television must create such an environment. If it is to move into the mainstream, it will need the exceptional talent of those eager to be free of Hollywood's formulaic straightjacket—who can only be attracted to a system where lines of responsibility are clear and precise and where decisions can be taken without a referendum or a vote.

The centralization of programming responsibility should not preclude but should actually increase independent production. The trend in that direction is already well established. *Bill Moyers' Journal, Adam Smith's Money World, Live from Lincoln Center,* the *Mac-Neil/Lehrer NewsHour,* and *Sesame Street,* as well as other PBS prime-time series, are produced independently of the stations. The trend should be pushed still further: stations should be removed from responsibility for national programming and should focus their attention and resources upon much-needed and largely neglected locally specific programming. Any number of production organizations are able to create national programming, oftentimes at lower costs, but only local stations are able to provide locally produced programming for purely local audiences.

As part of the marginalization of the public medium, Congress has promoted the notion that every local audience has quite different programming needs and tastes. Stations have been permitted, even encouraged, to treat PBS as a library by picking those programs that in the judgment of the management best suit local tastes and then airing them on a quixotic schedule of the station's choosing. The baleful result is program anarchy, a hodgepodge schedule that robs public television of a national identity and denies its producers and underwriters the advantages of national promotion. Local differences make sense with locally produced programs, tied as they are to specific events, people, and circumstances in a given community. But the notion runs off the rails when the effort is made to apply it to national programming; viewers everywhere enjoy the same popular programs on the commercial networks, and there is nothing to suggest they would treat public television any differently. Scheduling, the art of juxtaposing an evening's programming to create what the trade calls "audience flow," is practiced by the commercial networks with live-or-die intensity and with proven benefit to both the viewer and the programmer. Without challenging the statutory right of any station to refuse for any reason to air a given program, public television must devise *a rational approach to the scheduling of national programming* before it can become part of mainstream television.[15]

Implicit in the plot to reinvent and demarginalize public television is the assumption, at once wistful and desperate, that the dollars will be at hand to make the hope a reality. Countless recommendations to solve the system's chronic financial struggle have done little to ease the problem; the system continues to be grossly underfunded. How grossly can be gauged by a comparison of per capita annual support of public broadcasting in the United States ($6.34) with per capita support in Japan ($19.76), the United Kingdom ($37.31), and Canada ($48.86).[16] When the annual revenues of the world's top one hundred public and private broadcasting organizations are ranked by size, four public systems—Japan's NHK, Germany's ARD, Italy's RAI, and Britain's BBC—are among the top ten. PBS doesn't make the list at all. Putting aside for the moment the argument that America's money problem is due in some measure to the poor allocation of the resources it does have—too much for support of an inefficient structure and not enough for programming—more generous support is unquestionably essential if public television is to be responsive to the nation's needs.

Congress's failure to act on repeated recommendations for a stable and assured source of support, free of political influence, has driven the system to find its own solutions. Each solution has brought the trappings of new problems: Congressional appropriations have too often exerted political pressure on controversial programming; viewer support requires the periodic mind-numbing drumbeat of pledge weeks; and corporate underwriting increasingly narrows the crucial difference between the public and commercial media. In the search for alternatives, public broadcasters have turned their sights on the profits of private broadcasting, hoping to find a defensible claim upon a small piece of the industry's multibillion-dollar revenue. Two forms of a levy have been suggested. One, first advanced by former NBC president Joseph McConnell, would charge all private broadcasters a franchise tax (or "spectrum fee") for use of the "public airwaves." McConnell argued that "those who are licensed to use the airwaves in the 'public interest' . . . should at least share in the cost of Public Television . . . [and] should pay a franchise tax for that purpose."[17] Somewhat later, Joseph D. Hughes, an investment banker and charter member of the board of the Corporation for Public Broadcasting, echoed McConnell's call for a franchise tax. Hughes pointed out in a provocative 1977 "blueprint" for restructuring public broadcasting "that almost everything of a similar nature is now subject to charge . . . mining claims, timber-cutting rights in national forests, domestic and offshore oil leases, and even permits to graze cattle on public lands.''[18]

In a variation on the spectrum fee, some have proposed a license-transfer fee that would impose a levy on profits from the sale of a radio or television station. A brisk market emerged from the deregulation of the industry. But both the spectrum and license-transfer fees are opposed by commercial broadcasters, who feel increasingly at risk as cable and satellite technology cut heavily into their audience numbers and trim their profits. With a radically changed communications environment, the old formulas for funding the public medium no longer suffice. As an example, many if not most viewers of public television view their public station on a local cable system, particularly if their station is one of the two out of three public channels in the UHF band. The cable company charges a monthly fee for its services and shares that fee with the satellite-delivered cable networks—CNN, USA, MTV, and the others. Public broadcasting gets nothing (nor do any of the other over-the-air broadcast stations). All but the cable operators will find it ironic that viewers must pay cable companies $260 or more to a year to watch their public station beg for a $50 annual contribution. Cable's commendable assumption of the full support for non-profit C-SPAN may suggest a useful pattern for further exploration.

Those both inside and outside public broadcasting who would loosen the restraints on the amount and form of public television's corporate underwriting—who would, in effect, open the public medium to the acceptance of conventional commercials—must weigh the predictable consequences. Competition for advertisers leads inevitably to programming that serves the advertisers' and not the viewers' needs, raising questions about the need for a dual public-private system. Italians, who have seen their public system, once a monopoly, grow more and more to resemble its private competition, would understand. The British have astutely avoided this problem. By giving public and private television exclusive entitlement to distinctly different sources of income, they have, says the former chief of Britain's Independent Broadcasting Authority, "given both sides the incentive to match and out-match each other's programmes without being forced to pick each other's pockets."[19]

Public television's unrelenting search for an appropriate and practical mode of funding is less important than would be indicated by the time and studies devoted to it. The United States is well able to afford a public-television system, and the nation certainly has the wit and imagination to devise an appropriate means of funding it. It is neither money nor imagination that we lack, but a clear grasp of the concept and an all-out commitment to see it realized. Were that commitment to be made, public television's money problems would become, as media historian Erik Barnouw pointed out thirty years ago, "largely one of shifting our priorities."

Like it or not, within the next decade you and I are destined to move, or be pushed, into a new age of communication. The convergence of technologies—video, computer, fiber optics, digitalization, telephones, and the rest—promises to arm us with an astonishing array of communication tools, including a "superhighway" on which a seeming infinity of information will travel. The mind is boggled by the numbers. Which makes it all the more imperative that in our confused state we do not lose sight of what the numbers refer to: the potential volume of traffic, not the quality of its messages. We have no assurance that an exponential increase in the volume of messages will solve any of our basic problems, or for that matter, make life any more meaningful. In fact, says Neil Postman, information has become "a form of garbage that is not only incapable of answering the most fundamental human questions but barely useful in providing coherent direction to the solution of even mundane problems." In *Technopoly*, Postman chronicles what he believes is the surrender of our culture to the tyranny of technology—a technology that has transformed information into a "thing" in itself, a commodity to be bought and sold like soap. The result, he fears, is "a culture consumed with information," increasingly at risk not from a lack of information but from a glut of decontextualized data untied to human needs.[20]

Our home screens will bear the fruits of the coming revolution with more choice, more convenience, more everything—including interactivity and the chance to talk back (which is far more likely to be used simply for greater convenience in ordering the products and entertainments proffered on the screen). America's obsession with the myth that more is better has made a virtue of abundance itself. But having witnessed in my lifetime the concomitant growth in numbers and decline in quality of both radio and television, I fear the predicted explosion of channels will produce little more than debris—some of it diverting, most of it hardly worth the investment of time. The reason is the intensification of competition. With toothpaste and soap, competition for market share produces a better product. In broadcasting, competition drives the product downmarket. Those who pay the freight, the advertisers, measure success by the number of eyeballs focused on the screen. As the frenzy to win the numbers intensifies, producers are pressured to "dumb down" their product to broaden its appeal. The more competitors, the greater the competition, and the greater the pressures to find the lowest common denominator among a highly diversified universe of viewers.

Competition has created another phenomenon known as "narrowcasting"—the effort to reach smaller, more specialized "niche" audiences (groups of viewers who share a common interest and have an appealing demographic to advertisers). Much of cable and most of radio have moved in this direction. Whatever its appeal to individual viewers, the shift to narrowcasting poses a particular risk to our democracy, primarily because of its potential to weaken the social glue that binds our fragmented and pluralistic society. Social critic Benjamin Barber points out that network television, which once "offered perhaps the only truly common vision we have," helped to breach those differences. But with the trend toward narrowcasting, says Barber, factionalism—feared as "the scourge of democracy" by critics from James Madison to Walter Lippmann—"is given the support of technology."[21] Nor is Barber alone in seeing a threat to democracy in television's growing presence in our social and political fabric. James Reston, one of the nation's most respected journalists, confessed in a PBS retrospective of his career with the *New York Times* that "the influence of television on politics has really shaken my faith in democracy."[22]

The fears of both Barber and Reston were anticipated, in a sense, by another distinguished journalist. Writing almost three decades earlier, in 1959, Walter Lippmann voiced a concern that television was misusing a superb technical achievement by "monopolizing the air at the expense of effective news reporting, good art, and civilized entertainment." Lippmann, who did not believe the "evil" could be remedied by regulation, proposed that there be an alternative to private television, an option "practiced in one form or another in almost every other civilized country." The alternative was competition, "not for profit but for public service."[23] In the duality of our private-public system, we have the essentials for the Lippmann alternative. But the prescribed competition for public service cannot take place so long as each competitor plays a different game, under different rules, and with grossly unequal resources. Competition for public service becomes meaningful only when a reinvented public system, funded from a different source and armed with adequate resources, has the capacity to push into television's mainstream. When it does, we will see it set new and higher standards for all of television.

In the communications shakeout that is coming, there will be winners and losers. Some will survive and others will slip into limbo, victims of the inexorable economic forces that shape the fate of our mass media. Economic forces, however, are not the only arbiter of social needs. This nation, dependent as it is upon an informed electorate, must not permit its organs of enlightenment to be shaped by the same forces that determine its leading brands of beer, headache remedy, and dog food. Public television must be permitted to do what it has the power to do, not in its own interest but in ours.

It represents, as one observer has noted, "a claim of a present minority in behalf of a future majority."[24]

NOTES

Introduction

1. "An absolutely vital service" is quoted in Lloyd Grove, "Sound Bites over Substance: The Sorry End to PBS' Election Project," *Washington Post*, July 11, 1991.

2. David J. Brugger, president of the Association of America's Public Television Stations, quoted in Grove, "Sound Bites."

3. "Why Markle and PBS Split on Election '92," *Current*, July 22, 1991.

4. Ward Chamberlin, quoted in Grove, "Sound Bites."

5. The story of the federal government's seventy-year failure to understand and support the concept of public-service broadcasting is told in fascinating detail by Willard D. Rowland, Jr., in "Public Service Broadcasting in the United States: Its Mandate, Institutions, and Conflicts," in Robert K. Avery, ed., *Public Service Broadcasting in a Multichannel Environment* (New York: Longman, 1993).

6. Grove, "Sound Bites." Grove refers to public television as "the television equivalent of Yugoslavia."

7. George Gerbner, "Telling Stories in the Information Age," in Brent D. Ruben, ed., *Information and Behavior*, vol. 2 (New Brunswick, N.J.: Transaction, 1988).

8. *The Complete Essays of Montaigne*, trans. Donald M. Frame, bk. 2, no. 10 (Stanford, Calif.: Stanford Univ. Press, 1965), p. 304.

1. A New Medium, an Uncertain Mission

1. Willard D. Rowland, Jr., and Michael Tracey, "The Breakdown of Public Service Broadcasting," *Intermedia* 16, nos. 4–6 (autumn 1988).

2. "Such considerable identity between private and public interests" and "through the workings of enlightened, public-spirited, private

broadcasting leadership" are quoted from Willard D. Rowland, "Public Service Broadcasting in the United States," in Avery, *Public Service Broadcasting*, p. 160.

3. Powell, *Channels of Learning*, and Blakely, *To Serve the Public Interest*, both provide a detailed account of this period of educational television's birth and development.

4. The quotations on the aims of the Foundation are from Ford Foundation, *Ford Foundation Activities in Noncommercial Broadcasting, 1951–1976*, p. 2.

5. The aims of the Fund for Adult Education are cited in Blakely, *To Serve the Public Interest*, p. 84.

6. "More than any other person" quoted in Blakely, *People's Instrument*, in his dedication of his book to C. Scott Fletcher.

7. *Omnibus* references are cited in Ford Foundation, *Ford Foundation Activities*, p. 3, and in Blakely, *To Serve the Public Interest*, p. 84.

8. The constituent organizations of the Joint Committee on Educational Television (later the Joint Council on Educational Television) were the American Council on Education, the Association for Education by Radio, the Association of Land-Grant Colleges and Universities, the National Council of Chief State-School Officers, the National Association of Educational Broadcasters, the National Association of State Universities, and the National Education Association.

9. References to Hennock as the "mother protector" of educational television are from Richard B. Hull, "A Note on the History Behind ETV," in *Educational Television: The Next Ten Years* (Stanford, Calif.: The Institute for Communications Research, 1962), p. 340. Also quoted in Blakely, *To Serve the Public Interest*, p. 12.

10. The FCC specifications for educational television are found in the *Sixth Report and Order*, 17 Fed. Reg 3905, 3908; 41 FCC 148, 158, Apr. 14, 1952. See Frank J. Kahn, ed., *Documents of American Broadcasting* (Englewood Cliffs, N.J.: Prentice-Hall, 1984), p. 182.

11. Hennock argued that "educational TV stations, when established, will do more than furnish a uniquely valuable teaching aid for in-school and home use. They will supply a beneficial complement to commercial telecasting. Providing for greater diversity in TV programming, they will be particularly attractive to the many specialized and minority interests in the community, cultural as well as educational, which tend to be bypassed by commercial broadcasters thinking in terms of mass audiences. They will permit the entire viewing public an unaccustomed freedom of choice in programming. Educationally licensed and operated stations will, in addition, result in a substantial and beneficial diversification in the ownership and control of broadcast facilities. This would be closely

in line with established Commission policy, which has sought to achieve such diversification through the exercise of its licensing authority. Finally, educational stations will provide the highest standards of public service. Introducing noncommercial objectives and activities, they will be a leavening agent raising the aim and operations of our entire broadcasting system" (see Powell, *Channels of Learning*, p. 24). A more detailed account of Commissioner Hennock's role in the fight for educational reservations can be found in both Blakely, *To Serve the Public Interest*, pp. 12–17, and Powell, *Channels of Learning*, pp. 21–27.

12. The parallel story of how commercial radio broadcasters successfully blocked the efforts of educators to establish educational radio stations in the twenties and thirties is told in a series of articles—see Eugene E. Leach, "Snookered 50 Years Ago," *Current* 2, no. 1 (Jan. 14, 1983) and McChesney, *Telecommunications, Mass Media, and Democracy*.

13. Anne W. Branscomb, "A Crisis of Identity: Reflections on the Future of Public Broadcasting," in Cater and Nyhan, *Future of Public Broadcasting*.

14. An extensive treatment of the BBC's public-service philosophy as it was articulated by its first director-general is provided in Briggs, *History of Broadcasting*.

15. Fletcher's design for independent stations is quoted from Blakely, *To Serve the Public Interest*, p. 86.

16. Fletcher refers to the story of educational television as the "urgency-haunted struggle" in his introduction to Powell, *Channels of Learning*, p. v.

2. Building on the Bedrock

1. "The Time To Act Is Now," in Carroll V. Newsom, ed., *A Television Policy for Education* (Washington, D.C.: American Council on Education, 1952), cited in Blakely, *To Serve the Public Interest*, p. 90.

2. By the end of 1953, the staff of the Joint Committee on Educational Television included Ralph Steetle, executive director; David Stewart, his assistant; Cyril Braum, engineering adviser; Walter Emery, full-time general consultant; and Seymour Krieger, legal consultant.

3. Powell, *Channels of Learning*, p. 67.

4. Ibid., p. 79.

5. Ibid., p. 73.

6. Ibid., pp. 85–86. Powell quotes from an internal FAE memorandum from G. H. Griffiths to Fletcher dated June 6, 1952, and speculates that Fletcher underlined the portion on not retarding local initiative.

7. Lewis Hill's study of "Voluntary Listener-Sponsorship" was pub-

lished in 1958 by the Fund for Adult Education. The reasoning behind the Fund for Adult Education's requirement that recipients devote a reasonable amount of airtime to liberal adult education can be found in Powell, *Channels of Learning,* pp. 85–95.

8. Powell, *Channels of Learning,* p. 89.

9. Jack Gould, "It's More Blessed to Give than to Control," *New York Times,* May 12, 1970.

10. John Schwarzwalder's positions on public TV are contained in his thin book *ETV in Controversy,* in which he interviews twelve of the medium's leaders.

11. As aide-de-camp to Captain Hancock, Sener assisted his boss in his many interests outside television. As a consequence, he was often not where his public-television colleagues expected him to be. In one well-known incident, he failed to appear for a scheduled meeting in his Los Angeles office with a Ford Foundation executive who had flown across the continent to discuss a potential grant with him. The call went out to find him. He was sitting in New York—in the office of the Ford official waiting for him in Los Angeles.

12. Brief histories of other early stations can be found in Powell, *Channels of Learning,* pp. 121–63.

3. QED: The Search for Answers

1. George B. Leonard, Jr., "No Sponsors, No Censors, No Scandals," *Look* (western ed.), Feb. 16, 1960.

2. KQED's original transmitter was purchased from KPIX / Channel 5 for $25,250 with an additional $32,250 paid to convert it to Channel 9. Payments were to be made over several years, but a portion of the payments were forgiven when KQED was unable to meet them. The agreement was signed prior to the sale of KPIX to Westinghouse / Group W and has always been viewed by KPIX's then vice president and general manager, Philip G. Lasky, as a contribution.

3. In his organizational efforts to bring Channel 9 into being, Seidel drew heavily on the aid of his assistant superintendent, Raymond L. Smith. Smith later joined the KQED staff to build and direct its in-school service.

4. Of the two grants that put KQED on the air, the San Francisco Foundation gave $10,000 and the Rosenberg Foundation gave $60,000, half of which was paid when the station began regular broadcasting.

5. Dwight Newton, *San Francisco Examiner,* May 4, 1955.

6. Terrence O'Flaherty, "Something for Nothing," *San Francisco Chronicle,* June 28, 1955.

7. The KQED Auction grew over the years from the original one-day happening to an annual event that extended over ten days or more and that provided more than $1 million in annual income to KQED. The successful formula spread rapidly to other public-television stations until more than seventy of them adopted some variation of it as an annual fund-raising event.

8. KQED's audience support was a variation on the Pacifica pattern. But whereas KPFA's founder, Lewis Hill, saw viewers as subscribers, much as subscribers to newspapers and magazines, KQED's Seidel saw them as members of the corporation, each with a vote in electing the station's governing board. Seidel's view was laudably democratic but fraught with problems—as the board discovered years later when viewer voting produced factions and board meetings were devoted as much to politicking as to policy-making.

9. Minutes of the KQED Board of Directors, quoted in Linda Hawes Clever, "When Is a Program Policy a Policy?" pt. 2, *KQED in Focus* (Oct. 1979).

10. Bill Davidson, "I Wish I Had That Broad's Connections," *TV Guide,* June 8, 1974.

11. Nicholas von Hoffman is quoted in Adrian Taylor, "No Frills TV," *Washington Journalism Review* (Apr.–May 1979).

4. Go for Broke

1. "Independent Educational Television Plus Ten," an address by John F. White to the managers of the educational television stations at Edgewater Gulf Hotel, Gulfport, Miss., Mar. 6, 1958. National Public Broadcasting Archive (hereinafter referred to as NPBA), University of Maryland, College Park, Md.

2. Raymond Wittcoff's "bold and forthright" plan was proposed in a speech before the Television Programs Institute held at Pennsylvania State College in April 1952, NPBA.

3. For his "eyewitness account" of Fletcher's July 1952 meeting, Powell relied on the handwritten notes of Anne Spinney, who was present at the meeting as an FAE employee. Both Powell (*Channels of Learning*, pp. 78–79) and Wood ("First Decade of the 'Fourth Network,' " pp. 34–37) provide considerable detail on the discussion that took place, because, wrote Powell, "all the considerations raised are important." In fact, they laid down the basic principles on which the system operated for more than two decades and still, in large measure, honors today.

4. Dr. George Stoddard, as president of the University of Illinois, was not a wholly disinterested participant in the planning for educational

television. The University was a licensee at the time of two radio stations (AM and FM), was actively working to establish an educational television station, and had hosted two of the key planning sessions leading up to the fight for the reservation of the educational channels.

5. The two additional ETRC directors elected at the December 1952 meeting were Arthur H. Dean and Richard Hull. The election of Hull, the only professional broadcaster on the board (general manager of WOI-TV in Ames, Iowa), was a concession to the interests of the NAEB. A month later, the board elected a third new director, Kenneth Oberholtzer, superintendent of the Denver public schools.

6. Hudson's plans for the Center are contained in his memorandum to C. Scott Fletcher, "The Educational Radio and Television Program Development and Exchange Center," Nov. 16, 1952, NPBA.

7. Robert Hudson, "Producing for National Educational Television," *Journal of the University Film Producers Association* (winter 1958).

8. The three series produced and paid for by NBC in the first season of the cooperative arrangement were *American Government: Pursuit of Happiness*, with Professor E. E. Schattschneider of Wesleyan; *Mathematics*, with James Newman, editor of *The World of Mathematics*; and *Highlights of Opera History*, with Paul Henry Lang of Columbia. The remaining two series, produced and funded by the Center, were *The American Scene*, with guest authors hosted by Albert D. Van Nostrand of Brown, and *Geography for Decision*, with Albert E. Burke of the American Institute of Resource Economics. The fall 1957 series of ETRC-NBC programs included two produced by the Center—*The International Geophysical Year*, hosted by Frank Blair, and *Camera On Washington*, hosted by Bill Henry. NBC produced three program series: *Arts and the Gods from the Metropolitan Museum of Art*, hosted by Alexander Scourby; *Mathematics*, hosted by Clifton Fadiman; and *Survival*, hosted by Albert E. Burke. The ETRC-NBC programs in the spring 1958 series were *Decision for Research, Briefing Session*, and *The Subject Is Jazz*. The final two series, broadcast in the fall of 1958, were *Ten for Survival* and *Adventuring in the Hand Arts*.

9. Jack Gould, "TV: Professors on the Air," *New York Times*, Mar. 19, 1957.

10. "A Report from the Educational Television and Radio Center to the Ford Foundation, 1957," NPBA.

11. The original board of the ETRC included (in addition to Fletcher) Ralph Lowell, trustee of Boston's Lowell Institute; Robert Calkins, director of the Brookings Institute in Washington; George Stoddard, president of the University of Illinois; Harold Lasswell, professor of law and political science at Yale University; Arthur H. Dean, attorney; Kenneth Oberholtzer, superintendent of the Denver public schools; and

Richard Hull, general manager of WOI-TV (Ames, Iowa). Added later were Harry K. Newburn, president of the ETRC; Everett N. Case, president of Colgate University; Norman Cousins, editor of the *Saturday Review*; Leland Hazard, vice president and general counsel of Pittsburgh Plate Glass and chairman of WQED; Lloyd S. Michael, superintendent of the Evanston, Ill., public schools; Mark Starr, educational director of the International Ladies' Garment Workers' Union; Glenn T. Seaborg, chancellor of the University of California at Berkeley; and Raymond Wittcoff, vice president of the Carridine Hat Company and president of KETC / St. Louis.

12. The original Affiliates Committee of the ETRC, elected in 1956, consisted of John F. White (WQED / Pittsburgh), James Robertson (WTTW/ Chicago), Hartford Gunn (WGBH / Boston), William Harley (WHA / Madison), Loren Stone (KCTS / Seattle), and Earl Wynn (WUNC-TV / North Carolina).

13. "Independent Educational Television Plus Ten," an address by John F. White to the managers of the educational television stations at Edgewater Gulf Hotel, Gulfport, Miss., Mar. 6, 1958, NPBA.

14. In addition to Robert Hudson, the new vice presidents were Kenneth Yourd for business and legal affairs and Warren Kraetzer for development. In a later appointment, James Robertson was made vice president for station relations.

15. John F. White, interviewed by the author, New York, Sept. 17, 1981.

16. Hudson to Fritz Jauch, memorandum, July 6, 1962, quoted in Wood, "First Decade of the 'Fourth Network,' " p. 315.

17. "Discussion of General Objectives of the National Program Service," summary of NET seminar, Dec. 9–10, 1960, quoted in Wood, "First Decade of the 'Fourth Network,' " p. 322.

18. In the audience survey made for public television in 1952, a "regular viewer" was identified as one who could correctly identify at least one public-television show viewed in the past week.

5. 10 Columbus Circle

1. Richard O. Moore, "Public Television Programming and the Future: A Radical Approach," in Cater and Nyhan, eds., *Future of Public Broadcasting*.

2. James Armsey, interview with the author, New York, Nov. 17, 1984. Armsey asserted that he first suggested the endowment idea but that he dismissed it when he learned of the magnitude of White's request.

3. The "outside expert" brought in by the Ford Foundation to eval-

uate NET's program output was Charles Siepmann, one of the founders of the BBC, the author of the FCC's infamous "Blue Book" on broadcasters' public-service responsibilities, and the chairman of New York University's Communications Department.

4. "Instructions for Preparation of Grant Application Letter" is contained in a memorandum from James Armsey to John F. White and George Stoddard, June 24, 1963, NPBA.

5. Ford's request for "a plan and time schedule for the reorganization of NETRC" is contained in the memorandum from J. Armsey to White and Stoddard, June 24, 1963, NPBA.

6. NET's request for the Ford grant is in a letter from White and Stoddard to Henry T. Heald, July 19, 1963. Heald's response to Stoddard is a letter dated Aug. 29, 1963. Stoddard's thanks for Heald's "helpful letter" is in a letter from Stoddard to Heald, Sept. 6, 1963, NPBA.

7. The National Association of Educational Broadcasters (NAEB) sought take-over responsibility for representing the stations' interests, but the stations insisted on autonomy as a condition of remaining in the Association. In February 1964, they formed the Educational Television Stations (ETS) division of the NAEB and immediately recruited C. Scott Fletcher as their "executive consultant." The ETS board was first chaired by Robert Schenkkan, general manager of KRLN, the Austin, Tex., public station.

8. The *Denver Post* is quoted in the *Report to the Ford Foundation, 1967–68*, p. 9, NPBA.

9. Jack Gould, *New York Times*, quoted in *NET: A Progress Report, 1967–68*, NPBA.

10. The letter from Congress protesting the airing of Felix Greene's film on North Vietnam resulted from a request from Walter Judd, the former Minnesota congressman who figured prominently in the so-called China Lobby during the years when he and others were blaming communist influences in the State Department for the United States' "loss" of China. Judd, who also had not seen the film, asked his friends in Congress to sign the protest letter, arguing that the release of the Greene film was ill-timed "when American youth [were] giving their lives in a war against a ruthless enemy." Their quoted response is from Barnouw, *The Image Empire*, pp. 291–93.

11. Among the eighteen stations refusing to air *Inside North Vietnam*, the Milwaukee affiliate explained its position by saying the film's impact was "contrary to the best interests of our country, providing more fuel for the 'let's get out of it' movement at a time when national unity is

needed." (Otto Schlaak, general manager of wtvs / Milwaukee, to William Kobin, quoted in an article by Edwin Bayley in *Educational Broadcasting Review* [June 1969].) Stations in Buffalo, Duluth, St. Louis, Tampa, and Pensacola and the Alabama and South Carolina networks also refused to air it. Bayley reports that ktca (Minneapolis–St. Paul) carried the program but violated net's "take it or leave it" rule by cutting out net's introduction to the program then interrupting the show three times "to permit broadcast of a previously recorded interview with Vice President Humphrey, an analysis of propaganda by a local professor, and a diatribe by [Congressman Walter] Judd against Felix Greene, Ho Chi Minh and net." Other reasons for the show's cancellation are contained in a memorandum to John F. White, et al., from Fritz Jauch, July 10, 1969, "Survey of net Program Usage by Affiliates During January, February, and March 1968" (in net, *Semi-Annual Report to the Ford Foundation*, Jan.–June, 1969), npba.

12. White's statement about the positive response of the Committee on Foreign Affairs is contained in his letter to J. Day, Sept. 17, 1981, npba.

13. National Educational Television, *Semi-Annual Report to the Ford Foundation*, July–Dec. 1966, npba.

14. net's goals in drama production are contained in *National Educational Television Report of the Year 1964* (to Ford Foundation), Feb. 15, 1965, p. 19, npba.

15. Duke Ellington's opera, *Queenie Pie*, had its debut in September 1968 as a stage production under the aegis of Philadelphia's American Music Theater Festival. The quote about the Henze opera is from letter from C. W. Davis to J. Day, April 12, 1982, npba.

16. The purpose of Armsey's meeting with the net staff was stated in a letter from Ford Foundation secretary Joseph M. McDaniel Jr. to White, Oct. 8, 1963, npba. For an account of this meeting, I have relied upon detailed notes taken by Edwin R. Bayley, net's vice president (and a former newspaper reporter), contained in a memorandum from Bayley to White, June 15, 1963, and upon White's own notes of the meeting contained in a memorandum for the record, June 12, 1963, npba.

17. Armsey's consultant, Charles Siepmann, had his own "grand design" for public television, outlined in "Educational Television: Blueprint for a Network," one of the papers commissioned by the Foundation for its 1963 study of public television's future, npba.

18. White's delineation of "major problems" with the Ford Foundation is in his memorandum to Everett M. Case, Aug. 31, 1964, npba.

19. *Newsweek*, Mar. 27, 1967.

6. In a Friendly Fashion

1. Remarks by Fred W. Friendly to the PBS Annual Membership Meeting, Cincinnati, Ohio, June 29, 1981, NPBA.

2. Friendly, *Circumstances*, p. 306.

3. The invitations for comment on ABC's petition to launch a private satellite were in "FCC Notice of Inquiry," Mar. 2, 1966, FCC Files.

4. Friendly, *Circumstances*, p. 311.

5. Ibid., p. 319.

6. *Ford Foundation Annual Report*, 1967, Ford Foundation Files. The amount authorized for the first year's "startup" was $7.9 million.

7. Halberstam, *Powers That Be*, p. 135.

8. Friendly, *Circumstances*, p. 304. A detailed account of the PBL story is contained in Michael Golden, "The Great Experiment," *Emmy* (Nov.–Dec. 1983).

9. The ground rules for the NET-PBL relationship are from "Memorandum of Understanding, Between the Ford Foundation and the National Educational Television and Radio Center, May 11, 1967," NPBA. The committee members of the NET board named in the memorandum were George D. Stoddard, Edward W. Barrett, Everett N. Case, Norman Cousins, Philip D. Reed, and John F. White.

10. PBL's Editorial Policy Board comprised Edward W. Barrett (chair), dean of the Graduate School of Journalism, Columbia University; Norman Cousins, editor, *Saturday Review*; Lawrence Cremin, Frederick A. P. Barnard Professor of Education, Columbia University Teacher's College; John Fischer, editor, *Harper's*; James R. Dumpson, dean and professor of sociology, Fordham University; Richard Hofstadter, Dewitt Clinton Professor of History, Columbia University; Thomas P. F. Hoving, director, Metropolitan Museum of Art; Polykarp Kusch, professor of physics, Columbia University; Peter Mennin, president, Juilliard School of Music; William P. Rogers, former Attorney General of the United States; and John F. White, president, NET.

11. The policies of the PBL Editorial Board are set forth in a memorandum from Edward W. Barrett to the Public Broadcast Laboratory Editorial Policy Board, May 19, 1967, NPBA.

12. Westin to the PBL staff, memorandum, "The Concept," Dec. 30, 1966, NPBA.

13. Fred Friendly to Av Westin, memorandum, Oct. 10, 1967, NPBA.

14. Harriet Van Horne, "Back to the Lab," *New York Post*, Nov. 11, 1967.

15. Jack Gould, "A Noble Experiment: Nowhere to Go but Up," *New York Times*, Nov. 12, 1967.

16. Edward W. Barrett to Everett Case, McGeorge Bundy, Fred Friendly, Av Westin, and staff, draft memorandum, Nov. 10, 1967, NPBA.

17. Editorial Policy Board of *PBL* to Everett Case, memorandum, Apr. 25, 1968, NPBA.

18. Ibid.

19. A press release from NET on Sept. 30, 1968, announced the appointment of a *PBL* program advisory committee with Fred Bohen, chair; John F. White; Av Westin; John Fischer; Norman Cousins; Abram Chayes, professor of law, Harvard University; and William Gorham, president of the Urban Institute of Washington, D.C. Bohen's duties were outlined in a personal and confidential memorandum from Everett N. Case to John F. White, Av Westin, and Frederick Bohen, June 17, 1968, NPBA.

20. Stephanie Harrington, *Village Voice*, Jan. 23, 1969.

21. The criticism of *PBL*'s experiment with six independent filmmakers appeared as an unattributed quotation in "Can This Be America?" by Robert Lewis Shayon, *Saturday Review*, Feb. 22, 1969. Shayon scored the critics for overreaction. "Young filmmakers are very vulnerable . . . they need a sympathetic environment, encouraging, characterized by the respect and open-mindedness that ought to mark the democratic society."

22. Of the major participants in *PBL*, only Av Westin returned to commercial television, subsequently becoming vice president of ABC News. Among those who remained with the public medium were Lewis Freedman (*Hollywood Television Theater*), Stuart Sucherman (Media and Society Seminars), Tom Kennedy (*Sesame Street*), Joe Russin (*Inside Story*), and Gerald Slater (WETA).

23. *Variety*, Apr. 23, 1969.

24. The quotations from Freedman, Sucherman, and Bohen are excerpted from an undated draft memorandum from Fred Bohen to Fred Friendly ("I am happy to respond to your kind invitation to submit my personal views and recommendations concerning the future pattern and scale of foundation support in public television"), NPBA.

7. One for the Money

1. Carnegie Commission on Educational Television, *Program for Action*, p. 11.

2. Friendly, *Circumstances*, p. 303.

3. John E. Burke has provided a much more detailed account of events leading up to the Carnegie Commission in "The Public Broad-

casting Act of 1967, Part 1, Historical Origins and the Carnegie Commission," published in *Educational Broadcasting Review* 6, no. 2 (Apr. 1972). The article was drawn from Burke's Ph.D. dissertation for Ohio State University, 1971. Among other contributions to the historical record, Burke notes the key roles played by Hartford N. Gunn, Jr., and David Ives, both executives with Boston's WGBH, in the preparation both of Ralph Lowell's original proposal to the 1964 national conference and the subsequent submission to President Johnson.

4. In addition to Killian, Hobby, Hayes, and Kellam, the members of the Carnegie Commission on Educational Television were James B. Conant, former president of Harvard University; Lee A. DuBridge, president of the California Institute of Technology; Ralph Ellison, author; David D. Henry, president of the University of Illinois; Edwin H. Land, president, Polaroid Corporation; Joseph H. McConnell, president, Reynolds Metals Company; Franklin Patterson, president, Hampshire College; Terry Sanford, former governor of North Carolina; Robert Saudek, television producer; Rudolf Serkin, concert pianist; and Leonard Woodcock, vice president, United Automobile Workers of America. The Commission staff, headed by Hyman H. Goldin, included Stephen White, Gregory G. Harney, and Joan Cummings Solomon. White was the principal author of the resulting report.

5. See Carnegie Commission on Educational Television, *Program for Action*.

6. U.S. Congress, *The Public Broadcasting Act of 1967*. The Act called for "the extension of duration of construction grants" originally embodied in the Educational Television Facilities Act of May 1962, which established a program of federal matching fund grants "for the construction of television broadcasting facilities to be used for educational purposes." The funds were restricted to the purchase of equipment and required assurances that the recipient had sufficient funds to operate and maintain the equipment.

7. The argument over the phrase "strict adherence to objectivity and balance" is treated in more detail in Chapter 17.

8. In a letter endorsing the general objectives of the Commission, President Lyndon B. Johnson wrote: "From our beginnings as a nation we have recognized that our security depends upon the enlightenment of our people; that our freedom depends on the communications of many ideas through many channels. I believe that educational television has an important future in the United States and throughout the world. . . . I look forward with interest in the judgments which this Commission will offer" (quoted from the preface to Carnegie Commission on Educational Television, *Program for Action*).

9. The prospects for a dedicated tax to support public television were never favorable. Joseph D. Hughes, former board member of the Corporation for Public Broadcasting, recounts a Washington meeting held in Douglass Cater's office shortly after the CPB meeting when Stanley S. Surrey, Assistant Treasury Secretary, expressed to Pace, Hughes, and Chamberlin the Treasury's traditional opposition to dedicated taxes. Hughes notes that all hope for the tax was abandoned when the chair of the House Ways and Means Committee warned that a bill for a dedicated tax to support public television would not clear his committee. See Joseph D. Hughes, "Heat Shield or Crucible: A Blueprint for Carnegie II," *Public Telecommunications Review (PTR)* 5, no. 6 (Nov.–Dec. 1977).

10. Friendly's warning about government funding appears in U.S. Congress, "Senate Subcommittee on Communications, Committee on Commerce, Hearings to Accompany S. 1160" (Public Broadcasting Act of 1967), quoted in Blakely *To Serve the Public Interest*, p. 172.

11. James Killian, Jr., chairman of the Carnegie Commission, and Milton Eisenhower were named to the CPB board at the time the Public Broadcasting Act was signed. In March 1969, in addition to Pace, President Johnson named the following to the board of the Corporation for Public Broadcasting: Joseph A. Beirne, president of the Communications Workers of America; Robert S. Benjamin, attorney, Philips, Nizer, Krim & Ballon, and chairman, United Artists; Roscoe C. Carroll, corporation counsel, Golden State Mutual Life Insurance Company; Michael A. Gamino, Jr., president, Columbus National Bank of Providence, R.I.; Saul Haas, chairman, KIRO / Seattle (AM-FM-TV); Oveta C. Hobby, chair and editor, The *Houston Post* Corporation; Joseph D. Hughes, vice president, T. Mellon & Sons; Erich Leinsdorf, music director, Boston Symphony Orchestra; John D. Rockefeller 3d, chair, Rockefeller Foundation; Carl E. Sanders, former Governor of Georgia; Frank E. Schooley, director of broadcasting, University of Illinois; and Jack Valenti, president, Motion Picture Association of America. Of the fifteen appointees, eight were Democrats (Haas, Leinsdorf, Gammino, Sanders, Beirne, Pace, Benjamin, and Valenti), six were Republicans (Carroll, Rockefeller, Schooley, Hobby, Hughes, and Eisenhower), and one was an Independent (Killian).

12. Leonard Marks is quoted in Robertson, *Televisionaries*, p. 251.

13. "Assure the maximum freedom" is from U.S. Congress, *The Public Broadcasting Act of 1967*, sec. 396 (g)(1)(D).

14. The CPB board search committee that selected Macy comprised John D. Rockefeller 3d, Oveta C. Hobby, and Milton Eisenhower.

15. Macy, *Wasteland*, p. 32.

16. White resigned to accept the presidency of the fully endowed Coo-

per Union for the Advancement of Science and Art. His "farewell" message is contained in a memorandum from J. F. White to NET staff, Mar. 12, 1969, NPBA.

17. Robert Hudson to Sara Garland Frederickson, memorandum, "John F. White: One Man's Contribution to Educational Broadcasting," Nov. 17, 1971, NPBA.

18. Blakely, *To Serve the Public Interest*, p. 165.

19. Wood, "First Decade of the 'Fourth Network,' " p. 417.

20. J. F. White's address to the NET Affiliates, New York, Apr. 10, 1969. Reprinted in *Educational Broadcasting Review* (June 1969), NPBA.

8. Two for the Show

1. Public Broadcasting Service, *Long-Range Planning for Public Television*, vol. 1, p. 95.

2. "To assure the maximum freedom" appears in U.S. Congress, *Public Broadcasting Act of 1967*, sec. 396 (g)(1)(D).

3. "Public Television's Short Leash," *Washington Post*, May 1, 1969.

4. A complete transcript of the testimony before Senator Pastore's subcommittee is printed in "Hearings before the Subcommittee on Communications of the Committee on Commerce, United States Senate, on S. 1242, April 30 and May 1, 1969" (Washington, D.C.: U.S. Government Printing Office, 1969). The story of the "producer's revolt" is told in "The Producers Organize," *Nation*, May 19, 1969, and reprinted with an editorial reply by Ronald C. Bornstein in *Educational Broadcasting Review* (Oct. 1969).

5. The Public Broadcasting Act of 1967 provided that "nothing in the Communications Act of 1934, as amended, or in any other provision of law shall be construed to prevent United States communications common carriers from rendering free or reduced rate communications interconnection services for noncommercial educational television or radio services, subject to such rules and regulations as the Federal Communication Commission may prescribe." See U.S. Congress, *Public Broadcasting Act of 1967*, sec. 396 (h).

6. The members of the "Six Pack" were Robert Schenkkan, James Loper, and Presley Holmes from the NET Affiliates Council; and Hartford Gunn, Jr., Warren Kraetzer, and Lloyd Kaiser from the board of Educational Television Stations.

7. The quote "paranoia by the stations towards NET" is from Robert Pepper, "The Interconnection Connection: The Formation of PBS," in Avery and Pepper, *Politics of Interconnection*, pp. 3–4.

8. "NET Proposal for Interconnection Management," a planning paper submitted by NET to the Corporation for Public Broadcasting, July 24, 1969, NPBA.

9. Friendly's "U.S. 1" metaphor is contained in a letter from Fred Friendly to Frank Pace, Nov. 13, 1969 (quoted in Avery and Pepper, *Politics of Interconnection*, p. 7).

10. Everett N. Case to McGeorge Bundy, Sept. 16, 1969, NPBA.

11. The details of the plan to create PBS are contained in "The Management and Operation of National Interconnection for Public Broadcasting," an unsigned memorandum from the Corporation for Public Broadcasting, Oct. 1, 1969, NPBA.

12. The original PBS board was made up of five elected station representatives (Class A)—James Loper, chairman (KCET), Frank Barreca (KUAT), Howard Holst (WKNO), Jack McBride (KUON), and Lloyd Kaiser (WITF); two ex-officio members (Class B)—the presidents of CPB (Macy) and NET (Day); and two public members (Class C)—Clifford Wharton, president of Michigan State University, and Jerome Wiesner, provost of Massachusetts Institute of Technology. In March 1970, the president of PBS, Hartford Gunn, Jr., was added to the Board as a Class D director.

13. Gunn's decision to move the PBS headquarters to Washington had personal consequences that might have proved disastrous. Soon after moving there, he was severely beaten in a mugging.

14. The so-called Aspen Document was a letter dated June 18, 1971, to John W. Macy, Jr., and Hartford Gunn, Jr., from James Day (NET), David Ives (WGBH), Lloyd Kaiser (WQED), James Loper (KCET), William McCarter (WETA), and John Taylor (WTTW). A seventh member, Richard Moore (KQED), was not present at the meeting but indicated in a separate letter his "support of the intent of the Aspen Document." He added, however, that he felt "the bill of particulars in the Aspen Document fails to reveal the most fundamental problem we face, which is the institutional and essentially political structure both of CPB and PBS . . . the very things to which we object are inherent and inevitable in the nature of the system."

15. John Macy's comment on the Aspen Document is extracted from his letter to J. Day, July 14, 1971, NPBA.

16. Robert Pepper has detailed the involvement of the Ford Foundation in the creation of PBS. See Avery and Pepper, *Politics of Interconnection*.

17. John W. Macy, Jr., to Day, Mar. 26, 1971. On Apr. 27, 1971, the chairman of the merged NET-WNET, Ethan Allen Hitchcock, and the former NET chairman, Norman Cousins, met with John Macy, Fred Friendly, and David Davis to discuss these changes. Macy emphasized "the pro-

nounced and overriding need . . . to extend and enlarge programming from the nation's capital," and made the point that "the reorganization of public television is designed to maximize the capability of individual stations to represent their communities." Cousins expressed concern that the "national character" of NET-WNET "would be seriously weakened" and that its board was being asked to ratify a decision "without having participated in the decision-making." (Memorandum of the Minutes of Meeting, Apr. 27, 1971, NPBA).

9. The Street of the Eight-Foot Canary

1. *Sesame Street* theme. Music by Joe Raposo; lyrics by Raposo, Jon Stone, and Bruce Hart. "Sesame Street Theme" Courtesy of Children's Television Workshop.

2. Mayer, *About Television.*

3. Freedman's quote on television's potential is from Polsky, *Getting to "Sesame Street,"* p. 2.

4. Morrisett's letter to Freedman is quoted in Alan Sheldon, "Tuning in with Joan Cooney," *Public Telecommunications Review* (Nov.–Dec. 1978).

5. Alan Sheldon, "Tuning in with Joan Cooney," *Public Telecommunications Review* (Nov.–Dec. 1978).

6. Polsky, *Getting to "Sesame Street,"* p. 11.

7. The actual cost of the first year's production was closer to $7 million. The remaining $1 million was applied to the second year's show.

8. Aims of the Children's Television Workshop were announced in a press release, Mar. 21, 1968, issued jointly by the U.S. Office of Education, Carnegie Corporation, and the Ford Foundation, NPBA.

9. Jack Gould, "Educational TV Network to Teach Preschool Child," *New York Times,* Mar. 21, 1968.

10. The Children's Television Workshop was incorporated in April 1970 by Lloyd Morrisett, Joan Ganz Cooney, Gerald S. Lesser, Ralph B. Rogers, and James Day. The original board of trustees included, in addition to the five incorporators, Mrs. Emmett Rice, associate director of the College Entrance Board; the Honorable Terry Sanford, former governor of North Carolina; Eddie N. Williams, vice president for public affairs, University of Chicago; and Dr. Lawrence A. Cremin, Frederick A. P. Barnard Professor of Education, Columbia University Teacher's College.

11. David D. Connell, interviewed by the author, New York, June 24, 1983.

12. Polsky, *Getting to "Sesame Street,"* p. 33.

13. Connell, interview.

14. *Village Voice,* Nov. 10, 1969.

15. Jack Gould, "This 'Sesame' May Open the Right Doors," *New York Times,* Nov. 23, 1969.

16. Connell, interview.

17. "Who's Afraid of Big, Bad TV?" *Time,* Nov. 23, 1970.

18. Evelyn Davis, interviewed by the author, New York, June 1983.

19. The results of *Sesame Street*'s first year are in Ball and Bogatz, *First Year of "Sesame Street."*

20. Bogatz and Ball, *Second Year of "Sesame Street."*

21. G. Lesser, *Children and Television* (pp. 174–201), provides detailed criticisms of the Workshop's premises and goals, including its failure to close the advantaged-disadvantaged gap, its methods, and its effects on the target audience, together with his analysis and response to these criticisms.

22. Monica Sims's criticisms of *Sesame Street* were published in *The Guardian* (Manchester), Dec. 22, 1970. Lesser (p. 180) gives a brief account of her criticisms in his analysis of the show's critics.

23. G. Lesser, *Children and Television,* p. 134.

24. "Lightning in a bottle" is quoted from author's interview with Danny Epstein, New York, June 24, 1983.

25. Land, *Children's Television Workshop,* p. v.

26. "Long-Awaited *Sesame Street* Bows as Imaginative TV Head-Start Program," *Variety,* Nov. 12, 1969.

10. Dreams from a Machine

1. Carnegie Commission on Educational Television, *Program for Action,* p. 18.

2. I was in office less than a month when my NET colleagues persuaded me to stop over in London on my way to an international meeting in Florence and interview the entire cast of *The Forsyte Saga.* The resulting films were cut to fill out the oddly timed episodes to an even one hour in what can only be viewed as an exercise in husbanding limited production dollars.

3. The story of Jack Willis's remarkable recovery from his injury has been told in Jack and Mary Willis, . . . *But There Are Always Miracles* (New York: Viking, 1974). Their story has also been dramatized in a CBS made-for-television movie.

4. Percy Shain, "*Great American Dream Machine*: You're Never Bored," *Boston Globe,* Jan. 14, 1971.

5. Stanley Frank, "The Brat Is Back," *TV Guide,* Nov. 27, 1971.

6. William C. Woods, *Washington Post,* Jan. 6, 1971.

7. Terrence O'Flaherty, "Tell Me Your Dream . . . ," *San Francisco Chronicle,* Jan. 16, 1971.

8. Bernie Harrison, "An Uneven *Dream* And Unfunny, Too," *Evening Star* (Washington), Jan. 14, 1971.

9. The account of the referendum on showing the censored skit is reported in "WTTW Will Show Censored Segment," *Chicago Sun-Times,* Mar. 2, 1971.

10. Ron Powers, "Sad Mandate Supports Blow to Intelligence," *Chicago Sun-Times,* Mar. 12, 1971. The critics found it ironic that WTTW filled the time of the censored segment with an appeal for funds.

11. Leo Seligsohn, "TV Fatality: *The Great American Dream Machine,*" *Newsday,* Apr. 23, 1972.

12. NET's 1970 documentaries were aired under the generic title NET *Journal* until the merger with WNET / 13 in mid-year. After this time, they aired under the title *Realities.*

13. Prior to PBS, the rule for unauthorized editing was simple: stations were not compelled to air any show they did not like, but if they did air it, it was to be aired without changes. That wasn't acceptable to a majority of PBS stations. They demanded a membership agreement that permitted stations to edit programs, particularly when words or scenes failed to meet the station's program standards or, in the judgment of the station, failed to conform to FCC regulations. The conflict of interests between the producers and users of programs led to heated words and protracted negotiations. In the end a compromise was reached: "Stations shall not make any deletions, alterations, edits, replacements or other changes" in the content of programs "without prior permission of PBS." But to assuage the stations, PBS warranted its best efforts to obtain the necessary permission from the producing station—when possible.

14. John Leonard, "Does Money Think You're Dead?" *Life,* Oct. 23, 1970.

15. Public Broadcasting Service, "To All Station Managers and Program Managers from Samuel Holt re: *Realities* 5, 'Banks and Poor,' " telex, Nov. 8, 1970, NPBA.

16. Jack Gould, " 'The Banks and the Poor' Raises Major Issues," *New York Times,* Nov. 10, 1970.

17. Public Broadcasting Service, "Public Television Journalism," draft memorandum, Feb. 19, 1971. This document was a slightly revised version of another memorandum, "Public Broadcasting and Journalistic Integrity: A Policy Statement of Public Broadcasting Service," from Robert Schenkkan, general manager of KLRN (Austin, Tex.), to Hartford Gunn, Jr., Jan. 11, 1971, NPBA.

18. Public Broadcasting Service, "Statement of Policy on Program Standards," Apr. 15, 1971. The program standards were updated with PBS's "Report of the Special Committee on Program Policies and Procedures," Apr. 15, 1987, NPBA.

19. J. Edgar Hoover to John W. Reisor, NET assistant general counsel, Sept. 30, 1971, NPBA.

20. Rex Polier, "Public TV Censorship and Government Funds," *The Evening Bulletin* (Philadelphia), Oct. 7, 1971.

21. Ann Lee, "Public TV Suffers from Loss of Courage," *Memphis Press-Scimitar*, Oct. 7, 1971.

22. Fred Travis, "Education Body Asks Censoring of NET Shows," *Chattanooga Daily Times*, May 9, 1970. See also Larry Daughtrey, "NET's No-No Words Stir Board's Ire," *Nashville Tennessean*, May 9, 1970.

23. The problems of the Alabama ETV network are detailed in Christopher Lydon, "FCC Lets Alabama TV Setup Drop Black-Oriented Programs," *New York Times*, June 30, 1970; and "FCC Backs Alabama Ban on Bad-Taste ETV Films," *Birmingham News*, June 30, 1970. (Each newspaper presents a different approach to the story.) In 1974, the FCC voted 4–2 not to renew the licenses of the Alabama ETV stations because "they have a history of discrimination against blacks in both hiring and programming practices." See David Burnham, "Educational Stations in Alabama to Lose Licenses over Bias," *New York Times*, Sept. 20, 1974.

24. R. R. Garrett, director of staff marketing services of the 3M Company, to J. Day, Sept. 19, 1972, NPBA.

25. Bill Greeley, "Guess Who Loved 'VD Blues,' " *Variety*, June 6, 1973.

26. *Masterpiece Theater* was initiated by Arthur Calderwood, Hartford Gunn's successor as president of Boston's WGBH. With a background in corporate public relations (Land-Polaroid), Calderwood recognized immediately the entertainment value of the BBC's drama series and seized upon the success of the *Forsyte Saga* to fly to London and find out what else the BBC had for sale. Calls to his former colleagues in corporate public relations lined up Mobil Oil as the series underwriter. NET, on the other hand, failed to follow up on its own success because of an unwillingness to spend its Ford dollars on anything other than original productions. Not even the *Forsyte Saga* had claim on Ford dollars; special funds had to be raised to acquire it.

27. Craig Gilbert's experiences in producing *An American Family* are detailed in his essay, "Reflections on *An American Family*," *Studies in Visual Communications* (The Annenberg School of Communications, Univ. of Pennsylvania) (winter 1982).

28. Craig Gilbert to J. Day, June 11, 1971, NPBA.

29. "You have eminently justified the faith" is quoted in a letter from

Pat Loud to "Everyone Connected with This Series," Sept. 5, 1972, NPBA.

30. "An American Family," *Newsweek*, Jan. 15, 1973.

31. "Ultimate Soap Opera," *Time*, Jan. 22, 1973.

32. Frank Getlein, "A Family," *Washington Evening Star and Daily News*, Jan. 11, 1973.

33. Cecil Smith, "*An American Family* Opens a New Television Dimension," *Newark Star-Ledger* (New Jersey), Jan. 7, 1973 (from the *Los Angeles Times* Syndicate).

34. Jack Friedman, "Every Loud Has a Silver Lining," *Village Voice*, Jan. 18, 1973.

35. Steven V. Roberts, "An American Family Sees Itself on TV," and Stephanie Harrington, "An American Family Lives Its Life on TV," *New York Times*, Jan. 7, 1973.

36. *New York Times*, Jan. 13, 1973.

37. Fredelle Maynard, "An American Family: The Crack in the Mirror," *Image* (WNET) (Jan. 1973).

38. John O'Connor, "TV: *An American Family* Is a Provocative Series," *New York Times*, Jan. 23, 1973.

39. Margaret Mead's quote is from her article, "As Significant as the Invention of Drama or the Novel," *TV Guide*, Jan. 6, 1973.

11. Two into One Equals Thirteen

1. Edward R. Murrow, on-air inauguration of WNDT / New York, Sept. 16, 1962. "Tonight," he told Channel 13's viewers, "you join me in being present at the birth of a great adventure." In fact, the adventure was to be postponed for two weeks; immediately after the inaugural program, WNDT was closed down by a labor dispute.

2. NET's reluctance to use WNDT / 13's studios was in large measure due to what it saw as the poor quality of the station's technical staff. The studio crews, together with their labor contracts, were inherited from the New Jersey commercial channel as a part of WNDT's acquisition of Channel 13.

3. The assessment of Channel 13's performance appeared in "Supplemental Docket Item—Public Broadcasting," Mar. 23, 1970, and was an agenda item for a meeting of the Ford Foundation board of trustees, PA #710–0075, Ford Foundation Files.

4. An account of Newton Minow's involvement in the purchase of WNTA is contained both in Barnouw, *Image Empire*, and Blakely, *To Serve the Public Interest*, pp. 119–20. Both cite as their source Barbara S. Boekmeier, "The Genesis of WNDT: A Noncommercial Television Station on a Commercial Channel," Master's thesis, Columbia University, 1963.

5. The details of the transactions leading to the purchase of WNTA are contained in an interoffice memorandum from John F. White to Richard Catalano, NET's vice president of administration, May 8, 1969, NPBA. White uses 1959 as the date of the proceedings that led to the purchase rather than 1961. The agreement to broadcast a specified number of hours of New Jersey programming remains in effect today despite the presence of an all-UHF New Jersey public network and the transfer of RKO-General's WOR / Channel 9 from New York to New Jersey to ward off an FCC threat to rescind the license.

6. In addition to Sheperd, Houghton, Josephs, Rockefeller, and Stoddard, the original WNDT board included Henry C. Brunie, Walker G. Buckner, John D. Budinger, Joseph F. Cullman, Robert W. Dowling, H. C. Forbes, Samuel B. Gould (president), Justice Florence M. Kelley, James A. Linen, Governor Robert B. Meyner, Frederick N. Raubinger, William J. Saunders, Lawrence A. Wien, and David L. Yunich.

7. John White to his NET colleagues Gerard Appy, Robert Hudson, William Kobin, and Richard Catalano, confidential aide-mémoire, May 8, 1969, NPBA.

8. James Perkins, "Public Broadcasting: Some Recommendations to Channel 13, NET, The Corporation for Public Broadcasting, and the Ford Foundation," Jan. 5, 1970, NPBA.

9. Everett N. Case to John F. White, draft memorandum, n.d., NPBA. In a letter from James Perkins to Patricia Roberts Harris (Dec. 6, 1971), NPBA, Perkins defended his recommendations by saying that the regional concept followed on the facts, and the facts were that "the Ford Foundation had signalled an end to its large-scale support, and the Corporation for Public Broadcasting had also indicated that for political reasons alone it could not put all its programming money into one New York–based institution." From these "facts" he concluded that "NET as the single central programming facility for public television had no future."

10. Peter G. Peterson to J. Day, July 23, 1984. Peterson also commented that "throughout, Ethan Hitchcock was as charming as he was tough," NPBA.

11. "Notes on Outline of Proposal—Discussions with Ethan Allen Hitchcock, Monday, June 15, 1970," Peter G. Peterson, draft memorandum, NPBA.

12. David Davis, Ford Foundation, to Peter G. Peterson, June 19, 1970, NPBA.

13. Cousins to Hitchcock, July 7, 1970. On Aug. 4, 1970, Peterson wrote to Cousins warning him that he and Hitchcock had envisioned a more limited role for the advisory group. For the exchange of "if-you-

agree" letters, see Hitchcock to Cousins, Sept. 10, 1970, and Cousins to Hitchcock, Sept. 22, 1970, NPBA.

14. The members of the National Programming Council were Harry N. Abrams, president of his own publishing firm; Dr. Herman Branson, president, Lincoln University; Dr. Kingman Brewster, president, Yale University; Caroline Charles, chair, KQED board; Robert G. Chollar, president, Charles F. Kettering Foundation; Norman Cousins (chairman); James Day, president, WNET; Sy Gomberg, television writer; Denis Hayes, president, Friends of the Earth; Hazel Henderson, economist and writer; Ethan Allen Hitchcock, chairman, WNET; Joseph Iseman, attorney; Lloyd Kaiser, president, WQED, Pittsburgh; James Karayn, president, National Public Affairs Center for Television, Washington; Honorable Thomas Kuchel, former U.S. Senator from California; James Loper, president, KCET, Los Angeles; Dr. Herman Long, president, Talladega College; Leonard Marks, attorney; Dr. David Mathews, president, University of Alabama; William McCarter, president, WTTW, Chicago; Stephanie Mills; Dr. Maurice B. Mitchell, chancellor, University of Denver; Richard O. Moore, president, KQED, San Francisco; Raymond League, president, Zebra Advertising Associations, Inc.; Edward N. Ney, president, Young & Rubicam; Dr. James A. Perkins, chairman, International Council for Educational Development; Terry Sanford, president, Duke University; William Schuman, composer; Dr. Glenn T. Seaborg, Nobel Laureate chemist; Jennifer Jones, actress; Norton Simon, president, Norton Simon Industries; Donald Taverner; president, WETA, Washington; William Kobin, executive producer, Children's Television Workshop; and Alexandra Cincotta (executive director).

15. *Variety,* May 13, 1970.

16. "Merger Move for NET, WNDT," *Variety,* Nov. 26, 1969.

17. *New York Times,* Dec. 7, 1969.

18. Iselin's time in book publishing was not completely free of pressures. Chris Welles, "Poor Little Rich Station," *New York Magazine,* Oct. 9, 1978, relates the story of a one-day walkout of Harper & Row's editors to protest Iselin's treatment of them.

19. Nat Hentoff is quoted in WNET/13's "Annual Report on Local Programming, July 1, 1971, to June 30, 1972," p. 3, NPBA.

20. *New York Times,* Dec. 7, 1969.

21. *Variety,* Jan. 6, 1971.

22. John Beaufort, "Cops and Probers," *Christian Science Monitor,* Oct. 30, 1971.

23. *Variety,* Nov. 3, 1971.

24. Thomas Collins, "*The 51st State*: New Kid on the Block Isn't Making Friends Fast," *Bergen County Record,* June 18, 1972.

25. "*The 51st State*: A Freewheeling PTV Approach to Local News," *Broadcasting,* June 19, 1972.

26. Jack Willis, interviewed by the author, New York, Apr. 29, 1985.

27. U.S. Congress, *The Congressional Record,* H5154, June 1, 1972. Quote is from a news interview with Watson by Bill Jorgensen on WNEW-TV, May 11, 1972.

28. U.S. Congress, *Congressional Record,* H5154, June 1, 1972.

29. John W. Macy to J. Day, June 16, 1972, NPBA.

30. *Bergen County Record,* June 18, 1972.

31. Marvin Barrett, ed., *The Politics of Broadcasting: Survey of Broadcast Journalism, 1971–72* (New York: Thomas Y. Crowell, 1973), p. 28.

32. Jack Newfield, "On the Fate of *The 51st State*," *Village Voice,* Mar. 8, 1973.

33. Ibid.

34. "Justice Uncoiled," *Time,* Apr. 23, 1973.

35. Barrett, *Politics of Broadcasting.*

36. Nat Hentoff, "Even Bella Abzug Slipped Her Moorings," *New York Times,* Apr. 2, 1972.

37. Willis, interview.

38. John J. Iselin, interviewed by the author, New York, Feb. 22, 1985.

39. Newfield, "*The 51st State.*"

40. "Public TV's Depressing Condition Clues Call for Showdown at WNET," *Variety,* Feb. 7, 1973.

12. Humpty-Dumpty and the Nixon Years

1. Lewis Carroll, *Through the Looking Glass,* in *The Annotated Alice* (New York: Bramhall, 1960), p. 269.

2. Jefferson is quoted in Nat Hentoff, *The First Freedom* (New York: Delacorte, 1980), pp. 86–87.

3. The text of Agnew's attack upon broadcasters was published in the *Chicago Tribune,* Nov. 14, 1969.

4. Flanigin to Whitehead, memorandum, Nov. 3, 1969. See National Association of Educational Broadcasters, *The Nixon Administration Public Broadcasting Papers,* hereafter *Nixon Papers.* These papers were obtained under the Freedom of Information Act by the Carnegie Commission on the Future of Public Broadcasting and summarized by the National Telecommunication and Information Administration.

5. "Statement of Goals," James Karayn, NPACT press packet, 1975, NPBA.

6. Stone, *Nixon*, p. 84. Interestingly, in his book *Right Place* (p. 279), MacNeil characterized the National Public Affairs Center for Television as a title "so gloriously stilted that it seemed almost to be seeking anonymity in the Scrabble wasteland of Washington acronyms."

7. Stone, *Nixon*, p. 88. Nixon's characterization of Vanocur, and the charge that Vanocur's aggressive questioning in the first Nixon-Kennedy debate contributed to his defeat, are quoted from Nixon, *Six Crises* (Garden City, N.Y.: Doubleday, 1962), p. 339.

8. Jon Huntsman to Flanigin, confidential memorandum, Sept. 23, 1971 (*Nixon Papers*, p. 36).

9. "The Czar of the Airwaves," *Newsweek*, Feb. 7, 1972.

10. Whitehead's options for controlling public television are contained in Whitehead to the president, memorandum, Oct. 4, 1971 (*Nixon Papers*, p. 38).

11. Ehrlichman to Whitehead, memorandum, n.d., (*Nixon Papers*, p. 38).

12. Whitehead to Flanigin and Colson, "Action Memorandum," July 9, 1971 (*Nixon Papers*, p. 32).

13. The text of Whitehead's address to the National Association of Educational Broadcasters was transcribed and distributed to its members after the Miami Convention. Excerpts are quoted in Tom Zito, "Chastising Public TV," *Washington Post*, Oct. 21, 1971, and in "Collision of Politics and Public Television," *Broadcasting*, Oct. 25, 1971.

14. John Witherspoon, Corporation for Public Broadcasting to All Stations, memorandum, Nov. 5, 1971, NPBA.

15. Ibid.

16. "Carnegie Report Revisited," by Arthur L. Singer, Jr., in *Educational Broadcasting Review* 5, no. 4 (Aug. 1971). The article was adapted from Singer's address before the annual Public Television Development Conference at Boyne Highlands, Mich., June 28, 1971. Singer acknowledges the collaboration in the preparation of the address of Stephen White, one of the coauthors of the Carnegie Commission Report. See Carnegie Commission on Educational Television, *Program for Action*.

17. Interview over New York's WBAI and quoted in Macy, *Wasteland* (p. 75). It is quoted as well in Bruce E. Thorp, "White House Static over Structure, Funds Keeps Public Broadcasting Picture Fuzzy," *National Journal*, Apr. 29, 1972. Thorp attributes the interview to National Public Radio, Jan. 12, 1972.

18. *This Week with Bill Moyers*, Public Broadcasting System, Jan. 2, 1972. Quoted in *The Network Project*, Office of Telecommunications Policy (New York: The Network Project, 1973), p. 18.

19. The Administration's attitude toward the Ford Foundation's role

in public television was clearly stated in a memorandum from White House aide Jon Rose to Larry Higby of H. R. Haldeman's staff on Oct. 15, 1971. "Even if we go the Whitehead route and succeed in cutting off federal funds for liberal hour on public tv, no doubt Mac Bundy will be ready with Ford Foundation money to take up the slack. This is another battle for which I and a number of others would be eager to draft legislation if desired" (*Nixon Papers*, p. 42).

20. Flanigin to Albert Cole, memorandum, Nov. 9, 1970 (*Nixon Papers*).

21. Stone, *Nixon*, p. 66. Here he refers to an interview with Henry Goldberg, Jan. 28, 1981.

22. Whitehead to the president, memorandum, Oct. 4, 1971 (*Nixon Papers*).

23. Whitehead to the president, memorandum, Nov. 15, 1971 (*Nixon Papers*).

24. Whitehead to Haldeman, memorandum, Nov. 24, 1971 (*Nixon Papers*, p. 48).

25. Stone, *Nixon*, p. 153.

26. Ibid.

27. CPB Board minutes, Apr. 13, 1972.

28. In refusing to work the Republican National Convention, MacNeil said, "We felt it quite inappropriate for a news organization under attack by the Nixon White House to cover his renomination convention in full when we had not covered McGovern's. . . . Whatever NPACT's motives, I felt it would be widely perceived as an act of abasement." See MacNeil, *Right Place*, p. 284.

29. Stone, *Nixon*, pp. 187ff. He refers to an interview with Bill Moyers.

30. Jack Kuney, producer of *The Politics—and Comedy of Woody Allen*, has provided a more detailed account of the episode in "The Closing Down of Woody Allen," *Television Quarterly* 19, no. 4 (winter 1983). A full description of the show itself can be found in Eric Lax, *On Being Funny* (New York: Charterhouse, 1975), pp. 201–7. Details of the controversy surrounding its cancellation appeared in *New York Times*, Feb. 15, 1972; *Broadcasting*, Feb. 21, 1972; and *Variety*, Feb. 16, 1972.

31. Billy B. Oxley to All Stations, PBS telex, Feb. 11, 1972, NPBA.

32. *The Dick Cavett Show*, ABC-TV, June 17, 1972.

33. E. A. Hitchcock to J. Day, Feb. 15, 1972, NPBA.

34. "It was in bad taste," said Allen of his own show. "At the time I thought it was innocuous" ("Woody's Film Too Tasteless for TV," *New York Magazine*, May 21, 1979).

35. Stone, *Nixon*, p. 75.

36. Whitehead to Colson and Flanigan, "Action Memorandum," July 9, 1971 (*Nixon Papers*, p. 32).

37. Whitehead to the president, memorandum, Nov. 14, 1971 (*Nixon Papers*, p. 47).

38. Although William F. Buckley, host of the PBS show *Firing Line*, stood to gain from passage of the Macdonald Bill, his brother, Sen. James Buckley, cast the only dissenting vote in the Senate's 82–1 majority favoring passage.

39. President Nixon's Veto Message, June 30, 1972 (*Nixon Papers*, p. 75).

40. Fred Friendly, "The Politicization of Public TV," *Columbia Journalism Review*, (Mar.–Apr. 1973).

41. Bill Moyers, "Public TV: Up the Blandbox," *Washington Post*, Apr. 1, 1973.

42. Whitehead's "seeking funds and independence" quote is from Whitehead to the president, memorandum, June 26, 1972 (*Nixon Papers*, p. 75).

43. *New York Times*, Aug. 11, 1972.

13. The Man Who Saved Public Television

1. Moyers, "Up the Blandbox."

2. Carnegie Commission on Educational Television, *Program for Action*, p. 99.

3. Whitehead's preference for Kristol as Corporation president is contained in Whitehead to Flanigan, memorandum, July 5, 1972 (*Nixon Papers*, p. 81). Whitehead argued that "Kristol's personality and capabilities complement and reinforce Henry Loomis. . . . Kristol could be more readily elected as Chairman than Curtis." The reference to Henry Loomis as the presumed president of the Corporation occurred a month before Macy had decided to resign.

4. The quotation is attributed to CPB director Jack Valenti in Stone, *Nixon*, p. 191.

5. Transcript of Loomis's closed-circuit meeting with the PBS stations, Sept. 20, 1972, NPBA.

6. "A Novice for Public TV," *Time*, Oct. 16, 1972.

7. Harry Ashmore, *Fear in the Air* (New York: Norton, 1973), p. 113.

8. Stone, *Nixon*, p. 73.

9. "Profile," *Broadcasting*, Oct. 30, 1972.

10. Loomis to Whitehead, memorandum, Nov. 7, 1972 (*Nixon Papers*, p. 92).

11. The quote is generally credited to Jim Lehrer, then PBS's coor-

dinator of public-affairs programming. It appeared in the *New York Times*, Nov. 11, 1972.

12. "Several PTV's Nix NASA's Big Show," *Variety*, Nov. 22, 1972.

13. Resolution of the Board of Directors, The Corporation for Public Broadcasting, adopted at its regular meeting, Owings Mills, Md., Jan. 10, 1973. Quoted in John Carmody, "Public TV Takeover," *Washington Post*, Jan. 12, 1973.

14. "Public TV's Freedom Is Called Stunted," *New York Times*, Jan. 31, 1973.

15. "The Nixon Network," *Newsweek*, Jan. 1, 1973.

16. Cecil Smith, *Los Angeles Times*, Jan. 15, 1973, quoted in Stone, *Nixon*, p. 228.

17. Kay Gardella, "Public Broadcast Unit's Influence Seen Ended," *New York Daily News*, Dec. 22, 1972.

18. "Two Series Make End Runs to Get on CPB Schedule," *Variety*, Mar. 14, 1973.

19. "MacNeil Sees PTV in Danger of Being Nixon Mouthpieces," *Broadcasting*, Jan. 29, 1973.

20. Stone, *Nixon*, p. 195.

21. Goldberg to Whitehead, memorandum, Apr. 20, 1973 (*Nixon Papers*, p. 102).

22. Rose to Higby, Oct. 15, 1971, (*Nixon Papers*, p. 41).

23. Hearings of the U.S. Senate Committee on Commerce, Subcommittee on Communications, Mar. 28–30, 1973, No. 93–10, p. 8. Buchanan's charges against public television on the *Dick Cavett Show* were read into the record at the opening of Senator Pastore's hearings on public television.

24. "Public TV Affairs," *New York Times*, Jan. 19, 1973.

25. "Floppo Season for PTV Web," *Variety*, Nov. 29, 1972.

26. "PBS Board of Directors Statement Following Meeting of January 5, 1973," issued as an undated press release by PBS, NPBA.

27. Transcript of Gunn's remarks on PBS closed-circuit broadcast of Jan. 9, 1973, NPBA.

28. John J. O'Connor, "Moving in for the Kill?" *New York Times*, Jan. 21, 1973.

29. "Report CPB Flooded with Mail from Citizenry Deploring Govt. Control of Public TV and Squelching of News," *Variety*, Mar. 7, 1973.

30. According to Robert MacNeil, Loomis's reaction to the outpouring of mail was a disclaimer that "the number and emotional content of letters is not necessarily a good measure of audience size or interest." Said MacNeil, "I think this translates as 'To hell with what the public

wants.' " Quoted in Tom Shales, "Public TV: Debate Continues," *Washington Post*, Jan. 27, 1973.

31. Minutes of the Feb. 6, 1973, meeting of the Corporation for Public Broadcasting, NPBA.

32. The original members of the twenty-five-member lay Board of Governors of PBS were Edmund F. Ball (WLPB), Caroline Charles (KQED), Dollie Cole (WTVS), Phyllis Dennery (WYES), Salvatore Fauci (WSKG), Dr. William Friday (WUNC), Alfred C. Galloway (WDNC), James G. Harlow (WWVU), C. Bart Hawley (WCET), Ethan Allen Hitchcock (WNET), Sidney James (WETA), John Lowell (WGBH), Dr. Donald R. McNeil (WMEB), Barbara Roper (WFME), Dr. John Ryan (WTUI), Leonard E. Rosenberg (Maryland Center for PTV), H. Russell Smith (KCET), Irby Turner, Jr. (Mississippi ETV), Dr. Richard Vanhoose (Kentucky ETV), Robert G. Waldo (KCTS), Frank Wozencraft (KUHT), and Ralph B. Rogers (KERA), chairman.

33. "PBS: Only the Name's the Same," *Variety*, Apr. 4, 1973.

34. "Report of the CPB Ad Hoc Committee Commissioned to Negotiate with the Rogers Group," Apr. 5, 1973, NPBA. Also quoted in " 'Mutual Trust' as Victim of Fallout in Proposal for PTV Compromise; Acrimony Master of Ceremony," *Variety*, Apr. 25, 1973.

35. Avery and Pepper, *Politics of Interconnection*, p. 41.

36. Dr. Gloria Anderson, Neal B. Freeman, and Jack Wrather made up the new committee.

37. Thomas Curtis to James Killian, Apr. 16, 1973 (Stone, *Nixon*, p. 278).

38. "Public TV Licensees and CPB Head for Confrontation on Program Control," *New York Times*, Mar. 27, 1973.

39. John Carmody, "Public TV Fight: An Analysis," *Washington Post*, June 2, 1973.

40. "The CPB-PBS Agreement: 'In Order to Effect a Vigorous Partnership,' " *Public Telecommunications Review* (Aug. 1973). The article contains the complete text of the compromise agreement.

41. Henry Goldberg to Clay T. Whitehead, memorandum, Apr. 20, 1973 (*Nixon Papers*, p. 308).

42. Frank Carlucci to Henry Loomis, Jan. 1973 (quoted in Stone, *Nixon*, p. 258).

43. Thomas Curtis to Frank Carlucci, Feb. 1, 1973 (see Stone, *Nixon*, p. 260).

44. "Whitehead Bucks Pastore, Magnuson on CPB Funding," *Broadcasting*, Apr. 2, 1973.

45. U.S. Congress, *Record of Senate Hearings*, S. 1090, Mar. 28–30, 1973.

46. Whitehead to the president, draft memorandum, June 6, 1973 (*Nixon Papers*, p. 108).

47. Whitehead to the president, draft memorandum, Oct. 1973 (*Nixon Papers*, p. 112).

48. Patrick Buchanan to Hank Paulson, memorandum, Oct. 14, 1973 (*Nixon Papers*, p. 114).

49. Stone, *Nixon*, p. 290. He refers to an interview with James Karayn, Philadelphia, Dec. 10, 1980.

50. *Los Angeles Times,* June 20, 1973 (quoted in Stone, *Nixon*, p. 291).

51. MacNeil, *Right Place*, p. 288.

52. Ibid.

53. "Watergate Is Boon to Public Television," *Wall Street Journal,* June 15, 1973.

54. Stone, *Nixon*, p. 293.

55. "An Essay on Watergate," *Bill Moyers' Journal,* Public Broadcasting Service, Oct. 31, 1973.

56. Robert de Roos, "All Quiet along the Potomac," *Focus* (KQED) 19, no. 8 (Sept. 1973).

57. The resignation was not the end of my association with public television. I continued to serve on boards affiliated with the public medium, produced a nightly series of celebrity interviews (*Day at Night*), and taught undergraduate and graduate courses in public television for fourteen years.

58. *Nixon Papers*, p. 118 (quoting an Associated Press story of Apr. 4, 1974).

59. Stone, *Nixon*, p. 301 He refers to an interview with Clay T. Whitehead, New York City, Feb. 25, 1981.

60. Whitehead to the president, memorandum, Apr. 2, 1974 (*Nixon Papers*, p. 116).

61. Ibid.

62. Whitehead to Gen. Alexander Haig, memorandum, n.d. (*Nixon Papers*, p. 119).

63. Stone, *Nixon*, p. 312 (Whitehead interview).

64. Whitehead testimony before the Senate Communications Subcommittee, Aug. 6, 1974 (*Nixon Papers*, p. 123).

65. Stone, *Nixon*, p. 330 (Whitehead interview).

14. Great Noise. Big Wind.
Much Dust. No Rain

1. Les Brown, "He Sees a Bigger Picture for Public Television," *New York Times*, Sunday, Sept. 12, 1976.

2. John Friedman, "Nixon's the One," *Washington Journalism Review* (Apr.–May 1979).

3. John Carmody, " 'Lazy' Public Television Gets a 'Table-Pounding' President," *Washington Post*, Jan. 9, 1976.

4. Alan Sheldon, "The Grossman Style," *Public Telecommunications Review* (Jan.–Feb. 1976). According to Sheldon, Grossman's name was first suggested to Ralph Rogers by Robert Wilson, the Dallas station manager who failed to get the top PBS post.

5. Leo Seligsohn, "Public Television Finds a Dynamic Kingpin," *Newsday*, June 6, 1976.

6. "One Thing Is Made Perfectly Clear: Grossman Wants Better Programs for Public TV," *Broadcasting*, Feb. 16, 1976.

7. "Grossman States PBS Priorities: Programming and Plenty of It," *Variety*, Feb. 11, 1976.

8. "Lay aside this divisive [notion]" is quoted from "Grossman Asks PTV to Pull Together on National Programs," *Broadcasting*, June 28, 1976.

9. When the stations' contribution of $4 million to the experimental first year of the Station Program Cooperative proved inadequate, Rogers and Gunn went hat-in-hand to the Corporation and the Ford Foundation for a $10 million subsidy to launch the plan. The annual subsidy continued through its first three years. In later years, the SPC functioned entirely on station resources, which rose to over $30 million annually. Such expensive shows as *The MacNeil/Lehrer NewsHour, Great Performances*, and *Nova* were "discounted" to the stations because part of their production costs were covered by corporate underwriting. In the case of *Sesame Street*, half of the production costs are now borne by Children's Television Workshop out of its own revenue sources.

10. Jerry Krupnick, " 'Core' Strategy Helps PBS Chief Gain Viewership," *Newark Star-Ledger* (New Jersey), June 14, 1983.

11. Kay Gardella in the *New York Daily News*, Dec. 3, 1976.

12. Les Brown, "Public TV Aides Meeting to Settle Rift on Programs," *New York Times*, Dec. 2, 1976.

13. "Tug of War for Control of Public TV," *Variety*, Nov. 17, 1976.

14. Ibid. The Revolving Documentary Fund, designed to return its original investment by "selling" the documentaries to the stations, overestimated the stations' interest in documentaries and was soon abandoned.

15. Bill Greeley, "PTV Fight Is Whimper, Not Bang: Grossman Speech on CPB-PBS Followed by Clash Postponement," *Variety*, Dec. 8, 1976.

16. Bill Greeley, "Indians Have a Word for PBS-CPB Flap: Ugh," *Variety*, Dec. 15, 1975.

17. "The President's Message on Public Broadcasting," reprinted in *CPB Report* 8, no. 22 (Oct. 17, 1977).

18. "Gunn Guns for Carter Legislation," *Broadcasting*, Nov. 21, 1977. Rowland provides a detailed study of the 1978 legislation and its effects on public-broadcasting policy in "The Struggle for Self-Determination: Public Broadcasting Policy Problems and Reform," in Schement, Gutierrez, and Sirbu, eds., *The Telecommunications Policy Handbook* (New York: Praeger, 1982).

19. "Carter Asks 1B for Public TV," *New York Daily News*, Oct. 7, 1977.

20. Friendly to Rep. Lionel Van Deerlin, May 24, 1978, NPBA.

21. Van Deerlin's response is quoted from John S. Friedman, "Public TV—More Funds Without Strings," *New York Times*, July 30, 1978.

22. It was tacitly understood that Hartford Gunn, with his skills at forward planning, would be offered the presidency of NAPTS, but the offer came too late. He had already accepted the post of senior vice president and general manager of the Los Angeles station (KCET). The NAPTS presidency went instead to David Carley, a millionaire businessman from Wisconsin.

23. "CPB's Robben Fleming: A Time to Heal," *Broadcasting*, Apr. 23, 1979.

24. Ibid. Fleming's proposal to remove the board entirely from programming was modified when the board, unwilling to yield all of its power over programming, insisted on retaining its right to set the overall priorities of the newly created Program Fund and rejected the idea of an independent advisory board. The board did accept, however, the use of peer panels in the program selection process, a practice that continues to this day.

25. For the detailed chronology of events surrounding *Death of a Princess*, I am indebted to the Harvard Business School's case study of the program (no. 1–381–106), written by Laura L. Nash, research fellow, under the direction of Professor John B. Mathews, and copyrighted by the President and Fellows of Harvard College.

26. Richard Goldstein, "Did PBS Try to Kill 'Death of a Princess'?" *Village Voice*, June 2, 1980.

27. Lynn Darling, "Much Ado about PBS' *Death of a Princess*," *Washington Post*, May 12, 1980.

28. See Harvard Business School, case study no. 1–381–106, p. 477.

29. "Case of Saudi Princess," *Newsweek*, May 19, 1980. Excerpts from the Saudi Ambassador's letter to Warren Christopher and his covering letter to Lawrence Grossman are quoted from "Princess Aftermath," *Public Broadcasting Report* 2, no. 11 (May 23, 1980), p. 2. Grossman's response "that a free society requires open and candid discussion of

issues" is quoted from "A Man for All Media at NBC News," *Broadcasting*, Dec. 12, 1983.

30. "Carter Told of Senate 'Princess' Backing," *Public Broadcasting Report* 2, no. 10 (May 9, 1980), p. 1. Senator Percy's daughter, Sharon Percy Rockefeller, then a member of the CPB board, met briefly with CPB president Robben Fleming "just to talk through the matter" and "to make certain we were prepared for the ramifications." Later she said she believed the program should be aired, stressing that CPB has no say in program content.

31. "Case of Saudi Princess," *Newsweek*.

32. Tom Shales, "Ersatz Islam from a Confused Rabble Drowser," *Washington Post*, May 12, 1980.

33. *Public Broadcasting Report* 2, no. 10 (May 9, 1980), p. 2.

34. Patrick Buchanan, " 'Death of a Princess' . . . but Why Have Public TV at All?" *Philadelphia Inquirer*, May 19, 1980.

35. Natan Katzman, "Death of a Princess Diary," *Focus* (KQED) (July 1980).

15. Monumental Dreams on Shoestring Budgets

1. Edward Pfister, interviewed by the author, Washington, D.C., Apr. 10, 1985.

2. *Public Broadcasting Report* 3, no. 3 (Jan. 30, 1981).

3. *Public Broadcasting Report* 2, no. 22 (Nov. 7, 1980).

4. *Public Broadcasting Report* 3, no. 9 (Apr. 24, 1981).

5. *Public Broadcasting Report* 4, no. 7 (Mar. 26, 1982).

6. *Public Broadcasting Report* 3, no. 5 (Feb. 27, 1981).

7. Carnegie Commission on the Future of Public Broadcasting, *A Public Trust*. Also, "A Summary and Overview of the Findings and Recommendations of the Carnegie Commission on the Future of Public Broadcasting" issued by the Commission, Jan. 30, 1977. The members of the Carnegie Commission on the Future of Public Broadcasting (Carnegie II) were William J. McGill (chairman), president, Columbia University; Stephen K. Bailey, professor of education and social policy, Harvard University; Red Burns, executive director, Alternate Media Center, New York University; Henry J. Cauthen, president, South Carolina Educational Television Commission; Peggy Charen, president, Action for Children's Television; Wilbur B. Davenport, Jr., professor of communications and engineering, Massachusetts Institute of Technology; Virginia Duncan, independent producer; Eli N. Evans, president, Charles H. Revson Foundation; John Gardner, founding chairman, Common Cause;

Alex P. Haley, author; Walter W. Heller, Regent's Professor of Economics, University of Minnesota; Josie R. Johnson, vice president, General Alumni Association at Fisk University; Kenneth Mason, president, Quaker Oats Company; Bill Moyers, executive editor of *Bill Moyers' Journal*; Kathleen Nolan, president, Screen Actors Guild; J. Leonard Reinsch, chairman, Cox Broadcasting Corporation; and Dr. Tomas Rivera, author and poet.

8. Editorial in *Broadcasting*, Feb. 5, 1979, p. 30.

9. An analysis of how the Communications Act of 1978 (HR 13015) might affect public television is contained in a document prepared by the PBS General Counsel's Office and distributed to members of the PBS Board with a covering memorandum from Lawrence K. Grossman, "Rewrite of the Communications Act," June 22, 1978, NPBA.

10. "Final Report: Temporary Commission on Alternative Financing for Public Telecommunications, October 1, 1983" (printed in *Current*, Sept. 27, 1983).

11. The PBS standards for corporate underwriting were originally issued on April 15, 1987, as the *Report of the Special Committee on Program Policies and Procedures.* They have been updated periodically since, most recently in PBS *National Program Funding Standards and Practices*, issued by the Public Broadcasting Service, Alexandria, Va., Mar. 9, 1990.

12. The *MacNeil/Lehrer NewsHour*, originally a joint production of WETA and WNET, is now produced by an independent company, Mac-Neil/Lehrer Productions, Inc. However, executive producer Les Crystal (former president of NBC News) is employed not by MacNeil/Lehrer Productions but by the coproducing stations, WNET and WETA, as a part of the agreement between the independent producing agency and the public system.

13. Howard Rosenberg, "The *MacNeil/Lehrer NewsHour*, Longer and Better," *Washington Journalism Review*, Dec. 1983.

14. Arthur Unger, "*NewsHour* Looks Ahead," *Newsday*, Sept. 4, 1984.

15. Walter Karp, "Tiptoeing Through the Halls of Power," *Channels of Communication*, Mar. 1986.

16. Robert MacNeil announced his plan to retire from the *MacNeil/Lehrer NewsHour* in 1995.

17. Ben Brown, "PBS Chief Leaves Healthy Legacy," *USA Today*, Feb. 9, 1984.

18. Tom Shales, "Pledge Week Exacts a Stiff Price for Commercial-Free TV," *Paducah (Kentucky) Sun*, Mar. 8, 1984. Shales wrote that "Outgoing PBS president Lawrence Grossman helped give public TV a lobotomy, and he made it look more like network TV."

19. Penny Pagano, "New PBS Chief Lists Goals," *St. Louis Globe-Democrat*, Apr. 24, 1984 (from the *Los Angeles Times* Syndicate).

20. "America's First Television War," *Newsweek*, Oct. 10, 1983.

21. Tom Shales, "Vietnam: On PBS, A Landmark Journey Through 30 Years of Darkness," *Washington Post*, Oct. 3, 1983.

22. Fox Butterfield, "TV Returns to Vietnam to Dissect the War," *New York Times*, Oct. 2, 1983.

23. Davis resigned as Executive Director in 1990 and was succeeded by Ward Chamberlin.

24. Ellin Stein, "Quality Time," *American Film* (Jan.–Feb. 1986).

25. "Ten Years of Moving Pictures: American Playhouse 1982–1991," Public Playhouse, Inc., 1991, NPBA.

26. Carnegie Commission on Educational Television, *Program for Action*, p. 13.

27. Lee Margulies, " 'Sadness Begins' for Public Broadcasting," *Los Angeles Times*, May 13, 1982. The expression "the sadness begins" is from CPB president Edward Pfister.

28. Tom Shales, "The TV Year That Was," *Boston Globe*, Jan. 4, 1984.

29. The staples of the PBS prime-time schedule came into being by different routes. *Nova* was the brainchild of Michael Ambrosino, a WGBH / Boston producer, who worked with the BBC under a Corporation fellowship, developed a high regard for the BBC's science series (*Horizons*) and returned to WGBH with a deal to coproduce science shows with them. The *National Geographic Specials*, originally produced by Wolper Productions, began on CBS in 1965, shifted to ABC later, but ultimately lost their air time on the commercial networks. Gulf Oil and the National Geographic Society brought them to PBS a year later through WQED / Pittsburgh. *Great Performances* brought together two earlier series, *Dance in America* and *Theater in America*, both produced by Jac Venza at WNET / New York.

30. Sue Mullin, "PBS Chief Expects Best Season Ever," *Washington Times*, Aug. 4, 1984.

31. David Bergman, "PBS Prexy Forecasts Upbeat Future for Public TV," *Daily Variety*, May 29, 1984.

32. The members of the original CPB Board were Frank Pace, Jr. (chair), former Secretary of the Army; James R. Killian, Jr. (vice chair), chairman of the corporation, Massachusetts Institute of Technology; Joseph A. Beirne, president, Communications Workers of America; Robert S. Benjamin, chairman, United Artists Corporation; Roscoe C. Carroll, corporation counsel, Golden State Mutual Life Insurance Company; Michael A. Gammino, president, Columbus National Bank of Providence; Saul Haas, chairman, KIRO (AM-FM-TV), Seattle; Erich Leinsdorf, con-

ductor, Boston Symphony Orchestra; John D. Rockefeller 3d, New York; Frank E. Schooley, director of broadcasting, University of Illinois; Oveta C. Hobby, publisher, *Houston Post*; Joseph D. Hughes, vice president, T. Mellon & Sons; Carl E. Sanders, former Governor of Alabama; Jack Valenti, president, Motion Picture Association of America; and Milton S. Eisenhower, president, Johns Hopkins University.

33. *Television Digest*, Feb. 24, 1975.

34. Les Brown, "Benjamin to Quit Public TV Group," *New York Times*, Feb. 4, 1977. Benjamin's term as a director had expired eleven months before his resignation. His "lame duck" status may have been a factor in his decision to resign.

35. "Pfister Urges Public Broadcasting Unity," *Broadcasting*, Nov. 9, 1981.

36. The quotations from the Corporation's meeting of May 15, 1984, are taken from the minutes of that meeting, NPBA.

37. Steve Behrens, "Public Broadcasting's Unholy Link to Politics," *Channels*, July–Aug. 1985.

16. Let the Revolution Begin

1. Michael Tracey, "What Ails Public Broadcasting?" *Current*, Apr. 12, 1989.

2. "What They Said on Capitol Hill," *Current*, Dec. 8, 1987 (a reprint of transcripts of the House and Senate Hearings on the Twentieth Anniversary of the Public Broadcasting Act of 1967).

3. The Grossman quote used by Markey is from Lawrence Grossman, "Programming, Programming, Programming," *Current*, Nov. 3, 1987.

4. Stephen White, "Our Public Television Experiment: The Author of the First Carnegie Commission Report Looks at CPB and Public TV Twenty Years Later," *Current*, Oct. 20, 1987. Reprinted from *Public Interest* (summer 1987).

5. Ibid.

6. "Public TV: Looking Inward Toward the Future," *Current*, Mar. 30, 1988.

7. Ibid.

8. Richard Zoglin, "The Wisdom of Ms. Solomon," *Time*, Dec. 10, 1990.

9. The joint plan of the three organizations is contained in Corporation for Public Broadcasting, "Meeting the Mission in a Changing Media Environment," Jan. 1990, NPBA.

10. "PTV Program Development Will Remain Largely Collaborative, TV Critics Told," *Public Broadcasting Report* 12, no. 1 (Jan. 19, 1990).

11. Details of the Lawson plan for the National Program Service are contained in a memorandum entitled *National Program Service 1991 Annual Report*, Jan. 17, 1992, from Jennifer Lawson to station general managers, NPBA.

12. Public Broadcasting Service, *National Program Service 1992 Annual Report*, 1992, NPBA.

13. From a review by Jonathan Storm in the *Philadelphia Inquirer* (reprinted in *Current*, Oct. 21, 1991).

14. Lawson's reasons for cancelling *Edge* are quoted in "PBS backs over the *Edge*," the Marvin Kitman Show, *Newsday*, Mar. 30, 1992.

15. John Carman, "PBS Scared off of 'Tales' Sequel," *San Francisco Chronicle*, Apr. 12, 1994.

16. Ibid. Carman quoted from a PBS fax to its member stations suggesting responses to public and press inquiries about its decision on *More Tales of the City*.

17. Ibid. "The director of the state-run public broadcasting system [in Georgia] was dragged before a legislative appropriations hearing. . . . He courageously refused to withdraw the series or apologize for it. On the heels of a bomb threat, Chattanooga's WTCI-TV withdrew the series one hour before it was scheduled to air."

18. "Duggan Affirms Decision on 'Rights and Wrongs,'" *Current*, Sept. 5, 1994.

19. Ervin S. Duggan from Eleanor Holmes Norton et al., Aug. 17, 1994, NPBA.

20. *National Program Service 1992 Annual Report*, 1992, NPBA.

21. Letter from Lloyd N. Morrisett, president of the Markle Foundation, to selected participants in the Voters' Channel, July 1991, NPBA.

22. Public Broadcasting Service, "Programming for the Future: A National Programming Plan for the 1990's," June 1990, NPBA.

23. Quoted in Neil Hickey, "Public TV: Why Reports of Its Death Seem Premature," *TV Guide*, Dec. 11–17, 1982.

24. Public Broadcasting Service, *Long-Range Planning for Public Television*, vol. 1 (1978), NPBA.

25. Mahony et al., *Keeping* PACE, p. 1.

26. A description of the Grand Alliance can be found in "Proposal for a Grand Alliance," *Television Quarterly* (fall 1980). See also "PBS Unveils Public Subscriber Network," *Public Broadcasting Report* 3, no. 4 (Feb. 13, 1981).

17. The Indie's Six Million

1. Ben Davis, "The Right to Fail," *Emmy* (Sept.–Oct. 1983).

2. "A masterful, compelling achievement" (*Variety*), "a kind of

video miracle" (*Newsweek*), and "most accomplished documentary producer" (*New York Times*) are quoted in Rob Edelman, "An Epic of an Epoch: Ken Burns Discusses *The Civil War*," *The Independent* (Jan.–Feb. 1991).

3. The provision reserving a "substantial amount" of the Corporation's funds for independent production was written into the Public Telecommunications Financing Act of 1978 (Public Law 95–567, 95th Congress, Nov. 2, 1978), sec. 307, (k)(3)(B)(i).

4. Wiseman's first film, *Titticut Follies*, made in 1967, was not seen on television until 1992 after a long court battle. His stark look inside a Massachusetts mental hospital so embarrassed state authorities they had the film legally barred from public viewing during the intervening years. The description of *High School* as a "searing portrait of an institution" is from *Newsweek*, n.d., as quoted in Wiseman's promotional literature.

5. Ibid.

6. Tom Shales, "Struggle Nearly Closed *The Store*," *Los Angeles Times*, Dec. 13, 1983.

7. Quoted in "Neiman Marcus Producer Wiseman Speaks to CPB," *Current*, Jan. 17, 1984. Wiseman amplified his charges four years later in testimony before the Senate Subcommittee on Communication, reprinted in part in "Public TV Is a Mess: CPB's Panel Program Selection Is a Failure," *Current*, Mar. 30, 1988.

8. Quoted in J. J. Yore, "Relations Remain Strained Between Indies, Public TV," *Current*, Sept. 28, 1988.

9. Lawrence Daressa, "Independent Producers Propose New Program Service," *Current*, Sept. 22, 1987.

10. The original board members of the Independent Television Service were Linda Blackaby, Lawrence Daressa (chair), Julie Dash, David M. Davis, Eduardo Diaz, Ed Emshwiller, Virginia Gaines Fox, Laurence S. Hall, Cheryl Head, Lawrence M. Sapadin (president), and Joan Shigekawa.

11. Quoted in Martin Tolchin, "Public Broadcasting Bill Is Sidelined," *New York Times*, Mar. 5, 1992.

12. "Strict adherence to objectivity and balance" appears in the Public Broadcasting Act of 1967 (Public Law 90–129, Nov. 7, 1967).

13. Tuchman, *Making News*, p. 216. For a more specific approach on how objectivity is interpreted by those who cover the news and sometimes use it as a shield against criticism, see Tuchman's "Objectivity as Strategic Ritual: An Examination of Newsmen's Notions of Objectivity," *American Journal of Sociology* 77 (Jan. 1972). In *Basic Issues in Mass Communications: A Debate* (New York: Macmillan, 1984), John C. Merrill and Everette E.

Dennis debate whether journalistic objectivity is possible or not, with Merrill taking the position that it is not possible.

14. Wicker is quoted in Theodore L. Glasser, "Objectivity Precludes Responsibility," *The Quill* (Feb. 1984).

15. Russell Baker, *The Good Times* (New York: William Morrow, 1989).

16. Eric Alterman, *Sound and Fury* (New York: Harper-Collins, 1992), p. 306.

17. The City University of New York survey on PBS programming devoted to workers is cited in the film reviews of Stuart Klawans. See *Nation*, Mar. 30, 1992.

18. Marvin Kitman, "The Disquiet over Public TV," *New York Newsday*, June 4, 1992.

18. Intimations of Excellence

1. Carnegie Commission on Educational Television, *Program for Action*.

2. Corporation for Public Broadcasting study quoted in CPB Office of Communication Research, *News Brief* 1, no. 7 (Oct. 6, 1978), NPBA.

3. Willard D. Rowland, Jr., and Michael Tracey, "Lessons from Abroad: A Preliminary Report on the Condition of Public Broadcasting in the United States and Elsewhere," delivered as a speech to the International Communication Association in May 1993. The paper was preparatory to a larger report to be prepared under the auspices of the Hoso Bunka Foundation in Tokyo.

4. Barnouw, *Image Empire*, p. 339.

5. Les Brown, "Broadcasting's Vanishing Species," *Channels* (Sept.–Oct. 1985).

6. Carnegie Commission on Educational Television, *Program for Action*, p. 13.

7. Broadcasting Research Unit, *Quality in Television*.

8. Huw Wheldon, "The British Experience in Television" (Richard Dimbleby Lecture) (London: The British Broadcasting Corporation, 1976).

9. Barbara Tuchman, "The Decline of Quality," *New York Times Magazine*, Nov. 2, 1980.

10. "Can Television News Break the Understanding Barrier?" *Times* (London), Feb. 28, 1975. Birt and Peter Jay coauthored four subsequent articles for the *Times* on the same subject: "Television Journalism: The Child of the Unhappy Marriage Between Newspapers and Film" (Sept. 30, 1975); "The Radical Changes Needed to Remedy TV's Bias Against Understanding" (Oct. 1, 1975); "How Television News Can Hold the

Mass Audience" (Sept. 2, 1976); and "Why Television News Is in Danger of Becoming an Anti-Social Force" (Sept. 3, 1976).

11. William A. Henry III, "News as Entertainment," in Elie Abel, ed., *What's News: The Media in American Society* (San Francisco: Institute for Contemporary Studies, 1981).

12. Murrow's speech to the Radio-Television News Directors Association, Oct. 15, 1958, quoted in Sperber, *Murrow*, p. 539. Also in *Reporter*, Nov. 13, 1958.

13. Postman, *Amusing Ourselves*, p. 106.

14. Sydney S. Alexander, "Public Television and the 'Ought' of Public Policy," *Washington University Law Quarterly* (winter 1968).

15. Graham Murdock and Peter Golding, "Information Poverty and Political Inequality: Citizenship in the Age of Privatized Communications," *Journal of Communication* (summer 1989).

16. The *Times-Mirror* study and the study of the People for the American Way are both quoted in Michael Oreskes, "A Trait of Today's Youth: Apathy to Public Affairs," *New York Times*, June 28, 1990.

17. Alexander, "Public Television," p. 66.

18. A dissenting study of the *MacNeil/Lehrer NewsHour* by Fairness and Accuracy in Reporting concluded that "by and large the promise of broad, in-depth coverage on *MacNeil/Lehrer* remains unfulfilled." FAIR was particularly critical of the program's guest list, which it contended "represents an extremely narrow segment of the political and social spectrum." The study was based on viewings of the show over a six-month period in 1989. See the special issue of *Extra* (a publication of Fairness & Accuracy in Reporting) 3, no. 4 (winter 1990), "All the Usual Suspects: *MacNeil/Lehrer* and *Nightline*."

19. William A. Henry III, "News as Entertainment: The Search for Dramatic Unity," in Abel, ed., *What's News*.

20. Alterman, *Sound and Fury*, p. 307.

21. Alexander, "Public Television," p. 66.

22. Jeremy Isaacs, "Consensus and Dissent—or Freedom of Speech," *EBU Review* (European Broadcasting Union) (Mar. 1979), p. 28.

23. Justice Holmes's comment in *Gitlow v. New York* is cited in Anthony Lewis, *Make No Law* (New York: Random House, 1991), p. 85.

24. *Jack Gould*, "NET's Freedom Is Threatened," *New York Times*, April 12, 1971.

25. Quoted in Katherine Bouton, "Quest for Quality TV," *Saturday Review* (Feb. 1982), p. 28.

26. British Research Unit, "Quality in Television," p. 2.

27. Alexander, "Public Television," p. 66.

28. Ibid.

29. Hughes, *Culture of Complaint*, p. 5.

30. Rowland and Tracey, "Lessons from Abroad," p. 44.

Epilogue: Past Imperfect, Future Imperative

1. Barnouw, *Image Empire*, p. 340.

2. Lewis H. Lapham, "Adieu, Big Bird: On the Terminal Irrelevance of Public Television," *Harper's* (Dec. 1993).

3. See Twentieth Century Fund, *Quality Time?*, 1993.

4. Tom Shales, "Public Television—Tangled Up in Tape," *Washington Post*, Dec. 10, 1978.

5. Willard D. Rowland, Jr., and Michael Tracey, "Worldwide Challenges to Public Service Broadcasting," *Journal of Communication* (spring 1990).

6. Ibid. However, as one of the small band of civilian radio specialists in Tokyo at the time who was charged with implementing these policies, I would point out that it was also the Allied Occupation that introduced market-driven private broadcasting to Japan.

7. *TV Guide* quote cited in *U.S. News and World Report*, Oct. 3, 1977.

8. Tom Shales, "Public Television—Tangled Up in Tape."

9. Stuart Sucherman, "Old Enough to Get Its Act Together," *Channels* (Oct. 1987).

10. "Supplemental Comment from Eli N. Evans," in Twentieth Century Fund, *Quality Time?* (p. 60).

11. Lynne Cheney, "Uncivil Wars," *Washingtonian* (Feb. 1986).

12. David Puttnam, "Is There a Worldwide Future for Public Service Broadcasting?" *Combroad* (Commonwealth Broadcasting Association) (June 1993).

13. Ervin S. Duggan, "The Overture Ends," Address before Southern Educational Communication Association, Dallas, Tex., Oct. 17, 1994, NPBA.

14. Richard O. Moore, "Public Television Programming and the Future," in Cater and Nyhan, *The Future of Public Broadcasting*. Moore is the former president and chief executive officer of KQED / San Francisco and KTCA / Minneapolis–St. Paul.

15. Media writer Les Brown proposed a creative incentive to improve stations' carriage of national programs. Instead of distributing the system's federal funds to stations through annual Community Service Grants, Brown would have stations "earn" fees for each national program they aired, an interesting twist on the commercial network practice of sharing a show's advertising revenues with the stations that air it.

16. Per capita expenses for public television are for fiscal year 1990,

quoted in Corporation for Public Broadcasting, *Research Notes*, no. 44 (Aug. 1991).

17. Carnegie Commission on Educational Television, *Program for Action*, p. 72.

18. Joseph D. Hughes, "Heat Shield or Crucible: A Blueprint for Carnegie II," *Public Telecommunications Review* 5, no. 6 (Nov.–Dec. 1977). Hughes proposed a 3 percent tax on broadcast and cable revenues. Using 1976 as a base, he estimated revenues at $243 million annually. The balance of public broadcasting's needs would be met by Congressional appropriations to match the funds generated by the individual stations.

19. John Whitney, "The Pursuit of Excellence in British Broadcasting," *Combroad* (Commonwealth Broadcasting Association) (June 1985), p. 30.

20. Neil Postman, *Technopoly: The Surrender of Culture to Technology* (New York: Vintage Books, 1993).

21. Benjamin Barber, "The Second American Revolution," *Channels* (Feb.–Mar. 1982).

22. *James Reston: The Man Millions Read*, Public Broadcasting Service, Jan. 8, 1993.

23. Walter Lippmann, "The TV Problem," *New York Herald-Tribune*, Oct. 27, 1959. Lippmann is convinced that "the best line for us to take is . . . to devise a way by which one network can be run as a public service with its criterion not what will be the most popular but what is good."

24. Alexander, "Public Television."

BIBLIOGRAPHY

Alterman, Eric. *Sound and Fury: Punditocracy in America.* New York: Harper-Collins, 1992.

Arlen, Michael J. *Living Room War.* New York: Viking, 1966.

———. *The View from Highway One.* New York: Farrar, Straus & Giroux, 1974.

———. *The Camera Age.* New York: Farrar, Straus & Giroux, 1981.

Aspen Institute. *Aspen Notebook on Government and the Media.* New York: Praeger, 1973.

———. *Television as a Social Force: New Approaches to TV Criticism.* New York: Praeger, 1975.

———. *Television as a Cultural Force.* New York: Praeger, 1976.

Avery, Robert K., and Robert Pepper. *The Politics of Interconnection: A History of Public Television at the National Level.* Washington, D.C.: National Association of Educational Broadcasting, 1979.

Avery, Robert K., ed. *Public Service Broadcasting in a Multichannel Environment.* New York: Longman, 1993.

Ball, Samuel, and Gerry Ann Bogatz. *The First Year of "Sesame Street": An Evaluation.* Princeton, N.J.: Educational Testing Service, 1970.

Barnouw, Erik. *The Image Empire.* New York: Oxford Univ. Press, 1970.

———. *Tube of Plenty.* New York: Oxford Univ. Press, 1975.

———. *The Sponsor: Notes on a Modern Potentate.* New York: Oxford Univ. Press, 1978.

Blakely, Robert J. *The People's Instrument: A Philosophy of Programming for Public Television.* Washington, D.C.: Public Affairs Press, 1971.

———. *To Serve the Public Interest: Educational Broadcasting in the United States.* Syracuse, N.Y.: Syracuse Univ. Press, 1979.

Bogatz, Gerry Ann, and Samuel Ball. *The Second Year of "Sesame Street": A Continuing Evaluation.* Princeton, N.J.: Educational Testing Service, 1971.

Bower, Robert T. *Television and the Public.* New York: Holt, Rinehart, and Winston, 1973.

Briggs, Asa. *The History of Broadcasting in the United Kingdom.* Vol. 1: *The Birth of Broadcasting.* London: Oxford Univ. Press, 1961.

Broadcasting Research Unit. *The Public Service Idea in British Broadcasting.* London: Broadcasting Research Unit, 1987.

———. *Quality in Television: Programmes, Programme-makers, Systems.* London: John Libbey, 1989.

Brown, Les. *Keeping Your Eye on Television.* New York: Pilgrim, 1979.

———. *Televi$ion: The Business Behind the Box.* New York: Harcourt Brace Jovanovich, 1971.

Bryant, J., and D. R. Anderson, eds. *Children's Understanding of Television.* New York: Academic Press, 1983.

Burke, John Edward. *An Historical-Analytical Study of the Legislative and Political Origins of the Public Broadcasting Act of 1967.* New York: Arno, 1979.

Burns, Eric. *Broadcast Blues.* New York: Harper-Collins, 1993.

Carnegie Commission on Educational Television. *Public Television: A Program for Action.* New York: Harper & Row, 1967; New York: Bantam, 1967.

Carnegie Commission on the Future of Public Broadcasting. *A Public Trust.* New York: Bantam, 1979.

Cater, Douglass, and Michael J. Nyhan, eds. *The Future of Public Broadcasting.* New York: Praeger, 1976.

Children's Television Workshop. *"The Electric Company."* New York: The Children's Television Workshop, 1971.

———. *Sesame Street: 1000 Hours of a Perpetual Television Experiment.* New York: The Children's Television Workshop, 1976.

Coase, R. H., and Edward W. Barrett. *Educational TV: Who Should Pay?* Washington, D.C.: American Enterprise Institute, 1968.

Comstock, George. *Television in America.* Beverly Hills, Calif.: Sage, 1980.

Conrad, Peter. *Television: The Medium and Its Manners.* Boston: Routledge & Kegan Paul, 1982.

Cook, T. D., et al. *"Sesame Street" Revisited.* New York: Russell Sage Foundation, 1975.

Cooney, Joan Ganz. *The First Year of "Sesame Street": A History and Overview.* New York: Children's Television Workshop, 1970.

Corporation for Public Broadcasting. *CPB Annual Report.* Washington, D.C.: Corporation for Public Broadcasting, 1971–.

———. *Ten Years of Public Broadcasting, 1967–1977.* Washington, D.C.: Corporation for Public Broadcasting, 1977.

————. *Strategies for Public Television in a Multi-Channel Environment.* Washington, D.C.: Corporation for Public Broadcasting, 1991.

Corwin, Norman. *Trivializing America: The Triumph of Mediocrity.* Secaucus, N.J.: Lyle Stuart, 1983.

Crotts, G. Gail, and Willard D. Rowland, Jr. "The Prospects for Public Broadcasting." In Leonard Lewin, ed., *Telecommunications in the U.S.: Trends and Policies.* Dedham, Mass.: Artech, 1981.

Day, James, and Alden Whitman. *Report of the Task Force on Independent Documentaries and Public Television.* New York: National News Council, 1980.

Dennis, Everette E., and John C. Merrill. *Basic Issues in Mass Communication: A Debate.* New York: Macmillan, 1991.

Eastman, Susan Tyler. *Broadcast/Cable Programming: Strategies and Practices.* Belmont, Calif.: Wadsworth, 1992.

Esslin, Martin. *The Age of Television.* New York: W.H. Freeman, 1981.

Feinstein, Phylis. *All About Sesame Street.* New York: Tower, 1971.

Fishman, Mark. *Manufacturing the News.* Austin: Univ. of Texas Press, 1980.

Ford Foundation. *Ford Foundation Activities in Noncommercial Broadcasting, 1951–1976.* New York: Ford Foundation, 1976.

Ford Foundation Files, New York.

Friendly, Fred. *Due to Circumstances Beyond Our Control . . .* New York: Random House, 1967.

Geller, Henry, and Donna Lampert. *Charging for Spectrum Use.* Washington, D.C.: Benton Foundation.

Gibson, George H. *Public Broadcasting: The Role of the Federal Government, 1912–1976.* New York: Praeger, 1977.

Gitlin, Todd. *The Whole World Is Watching: Mass Media in the Making and Unmaking of the New Left.* Berkeley: Univ. of California Press, 1980.

————, ed. *Watching Television.* New York: Pantheon, 1986.

Goulart, Ron. *An American Family.* New York: Warner Paperback Library, 1973.

Greene, Sir Hugh. *The Future of Broadcasting in Britain.* London: Hurt-Davis, MacGibbon, 1972.

————. *Third Floor Front: A View of Broadcasting in the Sixties.* London: The Bodley Head, 1969.

Halberstam, David. *The Powers That Be.* New York: Alfred A. Knopf, 1979.

Hill, Lewis. *Experiment in Listener-Sponsorship.* Berkeley, Calif.: Pacifica Foundation, 1958.

Hoggart, Richard. *The Uses of Literacy.* London: Penguin, 1957.

————. *Speaking to Each Other.* Vol. 1: *About Society.* New York: Oxford Univ. Press, 1970.

Hoso Bunka Foundation. *Symposium 2: On The Public Role and Systems of Broadcasting.* Tokyo: Hoso Bunka Foundation, 1981.

Hoynes, William. *Public Television for Sale: Media, the Market, and the Public Sphere.* Boulder, Colo.: Westview, 1994.

Hughes, Robert. *Culture of Complaint: The Fraying of America.* New York: Oxford Univ. Press, 1993.

Institute of Communication Research. *Educational Television: The Next Ten Years.* Stanford, Calif.: Institute of Communication Research, 1962.

Katzman, Natan. *Program Decisions in Public Television.* Washington, D.C.: National Association of Educational Broadcasters, 1976.

Koenig, Allen E., and Ruane B. Hill, eds. *The Farther Vision: Educational Television Today.* Madison: Univ. of Wisconsin Press, 1967.

Krasnow, Erwin G., and Lawrence D. Longley. *The Politics of Broadcast Regulation.* New York: St. Martin's, 1973.

Kratochvil, D. W. *"Sesame Street": Developed by Children's Television Workshop.* Palo Alto, Calif.: American Institutes for Research in the Behavioral Sciences, 1971.

Kuney, Jack. *Take One: Television Directors on Directing.* New York: Praeger, 1990.

Land, Herman W. *The Children's Television Workshop: How and Why It Works.* Jericho, N.Y.: Nassau Board of Cooperative Educational Services, 1971.

Lashley, Marilyn. *Public Television: Panacea, Pork Barrel, or Public Trust?* New York: Greenwood, 1992.

Leach, Edward. *Tuning Out Education: The Cooperation Doctrine in Radio, 1922–38.* Washington, D.C.: Current Publishing, 1983; reprinted as "Snookered 50 Years Ago," *Current,* Jan. 14, 1983, et seq.

Lesser, Gerald S. *Children and Television: Lessons from "Sesame Street."* New York: Random House, 1974.

Lesser, Harvey, ed. *Television and the Preschool Child.* New York: Academic Press, 1977.

Loud, Patricia, with Norma Johnson. *Pat Loud: A Woman's Story.* New York: Coward, McCann & Geoghegan, 1974.

Lyle, Jack. *The People Look at Public Television 1974.* Washington, D.C.: Corporation for Public Broadcasting, 1975.

MacNeil, Robert. *The Right Place at the Right Time.* Boston: Little, Brown, 1982.

Macy, John W., Jr. *To Irrigate a Wasteland.* Berkeley: Univ. of California Press, 1974.

Magat, Richard. *The Ford Foundation at Work.* New York: Plenum Press, 1979.

Mahony, Sheila, Nick DeMartino, and Robert Stengel. *Keeping PACE with the New Television: Public Television and Changing Technology*. New York: Carnegie Corporation / VNU Books International, 1980.

Mander, Jerry. *Four Arguments for the Elimination of Television*. New York: William Morrow, 1977.

Mayer, Martin. *About Television*. New York: Harper & Row, 1972.

McChesney, Robert W. *Telecommunications, Mass Media, and Democracy: The Battle for Control of U.S. Broadcasting, 1928–35*. New York: Oxford Univ. Press, 1994.

National Association of Educational Broadcasters. *The Nixon Administration Public Broadcasting Papers: A Summary, 1969–1974*. Washington, D.C.: NAEB, 1979.

National Public Broadcasting Archives. University of Maryland, College Park, Md.

Network Project. *The Fourth Network*. New York: The Network Project, 1971.

———. *Office of Telecommunications Policy (The White House Role in Domestic Communication)*. New York: The Network Project, 1973.

———. *Government Television*. New York: The Network Project, 1974.

Netzer, Dick. *Long-Range Financing of Public Broadcasting*. New York: National Citizens Committee for Broadcasting, 1969.

———. *The Subsidized Muse: Public Support for the Arts in the United States*. Cambridge, Eng.: Cambridge Univ. Press, 1978.

Nielsen, Waldemar A. *The Big Foundations*. New York: Columbia Univ. Press, 1972.

Paley, William S. *As It Happened*. New York: Doubleday, 1979.

Palmer, Edward L. *Television and America's Children: A Crisis of Neglect*. New York: Oxford Univ. Press, 1988.

———. *Children in the Cradle of TV*. Lexington, Mass.: D. C. Heath, 1987.

Palmer, Edward L., and A. Dorr, eds. *Children and the Faces of Television*. New York: Academic Press, 1980.

Pepper, Robert M. *The Formation of the Public Broadcasting Service*. New York: Arno, 1979.

Perlmutter, Alvin H. *The Voters' Channel: A Feasibility Study*. New York: The John and Mary Markle Foundation, 1990.

Persico, Joseph E. *Edward R. Murrow: An American Original*. New York: McGraw-Hill, 1988.

Polsky, Richard M. *Getting to "Sesame Street": Origins of the Children's Television Workshop*. New York: Praeger, 1974.

Postman, Neil. *Amusing Ourselves to Death*. New York: Viking, 1986.

———. *Technopoly: The Surrender of Culture to Technology*. New York: Vintage, 1993.

Powell, John Walker. *Channels of Learning: The Story of Educational Television.* Washington, D.C.: Public Affairs Press, 1962.

Powledge, Fred. *Public Television: A Question of Survival.* New York: American Civil Liberties Union, 1972.

Public Broadcasting Service. *Long-Range Planning for Public Television.* 2 vols. Washington, D.C.: Public Broadcasting Service, 1978.

———. *Report of the Special Committee on Program Policies and Procedures.* Washington, D.C.: Public Broadcasting Service, 1987.

Rice, Michael. *Public Television Issues of Purpose and Governance.* New York: Aspen Institute for Humanistic Studies, 1981.

Robertson, Jim. *Televisionaries: In Their Own Words Public Television's Founders Tell How It All Began.* Charlotte Harbor, Fla.: Tabby House, 1993.

Rockefeller Foundation. *Independent Television-Makers and Public Telecommunications Policy: A Seminar Conference to Promote Telecommunications.* New York: Rockefeller Foundation, 1979.

Rose, Brian G. *Television and the Performing Arts.* New York: Greenwood, 1986.

Rowland, Willard D., Jr. "The Struggle for Self-Determination: Public Broadcasting, Policy Problems and Reform." In J. R. Schement et al., eds. *Telecommunications Policy Handbook.* New York: Praeger, 1982.

———. *The Challenges to Public-Service Broadcasting.* Queenstown, Md.: Aspen Institute, 1986.

Schramm, Wilbur, Jack Lyle, and Edwin B. Parker. *Television in the Lives of Our Children.* Stanford, Calif.: Stanford Univ. Press, 1961.

Schramm, Wilbur, Jack Lyle, and Ithiel de Sola Pool. *The People Look at Educational Television.* Stanford, Calif.: Stanford Univ. Press, 1963.

Schramm, Wilbur, and Lyle Nelson. *The Financing of Public Television.* Palo Alto, Calif.: Aspen Program on Communications and Society, 1972.

Schramm, Wilbur, ed. *National Educational Television and Radio Center.* Urbana: Univ. of Illinois, 1960.

———, ed. *Quality in Instructional Television.* Honolulu: Univ. of Hawaii Press, 1972.

Schwarzwalder, John C. *ETV in Controversy.* Minneapolis: Dillon, 1970.

Shooshan, Harry M., III, and Louis Arnheim. *Public Broadcasting.* Washington, D.C.: Benton Foundation, 1989.

Skornia, Harry J. *Television and Society.* New York: McGraw-Hill, 1965.

Smith, Mary Howard. *Midwest Program on Airborne Television Instruction.* New York: McGraw-Hill, 1961.

Sperber, A. M. *Murrow: His Life and Times.* New York: Freundlich Books, 1986.

Steinberg, Charles S., ed. *Broadcasting: The Critical Challenge.* New York: Hastings House, 1974.

Stone, David M. *Nixon and the Politics of Public Television*. New York: Garland, 1985.

Temporary Commission on Alternative Financing for Public Telecommunications. *Final Report*. Washington, D.C.: Federal Communications Commission, 1983.

Tressel, George W., et al. *The Future of Educational Telecommunications*. Lexington, Mass.: Lexington Books, 1975.

Tuchman, Gaye. *Making News: A Study in the Construction of Reality*. New York: Free Press, 1978.

Twentieth Century Fund. *Quality Time? Report of the Twentieth Century Fund Task Force on Public Television*. New York: The Twentieth Century Fund Press, 1993.

U.S. Congress. *The Public Broadcasting Act of 1967*. Public Law 90–129, 90th Cong. S. 1160, Nov. 7, 1967.

Williams, Raymond. *Technology and Cultural Form*. New York: Schocken Books, 1975.

Witherspoon, John, and Roselle Kovitz. *The History of Public Broadcasting*. Washington, D.C.: Current Publishing, 1987; reprinted as "Public Broadcasting: Origins and Themes," *Current*, Mar. 31, 1987, et seq.

Wood, Donald N., and Donald G. Wylie. *Educational Telecommunications*. Belmont, Calif.: Wadsworth Publishing, 1977.

Wood, Donald Neal. "The First Decade of the 'Fourth Network': An Historical, Descriptive Analysis of the National Educational Television and Radio Center." Ph.D. diss., Univ. of Michigan, 1963.

Woolery, G. W. *Children's Television: The First Thirty-Five Years, 1946–1981*. Part II: Live, Film and Tape Series. Metuchen, N.J.: Scarecrow Press, 1985.

GUIDE TO THE
PRINCIPAL PLAYERS

Aaron, Chloe: Senior vice president for programming, Public Broadcasting Service, from 1976 to 1980.

Armsey, James W.: Administered Ford Foundation's grants to public television from 1957 to 1966.

Baker, William F.: Former commercial television executive who became president of WNET / New York in 1987.

Barrett, Edward W.: While dean of Columbia's Graduate School of Journalism, he chaired the Advisory Board of PBL, the Public Broadcast Laboratory.

Benjamin, Robert S.: Attorney and chairman of United Artists who chaired the CPB Board of Directors from 1974 to 1977.

Bohen, Frederick M.: Was executive editor of PBL during its second season. Later joined WNET / New York as director of news and public affairs, 1973–74.

Bundy, McGeorge: President of the Ford Foundation from 1966 to 1979.

Case, Everett N.: President of the Alfred P. Sloan Foundation (and former president of Colgate College) who chaired the NET (National Educational Television) board from 1963 to 1969.

Chamberlin, Ward B., Jr.: The Corporation for Public Broadcasting's first executive vice president and the principal architect of PBS. Key figure in the merger of NET and Channel 13 as the executive vice president of WNET / New York. Became executive director of *American Playhouse* after serving seventeen years (1975–92) as president of WETA / Washington.

Christensen, Bruce: President of PBS from 1983 to 1993.

Cooney, Joan Ganz: Founding president of the Children's Television Workshop and creator of *Sesame Street*.

Cousins, Norman: Editor (*Saturday Review*) who chaired the board of NET at the time of its merger with the New York channel, and later headed the National Programming Council for Public Television.

Curtis, Thomas: Former Republican congressman from Missouri who chaired the CPB board in 1972 until his resignation the following year over differences with the Nixon White House.

Davis, Curtis P.: Played a large role in shaping public television's music and arts programming as a producer and head of cultural programming at NET for thirteen years.

Davis, David: Creator and the first executive director of *American Playhouse*; also a key figure in public television's development—first as the station manager of WGBH / Boston during the early decade of its rise, and later as the Ford Foundation's executive in charge of administering its grants to public television.

Dixon, Don: NET's director of public-affairs programs, and executive producer of its documentaries, from 1965 until its merger with Channel 13 in 1972.

Duggan, Ervin: Former FCC commissioner who became PBS's fourth president in 1993.

Flemming, Robben W.: The former president of the University of Michigan who served as president of the CPB from 1979 to 1981.

Fletcher, C. Scott: President of the Ford Foundation's Fund for Adult Education (1951–61) and a key figure in the early development of educational television. He backed the move to reserve the channels, helped to equip most of the earliest stations, and founded the Educational Television and Radio Center to distribute programming nationally. As consultant to the NAEB, he was the catalyst that led to the first Carnegie Commission.

Freedman, Lewis: Award-winning television producer and program executive (*Hollywood Television Theater*, WNDT / New York, and PBL). As the first director of CPB's Program Fund, he played an important role in the creation of *Frontline, American Playhouse,* and *Wonderworks.*

Friendly, Fred W.: Veteran program producer (*See It Now*) and network executive (president of CBS News) who became television adviser to the Ford Foundation's McGeorge Bundy in 1967. He later created at Columbia University the PBS Media and Society Seminars.

Grossman, Lawrence: President of PBS from 1976 to 1983. Resigned to become president of NBC News.

Gunn, Hartford N., Jr.: PBS's first president (1970–76), later vice chairman in charge of long-range planning. For fourteen years the president of WGBH / Boston (1956–70).

Heald, Henry T.: President of the Ford Foundation from 1956 to 1965.

Hennock, Frieda: Led the fight for the reservation of educational channels as the first woman on the Federal Communications Commission.

Hitchcock, Ethan Allen: Attorney and chairman of the board of WNET / New York before and after its merger with NET.

Hudson, Robert: Principal architect of public television's early program planning during the almost twenty years he was an executive with NET and a program consultant to the Fund for Adult Education.

Iselin, John Jay: President of WNET / New York from 1973 to 1987.

Karayn, James: Washington bureau chief of NET before heading the National Public Affairs Center for Television (NPACT) and, later, WHYY / Philadelphia.

Killian, James R., Jr.: President of MIT who led the first Carnegie Commission and later served on the board of CPB.

Kobin, William: For nine years NET's programming vice president before heading the public stations in Minneapolis–St. Paul and, since 1983, KCET / Los Angeles.

Landau, Sonia: CPB board member from 1981 and its chair from 1984 to 1986.

Lawson, Jennifer: Former director of CPB Program Fund. Was programming chief of PBS from 1990 to 1995.

Ledwig, Donald: President of CPB from 1986 to 1993.

Loomis, Henry: Former head of the Voice of America who succeeded Macy as president of CPB in 1972.

Macy, John W., Jr.: The first president of the Corporation for Public Broadcasting.

Moore, Richard O.: Former president of KQED / San Francisco and KTCA / Minneapolis–St. Paul and an independent documentary producer.

Morrisett, Lloyd D.: Foundation head (John & Mary Markle) who, with Joan Ganz Cooney, founded the Children's Television Workshop and has chaired its board since 1969.

Newburn, Harry K.: Former president of the University of Oregon who became the first president of NET in 1954.

Pace, Frank, Jr.: Former Secretary of the Army, appointed by Lyndon Johnson to chair the board of CPB in 1969.

Perlmutter, Alvin H.: Former program producer for NET (*Great American Dream Machine*) and later head of his own production company.

Pfister, Edward J.: President of CPB from 1981 to 1985 after five years as chief executive of KERA / Dallas.

Rice, Jonathan C.: KQED / San Francisco's pioneering program director.

Rockefeller, Sharon Percy: President of WETA / Washington since 1990 and former chair of the CPB board.

Rogers, Ralph: Texas industrialist and chairman of the KERA / Dallas board who brought about reorganization of PBS and served as its chairman until 1976.

Schwarzwalder, John: Manager of the nation's first public-television station, KUHT / Houston, and later president of KTCA / Minneapolis–St. Paul.

Tate, Sheila: Former press secretary to Nancy Reagan who was elected to head the CPB board in 1992.

Westin, Av: Executive director of *PBL* during its two seasons on PBS.

White, John F.: President of NET from 1959 to 1969 and former general manager of WQED / Pittsburgh.

Whitehead, Clay T.: Head of the Office of Telecommunications Policy during the Nixon Administration.

ACKNOWLEDGMENTS

To have produced a finished book is the dream of every ink stained scrivener. But the act of writing one—the solitary, agonizing hours of trying to force shapeless ideas into the rigid framework of language— well, that's another kettle of flounder. The hardest part, I am told, is getting started. I wouldn't know. My own start was eased, if not propelled, by visions of a return to Villa Serbolloni, the Rockefeller Foundation's study center on Italy's Lake Como. I had briefly known the Villa's delights of sight, taste, and talk as a participant in a week-long planning confer- ence. Extended stays at the Villa, it was explained, were reserved for those writing books. Thus did I resolve to reach the ineffable by tackling the impossible. With the encouragement and critical support of Howard Klein, whose skills as a catalyst to creative activity were unmatched during his years with the Rockefeller Foundation, I returned to the Villa a year later to begin writing.

Once begun, the task fed upon the kindness of friends. I have many to thank. Erik Barnouw, whose three-volume history of broadcasting has placed all chroniclers of the media in his debt, offered the helpful coun- sel of one who had gone this way before. Anne Mandelbaum, by volun- teering her editor's eye to an early draft, provided the confidence that fueled the writing effort for many months, if not years. Fred Friendly gave palpable support by reminding the writer that it is all up there in the head, it just needs decoding, even as his own books tumbled from the press at three times my decoding speed. Paul Kaufman and George Gerbner read early drafts and offered valuable suggestions. I am partic- ularly indebted to Willard D. Rowland, Jr., whose extensive writings, both alone and with Michael Tracey, have given me a critical perspective on the public medium. His detailed critique of this work helped to sharpen its focus and to link its story with earlier attempts to promote the public media in an America obsessed with the libertarian notion that only an enlightened and unfettered private enterprise can best serve the public interest. Rowland's chronicle of our failures in this regard should be required reading for those who make our laws.

A host of friends and former colleagues volunteered to check the details of this chronicle against their own recollections of events in which they were participants. Particular chapters were read by James Armsey, David D. Connell, Joan Ganz Cooney, Norman Cousins, Robert Davidson, Curtis W. Davis, Robert Hatch, William Kobin, Gerald Lesser, Lloyd Morrisett, Edward Palmer, Alvin Perlmutter, Peter G. Peterson, Stuart Sucherman, John F. White, Jack Willis, and Frederick Wiseman. Their suggestions added essential elements to the story.

Few of us welcome the word that we've tripped on our own tongue, misspoken, misspelled, or simply wandered off into the gaseous space of ambiguity, but, with good fortune, I have had the help of a cadre of text detectives whose meticulousness is matched by a genial and gentle manner. Beverley Day and Irma Commanday Bauman helped with early versions, and Meredith Johnson vetted a later draft. But it was in the final edit, administered with an awesome attention to detail by Julie Carlson and Suzanne Samuel of the University of California Press, that my metaphors were finally unmixed, my gender-specific nouns neutered, and my words burnished to a sharper clarity than is natural with me.

Other willing hands helped with the mundane work of producing a readable manuscript. Before PCs entered my life, Antonia Hyde spent many days on a Selectric, reducing chaotic pages to neat typescript, all of which would later be converted to a computer file by Sherry Delamarter. Once in the computer, only the intervention of Marian McDonald, who understands these things, saved the work from the mysterious void of accidental deletions.

Although public television has yet to produce a substantial body of critical and historical literature, two books, one by John Walker Powell and the other by Robert Blakely, were invaluable in searching out the details of public television's beginnings. No less valuable in chronicling the later years were NET's periodic reports to the Ford Foundation, an incidental contribution to the history of the period. I am much in the debt of David Stone for his kindness and generosity in making available to me his then unpublished manuscript on public television's troubled relations with the Nixon Administration; the 1985 publication of *Nixon and the Politics of Public Television* added a vital chapter to the public television story. To the WNET reference library and its small staff—Victoria Dawson, Harriet Obus, and Colin McQuillan—much is owed for help in searching out other files and articles. I am also grateful to Sharon Zechowski, a former graduate student, for her patience in organizing the archival photos.

An enterprise of this length feeds on the moral strength of a legion of helpful friends and colleagues, among them Win Murphy, John Boyer, Jeanne Alexander, Iñaki Zabaleta, Liz Dawson Lopez, and many others remembered if not recorded. The patience of my own family—my wife, Beverley, and four children—was tempered with a humor that helped to preserve sanity. Milton Stern aided me in finding a home for the manuscript on the campus where my undergraduate years were spent. And there, to my good fortune, it was put in the capable editorial hands of Naomi Schneider, whose caring patience and skill in transforming it into a book has the writer's everlasting gratitude. Notwithstanding the valuable help given by the editors and a host of friends, the writer bears the full responsibility for what appears in these pages.

INDEX

Compositor: Impressions
Printer/Binder: Edwards Brothers, Inc.
Text: 11/13.5 Baskerville
Display: Gill Sans